European Friends of the American Revolution

The Revolutionary Age

Francis D. Cogliano and Patrick Griffin, Editors

European Friends of the American Revolution

Edited by
Andrew J. O'Shaughnessy,
John A. Ragosta, and Marie-Jeanne Rossignol

UNIVERSITY OF VIRGINIA PRESS / Charlottesville and London

University of Virginia Press
© 2023 by the Rector and Visitors of the University of Virginia
All rights reserved

First published 2023

9 8 7 6 5 4 3 2 1

Library of Congress Cataloging-in-Publication Data

Names: O'Shaughnessy, Andrew Jackson, editor. | Ragosta, John A., editor. | Rossignol, Marie-Jeanne, editor.
Title: European friends of the American Revolution / edited by Andrew Jackson O'Shaughnessy, John A. Ragosta, and Marie-Jeanne Rossignol.
Description: Charlottesville : University of Virginia Press, 2023. | Series: The revolutionary age | Includes bibliographical references and index.
Identifiers: LCCN 2023011334 (print) | LCCN 2023011335 (ebook) | ISBN 9780813949888 (hardcover) | ISBN 9780813949895 (paperback) | ISBN 9780813949901 (ebook)
Subjects: LCSH: United States—History—Revolution, 1775–1783—Foreign public opinion, European. | United States—Foreign relations—1775–1783. | United States—History—Revolution, 1775–1783—Participation, Foreign. | United States—Foreign relations—Europe. | Europe—Foreign relations—United States.
Classification: LCC E249 E97 2023 (print) | LCC E249 (ebook) | DDC 973.3—dc23/eng/20230314
LC record available at https://lccn.loc.gov/2023011334
LC ebook record available at https://lccn.loc.gov/2023011335

Cover art: Detail from *The Siege of Yorktown* (1850–60), attributed to Henry LeGrand, after Louis-Charles-Auguste Couder. (Courtesy of the Museum of the American Revolution; object 2007.01.0148)

Contents

Acknowledgments   vii

Introduction   *Andrew J. O'Shaughnessy, John A. Ragosta, and Marie-Jeanne Rossignol*   1

Imagining an American, and a French, Revolutionary

American Nationality: A French Invention?   *Julia Osman*   17

Diplomacy: Friends, Allies, and Free Trade

Ideology *and* Interest: Free Trade, the League of Armed Neutrality, and the American Revolution   *Paul A. Gilje*   45

"Sir, I have not yet begun to fight!": John Paul Jones's Friends in the Dutch Republic, 1779–1780   *Victor Enthoven*   67

War at Sea: The Battle of the Chesapeake

Season, Winds, and the Sea: The Improbable Route of de Grasse to the Chesapeake   *Olivier Chaline*   99

The Battle of the Chesapeake from the Quarterdeck: From an Admirals' Quarrel to Scholars' Consensus   *Jean-Marie Kowalski*   123

Conflicted Allies: Spain and Portugal in the American War for Independence

Bernardo de Gálvez: Friend of the American Revolution, Friend of Empire   *Kathleen DuVal and Gonzalo M. Quintero Saravia*   147

Old Partners and Intersecting Interests: Trade and Diplomacy between Portugal and the United States during the Era of George Washington (c. 1781–1805)   *Timothy Walker*   175

Lafayette and French Nobles: Constitutional Reform in a Revolutionary Voice

Lafayette and the "More Perfect Union": Strengthening America in the Confederation Era, 1783–1789   *Robert Rhodes Crout*   209

Lafayette, the Lameths, and "Republican Monarchy," 1789–1791   *Munro Price*   242

Studying Atlantic History with Jacques Godechot and Robert R. Palmer

In Search of Global Democracy: Revisiting the Historical Work of Jacques Godechot and Robert R. Palmer, Founders of Atlantic History   *Marie-Jeanne Rossignol*   261

Contributors   279

Index   285

Acknowledgments

In honor of the arrival in America of the replica of the *L'Hermione*, the ship in which the Marquis de Lafayette sailed to the embattled colonies, the Sons of the American Revolution dedicated its annual conference in 2015 to the topic of "The Marquis de Lafayette and the European Friends of the American Revolution." The conference was held at the Fred W. Smith National Library at Mount Vernon on June 12–14, 2015. Arranged by Andrew O'Shaughnessy, as the Distinguished SAR Historian in 2014–15, the aim of the conference was to illustrate the importance of France, Spain, Holland, and other European nations in the American victory against Britain and the lasting and broad impact of both the American Revolution and the international alliances that accompanied it. In the tradition of the SAR annual conference, it also celebrated the memory of scholars who have advanced the study of the subject of the conference with a dedication to Jacques Godechot (1907–89) and Robert R. Palmer (1909–2002). Their role as leading pioneers in the field of Atlantic history highlights the central place of the European friends of the American Revolution not only to study of the Revolution and its impact in Europe but to build a firm foundation for that entire field of study.

The editors would like to acknowledge Joseph W. Dooley, who first proposed the idea of an annual scholarly conference under the auspices of the Sons of the American Revolution and who, in 2013, became the president general of the SAR. He has played a major role in instigating academic gatherings that have resulted in the publication to date of some six other volumes of proceedings, covering a range of subjects such as gender and race in the

American Revolution. These include a volume that supplements the essays on Spain in this work.[1]

The success of the conference owed much to the logistical support and hosting by Mount Vernon, especially Douglas Bradburn, Founding Director of The Fred W. Smith National Library for the Study of George Washington, and Stephen Macleod, Manager of the Library Programs.

It is an especial pleasure to thank other sponsors of the conference, including Miles Young, then CEO of Ogilvy & Mather and now Warden of New College, Oxford University; the Mount Vernon Ladies' Association and The Fred W. Smith National Library for the Study of George Washington; the Friends of Hermione-Lafayette in America; Ogilvy & Mather;[2] the Robert H. Smith International Center for Jefferson Studies at Monticello; Michael C. Quinn and the Museum of the American Revolution; the Richard Lounsbery Foundation; the George Washington Endowment Fund of the National Society of the SAR; George Knight–Kenneth C. Patty Memorial Trust Fund of the Virginia Society of the SAR; Arlington Blue Top Cabs; the WinSet Group LLC; the California Society SAR Ladies Auxiliary; J. Thomas Burch Jr.; Mr. & Mrs. John H. Franklin Jr.; Joseph R. Godfrey, PhD; S. John Massoud; Samuel C. Powell; Timothy E. Ward; the George Mason chapter of the Virginia Society SAR; and the George Washington chapter of the Virginia Society SAR. Of course, a special thanks is also due to the reviewers, editors, and staff of the University of Virginia Press; without their able assistance, this volume could not have been brought to fruition. In organizing the conference and completing this volume, the editors also express their appreciation for the work of Whitney Pippin, Andrew Vanderbilt, and Caitlin Lawrence.

The editors and authors particularly appreciate the support of this volume by the Mount Vernon Ladies' Association.

Notes

1. *Spain and the American Revolution: New Approaches and Perspectives,* ed. Gabriel Paquette and Gonzalo M. Quintero (New York: Routledge, 2020).

2. After Miles Young stepped down as CEO of Ogilvy & Mather, the new CEO, John Seifert, launched what he called the company's "re-founding" in June 2018, at which time the company changed its name from Ogilvy & Mather to Ogilvy.

European Friends of the American Revolution

Introduction

American independence would not have been possible without financial and military support from Europe. France funneled desperately needed military supplies and money to the rebelling colonies surreptitiously until it signed a commercial and military treaty with the United States in 1778. Spain, while not entering into a formal alliance with the new nation, declared war on Britain in 1779 (after it, too, quietly provided important supplies to the American cause). The Netherlands supported privateers and trade. Russia and other "neutral" countries demanded "neutral rights" at sea. Portugal, Britain's ally for centuries, worked quietly to maintain relations with the former British colonies. In a dynamic and interconnected Atlantic world, Great Britain found itself diplomatically and militarily isolated, unable to rely on any ally in a war that became a global conflict, while the British navy, which ruled the waves in the eighteenth century, was outnumbered by the combined fleets of America's friends.

Beyond that military and financial support, as the war progressed and its aftermath unfolded, European friends (led by France, Spain, and the Netherlands) encouraged recognition of the still-toddling new United States and its incorporation into the international fabric of nations as a means of opposition to imperious Britain. And without that recognition from powerful European states, the young country would never have achieved an independent status "among the powers of the earth" as promised (and hoped for) in the Declaration of Independence.

While each of these nations looked to its own interests, each effectively promoted America's, but many individual Europeans who became friends of the Revolution—like the brilliant Frenchman the marquis de Lafayette—were motivated by the ideals of liberty and equality expressed by the Americans to justify their revolt. Beyond the decisive impact in America, the consequences of the alliances and enthusiasm for reform from prominent individuals had a lasting impact on Europe and over centuries have inspired sympathetic revolutions across the Atlantic and the globe.

Though this may sound like an old story, it is a story worthy of reconsideration.

Recent historiography has opened new perspectives on the history of the American Revolution and of the War for Independence by focusing on their social and cultural dimensions. In doing so, historians have provided enormously important and helpful insights into the era and the war. They have also delivered a needed corrective by focusing study on topics that were previously largely ignored, including the roles of women, Native Americans, enslaved and free African Americans, dissenting religious communities, and the lower classes.

Thanks to this fine work on domestic factors and social history, we can revisit older narratives and give them new life. Inspired by global and Atlantic history, this volume offers an important additional international perspective that is essential for a fuller understanding of the outcome of the Revolutionary War. What necessarily follows is a reconsideration of critical issues of military power, diplomacy, politics, ideology, and war.

It is useful to remember that the entire field of Atlantic history began as a way to understand more fully the role of the American Revolution in an Age of Revolutions that engulfed Europe and other parts of the globe after American independence. As that field of inquiry has expanded beyond what was first imagined by its progenitors—now encompassing, for example, the Haitian Revolution—the firm foundation of Atlantic history in the transnational currents of the American Revolution is worth renewed and expanded exploration. The National Society of the Sons of the American Revolution (SAR) conference that generated the source material for this volume and the essays included herein provide an opportunity to renew those important conversations and offer new avenues and methods for fruitful study in Atlantic history and the Revolution itself.

This book addresses the history of the American Revolution as a war of independence in which military questions were central along with political, diplomatic, and social issues, not simply continentally, but globally. Through the presentation of innovative research, it offers a new understanding of the conflict. Fought with the material and diplomatic support of various European friends, the war between Britain and America did not merely reproduce traditional imperial conflagrations but pioneered new techniques and global realities anticipating later colonial conflicts.

The importance of the Continental European contribution to the war can be appreciated by looking at the war from the perspective of the British. A little-known historiographical debate between the late Oxford historian Piers Mackesy and University of Michigan professor John Shy about whether Britain could have won the American War for Independence suggests much about the role of European friends of the American Revolution.[1] It was a very amicable professional debate between friends and former army officers. Launching that debate, Piers Mackesy wrote the most detailed account of the British side of the conflict in his *The War for America*, published in 1976. His comprehensive coverage of all the theaters of the war over more than five hundred pages might give the reader the impression that he was attributing the British defeat in their war against France, Spain, and Holland to the empire's commitments elsewhere in the world. In reality, Mackesy was arguing that the war was winnable for Britain and that it was lost by poor military leadership. He clarified his view in a short essay, "Could the British Have Won the American War of Independence?" (delivered as the Chester Bland–Dwight E. Lee Lecture at Clark University in 1975), in which he absolved the politicians of responsibility and blamed the military leadership, maintaining that the generals were good tacticians and poor strategists.

John Shy, one of the most influential historians of the war, who was much influenced by the American experience of Vietnam, contested that interpretation. In the introduction to a second edition of Mackesy's book, Shy told the story of how Mackesy's father was blamed by Winston Churchill for the failure of an early attempt to create a beachhead in Europe in World War II by landing in Norway. By including a seemingly superfluous detail, he was gently suggesting that Mackesy was obsessed with leadership over what he (Shy) thought were more significant causal factors in the failure of the British. Responding to insurgencies, Shy understood, posed particular difficulties even for a powerful nation, difficulties that, in the case of the rebellion against British rule in America, were immensely complicated by the European friends of the Revolution.

In the American Revolutionary War, as Shy recognized, the British were fighting what today would be called counterinsurgency warfare of the type the United States faced in Vietnam and more recently encountered by Americans and their allies in Afghanistan. As this volume was being completed in 2021, the United States announced a withdrawal from Afghanistan—the longest war in its history—similar to its decision to cut its losses in Vietnam, both painful examples of America's military failures in the face of local insurgencies. There is a proliferation of literature showing the British have been similarly unsuccessful fighting counterinsurgencies in the twentieth and twenty-first centuries.[2]

Of course, before the American Revolution, the British and Americans shared many cultural, religious, ethnic, and economic ties that have tended to be absent in the twentieth and twenty-first century insurgencies fought by the United States and Britain, and the significance of these factors should not be discounted. Still, while the reasons for defeat in such circumstances are multiple and varied, there are several common factors, all relevant in the context of the American Revolution, including popular support for the revolt, the costs of a war of attrition, difficulties of terrain, and ultimately the political decision of the occupying power to withdraw. For Shy, then, the radicalization of ordinary citizens in state militias, legislatures, and courts was the key to understanding the success of the patriotic cause in the American Revolution.

There is another arguably essential factor in successful insurgencies: foreign support that the occupying power is often unable to challenge without risking escalation of the war. This was the case of the Americans in Vietnam, who were unwilling to bomb North Vietnam for fear of China, and in Afghanistan, where the Taliban had bases in neighboring Pakistan, an ostensible ally of the United States. While Mackesy cites one of the few examples of British successes in fighting a counterinsurgency, Malaysia (1948–1960), this was an aberration, an exception that proves the rule: first, the British were fighting an ethnic minority, the Chinese, who lacked support among the general population; and second, the insurgents had no foreign support. It was still a long war and involved brutal methods. As in the more common case, European friends of the American Revolution were likewise a major contributing factor in the success of the American insurgents.[3]

A standard interpretation holds that British resources were overstretched in America with the outbreak of war against France (1778), followed by Spain (1779), and the Dutch Republic (1780), while much of the rest of Europe formed a League of Armed Neutrality (1780) that was in fact hostile to British interests. Even Sweden sent a small army in support of America. The European allies of America were not necessarily motivated by American independence, a fact especially evident in the "support" for America from Spain (as seen, for example, in the essay in this volume concerning Bernardo de Gálvez). They were primarily concerned with restoring the balance of power in Europe to reverse the power-shifting, devastating British victories of the Seven Years' War (1756–1763). This is why the Revolutionary War was global and its last battle was fought in India. But the effect on British war efforts during the American Revolution was the same regardless of these European motivations: Britain lost the American war. In numerous international conflicts, Britain traditionally relied on allies because it had a small army compared to the major nations in Europe. This was one of the only wars in its history in which it fought alone, and the consequences were evident.

Even before the formal entry of France in 1778, the prospect of a war in Europe constrained the British war effort in America. This explains why Britain failed to mobilize fully its navy at the beginning of the war, despite the recommendations of the First Lord of the Admiralty, the Earl of Sandwich. The government was concerned not to provoke an arms race and not to antagonize France. Yet despite Britain's efforts not to antagonize the French, from the beginning of the war France's ports gave sanctuary to patriot privateers whose raids forced the British navy to introduce a convoy system for merchant ships that deflected ships that might otherwise have participated in a blockade of America. Perhaps even more importantly, France, especially, and other European nations provided vital armaments and supplies through front companies such as Hortalez and Company, arranged by the playwright and courtier Pierre-Augustin Caron de Beaumarchais. These were critical given the absence of saltpeter in America to make gunpowder, as well as serious deficiencies in other armaments and materials. According to one eyewitness, it would have been impossible to inflict more than a stalemate on the British at Saratoga (1777), for example, without muskets and ammunition from France.[4]

Beyond the munitions to engage in the war, the French and Spanish navies proved a decisive factor in the Revolutionary War. For the first time since the seventeenth century, their combined naval force outnumbered the British and threatened Britain itself with invasion in 1779. Their movements forced Britain to reallocate resources, sending more ships and troops to the Caribbean than America after 1778. And, of course, it was the French victory at the Battle of the Chesapeake (1781) and their naval blockade at Yorktown (the focus of two essays herein) that prevented Cornwallis and his army from being rescued by the Royal Navy and escaping to New York or Charleston, an event that sealed an American victory in the war.

In addition to the official support of France and other nations, individual Europeans provided essential military expertise, whether in military training and maneuvers, engineering forts, or siege tactics, when few patriots had any experience of military leadership or expertise.

Appreciation of the official and individual European roles in the military conflict is also important to counter a popular, simplistic myth among laymen, propagated today by some politicians, that the war was won by armed, private individuals shooting from behind stone fences and hedges, a myth that reinforces an exceptionalist and an isolationist narrative of the history of the United States at odds with a sound historic understanding. The popular obsession with the militia in these accounts also does an injustice to the Continental Army, since the decisive battles of the war were largely fought using conventional armies and tactics of the type deployed in Europe—in the case of Yorktown, with a large contingent of French troops. Indeed, George Washington wanted the nation's victory to be won by such methods to gain recognition of the United States as a nation on a par with European powers. The effort to obscure the role of the Continental Army and its European allies is not entirely happenstance. Since the warm embrace of nationhood formed in the Continental Army would prove essential in the coming battle to ratify the Constitution and increase the power of the federal government, the essential role of the army can be downplayed by those who hope to minimize acceptance of federal power in the early republic.

In any case, the Mackesy-Shy debate in the 1970s laid the groundwork for understanding the defeat of the British and the impact that European allies had on the result of the war itself, but relations with these European allies also tended to have important implications for the Age of Revolutions (and constitution making), on international law, trade, and diplomacy. While the impact of these relations on the French Revolution has been long debated (and this collection brings new insights to those critical questions), the broader impact of the first successful colonial revolution in modern times—made possible by European material support, encouraged by European friends of liberty, facilitated by ideas that brewed in the Atlantic environs—is undeniable. More particularly, notions of free trade that would be contested for years (erupting in the War of 1812 and still contested today) were developed in this context. Diplomatic protocols impacting new states, constitutional doctrines, citizenship norms, and other factors, all developed in this milieu and under the influence of the European friends. A proper understanding of these issues requires looking beyond America's shores.

In fact, as discussed in detail in this volume's final essay, the field of Atlantic history was originally grounded on the European influence on the Revolution. Reconsideration of the breadth of European allies and their influence on the war and postwar years in this volume provides another reason to reinvigorate and expand the study of Atlantic history, linking it even more intimately with the Age of Revolutions.

Such matters relating to European friends of the American Revolution, and some of the lasting impact of the resulting alliances and relationships, were the topic of the SAR conference that provided the impetus for this volume. The scholarly papers presented at the conference and collected in this volume, many plumbing largely untapped archives and new methodologies, represent original and important contributions from historians both in the United States and in Europe. Indeed, while the history of the American Revolution has been dominated by scholars in Britain and the United States (as has the field of Atlantic history), the majority of the authors here are from Europe, including Jean-Marie Kowalski and Olivier Chaline, both from the Sorbonne in Paris; Victor Enthoven of the Free University of Amsterdam; Munro Price of the University of Bradford in England; and Marie-Jeanne Rossignol of Université Paris Cité.

Of course, a single volume cannot encompass the breadth of issues relating to European participation in the war and its consequences.[5] Critical work is still to be done, for example, on the extent, origin, and use of foreign funding in the American war effort. Larrie D. Ferreiro, in a work published after the conference, claims that France and Spain contributed ninety percent of the arms used by the patriots and "close to $30 billion [current valuation] in direct monetary aid" for arms and munitions and that the French spent a total of "1 billion livres, about half a trillion dollars" (in 2017 dollars) on their total global war effort. In his *The Key to American Independence: Quantifying Foreign Assistance to the American Revolution*, William V. Wenger scaled down Ferreiro's estimates for arms, but calculated that total French aid to America—based on gifts, loans, credit, military aid, materials, shipping, troops, and naval support—amounted to the equivalent in 2010 of $69 billion and that from Spain $16 billion.[6] Others will certainly refine and expand on their work, exposing new topics to be considered, but whatever the precise level of financial support, French, Spanish, and Dutch grants and loans were ultimately vital for preventing the American Revolution from becoming a victim of its own antigovernment rhetoric and going bankrupt because the Continental Congress did not have the power to impose taxes.

While undoubtedly other topics will continue to present themselves, the essays in this volume cover a variety of issues: they probe the formation in Europe of ideological support for the war (with enormous implications for the subsequent French Revolution), as well as diplomatic history beyond France and Britain (including nonstate actors); they examine maritime history at a micro level by relying on previously untapped sources and a bottom-up approach; they take conflicted "allies" like Spain and Portugal into account and study how inspired French individuals who supported the war affected the postwar period both in America and France. In an important epilogue recognizing the foundational role of Robert R. Palmer's and Jacques Godechot's work on the American Revolution to the development of Atlantic history, the volume calls for a reconsideration of their effort, and the European friends of the American Revolution, as the scope of Atlantic history is expanded into new and exciting areas.

The first essay, by Julia Osman, asks how France (including especially the literate elite) was convinced to ally with the British North Americans who had been so thoroughly and effectively vilified only a few years previously during the French and Indian War. Osman's answer suggests much about the coming of the French Revolution and the making of French revolutionaries, adding a new chapter to the old debate about the influence of the American Revolution on the later upheaval in France.

The following two essays, in the section "Diplomacy," turn to the complex diplomatic chess games that consumed Europe for years during the American conflict, but in these essays the focus is away from Paris and London, the usual venues for study of Revolutionary War diplomacy. Paul A. Gilje, discusses the League of Armed Neutrality, sponsored by Catherine the Great of Russia, and how it played an important role in supporting American (and French) access to supplies while never formally allying with either side. Gilje also discusses how the League contributed to the long-term development of international legal principles of free trade (another important topic in Atlantic history). The equally complex but particular game that engaged John Paul Jones as he sought to refit his fleet in Holland after his victory over the British *HMS Serapis* on September 23, 1779—when the outgunned Jones reportedly responded to the British demand that he strike his colors with the retort, "I have not yet begun to fight"—is the topic of Victor Enthoven's essay. In both the specific (Enthoven) and the more general (Gilje) studies, the important contributions of European friends to America's ultimate victory are evident.

This volume also introduces scholars in America to a remarkable new research project: the work of the French Naval Academy, where Jean-Marie Kowalski and Olivier Chaline have undertaken a comprehensive study of French and British ship logbooks from 1781 to 1783, here relating to the critical role of naval battles and the worst naval defeat of the British in the eighteenth century at Chesapeake (1781), a decisive factor in the defeat of Lord Cornwallis at Yorktown. Consulting an important primary resource that has been undervalued, and in the case of French archives, largely ignored, they have opened a new archive that not only illuminates important details impacting naval warfare but evidences the useful work that can be done in reconsidering the naval history of the Revolution and the role of the European friends. Their detailed and particularized work with ships' logs parallels the type of town studies that have become popular and enriched the wider literature. Kowalski and Chaline's pioneering work, reflected in the section "War at Sea," reminds us of the role of chance in warfare, affected by factors such as the weather, a contingency that historians seeking cause and effect ignore at their peril. By comparing rarely consulted French logbook accounts with British ones, they retrace the movements of both fleets leading up to and during the Battle of the Chesapeake (1781), revealing important leadership decisions made during that critical military encounter but also the uncontrollable role of weather in the making of history. The project of the French Naval Academy, in cooperation with the United States Naval Academy in Annapolis, will undoubtedly provide grist for historians' mills for years to come as a major synthesis on the topic is being published in French (*Commander et naviguer*, forthcoming).

Beyond the direct support from France and the Netherlands, some of the American "allies" were not formally in alliance with the new nation and were reluctant to be so. Spain, for example, was never formally an ally of the United States but was part of the Bourbon alliance with France (1778). In the section "Conflicted Allies," the role of Spain, and especially of Bernardo de Gálvez, the Spanish governor of New Orleans during the war, is the subject of the essay by Kathleen DuVal and Gonzalo M. Quintero Saravia, the latter of whom wrote the authoritative biography *Bernardo de Gálvez: Spanish Hero of the American Revolution* (2018). Taking on an even less studied, and equally conflicted, diplomatic partner, Timothy Walker explores the role of Portugal, an English ally of many centuries that sought to protect its growing trading relationship with America during and after the war while not alienating its very long-term relationship with England. Both essays call on historians to look beyond the simple American-British-French triad.

Beyond these national, if sometimes ambivalent, "friends," individual Europeans contributed greatly to American success. The essays included here do not attempt to cover all of the many European adventurers who joined the American cause, such as Baron von Steuben of Prussia, Baron de Kalb of Bavaria, or Casimir Pulaski and Thaddeus Kosciuszko, both from Poland. Nor is the focus on the wartime contributions of Lafayette and other French allies. Instead, the essays presented in the section "Lafayette and French Nobels" expand our thinking about the role of individual Europeans both by widening our periodization—with Robert Rhodes Crout looking at the remarkable role that Lafayette played in postwar France and in America to promote US constitutional reform—and with Munro Price introducing a more thorough analysis of some characters who are not as well known as Lafayette, particularly the Lameth brothers of France, whose experience in America influenced their important role in the coming French Revolution.

The essays in the volume primarily focus on European activities in America and Europe, but we can arguably include the wider war in the Caribbean, India, Africa, and the Mediterranean as vital in assisting the Americans to overstretch and defeat the British; it is certainly an area worthy of additional study.

The final essay in this collection, by Marie-Jeanne Rossignol, pays homage to the work of Godechot and Palmer, who stressed the need to consider the European dimension of American history and similarly the American influence on European history, as does this volume. The approach represented by the contributors to this volume is indebted to their pioneering research and writings in Atlantic history. Looking at Palmer's and Godechot's contributions, Rossignol reminds us of the value of a classic historiography that is too easily missed in our voracious consumption of the newest monograph. She also suggests that the recent developments in Atlantic history, including especially a focus on the Haitian and other revolutions, may be closer stepchildren of Godechot's and Palmer's works than previously thought. Together, her essay and this volume demonstrate the need to continue expanding the scope of study in Atlantic history to maintain its vital contributions.

While no volume can provide the definitive word on a struggle as complex as the American Revolution, nor even on the intricacies of its international alliances, the contributions assembled here provide new insights and call for a renewed focus on the European friends of the American Revolution as an important means to better understand the war and its consequences and as a foundational element of Atlantic history. In doing so, the volume allows us to reconsider the essential nature of the ties across the Atlantic Ocean that made the American revolt not only successful, but of a much larger and long-lasting influence in the changing world. The breadth of issues considered—from the creation of a French revolutionary patriot to the development of the norms of modern free trade, from the impact of wind and waves to diplomatic efforts to assuage both parties to the conflict—reflects the continued potential for study not only of the Revolution but in the field of Atlantic history more generally.

Notes

1. Piers Mackesy, *The War for America, 1775–1783* (1964; reprinted, with an introduction by John Shy, Lincoln: University of Nebraska Press, 1993); Piers Mackesy, *Could the British Have Won the War of Independence?* (Worcester, MA: Clark University Press, 1976); John Shy, *A People Numerous and Armed: Reflections on the Military Struggle for American Independence,* rev. ed. (Ann Arbor: University of Michigan Press, 2000).

2. See, e.g., John Newsinger, *British Conterinsurgency,* 2d ed. (Basingstoke: Palgrave Macmillan UK, 2015).

3. Ibid., 33–66.

4. Larrie D. Ferreiro, *Brothers at Arms: American Independence and the Men of France and Spain Who Saved It* (New York: Vintage Books, 2017), 73.

5. A number of further publications on Europe and the American Revolution are under preparation, testifying to renewed interest in the field: see, e.g., Carine Lounissi and Bertrand Van Ruymbeke, eds., "The American Revolution in Europe: France, Italy, Germany, the Netherlands," *Revue Française des Etudes Américaines* (December 2022); Kevin Butterfield and Bertrand Van Ruymbeke, eds., "France and the American Revolution," *Early American Studies* (forthcoming, 2024); Jack Rakove and Bertrand

Van Ruymbeke, eds., "Studying the American Revolution in France," *Journal of Early American History* (forthcoming, 2023).

6. Ferreiro, *Brothers at Arms*, 335; William V. Wenger, *The Key to American Independence: Quantifying Foreign Assistance to the American Revolution* (El Segundo, CA: William V. Wenger, 2021), ix, 112, 113.

Imagining an American, and a French, Revolutionary

What makes a revolutionary? This is one of the central questions asked, implicitly or explicitly, as historians, political scientists, and military leaders have sought to understand the American Revolution since before the first shot was fired until our own day. The issue has been extensively studied by American historians (from Bernard Bailyn to Woody Holton to Gary Nash).

An equally complicated and extensively cogitated question is what effect the American Revolution had on the French.

Julia Osman, in her thought-provoking essay, confronts both questions anew. Looking beyond the problem of creating revolutionaries in America, her essay recognizes that making European friends of the American Revolution posed a somewhat different and particularly difficult problem. Of course, monarchies did not want to promote revolutionaries, much less democratic revolutions. An American revolutionary war against Great Britain was one thing; a war for independence from monarchy seemed another matter altogether. But obtaining the support of France—America's first and most important European friend in the Revolution—posed an additional problem: France had fought an extensive and bloody war against Britain and its American empire a few short years before in which the British, including the Americans, were vilified as barbaric, dishonorable, uncouth enemies. Bitter memories oozed from Paris, of course, but also from the shores of the Allegheny River near modern day Pittsburgh to the Plains of Abraham outside of Quebec to the seas surrounding France's Caribbean colonies. At the end of the Seven Years' War, a battered and humiliated France blamed

British Americans as much as natives of England for its costly and humiliating defeat.

As the American Revolution approached, this posed two related problems: the Continental Congress had to convince radical Protestants in New England who had fought against French Canada and its allied Indians decade after decade to acquiesce in an alliance with Europe's leading Catholic power. At the same time, changing the French perception of Americans was essential if France was to ally successfully with the new nation. Osman takes up this latter problem.

Even at the time of the Treaty of Paris of 1763, some in France saw the seeds for American colonials to challenge their British masters. This was one of several reasons why France relatively readily agreed in those negotiations to give up its territory in Canada and in the trans-Appalachian region in return for profitable Caribbean sugar islands: With Canada no longer French, a presumed threat to New England would be removed, and British military support would be far less needed by the American colonists. As a result, it was anticipated that it would be far more difficult for Britain to restrain independent-minded New Englanders who chafed under the transatlantic regulations of a swelling British Empire. But this left a critical question: How could France and the French people come to see its former bitter enemies in America as their friends and allies?

In the early 1770s, as conflict between Britain and its North American colonies heightened, some French officials perceived that a new war was in the offing. With British-American conflict portending a possible opportunity to humble the haughty British Empire, officials in France who hoped to support any American insurgency first had to go about systematically seeking to distinguish British Americans from the British and to rehabilitate and reform the image of the former among French citizens.

As Julia Osman explains in "American Nationality: A French Invention?," this was accomplished with the help of the comte de Vergennes. French officials were very successful in creating an image of an American patriot who was a victim of British atrocities, an honorable soldier, and a supporter of the Enlightenment, a character who was carefully distinguished in the emerging French literature not only from the British but from Native Americans and the enslaved. At the same time, seemingly unintentionally, the propagandists also created the image of a patriotic revolutionary fighting for his nation and liberty, an image that would come to the fore a few short years later in the

French Revolution. While France was a "friend" to America's revolutionary war against Great Britain, it found that it could not fully sequester that war from the War for Independence from monarchy; the images created to support the Americans could have a lasting influence on France's own people.

While many historians have sought to answer the questions of how one became a revolutionary and of how the American Revolution impacted the coming of the French Revolution, Osman presents a new and interesting way of exploring that topic and adds a new chapter to the existing volumes on the influence of the American Revolution on the French, reminding us all of historic paths yet to be explored.

American Nationality
A French Invention?

JULIA OSMAN

It is no secret among scholars of the eighteenth century that when the American Revolution erupted in the spring of 1775, it attracted the attention of the major powers of Europe and met with an especially enthusiastic reception in France, the rebelling colonists' future ally.

Certainly, one of the sources of this excitement was France's intense rivalry with Britain: by aiding the American rebellion monetarily and militarily, France would have a hand in severing Britain from her colonies and avenge her own loss to Britain during the Seven Years' War just twelve years earlier. To create an alliance with the Americans during the War for Independence, however, French elites, especially those in positions of political and military authority, had to reform and recast American identity, previously part of the "enemy," and they harnessed the power of printed texts and images to do so. These efforts not only provided a meticulously crafted American image for the French imagination, but even created a French Revolutionary language.

During the Seven Years' War, France and Britain had battled for territory in North America, and the French army had faced Anglo-American provincials as part of the enemy English. French writers had described these Anglo-Americans as evil barbarians to encourage and define French patriotism against "the other." In order to see these recent American enemies as allies, then, French writers in the 1770s had to refashion their ideas of what constituted an American. Charles Gravier, comte de Vergennes, the secretary of foreign affairs in France at the time, faced this challenge of turning public opinion from vehemently against the Anglo-Americans to strongly in their favor, and he used the *Affaires de l'Angleterre et de l'Amérique,* a propaganda paper he organized and disguised as an impartial Dutch gazette, to do so. This gazette presented an image of the Americans as virtuous farmers and philosophers who suffered grievously at the hands of the British army, and it caught French attention.

Even after the *Affaires* discontinued, with the French-American alliance, French public opinion had so embraced the American image presented therein that writers of all genres continued to sculpt and refine their construction of American identity. Not only did these fictitious Americans of the *Affaires* prove worthy allies, but they confirmed and fulfilled French preferences and philosophies. These texts, including poems and plays, positioned the Americans as victims of British barbarism; as grateful servants to Louis XVI, whose sovereignty they acknowledged and respected; and as honorable warriors whose culture, while remaining rugged, exhibited sufficient sensitivity to European delicacies. Through these texts, authors turned a recent enemy of France into an admirable ally, and in doing so created a national identity that not only rescued their old foe from infamy but revealed their own desire to reinvigorate their nation.

Making English enemies into American allies did more than just give French writers and readers positive if often inaccurate impressions of Americans. The act of writing and reading about these American revolutionaries came at a time of "collective soul-searching" in France—the loss of the Seven Years' War had resulted in humiliating concessions around the globe.[1] Men of letters questioned French patriotism, identity, and the very nature of French society, and French historians such as Sarah Maza, Deena Goodman, Jay Smith, Michael Kwass, and John Shovlin, not to mention Alexis de Tocqueville, have identified the roots of the French Revolution in these last decades before 1789.[2] This context of intense soul-searching and flurried writing about French social, military, and cultural reform, however, provides a charged prism through which to view these many and varied writings on American revolutionaries. The degree to which the American Revolution inspired the French Revolution is a thorny question that many historians have tackled—causality is always hard to place—but I argue that in inventing an American identity, French writers and readers also created the vocabulary, imagery, and aesthetic that spoke to their own desires for change. In constructing this American nationality, French writers and officials articulated and found inspiration for their own revolution.

The first time French writers purposely fashioned an "American" for their readers was during the Seven Years' War, which lasted from 1756 to 1763 and proved crucial to forming and encouraging French patriotism. Over the course of that war, French writers vilified the English as money-grubbing profit-seekers in order to create an opposing national image for the French as honorable and patriotic, contributing to a growing French identity of superior honor.[3] In these works, Anglo-American colonists shared in the reputation for British "barbarity," a trait exemplified by the killing of a Frenchman, Joseph Coulon de Villiers de Jumonville, who was hacked to death by an Amerindian ally of a young American colonist, George Washington. After Washington signed capitulation terms that cited him as Jumonville's murderer (Washington did not read French and later claimed he did not know what he was signing), his name and image became the target of many French publications that used him as the prototype of British savagery and aggression.[4]

French author Antoine Léonard Thomas, in his *Jumonville Poème* of 1759, cast Washington as the "butcher" who pierced Jumonville with a "murderous [shot of] lead." Jumonville, on the other hand, is depicted as a man with a "sacred character" who "represents the august corps of his nation." In the telling of Jumonville's death then, Thomas is implicating the entire nation of England in the attack of the honorable French; this incident merely represents the innate character of these two rival nations. By portraying Washington as killing Jumonville directly (most American historians blame his death on one of Washington's Amerindian allies), he is designating all English, including American colonists in this case, as murderous barbarians. As Jumonville's killers did not attack just him but the very "primitive laws of nations," it should attract universal revulsion.[5] Another history of the war that came out at the same time, by Etienne-Joseph Poullin de Lumina, tells not only how "Washington mercilessly assassinated" Jumonville but that Washington's Amerindian allies were so "horrified by the crime and were so ashamed of what they had done, that they abandoned [Washington] and offered themselves to the French, to help in their vengeance."[6] Again, Washington represents general English savagery. Such works portray the French as honorable and courageous next to the inherently dishonorable English and proved useful in inspiring French patriotism and helping to define an early French and English "nation."[7]

Despite the success of poems and other works like Thomas's to inspire French patriotism, readers would have to change their opinion very quickly about these Anglo-Americans. Just twelve years after the loss of the Seven Years' War, the colonial British subjects of North America, like the "murderous" George Washington, would have to become close French allies, and French writers would have to call on the power of their readers' imaginations once again.

Diplomatically, France had an interest in the potential of an American rebellion that would cause problems for Britain as soon as the Seven Years' War ended. Having ceded New France (Québec and Louisiana), French troops and French-Canadians no longer lurked in the North American theater, and Vergennes hoped that the absence of a common enemy would cause tensions to flare up between colonial Americans and their English overlords. When war did break out in 1775, Vergennes was eager to side with rebelling Americans, but he knew he would need to soften French attitudes toward their former Anglo-American enemies. American officials likewise welcomed opportunities to woo the French readers, and beginning in 1777 American and French administrators consciously tried to shape larger French perspectives of Americans with the periodical the *Affaires de l'Angleterre et de l'Amérique*.

The *Affaires*, while it printed its stories in the form of a newspaper, turned out to be more like Thomas's poem on the death of Jumonville than an actual gazette, as it acknowledged its propensity to exaggerate or invent things to heighten the readers' experience of the conflict. The comte de Vergennes, who oversaw its publication in Paris, heavily subsidized the paper, and Edmé-Jacques Genêt, a zealous advocate of the American cause, edited it and received several contributions to it from Benjamin Franklin and John Adams.[8] In the introduction to the *Affaires*, the editors explained how their publication differed from typical French-language periodicals by focusing on a single event and recording information that would be suitable for the history books as well as help its readers predict the outcome of the war. Like Thomas's poem about Jumonville, the writers also admitted, even embraced, that their own opinions would inevitably color their reports, as "you cannot write your exposé without embracing an opinion." If the *Affaires* tried to exist without any opinions, it would be limited "to a dry and boring enumeration of acts and petitions." Instead, it argued, "Why not fruitfully engage your readers?" After all, this English-American conflict was "a very great event for Europe."[9]

The writers behind the *Affaires* also noted that their aim was to explain American identity, especially since it was no longer useful for the Anglo-Americans at the heart of the American Revolution to embody English savagery. Other residents of North America with distinct identities already known to French readers included people of the many Amerindian nations, enslaved Africans or African descendants, and specific religious or political groups like the abolitionist Quakers of Pennsylvania. Each of these groups held precise identifiable qualities in French writings but still left the identity of the Anglo-Americans who had primarily occupied the role of villains in the previous war very much in question.[10] To this end, the *Affaires* made sure to distinguish them as neither "Indian" nor "Negro" nor "English," but a new people. For example, one letter in the *Affaires* reported a rumor that England was going to "raise the Indians and Negros and pay them 50 pounds sterling for each American head," thus distinguishing Americans from these two "other"-ed groups.[11] To ensure these Americans were no longer synonymous with the barbaric English, the *Avertisement* at the beginning of the first issue stated that the "Americans, as brothers of the English, can no longer be either their disciples or their slaves." Rather, they had become a separate people, still related to the English but no longer synonymous with them.[12]

The *Affaires* specified, through the observations of "Docteur Price" (likely a partially fictionalized version of Benjamin Franklin's English friend Dr. Richard Price), that Americans were "as enlightened" as the English "but more virtuous." Their number included thinkers who could hold their own with "the most renowned philosophers or politicians." One Englishman even expressed optimism via the *Affaires* that the Americans would be easily beaten because, after all, they were but "peasant philosophers." Americans' supposed philosophical edge did not mean, however, that they did not "produce extraordinary examples of courage and steadfastness." One story presented two soldiers from the country who were terribly wounded from a recent skirmish. As they lay dying in the hospital, they clasped their hands, and tore off their bandages, "declaring that they were too happy to die for the glorious cause of American liberty."[13]

Another report in the *Affaires* quoted from the *Boston Gazette* that "our militia are forming new armies; they will attack the tyrants in proper battle formation [*rangée*], and they will die with liberty on the field of honor, where a complete victory will assure their existence forever as an Independent people. These generous sentiments can only exalt in our hearts." Not only does this quote display Americans' eagerness to fight for Independence and the virtue therein, but it signals how they are going to fight: in proper battle formations that would honorably conform to European standards, not "à la Sauvage," like the Amerindians or European partisans. Such a highlight was important in the *Affaires*' attempts to establish an American identity, especially as the authors and Vergennes used the *Affaires* to angle for French military assistance to the embattled Americans. French officers could be assured that they would fight alongside disciplined, well-ordered troops, not reckless partisans.

These well-ordered American troops, tough and determined as they were, differed from the English in their practices of restraint and mercy. Their "principles of gentleness and humanity" in fact constituted their "distinctive character of bravery: each cruelty must be banned from the actions of a free people." The *Affaires* published multiple stories illustrating American mercy in war. In one of them, American soldiers showcased the "greatest proofs of humanity" to English prisoners of war that were trapped in a fire. At the approach of American rescuers, the prisoners thought they were going to be scalped and pleaded not to be massacred. One American replied, "Put your arms around my neck and let me help you." The Americans carried the prisoners gingerly to a British fort commanded by Captain Leslie. As the Americans entered the fort with the wounded British, the English thanked the Americans for their "humane and generous procedures."[14] The *Affaires* would have its readers believe that such patience and virtue in the army was widespread, as each "true American understood the precious advantages that an effort of virtue could make."[15]

In contrast, the *Affaires* preyed on French expectations for barbarous British violence and pointed to it as the most pronounced difference between Americans and Englishmen. One report printed a letter from an American who mourned his sad state as a victim of the British army. He lingered over "the appalling barbarism with which our enemies have conducted themselves . . . in burning our cities and towns . . . in exposing those who live there, without regard for age or sex, to all the calamities [of war]." Such excesses and "other horrors that will never please humanity" pushed even reluctant Americans to revolt against their cruel British overlords. The *Affaires* dwelt almost fiendishly on "the enormous excesses committed by the King's troops on the inhabitants of America." One letter detailed that "our virtuous children are massacred and our houses destroyed by the British troops." The most often reported act of British atrocity was the rape of American women and girls. According to a letter written by a "distinguished officer in the American army," one American civilian saw the "rape of his wife, as well as his ten-year-old daughter." The British then chased several other young women through the woods, and the letter describes in graphic detail the sexual assault of a thirteen-year-old girl. Yet another story followed a father who was shot while trying to save his daughter from becoming another victim of British lust. Even the American loyalists appeared to "conspire barbarous and infernal plots" against American patriots. One report even speculated that the entire reason behind the war was "the animosity of certain English against the Americans."[16] While other gazettes reported on supposed British atrocities as well, the *Affaires'* emphasis on destruction and rape must have elicited feelings of righteous outrage and wrestled the image of the Americans away from British allies to victims of such a vile enemy alongside the French.

Toward the end of the publication of the *Affaires*, the gazette gloried in the American victory at Saratoga. Titled, "Aux enfants de la patrie" (To the children of our homeland), which almost prophesized the "Marseillaise" still fifteen years in the making, a letter recounted the defeat of British general Burgoyne and the capture of his army. It is hard to tell how much of an influence the *Affaires* had in France's formal entry into America's War for Independence. Obviously, many factors were at work, including the painstaking efforts of American diplomats.[17] But Vergennes's efforts had succeeded in projecting a new concept and image of American identity, one that French writers would continue to develop.

The reaction of French writers to the alliance with these new Americans spoke to the *Affaires'* success in creating an image attractive to the French reading public. Historians, novelists, playwrights, and poets alike cited this new American as their muse. J. L. Le Barbier le Jeune indulged his American fantasies in his 1785 play based on a true incident of the last-minute redemption of an English officer who would have been hanged by the American army. In his *avertissement* preceding the play, he specified that "all that I have learned of interest about the Americans, their zeal . . . the inspiring gratitude [they have] for the[ir] [French] friends and generous liberators; has added a new interest that enflamed my imagination to the point that I dared to represent it."[18] The play that follows exhibits multiple moments of American mercy responding to British barbarity, especially in the fate of the titular character Asgill, himself a British officer who should have met his fate on the gallows but is reprieved at the last minute.

Writers would commandeer the Americans for serious endeavors, such as Joseph Cerutti's "The Eagle and the Owl" of 1783, an allegorical tale intended to instruct the young French prince, "whom others had dared to blame for his love of the Sciences and Letters." The poem features an eagle who flies about and incorporates lessons from the places he sees in order to be a wise ruler. When he flies over America, he witnesses Boston rebelling against England. Cerutti describes the American colonists as "a people forced to be slaves," but their "wisdom, without artifice triumph over obstacles." This "young land, imbued with miracles, [was] an independent world open to all mankind." The poem is so full of metaphor and symbolism that the publication is mostly footnotes explaining Cerutti's references. It is there that he has the most direct things to say about America. Not surprisingly, from the above description, Americans appear very wise. "The act of the declaration of independence," for example, "came from a congress . . . it is not an assembly that revolted against its masters, but a senate that judged them."[19] Such a point was vital for the young eagle/prince to learn: in the American Revolution, it "was not fanaticism nor even enthusiasm that declared war," but "reason" and "law."

Following the lead of the *Affaries de l'Angleterre et de l'Amérique*, Cerutti takes care to distinguish the Americans from the English by the violence they use and the way they respond to that violence: the British being excessive, and the Americans practicing restraint and mercy. To this end, Cerutti describes a story of General Burgoyne, who burned down the house of American general Schuyler. Eventually, Burgoyne is forced to surrender and is conducted to Schuyler's other house. There, he is welcomed as a guest by Schuyler's wife and children. Burgoyne recognizes with sighs and tears that "it is too much for someone who ravages their lands and burns their homes." In Cerutti's telling, his army was shown the same mercy from the Americans, who saw the British army pass before them "without making the slightest outrage, without letting escape an insulting gesture or smile." Americans were also good neighbors to each other, especially farmers who were trying to set up new settlements on the frontier. Cerutti describes them helping each other, for "in America, a man is never abandoned to himself alone."[20]

In tailoring their image of Americans, French writers were careful to note that even though Americans had fought against the English monarchy and formed a republic, they had nothing against monarchies in general, including the French monarchy. French writers glorified the debt that the newly independent American republic owed to Louis XVI for the funds, troops, and international support he had provided; French writers further claimed credit for their part in creating this laudable new race of Americans. LeManissier's poem "Le Docteur Franklin," published in 1787, exhibits all these elements. He opens the poem with Franklin's praise for the King's "supreme generosity." He explains, "The people of Boston, your old enemy / asks for your help today with my voice. . . . We are exposed to the most frightful obstacles / and you, great king, could break our chains." Franklin recounts that, like a nation of Cincinnati, Americans following the Seven Years' War "forgot the profession of war / Our soldiers' hands tilled the earth, / preferring harvesting grains to laurels." Like the people of Pennsylvania, a reference to the peace-loving Quakers, they all became pacifists, considering "the whole universe our country." "Humanity reigned; the Negro and the Indian were no longer distinguished from the most noble Christian." Trade blossomed as well. It was into this utopia that British troops arrived and imposed laws as if the Americans were "vile slaves." Franklin differentiates these Americans from current English people by, as is custom, describing them as virtuous heroes responding to terrible British atrocity. Franklin then returned his focus to Louis XVI, "the most powerful of kings."[21]

Pierre Duviquet added to this with some "Verses on the Peace [of 1783]," in which Louis XVI actively took part in inventing Americans. By "his good deeds . . . the world became French." The poet refers to the world, but it is America that Louis has recently helped. The poet is inferring that the Americans have become more like the French than the English.[22]

While historians can never really be certain how much of what one reads equates to how one thinks, reading and writing undoubtedly constituted powerful activities in eighteenth-century France. It was the century of the book, which readers could access in many ways, whether quietly in a private closet or heard in a boisterous public location like a café or the home of a friend. Over the course of the eighteenth century, "more numerous were those who owned books, and more numerous were the books that they owned." The eighteenth century saw a great increase in the number of readers in the lower classes—by the end of the century "shop owners, artisans, and laborers progressively tamed the book." Small towns in the country also obtained greater access to the printed word, especially as institutions began to lend books more readily, increasing the opportunities for even the poorest members of society to have access to publications. To quote Roger Chartier, even for humblest readers, appetites for reading "increased," even as they were "sated."[23]

And reading and writing produced powerful effects, especially regarding war. As Jill Lepore has shown in her book on King Philip's War (1675–1676), writing is a potent act in which writers try to "contain," "censure," or "organize" events, searching for truth while trying to establish a dominant narrative. "War," Lepore states, "is a contest of words as well as wounds," and in this contest, it is not unusual for people who were not directly involved in the conflict to write the most about it.[24]

Like King Philip's War, the American Revolution was rife with meaning, and French writers proved hugely influential in how the larger French citizenry understood that war, both on its own terms and its meaning for France. In writing and rewriting the American Revolution, authors invented a new but malleable world in which they could experiment with Enlightenment ideas and fantasies that had never been rooted in a real, contemporary case study. The world the gazettes presented was already rather fictional, which allowed for, even encouraged, writers to continue to play with and try to piece together what this revolutionary and postrevolutionary America looked like. After all, the *Affaires de l'Angleterre et de l'Amérique* had encouraged readers to engage their creative side and speculate. What did a former monarchy look like, having thrown off a king? What was this land of "peasant philosophers"? As much as America was supposed to be the embodiment of things that had previously only existed in French Enlightenment thinking, it was still a quasi-fictional and malleable world, ripe for imaginative interpretations from French writers and readers.

In this malleability are signs of French writers "trying Revolution on for size," for much of the language used to glorify the American Revolution found voice again in the French Revolution. In playing with and inventing America, these writers also invented a new identity for France in light of its American alliance. Authors who portrayed the French army in America, or imagined conversations between Louis XVI and Ben Franklin, or created epic poems that included American heroes crossing the Atlantic for French help, had to portray France as a country of liberty with a citizen-king. Certainly the Americans that writers had invented could not reasonably ask for or receive aid from a monarchy, or a monarch, as tyrannical as the one they were trying to escape. Just as French writers had contrasted the French from the English in the Jumonville literature, French writers drew direct distinctions between the French monarchy, one of freedom and reason, and the British monarchy, one of tyranny.

French writers could portray the French state and society as they would like it to be, so long as they referred to it as an ally to the Americans. Publications on America did have to be approved by a censor, but if writers were discussing America, they had greater freedom and flexibility since America was a French ally. So long as they discussed the French state relative to America, then, writers exercised a tremendous amount of freedom.[25] Some of their writings about America made that country seem more "French" in that French writers used America to draw what a revolutionized France itself might look like. The brief excerpts from the *Affaires de l'Angleterre et de l'Amérique* contain phrases that, in retrospect, may hint at the French Revolution to come, such as the previously mentioned letter reporting the battle of Saratoga, titled "Aux enfants de la patrie," which would later be the opening lines of the "Marseillaise." Likewise, an article from an actual (though far from impartial) Dutch gazette, the *Gazette de Leyde,* printed a story about the Connecticut militia, which was desperate for more troops. When the governor appealed to men who had extensive families, and thus were exempted from military service, they responded en masse. The reporter for the *Gazette* extolled them: "The example of these respectable citizens proves to what degree patriotism raises their hearts, and how difficult it will be to subjugate a people in which the vast majority know how to sacrifice their familial ties and their most valued personal interests to save the *patrie en danger.*"[26] These last three words, "*patrie en danger,*" appear frequently during the French Revolution, but more than that, this story and its lesson again seem to foreshadow events of that revolution: in this case, the *levée en masse.*

As Orville T. Murphy has noted, French readers seemed particularly entranced with the myth they propagated, and may have believed, about the American militias. All published materials about the American forces—newspapers, histories, fictions, and poetry—reported extremely high numbers of men fighting in them. The *Gazette de France* reported that out of a population of 2.4 million people, 600,000 men, or one colonist of every four, participated in either the American army or a local militia.[27] Even peace-loving Quakers reportedly constituted their own company of soldiers.[28] The remaining members of society contributed to the war effort by making saltpeter for gunpowder or clothing for the soldiers.[29] In Maryland, any person who "refused to contribute arms or ammunition was regarded as an enemy of America and would have his name printed in the [local] gazette," demonstrating that the Americans expected their fellow citizens to contribute to the war effort.[30] On an illustrative note, the *Gazette de France* published a letter from American general Lee to British general Burgoyne, informing him that "it would not be an exaggeration to say that all the boats in the world would not suffice to transport the forces . . . of three million men, unanimously resolved to sacrifice all for liberty."[31] This was a far cry from the 75,000 men Washington wished to have had in his ranks at one time but never got. (Don Higginbotham reports that Washington's maximum force in 1778, for example, was only 18,472 men.)[32]

Murphy likewise related an episode from 1777, in which the marquis de Lafayette counseled Washington not to call on the militia to protect Philadelphia against the encroaching British army, because "Europe has a great idea of our ability to raise when we please an immense army of militia, and it is looked upon as our last but certain resource. If we fall this phantom will also fall and you know that the American interest has always been since the beginning of this war to let the world believe that we are stronger than we ever expect to be."[33]

Murphy wondered, and was not the last to wonder, to what degree such a fascination with the militia and perpetuation of their high numbers at arms and effectiveness in battle influenced the *levée en masse*. The *levée en masse* intended to put the entire nation of France under arms in order to defend against foreign threats from Austria and other liberty-crushing monarchical states. All unmarried men between the ages of eighteen and twenty-five were to serve in the army, but all citizens had a role to play in the war. As the National Convention proclaimed on August 23, 1793,

> from this moment on . . . all Frenchmen are in permanent requisition for the service of the armies. The young men will go to combat; married men will forge weapons and transport food; women will make tents and uniforms and will serve in the hospitals; children will make bandages from old linen; old men will present themselves

at public places to excite the courage of the warriors, to preach the hatred of kings and the unity of the Republic.[34]

This type of imagery had already appeared in many discussions of the American Revolution. Did the American Revolution provide the expectation that, under the right conditions, the French could obtain this kind of uberpatriotic, unstoppable defensive force that would require little maintenance or training? Were these images in the back of peoples' minds when the decree for the *levée en masse* was issued? Such coincidences beg the question of the exact nature of the relationship between the American and French Revolutions. Were French writers inventing Americans or actually starting to articulate their own revolution?

George Washington as a literary character may be the key to understanding an answer to these questions, as writers used him to express multiple ideas or points of view, and his characteristics changed over time. Like Franklin, Washington was universally known and admired, but unlike Franklin, Washington had never set foot in France, and writers could imagine him as they liked. While people in America had varying opinions on Washington's leadership style, generalship, political maneuverings, and performance as first president, France was already turning him into a legend. All aspects of Washington were praiseworthy; by the time of the American Revolution, he had been thoroughly forgiven, even vindicated in the Jumonville incident of 1754. A veteran of the Seven Years' War in North America, M. Pouchot, declared as much in his memoirs of the war published in 1781. Describing the Jumonville incident, he describes how "the English," not Washington, "fired a discharge on [Jumonville's] detachment, killing Jumonville and several others." Washington only appears in a footnote of the incident, in which Pouchot says, "It is frustrating to remember that the famous general Washington was commanding the murderers of Jumonville. He only acted, in truth, by the precise orders of his court; but he could have executed them in a less odious manner."[35] Unlike the previous literature published on the Jumonville incident, in the era of the American Revolution, Washington is not a savage murderer but a young commander just following orders.

Since Washington represented such a positive figure, writers would assign him certain attributes in order to promote or try out potentially controversial views. In an early story about Washington that was published in the *Almanach Litteraire* in 1779, he appears as the perfect subject to his monarch. The editors of the *Almanach* situate their readers to believe they have intercepted a letter that Washington wrote to his wife, which they print as "one of the most precious pieces of our collection," exposing the "complete soul" of the "dictator of America." The letter was dated June 1776, just before America's declaration of independence. In it, "Washington" (and here I use quotes, as the letter was certainly fabricated) writes to his wife of his tender, personal feelings for her, asks her to inoculate the children, and mourns his status as a "rebel" in the American cause. "I love my king, you know it," he says; "A soldier, an honest man cannot help but love him. How cruel it is for us to be reputed as traitors to such a good king!"[36] The Washington myth's promonarchist sentiments were essential to France's creation of Americans before and during the Franco-American alliance. This letter allows supporters of the American Revolution to specify that it is not an antimonarchical movement, just one that is carried out against England's tyrannies.

Six years later, however, the same publication presented a small piece about Washington that exposed an entirely different attitude toward kingship. Describing a "Fête Liberté" in Philadelphia in 1785, the *Almanach* recounts the following:

> In the great hall, where the Legislature was assembled, there was an elevated chair on a platform, covered with a canopy. There one saw the Book of Laws, where the constitutions of America [were kept]. A jeweled crown covered this honorable book. It was in this session that General Washington solemnly retired the command that he had been honored with, a command that he had served with such glory for the happiness of his fellow citizens. When this ceremony had ended, the Fabius of North America took the crown on the Book of the Law, and ascending a balcony . . . he showed the crown to the People, broke it before their eyes, and threw all the pieces out to them. The history of the ancient republics could not offer anything comparable to the grandeur of this scene.[37]

This account of Washington differs strikingly from the impression left by Washington's supposed letter to his wife. Rather than a humble recognition of the worth of monarchies, this ceremony, also fictional, shows Washington condemning any monarchical system in favor of a republican one. The author of this fabrication emphasizes its "grandeur" and with the reference to Roman general Fabius finds Roman approval for Washington's actions. While Washington never participated in such a ceremony, it does closely echo a ritual that Thomas Paine proposed in his celebrated publication *Common Sense,* in which he illustrates that in America, as opposed to Britain, it is "THE LAW" that is king.[38]

That the author of this *Almanach* article would wish George Washington to preside over Paine's recommendation to exalt the law and break the crown shows that French writers are imagining, evening willing, these scenes to materialize in real time and place, not just in a writer's imagination. Reporting such a scene as actually happening brings French writers and readers closer to a similar action being realized on their own shores. Especially with the reference to ancient Rome, which would be extremely popular during the French Revolution, the scene bears an eerie familiarity to the festivals of the French Revolution that are yet to come.[39] French writers and readers may even have started to become familiar with the kind of language that, in less than a decade, would be used to challenge their own monarchy. This is not the only time, though, when French sources depict an American adopting a posture and attitude that one would not expect until the 1790s.

One of the symbols heavily associated with the French Revolution is the *bonnet rouge*, or the red Phrygian cap, that sans culottes (or insincere aristocrats) wore as a sign of their support for the revolution.[40] The cap would also perch on trees, maypoles, or pikes, depending on the period in the revolution or the festival or tableau in which it was used. The cap had previously appeared as a symbol for freedom or revolution in Dutch, English, and American protests, and it seems very likely that the French first started wearing them as a symbol of revolution based on the red cap's association with ancient liberty of the Greeks and Romans. J. David Harden emphasizes that while the cap appeared in French engravings to celebrate such early and foundational events of the French Revolution as the Declaration of Rights of Man and Citizen, it was also an important symbol for the American Revolution. Harden shows, for example, how a French artist placed the cap in an image that commemorated the French-American military alliance. In this image, France, in the form of a furious angel, chases the British army out of Philadelphia. While the British are denoted by a torn Union Jack among them, the Americans standing patiently behind the angel hold a striped flag and a liberty pole topped with a small cap. They dance around these poles in confidence that the angel has freed them. In another example, a French coin, probably minted in 1783 under the suggestion of Ben Franklin, commemorates the winning of the American War for Independence by displaying Lady Liberty, with a liberty cap perched on a pole in the background.[41] Harden sees these images as a sign that the American Revolution made use of the symbolic red cap for its own revolution and then the symbol crossed the Atlantic to become an important symbol for the French. I would add to his argument that since French artists use the hat so frequently to portray the American Revolution (Harden points to only a few examples of the Americans using it) that these artists must have consciously used this opportunity to fashion a revolutionary symbol.

French association of these liberty caps with the American Revolution was not rare or insignificant. The cap perched in the background of most images, usually as a prop to help the viewer properly identify the woman in Greek robes as Lady Liberty, who always accompanied the Americans. In 1777 the Abbé de Saint Non printed an image of Jean Honoré Fragonard's *le Docteur Franklin Couronné par la Liberté* (Dr. Franklin crowned by Liberty). In this image, Liberty, represented as a young woman in flowing robes, approaches a seated Franklin, who sits behind a globe showing America, with a cherub holding a sword. Liberty holds aloft two laurel wreaths, and behind her, from the center of light that shines about her head, is a small hat on a staff, underscoring her identity as Lady Liberty.[42] Another image by Jean Charles le Vasseur, based on the drawing by Antoine Borel of *L'Amérique Indépendante* in 1778, shows a serene Lady Liberty holding a pole and cap, standing beside Ben Franklin. Together, they watch as a Spartan in the foreground of the image clubs an avatar of England to death.[43] The cap made further appearances in dress fabrics popular with well-to-do French women. One fabric pattern from the celebrated fabric house Jouy,[44] titled *Hommage de l'Amérique à la France 1783–1789*, featured Lady Liberty and her mounted cap standing at the elbow of an Amerindian in deep conversation with a European figure.[45] Finally, another fabric called *Apotheosis of Franklin and Washington*, which was produced by an unknown English firm for French consumers, shows George Washington in a carriage pulled by leopards. Benjamin Franklin is walking calmly onto the scene with Lady Liberty, and together they carry a sign that reads, "Where Liberty Dwells, there is my Country." In her other hand, Lady Liberty holds the ever-present staff and cap.[46]

Figure 1. Detail of "The Apotheosis of Benjamin Franklin and George Washington," a popular British fabric in the late eighteenth century. Note the *bonnet rouge* atop Lady Liberty's staff. (Courtesy of the Society of the Cincinnati, Washington, DC)

In all of these cases, the cap in an important symbol, not just to demark Lady Liberty as she stands among a crowd of Americans or alongside Ben Franklin, but to show favor toward the rebelling Americans. With its roots in ancient Greek and Roman lore, the Phrygian cap communicated a measure of legitimacy for the American cause. The Americans and Lady Liberty who accompany the cap always bear a calm demeanor, which shows that the break with Britain is the Americans' natural right.

Harden points out that later writers of the French Revolution included America in the history of the liberty tree and cap. While it had at some point been in England, it was in America that it "recovered its primitive dignity."[47] In using the symbol of the cap repeatedly in the context of the American Revolution, French artists began the process of transforming the symbol from one of ancient or abstract liberty to one of contemporary revolution. While the *bonnets rouges* of the French Revolution are usually perched on heads, not poles, this trend did not begin until well into that revolution in 1792, when revolutionaries "crowned" Louis XVI with a bonnet to showcase his support for the revolution.[48] Until then, the liberty cap sat on poles, trees, or staffs as it did in all the French depictions of the American Revolution. French artists and potential revolutionaries found this symbol and honed its meaning, it would seem, during that earlier American Revolution. Thus, when the French Revolution began, they had a handy symbol at their disposal to signify the liberty, legitimacy, and "naturalness" of their own revolutionary endeavors.

To what degree did the American Revolution cause the French Revolution? The infinitely complicated French Revolution has many causes, and historians have offered plenty of food for thought for how France became embroiled in revolution on economic, political, social, cultural, and intellectual fronts.[49] Most of these causes come from inside the Hexagon itself, though more recent scholarship has looked outside France to see roots and causes of the French Revolution.[50] Suggestions for direct links between the two revolutions can be tentative at best, especially as they bore few similarities in the types of governments they eventually pursued and the cultures surrounding each. Susan Dunn and Patrice Higonnet, among others, have compared and contrasted the two revolutions and pointed to the lack of similarities between their goals and events.[51] R. R. Palmer, who took a wider view of the "democratic Revolutions" of the late eighteenth century, also came under fire for his arguments that the revolutions were so connected.[52] Forrest McDonald attempted to prove that veteran French soldiers may have been so inspired by fighting in the American Revolution that they caused the French, but his article could only suggest such a connection.[53] Agreeing that the French army played an important role in both the French and American Revolutions, Gilbert Bodinier and Sam Scott, in separate studies, combed through the military archives, searching for signs of direct revolutionary transference through the armies. Their research revealed, however, that outside of a few enthusiastic admirers from France's top ranks, most officers who had participated in the American Revolution opposed the French

Revolution, and a majority of them eventually emigrated for fear of their lives as the latter revolution progressed. Relatively few officers and soldiers crossed the Atlantic to America—even if they had been inspired in North America to encourage a revolution in their own country, it is unlikely they would have had a large effect.[54] Here, Lafayette always stands out as an individual who was particularly vocal in his support of the America Revolution, having fought directly under the command of George Washington long before France declared an official alliance with America. Lafayette continued to vocalize his support for the American Revolution when he returned to France and took a leading role in the early years of the French Revolution by leading the National Guard and participating in the early debates on the French constitution and political development.[55] His admiration, however, stands out in part because it was relatively unique. As Lee Kennett said in his study of the French army in America, "It is one thing to admire a people's institutions and quite another to imitate them."[56]

This cynical approach to the connections between the two revolutions has not always been the case. Especially in Napoleonic France, officers who had lived through and remembered both revolutions did not doubt their connection. Denis Jean Florimond de Langlois, marquis du Bouchet, for example, participated in the American Revolution as a volunteer under General Washington. When revolution broke out in France shortly after his return, he emigrated in fear of his life, only resuming his profession as a French officer once Napoleon had firmly established himself as emperor. Though he had been an eager supporter of the American Revolution, Bouchet condemned it in his memoirs, saying that "the English took their revenge on us and in the interest which we had in America, lighting the flame which embraced all of Europe, beginning with our own unfortunate country."[57] This observation about the American Revolution's effect on France continued to dominate perceptions of the late eighteenth-century relationship between France and America until the mid-twentieth century. As writers commemorated the centennial of the American and French Revolutions, numerous publications heralded the amity and influence between the two countries and their respective revolutions.[58]

In recent years, historians have taken up the probability of revolutionary transference again. Éric Peuchot and Marie-Jeanne Rossignol have remarked that revolutionaries used the state constitutions as potential models or sources of inspiration for the French government, as they tried to construct it in the beginning years of the French Revolution.[59] Jonathan Israel sees the revolutions connected, insofar as they largely drew from the European Enlightenment.[60] Marie-Jeanne Rossignol, again, has urged historians to continue to draw on the work of R. R. Palmer as well as Jacques Godechot, who in some ways spearheaded the study of Atlantic history.[61] As I have also argued, the context of the French army's reform attempts after the Seven Years' War set the stage for interest in the American Revolution when it broke out in 1775. As military reformers attempted to improve the army by elevating the soldier's status and increasing his sense of patriotism, they seemingly witnessed a tangible and contemporary example of victorious citizen-soldiers across the Atlantic. Nonmilitary readers and writers likewise embraced the American image of a citizen army fighting out of patriotism, and in their joint effort to create a citizen army, created revolution.[62]

It is in hopes of broadening the current literature that I highlight specific language and one powerful symbol to argue that the American Revolution did have a direct impact on the French Revolution by allowing French journalists and artists to draft an image of America that drew out the revolutionary ideas in France that were perhaps already embedded but not yet at work or given opportunity for expression. As writers and artists were allowed a certain freedom when they wrote about America that they did not have in other circumstances, they could either vent or experiment with ideas that they would not have had the license to explore if they were just writing about France. Beyond the simple license they had to publish such ideas and circulate them freely, writers, artists, and thinkers could "invent" the French Revolution as they "invented" an America that differed dramatically from the image that remained after the Seven Years' War. Writing, reading, and processing the American Revolution further worked revolution into the French mindset as something that could happen. Even as French writers invented or embellished American Revolutionary successes, their readers absorbed these stories as evidence that such lofty fantasies were in fact achievable goals. Writers discussing the American Revolution invented, at a time when the power of reading was at an all-time high, many of the words, symbols, and values that the French Revolution would come to embody. Additionally, they articulated an expectation of what a creature of a French revolution, born of the French Enlightenment, would embody and how he would behave. For the rest of the 1780s and 1790s, French readers and writers pursued that image and endeavored to make him a reality. In finding ways to describe and understand these revolutionary Americans, French writers created not just a new American nationality but a French revolutionary language, and with that, the French Revolution.

Notes

1. Jay M. Smith, *Nobility Reimagined: The Patriotic Nation in Eighteenth-Century France* (Ithaca, NY: Cornell University Press, 2006), 143.

2. Dena Goodman, *The Republic of Letters: A Cultural History of the French Enlightenment* (Ithaca, NY: Cornell University Press, 1994); Sara Maza, *Private Lives and Public Affairs: The Causes Célèbres of Prerevolutionary France* (Berkeley: University of California Press, 1993); John Shovlin, *The Political Economy of Virtue: Luxury, Patriotism, and the Origins of the French Revolution* (Ithaca, NY: Cornell University Press, 2006); Michael Kwass, *Privilege and the Politics of Taxation in Eighteenth-Century France: Liberté, Egalité, Fiscalité* (Cambridge: Cambridge University Press, 2000); Smith, *Nobility Reimagined*; Alexis de Tocqueville, *The Old Regime and the French Revolution*, trans. Stuart Gilbert (1856, reprinted, New York: Anchor Books, 1983). Timothy Tackett has presented an opposing view of the origins of the French Revolution in *Becoming a Revolutionary: The Deputies of the French National Assembly and the Emergence of a Revolutionary Culture (1789–1790)* (Princeton, NJ: Princeton University Press, 1997).

3. Smith, *Nobility Reimagined*, 142.

4. David Bell, "Jumonville's Death: War Propaganda and National Identity in Eighteenth-Century France," in *The Age of Cultural Revolutions: Britain and France, 1750–1820*, eds. Colin Jones and Dror Wahrman (Berkeley: University of California Press, 2002), 34.

5. Antoine Léonard Thomas, *Jumonville Poème* (Paris, 1759), 19: xvi–xvii.

6. Etienne-Joseph Poullin de Lumina, *Histoire de la Guerre contre les Anglais* (Genève, 1759), 14, 15.

7. For early patriotism in France being defined largely as anti-British, see Edmond Dziembowski, *Un nouveau patriotisme français, 1750–1770: La France face à la puissance anglaise à l'époque de la guerre de Sept Ans* (Oxford: Voltaire Foundation, 1998); see also Linda Colley, *Britons: Forging the Nation, 1707–1837* (New Haven, CT: Yale University Press, 2009).

8. For one of the many references to impartiality, see *Affaires de l'Angleterre et de l'Amérique*, vol. 4, section 20, ccxi–ccxx. The most recent publication that addresses the *Affaires* is George B. Watts, *Les Affaires de l'Angleterre et de l'Amérique and John Adams* (Charlotte, NC: Heritage Printers, 1965), 1–10.

9. *Affaires de l'Angleterre et de l'Amérique*, vol. 1, section 1, 81 (cited hereerafter as *Affaires* vol. #:section #, p. #). For more on conjecture in the *Affaires*, see William Slauter, "News and Diplomacy in the Age of the American Revolution" (PhD diss., Prince-

ton University, 2007); and William Slauter, "Forward-Looking Statements: News and Speculation in the Age of the American Revolution," *Journal of Modern History* 81 (December 2009): 759–92.

10. The Amerindian "Sauvage" was familiar to French readers as either "wildmen" native to North America or as symbolic figures who represented the law of nature and the essence of America. See Julia Osman, "Pride, Prejudice, and Prestige: French Officers in North American during the Seven Years' War," in *The Seven Years' War as a Global Conflict: Essays and Interpretations*, eds. Mark H. Danely and Patrick J. Speelman (Leiden: Brill Academic Publishers, 2012), 191–211; Élise Marienstras, *Les mythes fondateurs de la nation américaine: Essai sur le discours idéologique aux états-unis à l'époque de l'indépendance (1763–1800)* (Paris: François Maspero, 1976), 181, 184–95. French readers understood American slavery through the perspective of abolitionist Quakers and understood the latter through abolitionist efforts in France and Britain. See *The Atlantic World of Anthony Benezet (1713–1784)*, eds. Marie-Jeane Rossignol and Bertrand Van Ruymbeke (Leiden: Brill Press, 2017).

11. *Affaires,* vol. 1:2, 68.

12. The use of the word "people" in the Declaration of Independence had already raised interest among French readers, as translators of the Declaration, and Jefferson himself, referenced "un peuple" to designate not just a separateness from Britain, but the move from passive sufferers to sovereign agents. See Elise Marienstras and Naomi Wulf, "French Translations and Reception of the Declaration of Independence," *Journal of American History* 85.4 (1999): 1299–324, 1310–11.

13. *Affaires,* vol. 2:16, xlj; vol. 1:5, 40–41.

14. *Affaires,* vol. 1:5, 39.

15. *Affaires,* vol. 2:20, ccxxxix.

16. *Affaires,* vol. 1:5, 40 ("the appalling"); *Affaires,* vol. 6:25, 128 ("the enormous"); *Affaires,* vol. 2:10, 48 ("our virtuous"); *Affaires,* vol. 6:20, ccxv–ccvj ("distinguished officer"); *Affaires,* vol. 10:35, 69 ("conspire"); *Affaires,* vol. 6:26, liv ("the animosity").

17. For more on American diplomats and their important role in encouraging Franco-American alliance, see Larrie D. Ferreiro, *Brothers at Arms: American Independence and the Men of France and Spain Who Saved It* (New York: Knopf, 2016); Jonathan R. Dull, *A Diplomatic History of the American Revolution* (New Haven, CT: Yale University Press, 1985). For more on the comte de Vergennes, see Orville Theodore Murphy, *Charles Gravier, Comte de Vergennes: French Diplomacy in the Age of Revolution, 1719–1787* (Albany: State University of New York Press, 1982). For more on the American image in France more broadly, see Durand Echeverria, *Mirage of the West: A History of the French Image of American Society to 1815* (Princeton, NJ: Princeton University Press, 1957).

18. J. L. Le Barbier le Jeune, *Asgill, drame en 5 actes, en prose* (Paris, 1785).

19. Joseph Cerutti, *L'Aigle et le Hibou: Fable, écrit pour un jeune Prince que l'on osait blâmer de son amour pour les Sciences et les Lettres* (Paris, 1783), 32–35.

20. Cerutti, *L'Aigle et le Hibou,* 34–35.

21. LeManissier, *Le Docteur Franklin poème* (Paris, 1787), 8, 10. For more on how

the term "slavery" was employed in the American Revolution to refer to patriots, see Peter A. Dorsey, *Common Bondage: Slavery as Metaphor in Revolutionary America* (Knoxville: University of Tennessee Press, 2009).

22. Pierre Duviquet, *Vers sur la Paix* (1784), 6.

23. Roger Chartier, *Lectures et lecteurs dans la France d'Ancien Régime* (Paris: Editions du Seuil, 1982), 214.

24. Jill Lepore, *The Name of War: King Philip's War and the Origins of American Identity* (New York: Vintage, 1999), 47, 54, 68.

25. Raymond Birn, *Royal Censorship of Books in Eighteenth-Century France* (Stanford, CA: Stanford University Press, 2012); Joyce Appleby, "America as a Model for the Radical French Reformers of 1789," *William and Mary Quarterly* 28 (April 1971): 267–86.

26. *Gazette de Leyde,* May 13, 1777.

27. *Gazette de France,* December 13, 1776.

28. *Gazette de Leyde,* July 18, 1775.

29. *Gazette de Leyde,* January 9, 1776.

30. *Gazette de France,* April 17, 1775.

31. *Gazette de France,* March 1, 1776.

32. Don Higginbotham, *The War of American Independence: Military Attitudes, Policies, and Practice, 1763–1789* (Bloomington: Indiana University Press, 1971), 390.

33. Lafayette, *The Letters of Lafayette to Washington, 1777–1779,* ed. Louis Gottschalk (New York: American Philosophical Society, 1944), 12, cited in Orville T. Murphy, "The American Revolutionary Army and the Concept of Levee en Masse," in *Military Analysis of the Revolutionary War,* ed. Don Higginbotham, (Millwood, NY: KTO Press, 1977), 218.

34. Simon Schama, *Citizens: A Chronicle of the French Revolution* (New York: Knopf, 1989), 762.

35. M. Pouchont, *Memoires sur la derniere guerre de l'Amérique Septentrionale entre la France et l'Angleterre. Suivis d'Observations, dont plusieurs sont relatives au théatre actuel de la guerre, & de nouveaux détails sur les mœurs & les usages des Sauvages, avec des cartes topographiques.* Par M. Pouchot, chevalier de l'Ordre Royal & Miliaire de St. Louis, ancient Capitaine au Régiment de Béarn, Commandant des forts de Niagara & de Lévis, en Canada (Paris, 1781).

36. M. de'Aquin de Château-Lyon, *Almanach Littéraire, ou Etrennes d'Apollon* (1779), 158–59.

37. Ibid., (1785), 33–34.

38. Thomas Paine, *Common Sense,* ed. Isaac Kramnick (1776, reprint, New York: Penguin Classics, 1976), 98.

39. Mona Ozouf, *Festivals and the French Revolution,* trans. Alan Sheridan (Cambridge, MA: Harvard University Press, 1988).

40. Jennifer Harris, "The Red Cap of Liberty: A Study of Dress Worn by French Revolutionary Partisans, 1789–94," *Eighteenth-Century Studies* 14 (Spring 1981): 283–312, 285.

41. J. David Harden, "Liberty Caps and Liberty Trees," *Past & Present* 146 (February 1995): 66–102, 78–79, 81, 89.

42. In "Benjamin Franklin un Américain à Paris (1776–1785)," Paris musées, 203.

43. Ibid., 205.

44. Jouy was an important fabric house headed by Christophe Philippe Oberkampf, a German protestant who settled in France in the mid-eighteenth century and reintroduced a "painted fabric" tradition in France with great success. See Aziza Gril-Mariotte, "Christophe-Philippe Oberkampf (1738–1815) et l'industrie des toiles peintes en France: L'impact du protestantisme sur son parcours et la création," *Revue d'histoire du protestantisme* 1.2 (2016): 207–27.

45. "Benjamin Franklin," Paris musées, 103.

46. Whitney A. J. Robertson, "George Washington, Pulled by Leopards," *Cincinnati Fourteen* 49.1 (2012): 58–61.

47. Abbé Henri Grégoire, *Essai historique et patriotique sur les arbres de la liberté* Paris, an II 1793–4, in Harden, "Liberty Caps," 90.

48. Harden, "Liberty Caps," 100.

49. The literature is too exhaustive to list here, but some of the major works include: Tocqueville, *The Old Regime and the French Revolution*; Georges Lefebvre, *The Coming of the French Revolution*, trans. R. R. Palmer (Princeton, NJ: Princeton University Press, 1947); Francois Furet, *Interpreting the French Revolution*, trans. Elborg Forster (Cambridge: Cambridge University Press, 1986); Keith Michael Baker, *Inventing the French Revolution* (Cambridge: Cambridge University Press, 1990); Maza, *Private Lives and Public Affairs*; Timothy Tackett, *Becoming a Revolutionary: The Deputies of the French National Assembly and the Emergence of a Revoluionary Culture (1789–1790)* (Princeton, NJ: Princeton University Press, 1996); David Andress, *1789: The Threshold of the Modern Age* (London: Abacus, 2008).

50. E.g., Christopher J. Tozzi, *Nationalizing France's Army: Foreign, Black, and Jewish Troops in the French Military, 1715–1831* (Charlottesville: University of Virginia Press, 2016); Christy Pichichero, *The Military Enlightenment: War and Culture in the French Empire from Louis XIV to Napoleon* (Ithaca, NY: Cornell University Press, 2017). Pichichero does not dwell too much on the causes of the French Revolution but does much to show how French activity around the globe effects the Hexagon during the old regime and revolution.

51. Susan Dunn, *Sister Revolutions: French Lightening, American Light* (New York: Farber and Farber, 1999); Patrice Higonnet, *Sister Republics: The Origins of French and American Republicanism* (Cambridge, MA: Harvard University Press, 1988).

52. For example, M. S. Anderson said Palmer "pushes his argument too far." M. S. Anderson, review of *The Age of the Democratic Revolution, Vol. 2, The Struggle*, by R. R. Palmer, *English Historical Review* 81.320 (July 1966): 612–13.

53. Forrest McDonald, "The Relation of the French Peasant Veterans of the American Revolution to the Fall of Feudalism in France, 1789–1792," *Agricultural History Magazine* 51 (1951).

54. Gilbert Bodinier, *Les Officiers de L'Armée Royale: Combattants de la guerre d'Indépendance des Etats-Unis de Yorktown à l'an II* (Chateau Vincennes: Service Historique de L'armée de Terre, 1983); Samuel Scott, *From Yorktown to Valmy* (Denver: University Press of Colorado, 1998).

55. See Munro Price, "Lafayette, the Lameths, and 'Republican Monarchy,' 1789–1791," in this volume.

56. Lee Kennett, *The French Forces in America 1780–1783* (Westport, CT: Praeger Publishers, 1977), 169; and quoted in Bodinier, *Les officiers de L'Armée Royale,* 350.

57. Denis Du Bouchet, *Journal d'un emigré,* service copy, Rare and Manuscript Collection, 14853-5302, 51–52, Carl A. Kroch Library, Cornell University, Ithaca, NY.

58. For an excellent historiography of the nineteenth- and early twentieth-century works on the French and American Revolutions, see Martin Lathe Nicolai, "Subjects and Citizens: French Officers and the North American Experience, 1755–1783" (PhD diss., Queen's University, New York, 1992), 19–25.

59. Marie-Jeanne Rossignol, "The American Revolution in France: Under the Shadow of the French Revolution," in *Europe's American Revolution* (New York: Palgrave Macmillan, 2006), 57–59; Eric Peuchot, "L'Influence des idées américaines sur les constituants" in *La France de la révolution et les Etats-Unis d'Amérique,* ed. Gilbert Bodinier (Paris: Masson, 1995), 22–34.

60. Jonathan Israel, *The Expanding Blaze: How the American Revolution Ignited the World, 1775–1848* (Princeton, NJ: Princeton University Press, 2017). Israel also wanted to show the American Revolution's broader impact on world revolutions.

61. See Marie-Jeanne Rossignol essay in this volume: "In Search of Global Democracy: Revisiting the Historical Work of Jacques Godechot and Robert R. Palmer, Founders of Atlantic History."

62. Julia Osman, *Citizen Soldiers and the Key to the Bastille* (Basingstoke: Palgrave MacMillan, 2015).

Diplomacy

Friends, Allies, and Free Trade

Effectively engaging European friends of the American Revolution to support the American war effort and the new United States presented enormously challenging issues of diplomacy and finance, and not all diplomacy occurred in Parisian salons or at Benjamin Franklin's home in Passy. The essays in this section confront European diplomacy in support of the American Revolution outside of France, Spain, and Britain in several forms with varying degrees of success and, in one case, with long-term legal implications. These essays remind us of why an Atlantic perspective on the Revolution is necessary to understand more fully its progression and results.

As the impact of the American war spread well beyond its shores, nations across northern, eastern, and central Europe sought both to minimize any damage to their trade and to maximize any political and military advantages that could be achieved as Britain, France, Spain, and America engaged in the far-flung conflict of the American War for Independence. To protect the trade of these "neutrals," a group of nations coalesced around a plan by Catherine the Great of Russia to insist on free trade for nonbelligerents, warning at the same time that their League of Armed Neutrality could very effectively protect its own trade if any of its ships were attacked. While that threat applied to both Britain and France, it was a particular problem for Britain and its previously dominant navy that otherwise had the possibility of controlling maritime trade with France. Thus, while John Adams's desire for the United States to join the League never came to fruition, as a practical matter, it became an American friend.

Beyond the trouble that it caused for Britain's war effort, the League had other, longer-term implications. While international law always develops slowly, haltingly, Catherine's efforts strengthened a movement in international law toward free trade, a movement supported by such early modern legal scholars as Hugo Grotius and Emer de Vattel, Paul Gilje explains. At its founding, the United States also sought to adopt a policy of free trade, but the complicated diplomatic maneuvers that Gilje documents were based on parochial European interests rather than American principles. How these developments became entwined with the League of Armed Neutrality is discussed in "Ideology *and* Interest: Free Trade, the League of Armed Neutrality, and the American Revolution." As Gilje's other work demonstrates, the long-term consequences of these doctrines would be felt in American and European policies for years to come.

While intriguing nations engaged in complex diplomatic exchanges, Americans who found themselves in Europe during the war often were forced to negotiate a more immediate diplomacy involving local merchants, bankers, diplomats, and politicians, each pursuing their own varied interests. (The field of diplomatic history is increasingly focused on such multivalent relationships.) Such was certainly the case when John Paul Jones arrived in the Dutch port of Texel in desperate need of refitting his small fleet after his heroic and historic battle between the *Bonhomme Richard* and the *Serapis*. As Victor Enthoven shows in his essay, "'Sir, I have not yet begun to fight!': John Paul Jones's Friends in the Dutch Republic, 1779–1780," the mélange of shifting interests meant that, as an earlier author put it, "all Americans and their friends in the Dutch Republic were jealous and distrustful of one another. It was very much as at Passy, only worse." With a small fleet badly in need of repair and refurbishment after his victories at sea (and saddled with hundreds of British prisoners), Jones's squadron was left in limbo and his sailors in a most unwelcome interlude as British and French ambassadors and Dutch bankers, merchants, and politicians played their own game of diplomatic chess, rendering the American squadron just so many additional pieces.

These essays show that, at both macro and micro levels, many issues in the diplomatic history of the American Revolution and its Atlantic context are still to be explored fully.

Ideology *and* Interest
Free Trade, the League of Armed Neutrality, and the American Revolution

Paul A. Gilje

A mixture of ideology and interest led to the protection of neutral trade as free trade in the eighteenth century, the defense of this doctrine by the League of Armed Neutrality during the American Revolution, and the espousal of the same principle by the United States. Traditionally, the story of the organization that nonbelligerent European states formed to defend neutrality in 1780 was simple enough: during the War for Independence, Great Britain not only found itself in conflict with its American colonies, France, Spain, and the Netherlands, but also became diplomatically isolated when Catherine the Great of Russia proposed the League in an effort to protect neutral commerce and assert a leadership role in European diplomatic affairs. The provisions of the League stipulated that the member nations should be allowed to trade in their own ships with belligerents at war with each other. The League also insisted on a narrow definition of contraband—goods prohibited from neutral shipping would be limited to military equipment and exclude naval stores—and a restricted definition of a naval blockade. Before the close of the Anglo-French war that we associate with the American Revolution, as well as the Anglo-Dutch war that continued until 1784, a host of nations joined Russia in the League, including Denmark (July 9, 1780), Sweden (August 1, 1780), Prussia (May 19, 1781), Austria (October 9, 1781), Portugal (July 24, 1782), and Naples (February 21, 1783). Although the basic outlines of this interpretation are correct, it does not do full credit to the larger significance of the League within the context of the development of ideas about foreign affairs in the eighteenth century, or to the intricate nature of European power politics during the Revolutionary

War, nor to the meaning of the League and its position on neutral shipping in the diplomatic history of the United States.¹

This essay will explore each of these areas in an effort to better understand the context of the League in Europe and North America. In the mid-twentieth century, at a time when the world seemed to be divided by competing ideologies, Felix Gilbert wrote a little book on George Washington's Farewell Address that emphasized ideas over realpolitik. A few scholars have agreed with Gilbert. Many others, perhaps reflecting a cynical belief that American foreign policy in the second half of the twentieth century was more about interests than ideals, have minimized the impact of ideology.² This essay does not focus on determining which side is "right" in this debate. Rather, both motivations are part of a larger historical perspective providing a cultural context for understanding early American foreign policy. First, this essay examines the history of free trade, defined as allowing neutral trade with an enemy during a time of war, tracing this idea from its origins to the seventeenth century, through the Treaty of Utrecht and into the Enlightenment of the eighteenth century. The second section explores the complex diplomacy that lay behind the creation of the League in 1780. This section reflects a world where European interests trumped ideology and also reveals how the American Revolution was perceived by many powers on the other side of the Atlantic. Finally, the essay outlines how Americans, ignoring the machinations of European states, came to believe that free trade created a new kind of diplomacy, one that was based on ideals that they then applied to their foreign policy from the Revolution to the War of 1812. All three sections will demonstrate the odd and varying combination of ideology and interest in the claim that neutral ships had a right to trade with warring nations.

Free Trade

Catherine the Great and the other members of the League of Armed Neutrality did not create out of thin air their policy asserting that neutral ships make neutral goods. Instead, they built this notion of free trade on a set of ideas that reached back to the Middle Ages and had gained greater currency by the eighteenth century. Although the espousal of this protection of neutral rights had pragmatic roots, the emphasis on natural law and reason in the Enlightenment provided an intellectual rationale that made the policy ever more attractive.[3]

Before the mid-seventeenth century there was an international consensus concerning the status of neutral shipping. During the mediaeval period the Italian mercantile states supported what they called the *consolato del mare*, the belief that neutral products in neutral ships should be protected from seizure but that property owned by belligerents on that same neutral ship was not protected. Moreover, the neutral ship itself was free from seizure and was to be returned to the neutral owner once the property of the enemy had been removed. As a relatively weak state militarily, and as it began to expand its commercial interests, England adopted this policy. By 1600 most European nations, with the important exception of France, adhered to the *consolato del mare*. Although this approach to neutral shipping provided some protection, it also created difficulties. Ships were still liable to search and at least part of the cargo could be seized. In addition, drawing distinctions between goods owned by a neutral state or a belligerent state was not always easy. Even more problematical was the fact that a powerful military nation, France, refused to follow *consolato del mare* and claimed the right to seize the entire neutral ship and all of its goods if it attempted to trade with an enemy or carried property owned by merchants from a state with which France was at war.[4]

In the early seventeenth century ideas concerning the protection of neutral shipping began to be extended to protect all property aboard a neutral vessel, even if it belonged to an enemy. Between 1600 and 1780 European powers signed dozens of treaties accepting this expanded right of neutrals. Interestingly, France led the way with an agreement with the Ottoman Turks in 1604, followed by a Dutch-Turkish commercial treaty in 1612. The principle that neutral ships made neutral goods spread in the 1650s with treaties signed between the Netherlands and Spain in 1650, France and the Hanseatic League in 1658, as well as Spain and France in 1659. England also made several such agreements, starting with the Dutch in the Treaty of Westminster in 1654. As with all laws and treaties signed under the Interregnum in England, this pact was annulled with the restoration of the Stuart monarchy in 1660. Subsequent Anglo-Dutch treaties in 1667 and 1674 also protected neutral trade. The two nations issued a special "Explanatory Declaration" in 1686 to clarify that "ships and vessels" could "not only pass, traffic, and trade from a neutral port or place to a place in enmity with the other party, or from a place in enmity to a neutral place, but also from a port or place in enmity, to a port or place in enmity with the other party." By the time of this accord, Great Britain had signed a similar agreement with France in the commercial treaty of 1677 that stated that both countries could "traffick during the War, with the same Merchandizes with which they may trade in times of Peace," except when it came to contraband. Like the 1686 Anglo-Dutch Explanatory Declaration, this treaty explicitly allowed for a neutral to carry trade between the ports of belligerents. The pace of neutral trade agreements continued thereafter. Perhaps the most important treaty with a provision protecting neutral shipping during wartime was the Anglo-French commercial pact that accompanied the Treaty of Utrecht in 1713; it included the neutral rights stipulations in the earlier treaties and then succinctly summarized the principle in words that would be repeated or paraphrased in subsequent commercial agreements, especially later by Americans, "that free ships shall also give a freedom to goods."[5]

There remained practical limitations to this broad assertion of neutral rights. Besides the increasing number of treaties that allowed for free ships making free goods, there were also commercial treaties between nations that simply reasserted the older and more limited version of *consolato del mare*. Of the fifty-one separate trade conventions in Europe between 1650 and 1780, fifteen were based on *consolato del mare* and the rest had a "free ships make free goods" clause. The Anglo-Danish treaty of 1670 did not allow neutrals to carry enemy property, and all subsequent revisions and updates had the same limited provision throughout the eighteenth century. Similar restrictions on neutral trade appeared in the Dutch-Danish treaties after 1701, as well as Swedish treaties with England, France, and the Netherlands. Likewise, although the commercial agreements drawn up at Utrecht between Great Britain and Spain and between France and Holland had a free ships make free goods clause, the pacts between France and Savoy, Spain and the Netherlands, and Spain and Portugal did not. There was also the problem that regardless of treaty stipulations, the practice of privateers, naval vessels, and prize courts might vary. As they emerged as the two most powerful military and commercial empires in the eighteenth century, both Great Britain and France were more than capable of sidestepping protections of neutral trade. Often the opening wedge in this constriction of neutral trade was the definition of contraband. Treaties generally described contraband as implements of war, but the items listed as contraband might vary from treaty to treaty and include naval stores or even food. Moreover, during war a nation might lift its mercantilist restrictions limiting trade as a ruse to continue commercial contact with other nations or even its own colonies. To stop this practice during the Seven Years' War, and in reaction to similar restrictions imposed by the French, Great Britain issued its Rule of 1756 to prevent the Dutch from opening trade with France that had been previously restricted. In short, several nations in the eighteenth century pursued their own interests and limited neutral trade despite the multiple treaty provisions allowing that trade. Yet even when they did so, as was true with the Rule of 1756—a measure that in the early 1800s would be vehemently decried by Americans when the British used it to prevent trade between France and its colonies carried in American bottoms—almost all of these actions still allowed for some neutral trade.[6]

If interest sometimes dictated that practice deviated from principle, why assert the principle in the first place, especially during a seventeenth century marked by bloody religious warfare and intense civil discord? The answer may be that nations in this era had both pragmatic and principled reasons for supporting the sanctity of neutral trade. Perhaps we should not be surprised by this development as European commercial enterprise expanded in the seas around the continent and in the oceans across the world. The self-interest of nations engulfed in one war after another and anxious for access to trade goods to sustain these conflicts, as well as the self-interest of merchants eager to take advantage of the many military conflicts that erupted in this era, might well explain the willingness of the Dutch, the English, and even the French and the Spanish to sign agreements guaranteeing the sanctity of neutral shipping either through the *consolato del mare* or the assertion "that free ships shall also give a freedom to goods." But along with the practical needs of the interest of the state, there also emerged an intellectual rationale behind the protection of neutral shipping that began in the early seventeenth century with the work of Hugo Grotius and was continued in the eighteenth century during the Enlightenment, especially by Emer de Vattel.

In the early seventeenth century the Dutch political theorist Hugo Grotius viewed the ocean as an open avenue for commerce and thereby strengthened the ideological background to the *consolato del mare* and provided a rationale for enlarged neutral rights. First published in 1625, Grotius's *The Rights of War and Peace* became a classic on the law of nations. This huge treatise was read by nearly every educated person on both sides of the Atlantic, appearing on the bookshelves of Jean-Jacques Rousseau in Geneva as well as of George Washington at Mount Vernon.[7]

Grotius detailed the proper relations between nations, outlined the appropriate causes for war, and declared the sanctity of neutral property. Grotius argued that "the common Saying that Goods found in our Enemies Ships are reputed theirs"—part of the rules under *consolato del mare*—was not "a constant and invariable law of the Right of Nations" and should not necessarily be followed. Neither, for that matter "do the Ships of friends become lawful Prize, on the Account of the Enemies Goods." As Grotius explained later, "The Necessity must be really extream, to give any Right to another's Goods"; therefore, when "real Necessity urges us to take, we should then take no more than what it requires" and leave as much as possible to the original owner and compensate him if his property was consumed.[8]

This set of ideas implied that neutral property on the high seas ought to be protected from seizure, a point made even clearer in an earlier and shorter work by Grotius, *The Free Sea* (1609). At the time this book appeared, the Netherlands was still in the midst of its conflicts with Spain and Portugal while simultaneously pursuing its mercantile interests around the world. Combining astute business and commercial activity with swashbuckling enterprise, Dutch ships challenged the monopoly of distant seas claimed by the Spanish and Portuguese. Grotius wrote *The Free Sea* in defense of one incredibly successful Dutch seizure of a Portuguese East Indiaman in the Straights of Singapore in 1603. Grotius's argument, however, went beyond the particular case and the right of the Dutch to capture the Portuguese galleon. His legal brief asserted larger principles based in God-given natural law, legal precedent, and ancient texts to argue that no country had the right to control territory upon the high seas. Such claims might be made on the land, which was fixed and liable to both possession and improvement. Oceans, however, were by definition fluid and impermanent, and therefore "no part of the sea can be accompted in the territory of any people." Since the oceans were liquid highways free for all to travel, trade could not be inhibited. As Grotius explained: "The liberty of trading is agreeable to the primary law of nations which hath a natural and perpetual cause and therefore cannot be taken away." No nation, therefore, "may justly hinder two nations that are willing to trade between themselves." In short, since the sea was free for all to sail upon, and since property should not be seized willy-nilly, a neutral ship and its goods should be protected from capture.[9]

While Grotius talked about a God-given natural law, a century later Emer de Vattel, reflecting the Age of Enlightenment, couched his arguments more in terms of reason and nature, entitling his magnum opus *The Law of Nations, Or, Principles of the Law of Nature, Applied to the Conduct and Affairs of Nations and Sovereigns.* Even more than Grotius, Vattel became required reading for anyone interested in the relationship between natural law and the creation of states. Every major political thinker in Europe and North America read *The Law of Nations.* Vattel used reason to codify how nations should interact and described set rules for war that might avoid the bloodbath and destruction that had been wrought in the previous century. Equally important were regulations to guide commerce. Beginning with the idea that following the path of reason would lead to the greatest good for the greatest number, Vattel and other enlightened thinkers argued that the interchange of goods between regions and peoples benefitted all. One branch of this path led to the laissez faire economics of the physiocrats and Adam Smith; another led to a defense of neutral rights. Both branches might be labeled free trade. According to Vattel, "Man is so formed by nature, that he cannot supply all his own wants, but necessarily stands in need of the intercourse and assistance of his fellow-creatures." Thus "nations, as well as individuals, are obliged to trade together for the common benefit of the human race." Unlike Adam Smith, Vattel believed it was perfectly fine for a nation to limit and guide trade for its own good. Based on the belief that commerce benefits all, Vattel defended neutral trade: "Neutral nations should enjoy perfect liberty to trade" nonwarlike materials, and "the belligerent powers cannot with any reason refuse it, or prevent the importation of such goods into the enemy's country: the care of their own safety, the necessity of self-defence, does not authorise them to do it, since those things will not render the enemy more formidable." Vattel, however, conceded the right of search to any nation at war and acknowledged the right of a belligerent power to seize "an enemy's effects" aboard a neutral ship "by the right of war" if they were contraband. Even then, reason dictated that "we are naturally bound to pay the freight to the master of the vessel, who is not to suffer by such seizure."[10]

By the mid-eighteenth century neutral trade had a long history under both *consolato del mare* and in the idea that "free ships shall also give a freedom to goods." It also had an ideological rationale articulated by Grotius,

Vattel, and others that fit into the larger intellectual context of an Enlightened age based in the law of nature and reason.

Catherine the Great was fully aware of both the history of the practice of free trade and its ideological context when she issued her declaration "Regarding the Principles of Armed Neutrality" early in 1780. The czarina was an avid reader who was well versed in the works of the Enlightenment, including Diderot, Montesquieu, and Voltaire, and has often been called an enlightened despot—she used her absolute control of the state to help mold Russia according to enlightened precepts. It is no surprise therefore that she began her "Principles" by citing Russia's own respect for neutral trade in its recent war with the "Ottoman Porte" in terms that reflected enlightened ideas about commerce and that could just as easily have been written by Vattel or any number of the philosophes of the Enlightenment. She might have also reached further into Russian history and could have cited the Anglo-Russian commercial treaty of 1766, which protected neutral rights by granting permission "to the subjects of the two contracting parties to go, come, and trade freely with those states, with which one or the other of the parties shall at that time, or any future time, be engaged in war." As far as Catherine was concerned, in 1780 she was merely supporting "the rights of neutrality and the liberty of universal commerce." She believed that her previous conduct, as well as "the principles of impartiality" she followed during the current war, should have ensured that "her subjects would peaceably enjoy the fruits of their industry and the advantages belonging to a neutral nation." But neither her own policies "nor regard for the universal law of nations" had protected her subjects from the depredations of the current belligerents. For Catherine, the principles of neutrality were based on "the primitive law of peoples on which every nation is entitled to rely" as well as "the maxims" adopted by those nations at war "in different treaties and public engagements." Whatever calculating interest may have been behind the czarina's actions, she couched it in the most modern enlightened language of the day.[11]

European Diplomacy

From a European perspective, the American Revolution was just another episode in an ongoing struggle for power. Although the central protagonists remained France and Great Britain, unlike the previous and subsequent outbreaks—the Seven Years' War, the French Revolution, and the Napoleonic Wars—this conflict did not engulf all of Europe. Instead, it was marked by a shift in allegiance by many, but not all, of the English-speaking settlers on the eastern shores of North America, an alliance between the Bourbon powers of Spain and France, and British-instigated hostilities against the Dutch Republic. Despite the limited nature of this war, it could just have easily broken out into a general conflagration sucking into its inferno a host of nations large and small alike, including Russia, Austria, Prussia, Sweden, Denmark, the Ottoman Empire, as well as many German and Italian states. That it did not do so, and thereby perhaps alter the outcome for both the United States and Europe, was a very near thing and the result of a delicate diplomatic dance performed by Catherine the Great of Russia. Taking the hand of one partner after another, Catherine pursued Russian interests and led all of Europe in a carefully orchestrated minuet that culminated in the League of Armed Neutrality. France and Great Britain each had taken their turn on the dance floor with Catherine in her grand European ball, but both were left on the sidelines, exhausted by their efforts and compelled to end their conflict in a virtual stalemate. The Americans never even attended the dance and were so distant they misheard the music. Instead of understanding that the main chorus reflected Russia's own gambit for power and interest, they focused on the ideological prelude of neutral rights. No matter. The result of all the fancy footwork was a continued balance of power, more war in Europe, and, of course, the independence of the United States.[12]

To understand how and why this diplomatic dance took the form it did, we must first look at the world from the point of view of Catherine the Great. There were three major areas of diplomatic interest for Russia. In the late eighteenth century the number one priority was expansion to the south, toward the Black Sea and eventually into the Mediterranean to gain access to warm-water ports. Indeed, Catherine went so far as to dream of reestablishing Eastern Orthodox control of the Bosporus Strait and even named her grandson Constantine with the idea that he could one day be ensconced in the city that had once been the capital of the Eastern Roman Empire. Blocking her way was the Ottoman Empire, which retained control of the Black Sea. In an incredibly successful war that culminated in the Treaty of Kuchuk-Kainarji in 1774, Catherine gained several Black Sea ports and set up an independent Tartar state in Crimea. All of this territory had been controlled previously by the Turks. The situation remained tense.

Russia and Turkey almost went to war again over who would exert the most influence in Crimea in 1778. Had the British been willing to sign on to an alliance to help the Russians at the time, a general European war could have easily erupted. Instead, Austria and France stepped in and convinced the Turks to back off and allow the Russians to reinstall their client as head of the Crimean Tartars. The Russians were also interested in exerting control and influence to the west, stationing troops in Poland, signing an alliance with Prussia, and joining in the first partition of Poland in 1772. The War of the Bavarian Succession from the summer of 1778 to the spring of 1779 between Prussia and Saxony on one side and Austria on the other, offered Catherine a wonderful opportunity to act as a comediator with France and exert influence in the very heart of Europe. If instead of working to mediate the Austrian-Prussian conflict Catherine had merely joined her ally Prussia, a series of dominoes might have fallen that could have led to a general European war with Great Britain, Prussia, and Russia on one side, and France, Spain, Austria, and the Ottoman Empire on the other. In this case, the American War for Independence might well have been a mere sideshow. The third area of Russian interest was to protect and expand trade, especially in the export of naval stores like masts, pitch, tar, cordage, and canvas whether it was carried by Russian, Dutch, or even British ships. This last concern led to the development of the League of Armed Neutrality.[13]

Both before and after the formation of the League, Catherine's dance card was quite full. The British were most eager to partner with Catherine. There was good reason for the British to be hopeful. Catherine was an Anglophile who sought to balance French Continental power by having close ties to Great Britain. If Catherine had British sympathies, however, she was no fan of George III and his ministers, and she thought the British problem in North America resulted from bad policy. When the American colonists first began their rebellion, the British hoped to hire twenty thousand Russian soldiers to reassert royal control over North America. It was only after Catherine refused to send these troops that the British signed a series of agreements with small West German principalities to hire the soldiers we call the Hessian mercenaries. After France in 1778 and then Spain in 1779 began hostilities with King George, the British again turned to the Russians hoping to have the czarina's ships join his majesty's navy against the Bourbons. Rather than rejecting these overtures outright, Catherine behaved coyly, having her ministers send contradictory signals, asserting her confidence that the British could handle both the Spanish and the French, while refusing to make any commitments in 1778 and 1779. When the British asked her to adopt a policy of armed mediation, which meant threatening force against whatever power refused the mediator's suggested terms, Catherine simply insisted she was willing to serve as an honest broker without taking sides or threatening force. Catherine continued to string the British along. Only weeks before she issued her proclamation setting up the League of Armed Neutrality, she held a real, not metaphorical, ball that she told the British ambassador James Harris was to honor Admiral George Rodney's victory over the Spanish at Cape St. Vincent.[14]

Harris became convinced that the only reason Russia did not sign an alliance with Great Britain, especially after the British reluctantly agreed to help the Russians in the eastern Mediterranean against the Turks, was because of Prussian influence. Frederick II of Prussia, no doubt, wished Harris was right. He had an alliance with the Russians but found it did him little good. Catherine remained aloof from his moves against the Austrians in 1778, and Frederick began to feel more isolated as a result of the Franco-Russian mediation in the War of the Bavarian Succession. His name might have been inscribed on Catherine's official dance card, but he seemed unable to cut in and spend much time with her on the ballroom floor.[15] Instead, Catherine flirted with Austria and helped extricate the Hapsburg Empire from a potential military disaster during the Bavarian conflict. In turn, Austria hoped to woo Catherine away from her Prussian connection by suggesting support for Russian ambitions against the Turks. Given the geopolitical situation, with Hapsburg lands abutting the Ottoman Empire in the Balkans, there was a certain logic to this shift for Russia—at least for the time being. Moreover, Austria seemed more interested in consolidating its German holdings by moving into Bavaria than bringing additional Slavs into its empire. Hence, Catherine's willingness to intervene and mediate in the Austro-Prussian war over the Bavarian Succession. Likewise, in 1780 she secretly met the Austrian emperor and later signed a surreptitious treaty that annulled the Russo-Prussian alliance.[16]

France demonstrated some of the deftest dance moves at Catherine's diplomatic ball. The French exerted their influence to have the Turks back off on Crimea and worked with the Russians to mediate the Austro-Prussian conflict. Both actions were important to Catherine. The first furthered her southern ambitions and the second was a testament to her enhanced importance in Europe. Such flattery worked to keep the British diplomatically isolated. It also helped that the French reversed their edicts against neutral trade and seemed to accept Catherine's principles of neutrality. In short, the French demanded little of Catherine and were happy to keep her neutral and to obtain a supply of naval stores. Moreover, any effort to assert the ideal of free ships make free goods would accrue to French benefit.[17]

The final dance partner—or perhaps dance partners would be a better way to put it—were the northern states of Sweden, Denmark, and the Netherlands. The first two approached Catherine about some sort of neutrality league as early as 1778 but did so independently and in ways that suited their own interests. Catherine's initial response was to pursue her own course regarding neutral trade—one that did not coordinate with either Denmark or Sweden. She was not about to follow the lead of what she considered inferior dance partners. Russia merely sought to protect ships along her own coast, including British vessels carrying Russian products, while the other powers hoped to protect all neutral shipping and force the British to accept the idea that free ships make free goods. By the beginning of 1780, however, Catherine concluded that going her own way was not sufficient to protect her trade. Great Britain persisted in dragging Russian ships into its admiralty courts. France was more compliant, and more dependent on neutral shipping to obtain naval stores, but Spain had begun to seize neutral shipping. With both sides guilty of harassing neutrals, Catherine asked the three powers—Denmark, Sweden, and the Netherlands—to join her dance circle in the League of Armed Neutrality. Catherine announced this shift in policy in her declaration of principle in early 1780.[18]

The two Scandinavian countries quickly embraced this strategy but did so following their own interests. The Danes did not want the Dutch to be allowed into the League and, since the Danes were already allied to Catherine, they hoped that a joint declaration by Denmark and Russia would suffice. Catherine insisted on inclusion of the Dutch and equal treatment of Sweden. The Danes eventually concurred, but they then signed a separate agreement with Great Britain that defined naval stores as contraband, so long as provisions—think Danish hams—were excluded. In other words, despite written commitment to neutral rights, Denmark adhered to a more limited doctrine that protected its national interests in food production.[19]

Sweden, too, had its own agenda. The Swedes had hoped to use the upheaval in Europe caused by the Anglo-French war to seize Norway, which was part of the Danish kingdom. Those plans came to naught. Likewise, the Swedes sought to reassert some leadership in European affairs by pushing neutral rights in 1778 and 1779, but Catherine's initial rebuff of Sweden's suggestions left the Swedish navy to escort its convoys on its own. When Catherine offered to do almost the same thing the Swedes had originally proposed, the Swedes hesitated and claimed a bigger role for themselves, even seeking to become joint mediators with the Russians in the Anglo-Dutch war. Catherine would have none of these pretensions and insisted on the Swedes dancing to her tune.[20]

In the meantime, the Dutch dallied and before they could square the circle, Great Britain declared war on the Netherlands, creating a problem for Catherine and her league. Recognizing that the Dutch had the largest neutral merchant fleet trading with Spain and France, and that the Dutch West Indies island colony of St. Eustatius had served as a funnel for military shipments to the rebellious American colonies, the British hoped that by going to war with the Netherlands they could cut off naval stores to France and Spain and sever the supply network to North America. In short, an Anglo-Dutch war would minimize the threat the League of Armed Neutrality posed to Great Britain. Timing was everything. The Dutch officially acceded to the League on January 4, 1781, just weeks after the outbreak of hostilities with Great Britain but before knowledge of that conflict reached St. Petersburg. By rights, with a member of the League's ships liable to seizure by the British, the other powers of the League (Russia, Sweden, and Denmark) should have committed their navies to the protection of the Dutch. This action would have meant a wider war. Catherine was nothing if not nimble on her feet. Great Britain had timed its move against the Netherlands well. The British not only started the war before the Dutch officially signed onto the League of Armed Neutrality, they also had just asked Catherine to join her new friend Emperor Joseph II of Austria to act as comediators in the Anglo-Bourbon war—as far as the British were concerned the Americans were not to participate in the negotiations. They also offered Russia possession of Minorca—a British-owned island in the Mediterranean that had been seized from Spain earlier in the century—if the Russians supported their plan to return to the conditions of the Treaty of Paris in 1763 and let the British deal with the Americans without French interference. Although tempted, Catherine declined the offer, preferring to keep her status as a neutral untainted by any secret agreement. As for the Dutch, they were left out in the cold. Catherine offered to mediate the Anglo-Dutch conflict, an offer that the British declined since it would have meant accepting the idea that free ships made free goods. And then, in a nice example of splitting hairs, she decided that the Dutch were full members of the League of Armed Neutrality when it came to protecting their shipping from the French and Spanish—a meaningless gesture since Spain, France, and the Netherlands now were co-belligerents against the British. However, since the Anglo-Dutch war had technically commenced before the Netherlands agreed to join the League, Dutch ships would not be protected from seizure by the British. In short, the nation that had been the largest neutral trader was abandoned by its league partners.[21]

The subsequent history of the League of Armed Neutrality continued to reflect the interests of its individual components. Hoping to reassert his formal relationship with Catherine, Frederick brought Prussia into the League. Without much of a navy himself, Frederick also hoped that Prussian merchant ships could fill the vacuum created by the removal of the Dutch from neutral commerce. Not to be outdone by his Prussian rival, Joseph II of Austria soon followed suit, binding himself ever closer to Catherine. In fact, Austria did not technically join with the entire League, issuing an accession document that linked it only to Russia. Both Austria—which held provinces between the Netherlands and France (modern Belgium)—and Prussia reflagged hundreds of Dutch ships and became major carriers of naval stores from the Russian Baltic to France and Spain. To add even more force to her assertion of neutral rights and extend her leadership across Europe, Catherine convinced both Portugal and Naples to enter the League.[22]

The British reaction to Catherine's new dance moves was muted. Lord North's government refused to accept the principle that free ships made free goods and the limited definition of contraband pushed by the League. But it also sought to minimize friction with the members of the League. The British dealt most gingerly with the Russians, hoping to avoid a break with Catherine. The Russian merchant marine, which had only seventeen ships in 1775, more than doubled by 1780. These numbers were small by the standards of the day: the Dutch and British each had over a thousand ships in the Baltic trade before the outbreak of war. The British seized some Russian ships, sometimes purchasing the cargo for their own navy and thus compensating the owners, and other times releasing the Russian vessels to continue on to their destination, even if it was to an enemy port. The Danes and Swedes sidestepped the issue. Despite adhering to the principles of the League, neither power shipped any naval stores to the Bourbon monarchies for fear of British sea power. The growing Prussian and Austrian neutral trade was unanticipated and left the British government in a bind. The expanding merchant fleet of the Austrians and Prussians wiped out most of the advantages of going to war against the Netherlands for the British. Since Great Britain did not want to alienate a potentially hostile Prussia and a potentially friendly Austria, it limited its molestation of their merchant shipping. With the war apparently lost in North America after the surrender at Yorktown, the British continued to court Catherine. Indeed, once the North administration collapsed in March 1782, to placate Catherine the new administration was willing to pursue a second effort at Russian mediation of the Anglo-Dutch conflict, although it meant accepting a provision protecting neutral trade. The negotiations, however, came to naught, as did the proposed Austrian-Russian mediation in the war against France and Spain. Instead, the British began direct negotiations with the Americans and then, in turn, with the other belligerents.[23]

As this brief outline of diplomatic maneuvers suggests—and it does not do full justice to the complex negotiations, backdoor deals, cloak-and-dagger operations that marked eighteenth-century European diplomacy—the League of Armed Neutrality was not a monolith with a clearly articulated and unified policy. Nor was it established simply to isolate the British who then had to confront the hostility of not only their declared enemies but also an ever-increasing array of neutral and united powers. Instead, it was a patched-together organization that reflected the interests of the many different nations who signed on, although first and foremost it reflected the interests of Catherine the Great. But however tainted by the hard-nosed realpolitik of the Ancien Régime the League of Armed Neutrality might appear, it had been inspired by and had been cast in terms reflecting the ideals of the Enlightenment. In the process, despite the many and varied moves of the czarina, she doggedly clung to the idea that by her will alone she was going to establish free trade principles in her League of Armed Neutrality. Whatever the League's sordid origins, whatever the bigger diplomatic games played by Catherine, revolutionary Americans seized on the same ideals outlined by the League and made them their own.

The Americans

Americans greeted the League of Armed Neutrality with enthusiasm. In April 1780 John Adams referred to Catherine's plan as a "great event" marking an "improvement in the law of nations" that was "hurtful to England," just as it was "beneficial to all other nations, and to none more than the United States." As far as Adams was concerned, "The principle which the neutral powers are contending for is evidently laid in the common good of nations, in the ease, safety, convenience, happiness, and prosperity of mankind in general."[24]

Benjamin Franklin concurred, referring to the Russian proposal "for protecting the Liberty of Commerce" as "the great publick Event in Europe of this Year [1780]." Franklin declared that not only was "the Proposition . . . accepted now by most of the Maritime Powers," but that it was also "likely to become the Law of Nations that free Ships should make free Goods." Given the importance of this move, Franklin suggested that Congress issue "Orders to their Cruizers not to molest Foreign Ships, but conform to the Spirit of that Treaty of Neutrality."[25]

The Continental Congress was quick to respond. On October 5, 1780, Congress, in testimony to "the rights of commerce, and their esteem for the sovereign [Catherine]," passed a resolution to respect neutral trade. Oblivious to whatever interest lay behind Catherine's motives, Congress gave full credit to the czarina as a defender of high-minded ideals and declared that the Empress of Russia was "attentive to the freedom of commerce, and the rights of nations." As far as Congress was concerned, her proposal was "founded upon principles of justice, equity, and moderation." Moreover, Congress empowered the "ministers plenipotentiary from the United States, if invited thereto . . . to accede to such regulations, conformable to the spirit of the said declaration," pending congressional approval. In other words, cutting through the diplomatese, Congress was willing to join the League itself![26]

Americans believed that the League of Armed Neutrality had been created just for them. As Adams explained: "I confess the wonders of this revolution exceed all that I foresaw or imagined. That our country, so young as it is, so humble as it is, thinking but lately so meanly of itself, should thus interest the passions, as well as employ the reason, of all mankind in its favor, and effect, in so short a space of time, not only thirteen revolutions of government at home, but so completely accomplish a revolution in the system of Europe and in the sentiments of every nation in it, is what no human wisdom . . . could foresee."²⁷

Similar expressions appeared in American newspapers. The *Massachusetts Spy* included a report exclaiming that "the end and basis of the whole plan" was "free trade for all the world with the new States of America." In 1783 the *Boston Evening-Post* published a letter from a correspondent in Europe who declared that "the spirit of commerce seems to pervade the nations of Europe, and to form a complexion of the present age" that "happily for mankind," opened "a friendly intercourse between distant nations" that rendered "them reciprocally dependent." The writer continued, in language redolent with the Enlightenment, to claim that this effort "enlarges and polishes the human mind; checks ferocity; abates bigotry; softens the rage of war; makes us citizens of the world, and surprizingly changes that self interest from which it springs into the means of promoting the benevolent affections, and the pleasures of human society." The League of Armed Neutrality wanted to make free trade "the basis of a new general system," while "America, without doubt, wishes to trade with all the world upon the most liberal and extensive plan," and in turn "every nation would be glad to have as large a share as may be in the trade of America."²⁸

The League and its protection of neutral shipping seemed part of an ongoing diplomatic revolution spawned by the Enlightenment and espoused by American revolutionaries. Indeed, Americans believed that they were in the vanguard of a movement that most of the leading nations of Europe had now joined. When John Adams wrote the Plan of Treaties in 1776, he used the language of the free ships make free goods provision of the Treaty of Utrecht and the earlier Anglo-Dutch treaties. To sustain this momentum, American diplomats thereafter sought to include a free ships make free goods clause in its commercial treaties. The French commercial agreement of 1778 had such a provision, as did the next three commercial treaties signed by the United States, those with the Netherlands, Sweden, and Prussia.²⁹

Lurking just beneath this talk of a revolution in diplomacy and the declaration of a new order based on enlightened ideals that viewed commerce as a means to benefit humanity, was a strong dose of self-interest. By breaking out of the mercantilist constraints of the British Empire, Americans almost had to embrace the freedom of neutrals to trade with nations at war. That so many European nations seemed to agree with this goal appeared like a dream come true. Americans had written the model treaty hoping to avoid a more formal alliance, and only the exigencies of war, and the disastrous campaign of 1776, convinced them otherwise. Yet the hope persisted that once independence was won the United States could remain aloof from the divisive wars of Europe. Thomas Paine had said so in *Common Sense,* and John Adams repeated these sentiments in 1780, declaring that "our business with them [European nations], and theirs with us, is commerce, not politics, much less war; America has been the sport of European wars and politics long enough." In such a world the United States could reap huge profits from its neutrality. If Europe again became engulfed in war, the American merchant marine could expand and enrich the nation. No wonder both Adams and Franklin had wished for even greater neutral rights. Adams went so far as to suggest that "as human reason advances, and men come to be more sensible of the benefits of peace . . . all neutral nations will be allowed, by universal consent, to carry what goods they please in their own ships," and Franklin wanted to protect all merchants, as well as farmers and fishermen, since they were "working for the common Benefit of Mankind."[30]

The opportunity to take advantage of these "principles" began in earnest early in 1793 when Great Britain and France renewed their century-long conflict—with France this time representing a new and revolutionary regime. Remaining neutral in a world at war was not easy as the United States lurched from one crisis to another with each of the belligerents over the next nineteen years until James Madison and the Democratic-Republicans stumbled into the War of 1812 against Great Britain. There is no need here to rehearse the zigging and zagging of American foreign policy during those years except to say that at least until the Embargo of 1807, neutral commerce under the aegis of free ships make free goods was the driving force behind much of the growth of the US economy. Moreover, however much Americans focused their attention on Great Britain and France, always in the background hovered the legacy of the League of Armed Neutrality. Europeans attempted to revive the League at least twice: once in 1794 and again in 1800. The United States even considered joining these efforts but ultimately decided not to do so for fear of entangling alliances. An even more important reflection of the League's heritage appeared at the opening of the War of 1812 when Czar Alexander offered to mediate the second Anglo-American war. Remembering that it was Russia that had led the League during the American Revolution, James Madison quickly accepted this offer and dispatched a team of diplomats to St. Petersburg because he was convinced that the American position on neutral shipping would be defended by the Russians.[31]

The League of Armed Neutrality represented a pivotal moment in both American and European history when Old World diplomacy and realpolitik combined with a set of principles to offer a protective umbrella for neutral rights under the guise of free trade. Ideology and interest combined to give birth to the defense of neutral rights whether under the guise of *consolato del mare* or the rubric of free ships make free goods. Commercial nations embraced neutral rights in the seventeenth and eighteenth centuries seeking to profit as other nations waged war, while political theorists like Grotius and Vattel articulated a rationale for those rights based in the law of nations. Ideology and interest together lay behind Catherine the Great's formation of the League of Armed Neutrality. The czarina may have turned to neutral rights in a calculated move to obtain prestige and influence, but she labeled her actions a defense of the "liberty of universal commerce." Ideology and interest appeared yet again when the United States proclaimed the advent of a revolutionary diplomacy free from the constraints of the past that released American merchants to open new markets even as Europe continued to fight its wars.

Notes

1. For standard coverage of the League of Armed Neutrality, see Samuel Flagg Bemis, *The Diplomacy of the American Revolution* (Bloomington: Indiana University Press, 1957), 149–63; Richard B. Morris, *The Peacemakers: The Great Powers and American Independence* (New York: Harper & Row, 1965), 165–68. For an argument from the British perspective that views its diplomatic isolation as a result of British success in the Seven Years' War, see H. M. Scott, *British Foreign Policy in the Age of the American Revolution* (New York: Oxford University Press, 1990).

2. Felix Gilbert, *To the Farewell Address: Ideas of Early American Foreign Policy* (1961; reprinted, Princeton, NJ: Princeton University Press, 1970). For other scholars emphasizing ideals, see Jonathan R. Dull, "Benjamin Franklin and the Nature of American Diplomacy," *International History Review* 5 (August 1983): 346–63; Lawrence S., Kaplan, *Colonies into Nation: American Diplomacy, 1763–1801* (New York: Macmillan, 1972). For an emphasis on early American diplomats as realists, see Bemis, *Diplomacy of the American Revolution*; Morris, *The Peacemakers*; James H. Hutson, *John Adams and the Diplomacy of the American Revolution* (Lexington: University of Kentucky Press, 1980). See also Alexander DeConde, "Historians, the War of American Independence

and the Persistence of the Exceptionalist Ideal," *International History Review* 5 (August 1983): 399–430; Lawrence S. Kaplan, "The Treaty of Paris, 1783: A Historiographical Challenge," *International History Review* 5 (August 1983): 431–42; and Kaplan, "Foreign Policy in the Early Republic Reconsidered: Essays from a SHEAR Symposium," *Journal of the Early Republic* 14 (Winter 1994): 453–57. For a discussion that sees an interplay between ideas and interests but that leans toward arguing interests predominated, see Bradford Perkins, *The Cambridge History of American Foreign Relations: Vol. I, The Creation of a Republican Empire, 1776–1865* (Cambridge: Cambridge University Press, 1993).

3. For a fuller exploration of different meanings of free trade, see Paul A. Gilje, *Free Trade and Sailors' Rights in the War of 1812* (New York: Cambridge University Press, 2013).

4. Francis Taylor Piggott, "The Freedom of the Seas, Historically Treated," *Peace Handbooks: International Affairs*, 23:148 (London: H. M. Stationary Office, 1920), 14–28; Carl J. Kulsrud, *Maritime Neutrality to 1780: A History of the Main Principles Governing Neutrality and Belligerency to 1780* (Boston: Little, Brown, and Co., 1936), 107–23.

5. *A General Collection of Treatys of Peace and Commerce . . .* , 4 vols. (London: J. J. and P. Knapton, 1732), 3:68–69, 1:171–72; George Chalmers, *Collection of Treaties between Great Britain and Other Powers*, 2 vols. (London: John Stockdale, 1790), 1:189–91. See also Kulsrud, *Maritime Neutrality to 1780*, 123–50; Scott, *British Foreign Policy*, 277–80.

6. Scott, *British Foreign Policy*, 278; Kulsrud, *Maritime Neutrality to 1780*, 132–47; Gilje, *Free Trade and Sailors' Rights*, 149–51.

7. Hugo Grotius, *The Rights of War and Peace*, ed. Richard Tuck, 3 vols. (Indianapolis, IN: Liberty Fund, 2005; orig. pub. 1625), 1:6–7.

8. Grotius, *Rights of War and Peace*, 3:1324–25, 1519.

9. Hugo Grotius, *The Free Sea*, ed. David Armitage (Indianapolis, IN: Liberty Fund, 2004; orig. pub 1609), 30, 51.

10. Emer de Vattel, *The Law of Nations*, eds. Béla Kapossey and Richard Whatmore (Indianapolis, IN: Liberty Fund, 2008; orig. pub. 1758), 71, 135, 529, 532.

11. Although the principles outlined by the Russian proposal were nearly identical to a Danish proposal in 1778, this discussion assumes that since Catherine issued the principles under her own name, she had made them her own. See "Declaration of the Empress of Russia Regarding the Principles of Armed Neutrality," in H. M. Scott, ed., *The Armed Neutralities of 1780 and 1800: A Collection of Official Documents Preceded by the Views of Representative Publicists* (New York: Oxford University Press, 1918), 273–74; Chalmers, *Collection of Treaties*, 1:7; Nikolai N. Bolhovitinov, *Russia and the American Revolution*, ed. and trans. C. Jay Smith (Tallahassee, FL: Diplomatic Press, 1976), 31–40; Bolhovitinov, *The Beginnings of Russian-American Relations, 1775–1815*, trans. Elena Levin (Cambridge, MA: Harvard University Press, 1980), 13–15; Scott, *British Foreign Policy*, 300–304.

12. This essay identifies Catherine as the progenitor of Russian foreign policy. Admittedly this approach is an oversimplification of a much more complex process in which different Russian officials pursued different policies, sending mixed signals. Regardless of this larger complexity, in the final analysis, Russian policy reflected the ideas and interests of Catherine. For a fuller examination of the intricacies of Russian foreign policy during the era of the American Revolution, see Isabel de Madariaga, *Britain, Russia, and the Armed Neutrality of 1780: Sir James Harris's Mission to St. Petersburg during the American Revolution* (New Haven, CT: Yale University Press, 1962).

13. Isabel de Madariaga, *Russia in the Age of Catherine the Great* (New Haven, CT: Yale University Press, 1981), 187–236, 377–92; John T. Alexander, *Catherine the Great: Life and Legend* (New York: Oxford University Press, 1988), 121–42, 227–55; Robert K. Massie, *Catherine the Great: Portrait of a Woman* (New York: Random House, 2011), 371–83, 484–89.

14. Scott, *British Foreign Policy*, 216–20; De Madariaga, *Britain, Russia, and the Armed Neutrality*, 21–56, 96–139; Bolhovitinov, *Russia and the American Revolution*, 1–29; David M. Griffiths, "Catherine the Great, the British Opposition, and the American Revolution," in *The American Revolution and "A Candid World,"* ed. Lawrence S. Kaplan (Kent, OH: Kent State University Press, 1977), 85–110.

15. De Madariaga, *Britain, Russia, and the Armed Neutrality*, 26–27, 48–49, 53–55, 97–98.

16. Ibid., 97–98, 216–17, 261–62, 280–81, 295, 300–301.

17. Ibid., 25–29, 42, 90–92, 184–85, 223.

18. Scott, *Armed Neutralities of 1780 and 1800*, 275–77.

19. De Madariaga, *Britain, Russia, and the Armed Neutrality*, 185–89; Scott, *Armed Neutralities of 1780 and 1800*, 290, 295–307, 308–10, 320–21.

20. H. A. Barton, "Sweden and the War for American Independence," *William and Mary Quarterly*, 3rd ser., 23 (July 1966): 423–25; Raymond A. Lindgren, "The League of Armed Neutrality," in, *Scandinavian Studies: Essays Presented to D. Henry Goddard Leach on the Occasion of His Eighty-fifth Birthday*, eds. Carl F. Bayerschmidt and Erik J. Friis (Seattle: University of Washington Press, 1965), 395–409; De Madariaga, *Britain, Russia, and the Armed Neutrality*, 189–90; Scott, *Armed Neutralities of 1780 and 1800*, 288–90, 307–8, 311–19, 322–23.

21. Jan Willem Schuilte Nordholt, *The Dutch Republic and American Independence*, trans. Herbert H. Rowen, (Chapel Hill: University of North Carolina Press, 1982), 144–57; De Madariaga, *Britain, Russia, and the Armed Neutrality*, 216–312; Scott, *Armed Neutralities of 1780 and 1800*, 277–79, 281, 283, 325–28, 330–45, 346–90; Scott, *British Foreign Policy*, 277–309.

22. De Madariaga, *Britain, Russia, and the Armed Neutrality*, 306–7, 340–41; Scott, *Armed Neutralities of 1780 and 1800*, 391–436.

23. De Madariaga, *Britain, Russia, and the Armed Neutrality*, 287, 336–412; Scott, *British Foreign Policy*, 310–38; David Syrett, *The Royal Navy in European Waters during the American Revolution* (Columbia: University of South Carolina Press, 1998), 95–132.

24. John Adams to the President of Congress, April 26, 1780, in *The Revolutionary Diplomatic Correspondence of the United States,* ed. Francis Wharton, 6 vols. (Washington, DC: Government Printing Office, 1889), 3:631–32; Adams to the President of Congress, April 28, 1780, ibid., 639.

25. Benjamin Franklin to Samuel Huntington, August 9, 1780, *The Papers of Benjamin Franklin,* ed. Leonard Labaree et al. (New Haven, CT: Yale University Press, 1959-present), 33:160–66.

26. *Journals of the Continental Congress, 1774–1789,* ed. Worthington C. Ford (Washington, DC: GPO, 1904–37), 18:864–66, 905–6; Scott, *Armed Neutralities of 1780 and 1800,* 323–24; Bolhovitinov, *Russia and the American Revolution,* 41–43.

27. Adams to the President of Congress, April 28, 1780, in *Revolutionary Diplomatic Correspondence,* 3:639.

28. *Philadelphia Pennsylvania Packet,* April 4, 1779; (Worcester) *Massachusetts Spy,* December 27, 1781. See also *Philadelphia Pennsylvania Packet,* July 11, 28, 1780; June 27, 1782; *Philadelphia Pennsylvania Evening Post,* July 28, 1780; and *Boston Independent Ledger,* November 27, 1780; *New-York Gazette,* March 18, 1782; *Boston Evening-Post,* September 20, 1783.

29. Hunter Miller, ed., *Treaties and other International Acts of the United States of America,* 8 vols. (Washington, DC: GPO, 1931), 2:3–29, 59–90, 123–49, 162–84. See also George L. Lint, "The Law of Nations and the American Revolution," in Kaplan, *American Revolution and "A Candid World,"* 111–33.

30. Plan of Treaties (September 17, 1776), *Journals of the Continental Congress,* 5:768–69; Thomas Paine, *Common Sense,* ed. Isaac Kramnick. (New York: Penguin Books, 1976; orig. pub. 1776), 87; John Adams to the President of Congress, April 18, 1780, *Revolutionary Diplomatic Correspondence,* 3:623; Adams to the President of Congress, April 14, 1780, ibid., 3:612–13; Benjamin Franklin to Robert Morris, June 3, 1780, *Papers of Benjamin Franklin,* 32:46–67. See also James Sofka, "American Neutral Rights Reappraised: Identity or Interest in the Foreign Policy of the Early Republic?," *Review of International Studies* 26 (October 2000): 599–622; Gilbert, *To the Farewell Address,* 44–75; Hutson, *John Adams and the Diplomacy of the American Revolution,* 26–31; William C. Stinchcombe, *The American Revolution and the French Alliance* (Syracuse, NY: Syracuse University Press, 1969), 1–31; William Stinchcombe, "John Adams and the Model Treaty," in Kaplan, *American Revolution and "A Candid World,"* 69–84.

31. Douglass C. North, *The Economic Growth of the United States, 1790–1860* (Englewood Cliffs, NJ: Prentice Hall, 1961); Gilje, *Free Trade and Sailors' Rights,* 53, 63, 251–55.

"Sir, I have not yet begun to fight!"
John Paul Jones's Friends in the Dutch Republic, 1779–1780

VICTOR ENTHOVEN

In the summer of 1780 John Adams arrived as the first ambassador plenipotentiary of the US Continental Congress to the Dutch Republic. He carried with him a kind of shopping list of whom to meet in Amsterdam, and the names are mostly those of Amsterdam merchants or bankers who had American interests. Top of the list was Mr. John de Neufville of the firm of De Neufville & Fils. De Neufville was the most zealous advocate of the American cause in the Netherlands. The list also included firms like Fizeaux, Grand & Co., John Hodshon & Zoon, Nicolaas & Jacob van Staphorst, Daniël Crommelin & Zoonen, and individuals including Jan Gabriel Tegelaar.[1]

A few months earlier Captain John Paul Jones had arrived at the Texel in the Netherlands with his battered squadron. He had acted as a kind of pathfinder for Adams's mission and had met most of the persons named on Adams's list. In fact, John de Neufville acted as his agent or "fixer," and his network, supplies, and credit aided Jones in repairing his ships and, after some delay, leaving the Texel safely. In the vast literature on this American legend, the Texel episode plays an insignificant role, but Jones's experience at the Texel is representative of the complex private and state diplomacy that Americans in Europe had to navigate as nations grappled with how and when to respond to the American Revolution.[2]

The arrival and stay of the American squadron at the Texel created a many-faceted incident that epitomizes American and Dutch relations in the period. First, it was a long time in the making, starting in 1776. Second, it reveals for the first time a kind of "American" support group in the Netherlands. Third, it deepened an existing rift between the pro-British *stadhouder* (Orange party) and the patriotic movement and consequently soured relations between the United Kingdom and the Dutch Republic.³ Fourth, it cast a long shadow on future events.

Studying the incident also presents unique challenges and opportunities to historians. The European friends of the American Revolution spanned two continents and covered a wide variety of different languages. This diversity of characters and historic materials certainly applies to the Dutch friends. On the one hand, American researchers, even relatively modern writers like James A. Lewis, did not consult Dutch sources. One exception is, of course, Jared Sparks. However, his work not only is almost two hundred years old but is also very limited in scope. He consulted a small portion of the archives of the States General—the highest executive power in the Dutch Republic. Friedrich Edler, too, only consulted the archives of the States General. On the other hand, Dutch authors like P. J. van Winter, F. W. van Wijk, and Jan Willem Schulte Nordholt have used the correspondence of the founding fathers in a rather limited manner. Due to the many digitization projects, these correspondences are now easily accessible. Thus, many of the American sources relating to the Dutch friends of the American Revolution used here are new, at least in terms of their ease of accessibility (especially for European historians), as is the cast of most of the Dutch sources relating to John Paul Jones.

Prelude

After the Declaration of Independence (July 4, 1776), the Americans were in desperate need of heavily armed ships that would be a match against the mighty warships of the Royal Navy. The American commissioners in Paris, Silas Dean, Benjamin Franklin, and Arthur Lee, were instructed by the Continental Congress to obtain eight ships of the line from the French government, which declined politely. After the French refusal, the Americans were introduced to Jacques Boux, a prominent French naval officer, through their trusted Paris contacts: Jacques-Donatien Le Ray de Chaumont, a shipping magnate and governor of Les Invalides, and bankers George and Ferdinand Grand.⁴

L'Indien

In early 1777 the three American commissioners signed a contract with Boux for the construction of several frigates in neutral Amsterdam. Although the commissioners could not understand all the details of the plan, they were persuaded that the frigates could be built most quickly and cheaply in the Netherlands. No time was wasted.[5]

Boux arrived in Amsterdam by late February 1777 and contracted Arie Staats of the shipyard Vergulde Schol on Realeneiland. They signed a contract for a 160-foot (45.5 meter) frigate with forty guns on May 6.[6] By August the keel had been laid, and by September the frigate *L'Indien*, as the French called it, which would become the *South Carolina*, was well underway. By that time, however, the Americans had run out of money. But the French government, whose money was really building the ship anyway, was willing to take over the frigate and complete it. By the end of 1777 ownership of *L'Indien* was in the hands of Versailles. In February 1778 the ship slid off the stock, and the French made a half-hearted attempt to get the ship to sea. For a while the frigate was ostensibly owned by the Amsterdam firm Horneca, Fizeaux & Co. In 1779 the name of the company changed to Fizeaux, Grand & Co., including George Grand from Paris. The firm claimed that the vessel was an East Indiaman intended for Asia.[7]

Almost from the start the British were informed in detail of the covert operation. Not only was the Paris entourage of Franklin, Dean, and Lee riddled with British informers, but after Arthur Lee's papers were stolen by British agents in mid-1777, Whitehall probably had a copy of the Boux contract. In the Dutch Republic, British ambassador Joseph Yorke, 1st Baron Dover, had an extensive network of informers and spies. From his Amsterdam agent Yorke was informed almost daily on the progress of the ship. As he sought to stop any effort to sail her under French colors, he demanded from the States General strict assurances that the vessel's purposes were commercial and not military.[8]

At that point the Dutch government was in no mood to provoke Britain unnecessarily. The Dutch were much more interested in supplying the Americans with arms via St. Eustatius than the whereabouts of a French frigate in Amsterdam. As early as 1775 Dutch merchants exported large quantities of ammunition to the West Indies that eventually ended up in North America.[9] So the States General required guaranties from Fizeaux c.s. that no military intention was associated with the ship. For the French government at that moment, Dutch goodwill was more important than the sailing of one frigate; as a result, the ship rotted away in Amsterdam.

John Paul Jones apparently heard about *L'Indien* in December 1777. By that time Jones had crossed the Atlantic Ocean from Portsmouth (New Hampshire) to Nantes with the *Ranger* with a commission issued under authority of the Continental Congress. It was understood by Jones before he left Portsmouth that the American commissioners in Paris were to purchase a frigate for him.[10] On December 15 Jones was summoned to Paris. With respect to *L'Indien,* he got nothing but vague promises; the French government could not be pressed while other more important and delicate negotiations were underway. After pulling all the strings that he could think of, Jones received word from Franklin in June 1778 that he would be given command of the *L'Indien* as soon as she reached a French port. That never happened.[11]

On Franklin's invitation, Jones came to Passy, Franklin's retreat near Paris (now the 16th arrondissement) and remained until August 7, 1778. In Passy, Jones's host was Jacques-Donatien Le Ray de Chaumont, who would become Jones's main financier and supplier. Men like Chaumont gave the French government camouflage, acting as frontmen, funneling war supplies to the Americans without direct involvement by the Crown.[12] With *L'Indien* laid at Amsterdam all but ready to sail and wanting only a fortnight's work to float her out to the Texel road, Franklin informed Jones about the conditions attached to his new command. French sailors would man the ship, but he could supplement the crew by exchanging British prisoners that he had taken on earlier voyages for American captives held in England. Furthermore, the German-French prince Karl Heinrich Nassau-Siegen, a noted adventurer and colonel of a regiment, would sail with him. Nassau-Siegen was apparently chosen because of his remote kinship to Prince William Oranje-Nassau, the *stadhouder,* cousin of the King of England, and the leader of the pro-British Orangists.

Nassau-Siegen was sent to Holland to try to reverse the attitude of the States General concerning the sailing of *L'Indien*. Jones promised that if he effected this, he should have a commission under him, but Nassau-Siegen accomplished nothing while the Dutch remained obdurate. The States General still had other American interests to defend: namely, St. Eustatius, which Admiral George Brydges Rodney, 1st Baron Rodney, would later call the "rock of only six miles in length and three in breadth [that] has done England more harm than all the arms of her most potent enemies and alone supported the infamous American rebellion."[13] The Dutch government could not afford the embarrassment and diplomatic turmoil with Whitehall that would result from a French man-of-war fitting out in their ports. By the end of 1778 *L'Indien* had gone nowhere, and Jones was stuck in France without a command. But soon, both would meet.¹⁴

THE *BONHOMME RICHARD*

In 1778 James Moylan, an Irish merchant in Lorient, found the French East Indiaman *Le duc de Duras* for the Americans. On December 7, 1778, Jones arrived in Lorient to inspect the vessel and was told that the French king was willing to purchase the ship. Jones charged himself with the entire expense of fitting the ship out and meeting its payroll. The forty-gun ship was renamed *Bonhomme Richard*, a reference to Franklin's *nom de plume* for his famous almanacs, and Jones was given command in February 1779. She would sail under American colors, but Jones was allowed to enlist a French crew. Before long Jones's command was expanded with the new American-built frigate *Alliance* (thirty-six guns), under command of Pierre Landais, and the French government assigned to him three armed ships: the frigate *Pallas* (twenty-six guns), commanded by Dennis-Nicolas de Brulôt Cottineau de Kerloguen; the brig *Vengeance* (twelve guns), commanded by Philippe Ricot; and the fast cutter *Cerf* (eighteen guns), commanded by Joseph Varange.¹⁵

On August 9 *Bonhomme Richard, Pallas, Cerf,* and *Vengeance* sailed from Lorient to join the *Alliance* off Île de Groix. Two French privateers—*Monsieur* (twenty-six guns), commanded by Nicholas Guidelou, and *Granville* (ten guns), commanded by Louis Pierre Etienne Le Pelley—had decided to join Jones. Of these, Jones, Landais, Ricot, Varange, and Cottineau had US commissions and signed a contract that the ships would be considered as belonging to the US Navy, would fly the American ensign, and would operate under US regulations. All prizes were to be consigned to M. de Chaumont, and the portion of each prize taken by any vessel of the squadron would be determined by the American minister at the Court of Versailles and the French minister of the navy.¹⁶ The squadron left Groix on August 14, 1779.

In the early hours of September 23, 1779, Jones's squadron, comprising *Bonhomme Richard, Alliance, Pallas,* and *Vengeance* (the *Cerf* had returned to Lorient), and two British prizes encountered the Baltic fleet of more than forty merchantmen under convoy of HMS *Serapis* (forty-four guns), commanded by Richard Pearson, and HMS *Countess of Scarborough* (twenty guns), commanded by Thomas Piercy, near Flamborough Head. *Bonhomme Richard* and *Serapis* entered a bitter engagement lasting over four hours, which cost the lives of nearly half of the American and British crews. Initially, British victory seemed inevitable. Pearson called on Jones to surrender, who allegedly replied, "Sir, I have not yet begun to fight!" An attempt by the Americans to board *Serapis* was repulsed, as was an attempt by the British to board *Bonhomme Richard*. Finally, after the *Alliance* joined in the fight, Pearson surrendered. Jones abandoned the sinking *Bonhomme Richard* and transferred to the *Serapis*, taking Pearson and his men prisoner. In the meantime, the Baltic fleet had escaped safely.[17]

Jones's squadron, more or less intact and composed of the heavily damaged *Serapis, Alliance, Countess of Scarborough, Pallas,* and *Vengeance,* sailed straight across the North Sea to the Dutch Republic—or, more accurately, the French captains led the squadron there. They had been instructed by Chaumont that the cruise should end by the first of October at the Texel, the shipping roads that served Amsterdam, so that they could escort a fleet of merchantmen waiting there avoiding British cruisers. Jones preferred Dunkirk as a French, not a neutral, port where he could land his more than five hundred prisoners and then to proceed to Texel. But as the prisoners were distributed among all four ships, he had no choice but to follow the French. According to his instructions, Jones had to hand over British prisoners to Paul François de Quélen de Stuer de Caussade, duc de la Vauguyon, France's ambassador in the Dutch Republic.[18] The prize ships were sent to Bergen (Norway), and Jones safely reached Dutch waters on October 3, 1779.

The American Friends in Holland

When Jones arrived at the Texel, a loose network of all sorts of individuals living in the Netherlands were sympathizing with the American cause: Dutch merchants and *regenten* (politicians and officials), visiting American agents (both Dutch-born and British subjects) in search of financial support and military supplies, and French representatives. Jones's most valuable contacts among these groups were Guillaume-Frederic Dumas in The Hague and John de Neufville in Amsterdam, but a review of the groups and the individuals vying for influence on American affairs gives some sense of the complex matters of private and state diplomacy that Jones had to navigate.

The Dutch Friends

Probably as early as 1775 several influential Dutch politicians and merchants began to take up the American rebels' cause. In 1778 and 1779, Dutch pro-American journals included the *Gazette de Leyde* and the *Lettres Hollandaise [. . .] de la République des Sept Provinces-Unies*. Under the influence of Jones's arrival and the political and social upheaval it caused, by 1780 a significant portion of the Dutch elite had made a pledge to the American cause.[19]

By far the most visible and prominent member of the group was Joan Derck van der Capellen tot den Pol, a nobleman from rural and less wealthy Gelderland. Not only did he have contact with Amsterdam merchants, but as a member of the Dutch elite he had also a network in Holland, including the prominent patriot Cornelis de Gijzelaar, councilor and burgomaster of Dordrecht;[20] arms dealer Egbert de Vrij Temminck, burgomaster of Amsterdam;[21] publisher and patriot J. G. Tegelaar;[22] and C. W. Visscher, second Pensionaris of Amsterdam.[23] Van der Capellen's 1781 American-inspired pamphlet *Aan het volk van Nederland* (To the people of the Netherlands) was an important factor in sparking the Dutch support for the American cause. One of his contacts was Dutch-born lieutenant colonel of the Continental Army, Jacob Gerard Dircks, whose mother was the daughter of a burgomaster of the town of Deventer. In the fall of 1778 Dircks was on leave in the Dutch Republic, carrying letters from Jonathan Trumbull, Governor of Connecticut; William Livingston, Governor of New Jersey; and General-Major Horatio Gates, all addressed to Van der Capellen. They all praised the Dutch efforts in support of their struggle, but they would all have liked to see the Dutch reach for their wallets. By August 31, 1779, Dircks left the Dutch Republic but not before he had handed over a parcel of letters to Van der Capellen from Goswinus Erkelens, another of his American contacts.[24] In the summer of 1777, Erkelens, a Dutch gentleman living in Philadelphia, had written to Van der Cappelen on behalf of the Continental Congress, at least according to his letters. For the next five years Erkelens and Van der Capellen had regular contact.[25]

American Visitors

When Dircks left the Dutch Republic in the summer of 1779, Stephen Sayre arrived. He had acted for a short while as Arthur Lee's secretary, but he came to Amsterdam on May 17, 1779, in search of a ship to command. British ambassador Yorke kept an eye on "the noted American agent." But without

Table 1. Merchants and trading houses visited by Jacob Gerard Dircks in 1779

John de Neufville & Son, early and uniformly active	Guisebert Wilhelminus Willemson
De La Lande & Fijnje	Jan Gabriel Tegelaar
Lever & De Bruine	Abraham van Loghem, a great chemist
Evert de Burlet	Van Brant, d° Druggist
Hendrick Steenbergen	Van Tarelinck
Mijnheer Splithoft	The Widow Chabanel and C°
François Abrahams	The widow Erkelens
Gulicher & Mulder	Crommelin, senior
Jacob van Bunschoten	Horneca, Fizeaux & C°

Source: Van der Capellen to Adams, April 20, 1783, *Brieven Van der Capellen*, 583–86.

an order or commission, Sayre approached the Dutch and tried to sell Continental Congress bonds and wild lands in America that he did not possess. Sayre was openly received at first only by the merchant John de Neufville, who introduced him to Van der Capellen in July.[26]

During the fall of 1779 Sayre was busy acquiring and equipping an armed vessel that could operate as a privateer. In this context, strangely enough, there is no mention of *L'Indien*, although Sayre was in contact with shipwright Staats about building a vessel. It is most likely that Sayre acquired his "little frigate" with the cash and credit assistance of the De la Lande & Fijnje, a young and not very powerful but active and fiercely patriotic firm involved with the shipyard De IJhoek of the firm Ten Cate. Later De la Lande & Fijnje delivered much of the means for building another ship, which Sayre undertook in partnership with some Russians.[27]

When Jones arrived in October, Sayre spread the rumor to the effect that the *Richard*, *Pallas*, and *Vengeance* were Le Ray de Chaumont's privateers, and he even had the impudence to propose himself as captain of the *Alliance* when Captain Landais was relieved of her command. Jones was appalled. Many people must have been relieved when Sayre left the Dutch Republic with his little frigate in January 1780.[28]

THE FRENCH

In December 1776 Paul François de Quélen, duc de la Vauguyon, was appointed French minister to the States General. His primary task was to see that the Dutch Republic remained neutral in the rising tensions between France and Great Britain over the American cause because Dutch merchants were the chief sources of French naval stores and provisions. Besides his diplomatic activities with the States General in The Hague, the main field of his business was in Amsterdam. Over time he succeeded in convincing the political elite to follow his suggestions and the Dutch Republic drifted toward France. His British counterpart and adversary, Joseph Yorke, spoke of Vauguyon as being "of the right cut for this Embassy, being as *squab* [a young pigeon] as anything in Holland."[29]

In the summer and fall of 1779 a French naval agent by the name of M. de Livoncourt was active in Amsterdam, but his particular activities have yet to be disclosed. In December 1779 he stayed in Den Helder in support of Jones.[30]

The third and final French forward base of operation was the earlier mentioned banking house of Fizeaux, Grand & Co.; the partner George Grand was the brother of Ferdinand Grand, the Paris banker for the United States.[31]

Guillaume-Frederic Dumas

The first friend in the Dutch Republic to welcome Jones was Guillaume-Frederic Dumas, a Frenchman born in Brandenburg and educated in Switzerland. In 1768 Dumas had taken up the idea to settle in one of the British North American colonies. He consulted Benjamin Franklin, whom he presumably had met during the latter's visit to the Netherlands with Sir John Pringle in 1766.[32] The plan did not materialize, but the two men remained in contact, which resulted in Dumas's interest in the American cause.

By the end of 1775 there was "not in Europe a better Station to collect Intelligence from France, Spain, England, Germany, and all the Northern Parts; nor a better Situation from whence to circulate Intelligence" than the Netherlands.[33] On December 9 Franklin wrote, as member of the Committee of Secret Correspondence, to his old Dutch friend Dumas and offered him an opportunity to devote himself to the service of the American cause. Dumas enthusiastically accepted and became the first American agent on the Continent. He lived in The Hague, where the States of Holland and States General met; in Amsterdam he stayed at the patriotic firm De la Lande & Fijnje.[34]

During 1777 Dumas furnished the American commissioners in Paris with addresses of Dutch firms with whom the Americans could deal; unfortunately, at the time there was no prospect of any credit for the Americans. A few weeks later, however, Van der Capellen suggested a plan for a loan. It would serve both to separate the Dutch gradually from the British and to attach them more and more to the interests of the Americans. Consequently, Dumas published an essay written by Arthur Lee advocating that for the American cause a new avenue could be opened via a Dutch loan.[35]

While in Paris, Franklin, Adams, and Lee were working on a loan from the Netherlands; they also tried to open some diplomatic channels by dispatching a parcel of letters to their trusted friend in The Hague, including a letter addressed to the influential *Raadpensionaris* Pieter van Bleiswijk.[36] (The *Raadpensionaris* was the highest executive office in the service of the States of Holland, the most powerful province.) Unfamiliar with the political practices in the Dutch Republic, the Americans could not address Van Bleiswijk directly; instead, their letter was sent to Dumas and included the information that France had recognized the United States and concluded a treaty of amity and commerce. The commissioners expressed their hopes that soon there would be friendly relations and mercantile dealings between the two republics. Dumas handed the letter to Van Bleiswijk.[37] The *Raadpensionaris* showed the letter to other representatives of the States of Holland, including Cornelis de Gijzelaar and Amsterdam burgomaster Egbert de Vrij Temminck. Van Bleiswijk never replied to the letter formally.

Amabassador Yorke had got wind of the letter and prevented the States of Holland and the States General from entering into any official relation with the commissioners in Paris. While Vauguyon, France's ambassador, had suggested a Dutch-American treaty of amity and commerce, during the whole affair he remained in the background and Dumas acted as his proxy. Just as Chaumont gave the French government camouflage in dealing with Jones, Dumas also acted as front man for the French ambassador. But Dumas did not like Vauguyon, whom he referred to disparagingly as "the Great Man."[38]

Already in early September 1779, even before the battle that made Jones a legend, Chaumont had informed Dumas that Jones was ordered to sail to the Texel. In the same letter Chaumont advised Dumas to contact the Amsterdam merchant John de Neufville if the squadron was in any need of provisions.[39] On October 3 Dumas arrived in Den Helder, opposite the Texel, where the sight of the Stars and Stripes flying over a former British man-of-war thrilled him: "My telescope, if not my imagination, gives me red & white lines, & a blue square in the head quarter." The next day

Dumas visited Jones on board the *Serapis,* inviting him to The Hague to meet the French ambassador as well as to Amsterdam to meet merchant John de Neufville.⁴⁰

JOHN DE NEUFVILLE

John de Neufville was trading with New York merchant Gerard G. Beekman in the 1750s; over time he developed an extensive trade network covering most of the North American East Coast. His contacts included Storer, Waldo, Brown, Church, Philips, Lee & Jones, Throgmorton, Cartwright, Powel, Dunkin, and Bumstead in Boston; Hooper, Armstrong, and Dalton in Newbury (Massachusetts); and Daniel & Joseph Parker in Germantown, south of Boston. He also traded with Virginia and Philadelphia.⁴¹

De Neufville was appalled by the severance of these trade connections because of the British-American conflict and saw America as threatened with "absolute slavery." He supported the rebels from the start. All Americans visiting Amsterdam met him. On the other hand, his zeal to profit from the rupture between England and its colonies was relentless. His desire to become the Dutch pivot of all American activities made him quite intrusive, and after a while he acquired the status of a sort of semiofficial American agent, this to the dismay of Dumas and Franklin.⁴²

In the summer of 1778 De Neufville travelled to Germany to sell tobacco. In Frankfurt he met William Lee, a brother of commissioner Arthur Lee, and his secretary Samuel Witham Stockton and told them of his hopes of reestablishing trade with the United States. De Neufville saw the opportunity for a close cooperation between the two republics, "independent of any French influence." Furthermore, the plan of a loan of some 700,000 guilders was discussed. For the Lee brothers, who did not appreciate Franklin and his strong pro-French stance, this was an opening to outmaneuver Franklin and to put aside banker Ferdinand Grand. For De Neufville this was an opportunity to fulfill his ambition to become America's financial commissioner. But to realize the plan, it was essential that the Netherlands show some official willingness to enter into friendship and trade relations with Congress.⁴³

Upon his return to Amsterdam, De Neufville contacted the influential and fiercely anti-British pensionaris Engelbert François van Berckel, who was closely connected with (presiding) burgomaster Egbert de Vrij Temminck. Probably influenced by the April letter sent by the American commissioners to Van Bleiswijk or prompted by Ambassador Vauguyon, hoping that there would be friendly relations between the two republics, Van Berckel and De Neufville likely drafted the treaty of commerce and amity. De Vrij Temminck discussed the matter with the other burgomasters, Hendrik Daniëlsz Hooft, Willem van Heemskerck, and Jan van Tarelinck. De Vrij Temminck was anti-Orangist, while Hooft was a more radical patriot.[44]

What was discussed in the mayor's chamber is still unknown because the minutes for the year 1778 are lost—as we will see, this is no coincidence. Around August 26 De Vrij Temminck ordered Van Berckel, on behalf of the burgomasters, to open negotiations in secret with the Americans. On September 3 Van Berckel wrote Dumas that the burgomasters followed the developments in America with great interest and that they were prepared to take the necessary steps to urge the States General to recognize the United States. Subsequently De Neufville travelled to Aix-la-Chapelle (Aachen) to meet William Lee. They signed the "Plan of Treaty of Commerce to be entered into between their High Mightinesses the States of the Seven United Provinces of Holland and the thirteen United States of North America" on September 4, 1778. Neither the States General nor the Continental Congress were involved in this, and the treaty never came into effect. Shortly thereafter, Dumas sent a copy to Franklin in Paris and to Congress. A direct consequence was the appointment of Henry Laurens (a South Carolina planter and merchant who had served as president of the Continental Congress) as the first plenipotentiary of the Continental Congress to the United Provinces on October 21, 1779.[45]

Shortly after this extraordinary treaty was signed, and to the dismay of De Neufville, the Paris commissioners' earlier financial initiative materialized in a loan when they deposited bonds worth over 200,000 guilders with Fizeaux c.s. at a 5 percent interest with a term of ten years. Earlier De la Lande & Fijnje had vaguely promised 100,000 guilders; now they tried to get a piece of the action by repeating the same figure, on the condition they would be co-issuers. Van Berckel asked the same for his protégé De Neufville. The latter even wrote directly to Franklin offering his services: "If I enjoy'd the pleasure Yr: Ee. ever heard of me, she would know my Zeal for the new Republicq of the Thirteen United States."[46]

However, Franklin, in conjunction with Ferdinand Grand, blocked these initiatives. The Fizeaux c.s. loan was not a success: only a limited number of bonds were sold. Van der Capellen tendered 10,000 guilders to purchase bonds, and he persuaded Hendrick Bicker of the firm Andries Pels for three times that amount. Even though the bonds remained in deposit at Fizeaux c.s. till 1781, only 51,000 guilders were subscribed for. Most of America's friends rejected the initiative.[47]

During the spring and the summer of 1779, the mood among the Dutch supporters of the American cause was rather agitated. Dumas was frustrated because everything was handled from Paris, and he took revenge on George Grand of Fizeaux c.s., who ignored him by suggesting that they did not succeed with a loan because they were British agents, like all Swiss merchants in Holland and France. Dumas urged that De Neufville—as the merchant most active on the Exchange (Beurs)—should be trusted, although he was a bit ambitious.[48] Franklin, on the other hand, was most suspicious of De Neufville. In the spring of 1779 De Neufville visited Franklin and offered an extensive loan if he and his son could become Congress's bankers in Europe instead of Grand. Franklin saw no reason to change his banker, but if De Neufville could produce a list of subscribers amounting to the sum he offered, Franklin was willing to consider the proposal. After three months De Neufville came up with nothing, and Franklin terminated the correspondence with this "vain Promiser."[49]

Thus, on the eve of the arrival of John Paul Jones at the Texel in October 1779, "all Americans and friends of America in the Netherlands were jealous and distrustful of one another. It was very much as at Passy, only worse."[50]

John Paul Jones at the Texel

As Jones's ships anchored at the Texel on October 3, 1779, the only thing the commodore wanted was permission to repair and replenish his battered ships, land and exchange his prisoners, and, in short, do everything that he might have done in an allied port. Under international law it was customary that in a time of war a damaged ship of one of the belligerents was allowed to enter a neutral port for repairs. After the damage was repaired, the ship had to leave immediately. This rule, however, did not apply to Jones's squadron, which flew the American flag. Since the United States was not a recognized country but a bunch of rebellious colonies, they had no belligerent rights.[51] To complicate matters, after Jones's arrival, a Royal Navy squadron blockaded the Texel. So if the Dutch authorities welcomed Jones and allowed him to repair his ships, that would harm relations with Great Britain; on the other hand, if they sent the ships away, that would damage relations with

France. Anyway, Dumas welcomed Jones and took him first to The Hague and later to Amsterdam.

Popularity

There can be no doubt that Jones was popular in the Dutch Republic. After all, the Dutch had a long tradition of *zeehelden* (naval heroes). When he visited the Amsterdam Exchange a large crowd gathered, and he was followed on the streets and huzzaed. In many newspapers Jones's stay in Amsterdam made headlines. When Jones attended the theater he received a public ovation, and artist Simon Fokke made a silhouette of him. There was even a ditty written in his honor, with a strong patriotic note.[52]

But not everybody was so cheerful. According to Ambassador Yorke, when Jones and De Neufville left the Exchange, bystanders reacted with displeasure. They were even approached by a merchant who accused Jones of plunder and looting and De Neufville of protecting thieves and pirates. According to Yorke, it made the men leave in haste.[53]

Assistance

At his arrival at the Texel, Jones's ships and crew were in need of many things, including repairs and fresh provisions. On October 5 Jones received a letter from John Ross, US commercial agent at Nantes, stating that Dumas and De Neufville had received instructions from Chaumont to come to Jones's assistance. The same day Jones wrote De Neufville that he had received instructions to apply to him for "public wants of every kind." Jones requested canvas, provisions, workmen, and all sorts of materials to make his ships fit for sea, especially the *Serapis*. But his first concern was to land the sick and 504 British prisoners.[54]

The Dutch authorities and prisoner of war Captain Pearson were not very helpful in this respect. Jones offered to release the six British officers on parole, but Pearson declined, fearing that his men, if left on board without their officers, would join the Americans. (Jones hoped to exchange Pearson for Captain Gustavus Conyngham, an American privateer who had escaped from a British prison and fled to Holland.) Initially the authorities prohibited the wounded and sick from being cared for on land, and the States General did not authorize the two captive captains to stay ashore, although this could have improved relations with the British and Yorke significantly.[55]

It was a dull autumn and winter for the American sailors at the Texel. No shore leave, no prize money, except one ducat per head, which some of them contemptuously tossed overboard. Word spread that Jones had been gallivanting and having a good time in Amsterdam and The Hague, entertaining Dumas's thirteen-year-old daughter Anna, while his officers and men, many of them nursing terrible wounds, suffered on board his ships. The prisoners schemed to kill Jones within a few days after his return: "Last night I very fortunately discovered a plot that had been formed by the prisoners on board here to play a game at throat cut. They will not find opportunity a second time."[56] Only after an intervention by Yorke writing to the States General was Jones permitted to land the wounded prisoners and to house them in a fort on Texel, guarded by French marines. Jones's efforts to arrange a prisoner exchange failed, however, altogether.[57]

With the British blockading squadron plainly visible, the Americans did not go anywhere. During one of Jones's visits ashore, a score of sailors made a run for it in a stolen boat, and five of them drowned before they could be recaptured. Jones complained to De Neufville about the steady trickle of deserting men, and the next day De Neufville got permission from Van Berckel to apprehend the deserters, but Van Berckel advised De Neufville to be lenient. In December four sailors fled. Jones insisted that if they were caught after his departure, De Neufville should put them on an American ship that would deliver them to the proper authorities.[58]

Jones spent much time at Amsterdam, arranging through De Neufville for supplies and carpenters to fit *Serapis* for sea. A steady stream of barges sailed from Amsterdam to the Texel filled with craftsmen, ship supplies, provisions, and all sort of private requisites. By October 18 De Neufville had found a new mast for *Serapis*. On the other hand, he warned Jones that the "ten thousand weight of bread" sought was not due for a fortnight because such a large consignment was not available at the moment. For the sick and wounded, De Neufville provided sweet oranges, pears, apples, *pippelendooren*, and rice. Furthermore, there was a special request by Dennis Cottineau, captain of the *Pallas*, for a portrait painter; he wanted to be painted on his sickbed. De Neufville also had to deal with local authorities to negotiate all sorts of red tape, excises, and fines Jones did not intend to pay. By November 4 the conditions turned foul, with "thick cloudy weather and hard rain" and the Dutch carpenters refused to work on *Serapis*. It was too rough to send barges from Amsterdam. The supplies of fresh water ran low. Jones even petitioned Ambassador Vauguyon to pay, clothe, and feed

Table 2. Total expenses paid by De Neufville for Jones's ships, 1779

Expenses	Guilders
Serapis	61,502
Pallas	10,466
Vengeance	2,651
Countess of Scarborough	8,080
Alliance	36,696
General costs	3,384
Total	122,779

Source: Peter Force Papers series 80, container 110, no. 53, Factuur book no. 2, f. 200–212; Lincoln, *Calendar of John Paul Jones Manuscripts,* Dumas to Franklin, February 18, 1780; Van Wijk, *De Republiek en Amerika,* 77.

his men: "The bread that has been twice a week sent down from Amsterdam to feed my people has been literally speaking *rotten.*"[59]

Who had to pay for all of this remained unclear: Chaumont, as investor of Jones's squadron, or Congress?[60] Let us take the example of Dumas's travel expenses from The Hague to Den Helder; if De Neufville would not pay for them, Dumas would send the bill to Chaumont in Paris.[61] Franklin assured De Neufville: "America will remember, and one Day be in a Condition to return with Gratitude, the Kindnesses she receives from other Nations in her infant State." On the eve of his departure from the Texel, Jones hoped for "a more sure method in the arrangement of accounts," but nothing came of that.[62] De Neufville had spent a small fortune on Jones's account, although the invoice De Neufville sent to Franklin at Paris included a handsome 5 percent commission for De Neufville (see table 2). The following years, De Neufville asked Franklin several times for his money, but in vain. Over time, the tone of their correspondence soured, and the Jones account was not settled during De Neufville's lifetime. The United States were less grateful than hoped for.

Politics

Strategically, the Dutch Republic was situated between the devil and the deep blue sea. Compliance with the demands of Britain would eventually involve the Dutch Republic in a land war with France. On the other hand, to choose the side of the American rebels and their French allies would lead to the disruption of Dutch trade and navigation and loss of empire. To complicate matters, economically the Dutch were dependent on both France and Britain. So when Jones arrived with his squadron at the Texel, Dutch diplomacy had only one option: to remain neutral. Ambassador Yorke was aware that the Dutch authorities would neither force the American ships to go to sea in the state they were in, nor would they take such drastic action as handing over the former Royal Navy ships *Serapis* and *Scarborough* to the British, but he could try to exert enough pressure to have Jones's squadron forced out into the waiting Royal Navy ships. But if the repairs were prolonged, the British blockading squadron would eventually return to port. The French, on the other hand, did not want to see an open breach between Holland and Britain; Paris wanted the Dutch to remain neutral so they could continue to ship naval stores to France without interference by the Royal Navy.[63]

The first thing Yorke did after he heard of the arrival of Jones was to call on *Stadhouder* Oranje-Nassau, *Raadpensionaris* Pieter van Bleiswijk, and the president of the States General. He got sympathy from the prince but no assurances from anyone. Yorke tried to arrange the arrest of Jones for robbery, but sheriff W. G. Dedel of Amsterdam would not allow it.[64] In the meantime the States General looked into the affair and assembled over and over again. On November 5 Yorke complained about "the slow and dilatory conduct of the States, who have determined nothing yet, and many probably hope that before they can do it, the whole may be gone from Texel."[65]

Ambassador Vauguyon, on the other hand, claimed that the entire squadron was French; surely the States General would not offend His Majesty? A Dutch navy officer came on board to get a look at Jones's alleged French commission. Now that the French government had decided to take responsibility for the squadron (except *Alliance*), Jones moved his flag to this ship. On November 12, finally, the States General ordered a Dutch squadron under command of Captain Nicolaas Riemersma to sail to the Texel to intimidate Jones and to give the impression they were doing something. Vauguyon instructed Jones not to sail until further notice. In the eyes of Oranje-Nassau, Riemersma was too pro-American; he replaced him with Vice Admiral Pieter Hendrick Reynst, who started to pester Jones with all sorts of inconveniences and insults. After the wind had changed, for instance, he anchored his ships in a sheltered outlet so the Americans were hindered by more swell.[66] In response, Vauguyon ordered *Pallas* and *Vengeance* to show French instead of American colors, later to be followed by *Serapis* and *Scarborough*. Shortly, the *Scarborough* and the *Vengeance*, together with two French cutters, left with 191 prisoners. To Jones's resentment, they were exchanged in England for French and not American prisoners. On November 16, finally, the States of Holland adopted a resolution to compel Jones to depart.[67]

It was indeed time to depart, but westerly gales kept *Alliance* wind bound. The convoy carrying French naval stores from the Baltic, which had been waiting for months for Jones to escort them to Brest, was also still at the Texel. As yet, Jones had no orders from Franklin, or Congress, or the French as to what he should do or whether he should sail. Finally, the wind backed around to the east and blew a frozen gale that drove off the British blockading squadron, and Jones prepared for departure.[68] In the meantime, Vice Admiral Reynst sat idle. At last, on December 27, the wind came fair to sortie. At eleven a.m. John Paul Jones raised the American colors, and the *Alliance* departed the crowded Texel road.[69] Once safely at sea, he wrote Dumas: "I am here, my dear Sir, with a good wind at East, under my best American colors. What may be the event of this critical moment, I know not. I am not however without good hopes." Dumas was clearly relieved by the departure of Jones: "While here has caused me much anxiety as trouble."[70]

Aftermath

By New Year's Eve all the ships from Jones's squadron had safely left the Texel. The *Countess of Scarborough* and the *Vengeance* were sold at Dunkirk. Chaumont wanted *Pallas* to be made a dispatch boat. And the *Serapis* was purchased at Lorient by a merchant who sold her to King Louis XVI, who sent her to the Indian Ocean as a privateer (where she was shipwrecked). In total the prize proceeds were around 353,367 livres or $70,673 in gold; Jones's share was $2,658. The final account was settled by Congress in 1848.[71] But there were more unpleasant accounts to be settled.

ALLIANCE AND JONES

A few days after his departure, the *Alliance* intercepted the Dutch merchantman *Berkenbosch,* master Arie de Neif, on its way from Liverpool to Livorno with a cargo of salted herring owned by Van de Perre & Meyners from Middelburg. Van de Perre was a patriot and related to Van Berckel. Jones ordered the master to sail to Boston. This was clearly in breach of the Treaty of Commerce. On its way to Boston, the *Berkenbosch* was intercepted again near St. Eustatius, now by two British frigates, and brought to Barbados and condemned as good prize. This incident dampened the already deteriorating relations between the Americans and their Dutch friends.[72]

The Victims

The main victim of Jones's stay at the Texel was De Neufville. On June 17, 1782, De Neufville retired from his business. In a sense, he had achieved most of his aims: the States General had recognized the United States of America; the road was paved for free trade between the two republics, and a loan was negotiated with Congress and approved by John Adams, the American Minster to the Dutch Republic. He felt that he could leave his business with confidence to his son. In May 1785 De Neufville and his family moved to Boston. He spent the last years of his life in loneliness and poverty, deeply disappointed in Congress, which failed to reimburse his advances, let alone thank him for all his efforts. He died in West Cambridge on December 5, 1796. In 1851 his granddaughter, Anna G. de Neufville-Evans, was awarded by Congress some $16,976 dollars (40,295 guilders).[73]

Another inadvertent victim was Henry Laurens, who was appointed the first plenipotentiary of the Continental Congress to the United Provinces. On September 3, 1780, the packet *Mercury*, bound for the United Provinces from Philadelphia carrying Laurens, was intercepted by HMS *Vestal*. On the approach of the *Vestal*'s boarding party, Laurens threw a weighted bag overboard, but it remained afloat long enough to be salvaged. It contained the Amsterdam Pact of Amity and Commerce, as well as correspondence between American and Dutch officials concerning financial aid to the colonies. Laurens was taken to England and imprisoned in the Tower of London for fourteen months. As a consequence, John Adams replaced Laurens as America's minister in Holland.[74]

The third victim was Amsterdam *pensionaris* Van Berckel. The papers confiscated from Laurens were sent to Yorke in The Hague. This was the right kind of ammunition to curtail the pro-French party, destroy the prestige of Amsterdam, and elevate the *stadhouder* and his pro-British followers as the true guardians of Dutch interests. The States of Holland declared that they had no knowledge of the matters and demanded an explanation from the city of Amsterdam. On November 10, 1780, Yorke asked the States General formally to disavow the secret pact and demanded that De Neufville and Van Berckel be punished. If this was not done immediately, His Majesty would take such measures as "his own dignity and the essential interests of his people demand." The States General distanced itself from the treaty but failed to punish Van Berckel and De Neufville. On December 22, 1780, the States General resolved that only the provincial court of Holland was competent in judging the culprits, the papers taken from Laurens contained nothing that, according to the constitution of the United Provinces, would justify criminal charges against the burgomasters of Amsterdam and their *pensionaris*. Yorke refused to accept this decision. In the meantime, the burgomaster's minutes of 1778 had disappeared![75]

The fourth victim was peace. On December 16, 1780, the British government learned that the States General planned to join the League of Armed Neutrality. For the British cabinet, the Dutch decision was equivalent to entering the war on the side of France and Spain. On December 20 the British government sent Yorke a manifesto severing diplomatic relations with the Dutch Republic and declaring war. As the Dutch government had not yet announced its formal accession to the treaty, the Laurens affair would become the excuse for war. An assault upon the Dutch at this time without this pretext would have been difficult to defend in Parliament, and an attack upon the Dutch Republic openly based upon their accession to the League would have suggested a hostile attitude toward the other armed neutrals. And the United Kingdom was almost completely dependent upon Riga and the northern powers for vital naval stores.[76]

L'INDIEN

During Jones's Dutch intermezzo the matter of the frigate *L'Indien* was still unresolved. Initially the project was started by the Americans; they sold her to the French Crown; finally, the frigate returned to American hands through French intervention in May 1780. Rotterdam-born Alexander Gillon, now an American merchant and ship captain living in South Carolina, succeeded as the captain of the *L'Indien* where Jones had failed.

Early in 1779 Gillon arrived in Europe in the service of South Carolina in search of military supplies. In contrast to most American propagandists and agents traveling through Europe, he was armed with a cargo of indigo and rice estimated to be worth £500,000. In April Franklin arranged an interview for Gillon with Antoine Sartine, the French Minister of the Navy. In December Gillon came up with the idea to buy the frigate on credit for 600,000 livres and to combine her with Jones's ships at the Texel.[77] For reasons not yet fully disclosed, in March 1780 the French crown granted control over *L'Indien* to Anne Paul Emmanuel Sigismond de Montmorency, chevalier de Luxembourg. By that time Gillon had concluded his business for South Carolina, having invested in a cargo of military and naval stores to be sent to Charleston via St. Eustatius. On May 1 the chevalier and Gillon signed a contract, and Gillon received control over the frigate, now renamed *South Carolina*. The frigate had to be used exclusively for privateering and chasing lightly armed merchantmen. Gillon saw no problem with this, for he had no illusion about taking on the Royal Navy with just one frigate, no matter how fast and powerful. This explains, though, why Jones was not considered a suitable commander of *L'Indien*. For Jones a warship was just another military tool, expendable and replaceable in his striving for glory. Finally, the frigate pulled up its anchors at the Texel on August 4, 1780, leaving the Netherlands after all those years. The unlucky life of the *South Carolina* and the tedious settlement of the affair are beyond the scope of this essay.[78]

Conclusion

When Jones arrived at the Texel, already a loose network of sympathizers with the American cause was active. But to quote Morison, "all Americans and friends of America in the Netherlands were jealous and distrustful of one another. It was very much as at Passy, only worse."[79] Jones found himself trapped in the complex relations of Dutch, French, American, and British merchants, bankers, and officials. Looking at the correspondence of Jones, three Dutch friends really stand out: Joan Derck van der Capellen tot den Pol, Guillaume-Frederic Dumas, and John de Neufville.

Van der Capellen, who described himself as "an old and tried friend of America," had heard about Jones's adventures from De Neufville, and he requested from Jones an account of his life and exploits to counteract the "dispictable party spirit" of the pro-British Orangists.[80] Jones sent him a copy of his action report and stated that he had drawn his sword "only in support of the Dignity of Freedom." Van der Capellen intended to publish the information Jones disclosed to him in one of the newspapers or journals, but Jones declined the offer. Some of the information concerned a young lady and was rather private. Later, two pamphlets on Jones's exploits were printed in Holland, but it is not clear if Van der Capellen was involved.[81] There are, however, serious doubts about the sincerity of Van der Capellen's commitment to the American cause. As it came time to do something substantial for the Americans, was he not a poseur who hid behind his pretended poverty, poor health, and the opposition of his enemies? Franklin, Dumas, and Sayre doubted his sincerity. Anyway, for Jones he did very little.[82]

Dumas's function as American agent was twofold. First, he provided the commissioners in Paris with invaluable information on Dutch politics. Furthermore, he acted as intermediary between the Amsterdam burgomasters and the Paris commissioners. Second, when it was not opportune for Ambassador Vauguyon to act too openly and embarrass the Dutch authorities, Dumas gave Vauguyon camouflage, acting as front man for the French. Jones seemed to be very fond of Dumas, but probably that had more to do with thirteen-year-old Anna Dumas.[83]

Jones's best friend in Holland was John de Neufville. Despite the distrust among the American representatives in Europe, De Neufville became Jones's mainstay. Without his contacts, supplies, and credit, Jones would have been stuck at the Texel much longer. Their relationship began on a hopeful note, but uncertainties resulted in mutual irritations: uncertainty about Jones's unwelcome position in the republic, the British prisoners, the sluggish workmen slowly repairing his ships, and the many deserters. De Neufville, on the other hand, had to deal with a most uncertain financial situation. Who would settle Jones's account? John Paul Jones does not mention De Neufville in his memoirs, let alone thank him for his services. Congress proved even more ungrateful. Despite all the nice words and promises from the Americans, De Neufville never got his money back; his granddaughter did not receive any recompense until 1851. He died as a lonely and bitter man in his admired and beloved adopted country.

Jones, of course, became an American hero. Preferring to make his reputation from the quarterdeck, he had never anticipated the swamp of public and private diplomatic relations that would delay him for so long in the Netherlands after his most famous victory.

Notes

I am grateful to Pauline Wittebol who most kindly agreed that I could use her paper "John Paul Jones, Reuring in de Republiek" (research paper, Vrije Universiteit Amsterdam, 2013). In a sense this essay is a joint effort.

1. List of Persons and Firms to Be Consulted in the Netherlands, July–August

1780, Founders Online, https://founders.archives.gov/documents/Adams/01-02-02-0010-0005-0001, cited in Jurriën Cremers, "Lessons Learned: American Diplomats in the Netherlands, 1780–1801" (thesis, Universiteit Leiden, 2012), 30–44.

2. Samuel Eliot Morison, *John Paul Jones: A Sailor's Biography* (Annapolis: U.S. Naval Institute Press, 1999); Evan Thomas, *John Paul Jones: Sailor Hero, Father of the American Navy* (New York: Simon & Schuster, 2003); Joseph Callo, *John Paul Jones: America's First Sea Worrior* (Annapolis: U.S. Naval Institute Press, 2006).

3. The *stadhouder* was the highest executive office in the Dutch Republic; held by a member of the Oranje family, its responsibilities included commander-in-chief of the army and the navy.

4. Agreement between the American commissioners and Jacques Boux, February 12, 1777, Founders Online, accessed November 12, 2022, https://founders.archives.gov/documents/Franklin/01-23-02-0195; Thomas J. Schaeper, *France and America in the Revolutionary Era* (New York: Berghahn Books, 2005).

5. James A. Lewis, *Neptune's Militia: The Frigate* South Carolina *during the American Revolution* (Kent, OH: Kent State University Press, 1999), 7.

6. Ron de Vos, *Nederlandse fregatschepen & Barken* (Franeker: Uitgeverij Van Wijnen, 2012), 58; F. W. van Wijk, *De Republiek en Amerika* (Leiden: Brill, 1921), 64; Stadsarchief Amsterdam, Amsterdam (cited hereafter as SAA), Collectie Hart [883] no. 281, "Staat"; SAA, Archief van het Bevolkingsregister [5422] no. 1408; SAA, Notariële archieven [5075] no. 12435/245, Bestek, May 6, 1777.

7. Lewis, *Neptune's Militia*, 8–9; P. J. van Winter, *Het aandeel van den Amsterdamschen handel aan den opbouw van het Amerikaansche Gemeenebest*, 2 vols. (The Hague: Martinus Nijhoff, 1933), 1:60; Johan E. Elias, *De Vroedschap van Amsterdam, 1578–1795*, 2 vols. (Amsterdam: N. Israel, 1963), 2:1057.

8. Lewis, *Neptune's Militia*, 10.

9. Nationaal Archief, The Hague (hereafter NA), Archief Pieter Van Bleiswijk (PvB) [3.01.25] no. 461, Memorie of Joseph Yorke, December 14, 1774; no. 464, Lijst met verzoeken gedaan uit St. Eustatius om munitie te mogen verschepen, 1775; no. 465, Lijst van en naar St. Eustatius door J. Luyt op verzoek van diverse inwoners verscheepte munitie, 1775; Victor Enthoven, "'That Abominable Nest of Pirates': St. Eustatius and North America, 1680–1780," *Early American Studies*, 10.2 (2012): 239–301; Daniel A. Miller, *Sir Joseph Yorke and Anglo-Dutch Relations, 1774–1780* (The Hague: Mouton, 1970), 49–59.

10. Morison, *Sailor's Biography*, 145, 147, 152; Thomas, *John Paul Jones*, 143.

11. Morison, *Sailor's Biography*, 156; Lewis, *Neptune's Militia*, 11; Thomas, *John Paul Jones*, 143–47.

12. Thomas, *John Paul Jones*, 97–98; Schaeper, *France and America*.

13. J. Franklin Jameson, "St. Eustatius in the American Revolution," *American Historical Review* 8.4 (1903): 683–708, esp. 695; Andrew J. O'Shaughnessy, *The Men Who Lost America: British Leadership, the American Revolution, and the Fate of the Empire* (New Haven, CT: Yale University Press, 2014), 289–319.

14. Morison, *Sailor's Biography*, 214–15; Lewis, *Neptune's Militia*, 11, 21.

15. Morison, *Sailor's Biography*, 223–25, 228–35.

16. Ibid., 240, 241.

17. For a discussion of what Jones had said, see Morison, *Sailor's Biography*, 263–94.

18. Ibid., 302; Thomas, *John Paul Jones*, 177; *John Paul Jones' Memoir of the American Revolution: Presented to King Louis XVI of France*, ed. Gerard W. Gawalt and John R. Sellers (Washington: American Revolution Bicentennial Office, Library of Congress, 1979), 43–44.

19. For an overview of the published pamphlets and newspapers, see Van Wijk, *De Republiek en Amerika*, 37–43; Nathan Perl-Rosenthal, "Corresponding Republics: Letter Writing and Patriot Organizing in the Atlantic Revolutions, circa 1760–1792" (PhD diss., Columbia University, 2011), 164; Van Wijk, *De Republiek en Amerika*.

20. See the webpage of the Regionaal Archief Dordrecht, accessed May 2015, http://www.regionaalarchiefdordrecht.nl.

21. P. J. Blok and P. C. Molhuysen, *Nieuw Nederlandsch biografisch woordenboek*, 10 vols. (Leiden: A. W. Sijthoff, 1911–37) 5; NA, Familiearchief Van Slingelandt-De Vrij Temminck [3.20.52]. The burgomaster was the highest elected officials of Amsterdam.

22. S. R. E. Klein, *Patriots Republikanisme. Politieke cultuur in Nederland, 1766–1787* (Amsterdam: University Press, 1995), 96, 337.

23. H. Wildeboer, "Carel Wouter Visscher, 1734–1802: Portret van een Patriots pensionaris," *Jaarboek Amstelodamum* (1989), 139–74. The *pensionaris* was the highest executive office of the city of Amsterdam, in this case his deputy.

24. *Journals of the Continental Congress*, 27:38, 151, 464, Library of Congress, accessed March 2021, https://memory.loc.gov/ammem/amlaw/lwjclink.html; NA, Collectie J. D. Van der Capellen tot den Poll [1.10.18] no. 19, letters from J. G. Dericks, July 15, 1779–April 7, 1783; Van Wijk, *De Republiek en Amerika*, 61; Van Winter, *Het aandeel*, 1:38.

25. NA, Collectie J. D. van der Capellen no. 25, Erkelens to Van der Capellen, 1777–82; Matthijs Tieleman, "'No Intrigue Is Spared': Anglo-American Intelligence Network in the Eighteenth-Century Dutch Republic," *Itinerario. Journal of Imperial and Global Interaction* 45.1 (2021): 99–123, esp. 113–15.

26. Friedrich Edler, *The Dutch Republic and the American Revolution* (Madison, WI: AMS Press, 1971), 80–81; John R. Alden, *Stephen Sayre: American Revolutionary Adventurer* (Baton Rouge: Louisiana State University Press, 1983), 116; Van Wijk, *De Republiek en Amerika*, 63–64; J. A. Sillem, ed., *Brieven van en aan Joan Derck van der Capellen* (Utrecht: Kemmink & Zoon, 1883), 106, 154–57.

27. Sillem, *Brieven van en aan Joan Derck van der Capellen*, 158: Sayre to Van der Capellen, October 24, 1779; Vereniging van de Binnenvaart, see Fa. Staal en Haalmeijer, accessed May 2015, www.debinnenvaart.nl/binnenvaarttaal/lijsten/lijsten.php?lijst=werven#s; Alden, *Stephen Sayre*, 115, 120, 125, 127, 132, 151–52; Van Winter, *Het aandeel*, 1:32; Nederlands Economisch-Historisch Archief, Amsterdam, Bijzonder Collecties, Jac. De la Lande [256].

28. Alden, *Stephen Sayre*, 115–21; Morison, *Sailor's Biography*, 304; Van Winter, *Het aandeel*, 1:40; NA, Collectie Van der Capellen no. 68, Sayre to Van der Capellen, January 9, 1780–December 27, 1781.

29. Edler, *Dutch Republic*, 19–20; Herman T. Colenbrander, *De Patriottentijd*, 3 vols. (The Hague: Martinus Nijhoff, 1897), 1:120–21.

30. Edler, *Dutch Republic*, 68; Charles H. Lincoln, ed., *A Calendar of John Paul Jones Manuscripts in the Library of Congress* (Washington: GPO, 1903): Jones to De Livoncourt and De Neufville to Jones, December 17, 1779; Jared Sparks, ed., *The Diplomatic Correspondence of the American Revolution*, 12 vols. (Boston: N. Hale and Gray & Bowen, 1829–30), 9; De Livonvourt to Jones, December 17, 1779.

31. Lewis, *Neptune's Militia*, 8–9; Van Winter, *Het aandeel*, 1:60; Elias, *Vroedschap*, 2:1057.

32. Franklin to Dumas, July 25, 1768, Founders Online, accessed November 5, 2022, https://founders.archives.gov/?q=Franklin%20to%20Dumas%2C%20July%2025%2C%201768&s=1111311111&r=1; Tieleman, "No Intrigue Is Spared," 109.

33. Sparks, *Revolutionary Diplomatic Correspondence*, 4:30.

34. NA, Archief C. W. F. Dumas [1.10.26], introduction; US Department of State, Office of the Historian, accessed May 2015, https://history.state.gov/milestones/1776-1783/secret-committee; Van Winter, *Het aandeel*, 1:32; Bob Ruppert, "Charles Dumas Deals with the Dutch," *Journal of the American Revolution* (April 2015), http://allthingsliberty.com.

35. Houghton Library, Harvard, Arthur Lee Papers, Series III, bMS Am 811.2 no. 71, Dumas to Arthur Lee, September 23, 1777; Sparks, *Revolutionary Diplomatic Correspondence*, 2: 545; Edler, *Dutch Republic*, 74–76.

36. A. J. C. M. Gabriëls, *De heren als dienaren en de dienaar als heer: Het stadhouderlijk stelsel in de tweede helft van de achttiende eeuw* (The Hague: Stichting Hollandse Historische Reeks, 1990), 150–51.

37. NA, PvB no. 483, Letters of Benjamin Franklin, Silas Deane, and Arthur Lee, April 19–May 11, 1777.

38. Edler, *Dutch Republic*, 84–90; Morison, *Sailor's Biography*, 304–5; Van Wijk, *De Republiek en Amerika*, 44–45, 58–59.

39. Sparks, *Diplomatic Correspondence of the American Revolution*, 3: Chaumont to Dumas, September 2, 1779; Van Wijk, *De Republiek en Amerika*, 64–65.

40. Dumas to Franklin, October 3, 1779, Founders Online, accessed November 12, 2022, https://founders.archives.gov/documents/Franklin/01-30-02-0365; Dumas to Franklin, October 6, 1779, ibid., https://founders.archives.gov/documents/Franklin/01-30-02-0374.

41. Philip L. White, ed., *The Beekman Mercantile Papers, 1746–1799*, 3 vols. (New York: New York Historical Society, 1956), 2:600–603; Cathy Matson, *Merchants and Empire: Trading in Colonial New York* (Baltimore: Johns Hopkins University Press, 1997), 147; New York Historical Society, BV De Neufville, De Neufville Letterbook and De Neufville Journal; Blok and Molhuysen, *Nieuw Nederlands Biografisch Woordenboek*, 1211; Van Winter, *Het aandeel*, 1:89n.2; Van Wijk, *De Republiek en Amerika*,

47; A. C. de Neufville, *Histoire Généalogique de la Maison de Neufville: D'après d'anciennes chartes et des documents inédits* (Amsterdam, 1869).

42. De Neufville to John Jay, July 28,1779, Papers of John Jay online, accessed November 2022, https://dlc.library.columbia.edu/jay?utf8=%E2%9C%93&search_field =all_text_teim&q=12596; Van Winter, *Het aandeel*, 1:33–34; New York Historical Society, BV De Neufville, De Neufville Letterbook.

43. William Lee and John de Neufville to Continental Congress Secret Committee, October 15, 1778, accessed November 2022, https://www.loc.gov/item/mtjbib000304; Van Winter, *Het aandeel*, 1:34–35; Van Wijk, *De Republiek en Amerika*, 51.

44. Gabriëls, *De heren als dienaren*, 296.

45. SAA, Archief Burgemeesters [5028] no. 538 (folder Amerika), Declaratoir of Pensionaris E. F. van Berckel; Van Winter, *Het aandeel*, 1:34–5; Edler, *Dutch Republic*, 88–91; Van Wijk, *De Republiek en Amerika*, 46, 184–85; Jan Willem Schulte Nordholt, *Voorbeeld in de verte: De invloed van de Amerikaanse revolutie in Nederland* (Baarn: In den toren, 1979), 61–71; Peter Force Papers series 8D, container 31, no. 37, Journal of Dag Register Van den Beginne des tegenwoordige Oorlog tussen de seven Vereenigde Provincien, en England, Library of Congress.

46. De Neufville to Franklin, December 24, 1778, Founders Online, accessed November 12, 2022, https://founders.archives.gov/documents/Franklin/01-28-02-0214.

47. Van Winter, *Het aandeel*, 1:35–36; Edler, *Dutch Republic*, 78–80, 82.

48. Dumas to Franklin, January 25, 1779, Founders Online, accessed November 12, 2022, https://founders.archives.gov/documents/Franklin/01-28-02-0360; Dumas to Franklin, March 23, 1779, ibid., https://founders.archives.gov/documents/Franklin /01-29-02-0157; Dumas to Franklin, May 10, 1779, ibid., https://founders.archives .gov/documents/Franklin/01-29-02-0390; Dumas to Franklin, May 17, 1779, ibid., https://founders.archives.gov/documents/Franklin/01-29-02-0422; Dumas to Franklin, June 24, 1779, ibid., https://founders.archives.gov/documents/Franklin/01-29-02 -0586; Van Winter, *Het aandeel*, 1:36–37; Sparks, *Diplomatic Correspondence*, 9:367, Dumas to Committee of Foreign Affairs, September 20, 1779.

49. Franklin to Jay, October 4, 1779, Founders Online, accessed November 2022, https://founders.archives.gov/documents/Franklin/01-30-02-0369; Van Wijk, *De Republiek en Amerika*, 60–61.

50. Morison, *Sailor's Biography*, 304–5.

51. Ibid., 305; Sparks, *Diplomatic Correspondence*, 9: Admiraliteit Amsterdam to States General, October 8, 1779.

52. Morison, *Sailor's Biography*, 307; Thomas, *John Paul Jones*, 202; Isaac Grand to Franklin, October 11, 1779, Founders Online, accessed November 2022, https:// founders.archives.gov/documents/Franklin/01-30-02-0402; Dumas to Franklin, October 12, 1779, ibid., https://founders.archives.gov/documents/Franklin/01-30-02-0409; Koninklijke Bibliotheek, The Hague, *De Maandelyks Nederlandse Mercurius*, vols. 44–47 (October, second part, 1779), 161; Koninklijke Bibliotheek, Brussels, *Gazette de Leyde* (October 26, 1779), 3; Koninklijke Bibliotheek, The Hague, *Hollandse Historische*

Courant (December 14, 1779); D. F. Scheurleer, "Het liedje van Paul Jones," *Tijdschrift der Vereeniging voor Nederlandse Muziekgeschiedenis* 9 (1914): 77–97.

53. Houghton Library, Harvard, MS Parks no. 72 f. 146, Report of Joseph Yorke, October 8, 1779.

54. NA, Archief C. W. F. Dumas no. 78, a return of prisoners, November 4, 1779.

55. NA, PvB no. 409, Admiraliteit Amsterdam to States General, October 8, 1779; Sparks, *Diplomatic Correspondence*, 9: Admiraliteit Amsterdam to States General, October 8, 1779.

56. Morison, *Sailor's Biography*, 313; Dumas to Franklin, November 5, 1779, Founders Online, accessed November 2022, https://founders.archives.gov/documents/Franklin/01-31-02-0021; Thomas, *John Paul Jones*, 207.

57. NA, PvB no. 409, Letters from Jones and Yorke to Van Bleiswijk, October 15, 1779; Morison, *Sailor's Biography*, 310; Thomas, *John Paul Jones*, 206–7; Sparks, *Diplomatic Correspondence*, 9: Admiraliteit Amsterdam to States General, October 12, 1779.

58. Lincoln, *Calendar of John Paul Jones Manuscripts*: De Neufville to Jones, October 18, 1779; Jones to De Neufville, October 18, 1779; De Neufville to Jones, October 19, 1779; De Neufville to Jones, October 20, 1779; Jones to De Neufville, December 21, 1779; Thomas, *John Paul Jones*, 207.

59. Lincoln, *Calendar of John Paul Jones Manuscripts*, Correspondence between De Neufville and Jones; Thomas, *John Paul Jones*, 207; Morison, *Sailor's Biography*, 314.

60. Peter Force Papers series 8D, container 110, no. 53, Factuur book No. 2, John D' Neufville & Son, Amsterdam, containing list of articles furnished and bills paid for American Squadron under command of John Paul Jones, 1779–1780, Library of Congress.

61. Papers of the Continental Congress, 301686 no. 103 f. 5, Jones to De Neufville, October 5, 1779, National Archives, Washington, DC; Lincoln, *Calendar of John Paul Jones Manuscripts*, Dumas to Jones, October 11, 1779.

62. Franklin to De Neufville, October 15, 1779, Founders Online, accessed November 2022, https://founders.archives.gov/documents/Franklin/01-30-02-0422; Lincoln, *Calendar of John Paul Jones Manuscripts,* Jones to De Neufville, December 17, 1779.

63. Victor Enthoven, "Dutch Maritime Strategy," in *Strategy in the War for American Independence: A Global Approach*, eds. Donald Stoker, K. J. Hagan, and M. T. McMaster (London: Routledge, 2009), 176–201, esp. 178; Thomas, *John Paul Jones*, 207; Morison, *Sailor's Biography*, 309, 314.

64. Morison, *Sailor's Biography*, 309, 314; Van Wijk, *De Republiek en Amerika*, 71.

65. NA, PvB no. 409, Extract resolutie Staten van Holland, October 21, 1779; NA, Archief Gerard Brantsen [1.10.12] no. 9, Extract resolutie Staten-General, October 25, 1779; NA, PvB no. 409, Extract resolutie Staten-General, October 29, 1779; Sparks, *Diplomatic Correspondence*, 9: Yorke to States General, October 29, 1779; MS Sparks no. 72 f. 161, Report Yorke, November 5, 1779, Houghton Library, Harvard.

66. Morison, *Sailor's Biography*, 314–15; Jones, *Memoir of the American Revolution*, 44; Jones to Franklin, November 13, 1779, Founders Online, accessed November 2022,

https://founders.archives.gov/documents/Franklin/01-31-02-0054; Van Wijk, *De Republiek en Amerika*, 72–73.

67. Morison, *Sailor's Biography*, 315; Sparks, *Diplomatic Correspondence*, 9: Vauguyon to Dumas, November 17, 1779; Van Wijk, *De Republiek en Amerika*, 73–75.

68. Morison, *Sailor's Biography*, 316; Thomas, *John Paul Jones*, 208–9.

69. NA, PvB 418, Extrat resolutie Staten-Generaal, December 22, 1779; C. W. van Maanen, "Pauwel Jones," *Maandblad Amstelodamum* (1982), 108–9; Morison, *Sailor's Biography*, 316.

70. Lincoln, *Calendar of John Paul Jones Manuscripts*, Jones to Dumas, January 16, 1779; Papers of the Continental Congress, 1938489, no. 306, Dumas to Congress, December 28, 1779, National Archives, Washington, DC; Thomas, *John Paul Jones*, 209–10.

71. Morison, *Sailor's Biography*, 318–20; Thomas, *John Paul Jones*, 213.

72. Van Wijk, *De Republiek en Amerika*, 83–84.

73. Papers of the Continental Congress, 1938489, no. 156, De Neufville to Congress, June 1, 1782, National Archives, Washington, DC; Blok and Molhuysen, *Nieuw Nederlandsch biografisch woordenboek*, 4:1211–14; MHS, Anna G. de Neufville Evans papers [N-1196], Petition of Mrs. Anna C. De Neufville-Evans to the Senate and House of Representatives, December 1851, 32d Congress, 1st Session, S.R. 51, Joint Resolution, July 15, 1852; A.H.N, "John De Neufville," *The Collector* 6.2 (1892): 16–17; Maria de Neufville, *Verhaal van myn droevig leeven*, ed. Tony Lindijer (Hilversum: Verloren, 1997).

74. Ronald Hurst, *The Golden Rock: An Episode of the American War of Independence* (London: Leo Cooper, 1996), 55; Edler, *Dutch Republic*, 151; Miller, *Sir Joseph Yorke*, 95.

75. Enthoven, "Dutch Maritime Strategy," 185; Edler, *Dutch Republic*, 151–64; Miller, *Sir Joseph Yorke*, 100–101; Blok and Molhuysen, *Nieuw Nederlandsch Biografisch Woordenboek*, 4; NA, PvB nos. 480–82; NA, Stadhoudelijke Secretatie [1.01.50] no. 793, Stukken over de onderhandelingen tussen de regering van Amsterdam en de Amerikaanse agent William Lee, 1780–81.

76. Edler, *Dutch Republic*, 157; Enthoven, "Dutch Maritime Strategy," 185.

77. Gillon to Franklin, December 1, 1779, Founders Online, accessed November 2022, https://founders.archives.gov/documents/Franklin/01-31-02-0114; Morison, *Sailor's Biography*, 317–18.

78. Lewis, *Neptune's Militia*, 15, 18, 20–21, 22–23, 34; Van Wijk, *De Republiek en Amerika*, 84–85; Priscilla H. Roberts and Richard S. Roberts, *Thomas Barclay, 1728–1793: Consul in France, Diplomat in Barbary* (Bethlehem: Lehigh University Press, 2008), 78–80; D. E. Huger Smith, "The Luxembourg Claims," *South Carolina Historical and Genealogical Magazine* 10.2 (1909): 92–115.

79. Morison, *Sailor's Biography*, 305.

80. Richard Price, *Aanmerkingen over den aart der burgerlyke vryheid, over de gronden der regeering, en over de regtveerdigheid [. . .] van den oorlog met Amerika*, translated after the 11th corrected enlarged English impression by J. D. van der Capellen tot den Poll (Leiden: Leendert Herdingh, 1776).

81. Morison, *Sailor's Biography*, 311; Sillem, *Brieven van en aan Joan Derck van der Capellen*, 123–50; Van Wijk, *De Republiek en Amerika*, 80–82; Theophilus Smart, *Echt verslag der voornaamste levensbyzonderheden van John Paul Jones [. . .] behelzende deszelfs menigvuldige krygsbedryven*, trans. from the English (Amsterdam: D. Schuurman, 1780); John Paul Jones, *Paul-Jones, ou Prophéties sur l'Amerique, l'Angleterre, la France, l'Espagne, la Hollande, &c* (Basel: s.n., 1781).

82. Van Wijk, *De Republiek en Amerika*, 85; Sillem, *Brieven van en aan Joan Derck van der Capellen*, 170–71; Sayre to Van der Capellen; Alden, *Stephen Sayre*, 120–21.

83. Ruppert, "Charles Dumas Deals with the Dutch;" Van Wijk, *De Republiek en Amerika*, 54, 58–59, 76.

War at Sea

The Battle of the Chesapeake

The Sons of the American Revolution conference on European friends of the American Revolution that produced these essays was not focused exclusively, or even primarily, on the military support provided by the European friends. But nowhere is the European impact on the American War for Independence more readily seen than in that military assistance. Reinvigorating the study of the Revolution as central to Atlantic history, then, requires some consideration of that aid. And while the essential nature of that military support to American independence—from military supplies to infantry training and artillery expertise to "boots on the ground"—has been broadly recognized and extensively studied and discussed in previous books and conferences, new innovative research methods pursued by scholars in France allow reconsideration here of the essential role of the French navy—and of wind, weather, and sea—in the final, decisive campaign at Yorktown.

Through a detailed analysis of wind, weather, and ship movements, Olivier Chaline and Jean-Marie Kowalski show how difficult and contingent was the essential French victory at the Battle of the Chesapeake, creating the circumstances that permitted Washington and Rochambeau to succeed at Yorktown and, as a result, bring the war to a successful conclusion. Not only is the very detailed look at the fleet's positioning before and during the battle important in its own right for a better understanding of the maritime military history—and an excellent example of both individual agency and contingency—but it also draws on previously underutilized resources (both French and English ships' logs), reminding scholars again of how much research is yet to be done, how many archives yet to be explored, how many stories yet to be discovered, and how many histories yet to be written.

Getting the French fleet to the Chesapeake is explored in Chaline's "Season, Winds, and Sea: The Improbable Route of de Grasse to the Chesapeake," while Kowalski, in "The Battle of the Chesapeake from the Quarterdeck," explores the intense days and moments leading up to and through the battle as ships sought to position themselves to gain some advantage from the wind and sea.

Applied here to the movement of ships, Chaline's and Kowalski's work also suggests how a bottom-up review of military and maritime history, a type of analysis that may be presaged in parallel developments in social and cultural history, can provide important new insights.

Seasons, Winds, and the Sea
The Improbable Route of de Grasse to the Chesapeake

OLIVIER CHALINE

> Other intelligence besides Monsieur Barras' letters makes it highly probable that Monsieur de Grasse will visit this coast in the hurricane season and bring with him troops as well as ships.
> —Sir Henry Clinton to Earl Cornwallis, New York, June 19, 1781

An alliance among nations at war is not only a matter of diplomatic preparations and treaties. Its military implementation is something more complicated, especially when allies have to cope with the sea and great distances. Such practical difficulties, as obvious as they may be, appear to have been largely neglected by the historiography of the French intervention in the American Revolution. It may be that an excessive focus on the consequence of the battle—the victory at Yorktown and American independence—has led to underestimating the complexity of the strategic rendezvous at the Chesapeake Bay at the end of the summer of 1781. But at the time, and for the commanders involved, victory could not be taken for granted. It is thus worth examining again the few months of naval operations between de Grasse's departure from Brest, March 22, 1781, and his mooring near Cape Henry at the entrance of the Chesapeake Bay on August 30.

That crucial period before the Battle of the Capes (September 5) has received less attention than the famous events later in September and October. This is rather unfortunate because answering the question—"Why and how did de Grasse sail to the Chesapeake?"—is very useful if one wishes to understand the inappropriate British response to the French threat in North America. Revisiting this topic involves not only traditional military or naval history but also diplomatic history (French-American and French-Spanish relations) as well as technological history (sailing and longitudes). The diplomatic side and the French navy's specific assignment are well known since Henri Doniol published many volumes concerning France's role in American independence at the end of the nineteenth century, and Jonathan R. Dull gave the best synthesis concerning it. Narrative histories as well as other analyses now use their work.[1] This paper will be concerned with the less-considered aspects of the naval history of the period, and especially the less-investigated French side of the events.

As surprising as it may appear, the French admiral François Joseph Paul de Grasse was neglected for a long time by historians, especially in France. This can be explained by his defeat at the Saintes (April 12, 1782) and his trial at Lorient after his return to France, when he publicly accused some of his subordinates of having abandoned him in front of the enemy. These accusations caused a dangerous turmoil inside the navy, and de Grasse was dismissed from favor by the king and died soon afterwards (1788). As a result, his historic memory fell into suspicion or oblivion until after the First World War. In his own country he remained the vanquished of the Saintes more than the Chesapeake's victor. But American historians like James Brown Scott, who in 1931 published Washington's correspondence with de Grasse, or Charles Lee Lewis, who in 1945 dedicated his book to his French ancestors, recognized the admiral's real importance.[2] Only in 1931 was a rather discrete de Grasse memorial erected in Paris near the Palais de Chaillot, in front of the Eiffel Tower. The construction of the first ship in the French navy named *De Grasse* began in 1938, but the ship itself was launched only in 1946 and waited until 1956 for combatant service before being decommissioned in 1974.[3] Today the first and unique biography in French of the admiral remains the book by Jean-Jacques Antier (1965), which does not really qualify as a research monograph.[4] Nevertheless, de Grasse's relative obscurity in France did not prevent American, French, and British historians from studying the Battle of the Capes.[5]

It was necessary to fill this gap in naval historical research, which is why the PRODROMES project was initiated in 2013 by Sorbonne University and the French Naval Academy. Jean-Marie Kowalski, whose essay follows this one, has played a major role in the project. The PRODROMES project takes its name from the "prodromus," a favorable wind blowing from the north-northeast in antiquity. The program's purpose is to address major historical issues concerning the naval expedition led by Admiral de Grasse in 1781–1782 and then by Admiral Vaudreuil from the defeat of the Saintes to the peace of 1783. Evidencing the interdisciplinarity that scholars increasingly seek, PRODROMES federates multidisciplinary skills provided by the members of this project (Sorbonne University, French Naval Academy, US Naval Academy, Defense Acquisition University, French National Archives) in such various fields as history, geographic information systems (GIS), leadership, navigation techniques, and naval architecture. This innovative approach is meant to bring a major contribution to the understanding of the operational aspects (especially the decision-making processes) of this expedition from 1781 to 1783. Having a better understanding of these very particular operations will undoubtedly provide an opportunity for a better appreciation of their roles in a much broader historiography as well as providing a valuable example of new areas of technical and historic cooperation in other areas of study. The first results have been presented in various conferences and symposia, and they already provide important new information about de Grasse and his fleet.[6]

De Grasse's northward progress from the West Indies to the Capes of Virginia may be studied with precision thanks to his ships' logbooks preserved at the French Archives Nationales in Paris. Such rather neglected sources, especially when compared to British logbooks, allow scholars to develop a clear knowledge of that brief but decisive period.[7] For a long time the only logbook to be published, and for that reason quoted, about de Grasse's fleet was that of Karl Gustav Tornquist, a Swedish officer on French duty.[8] But for almost all of de Grasse's ships of the line, at least one and sometimes many logbooks are available. Each midday, officers had to calculate their position and estimate the distance they had covered. They also noticed all remarkable events as well as winds and weather. These sources allow researchers to track the ships' sailing daily and accurately.

Many books have been written about war at sea during the American Revolution, but these have been written from either a narrative or global perspective and are either histories of the war or works about the main navies.[9] Another approach is worth being used: a history from below—in this case from the perspective of the ships at sea and not from seapower analysis or state history. Looked at on a more micro level, people can prepare fleets, but the sea decides. The role of ships' condition, naval lanes, weather, and the calculation of positions are thus given pride of place in such an analysis.

Today, these type of concrete sailing conditions are better understood.[10] But during the eighteenth century, in France as well as in Britain, understanding these factors was far more difficult. For example, how to calculate longitude at sea was a major and exciting issue in the eighteenth century.[11] Even after Harrison, Le Roy, or Berthoud invented maritime clocks, sea practice remained complicated—and surprising, as shall be seen. These sailing conditions, though, could easily decide the fate of a ship or the result of a battle.

Despite Sir Henry Clinton's note (quoted at the beginning of this chapter), finding twenty-four French vessels moored in the Chesapeake Bay on August 30 was a doubly unpleasant surprise for Earl Cornwallis, the British commander at Yorktown.[12] Nobody on the British side had thought it possible that de Grasse's fleet could sail to the Capes of Virginia or do so with so many ships. Not only did the French enjoy naval superiority, but by mooring at the entrance of the bay, they separated the British troops stationed at Yorktown from the relief expected from the Royal Navy.

Nevertheless, despite its clear strategic advantages, de Grasse's arrival in the Chesapeake was not obvious at all. Not only was his destination unexpected, but his road to the Capes of Virginia was something quite improbable. This feat must not be underestimated. Improbable means unpredictable, unthinkable, and implausible at the same time: neither French nor British ministers foresaw de Grasse's sailing to the Capes of Virginia, but the former allowed de Grasse the flexibility to sail to North America, and he decided to steer to the capes. Even if the British admirals and generals were convinced of the military value of the Chesapeake, they were far from imagining that the full French fleet would end up mooring in it in August 1781. Why could they not expect this decision? Because Admiral Rodney, commander of the Leeward Islands naval station, thought it highly unlikely that de Grasse would steer to North America with his full force, leaving the French West Indies and French trade undefended.

The outcome was the result of a series of surprises, both for the British and the French. For the former, the surprise concerned the number of their enemies as well as their true destination; for the latter, on an operational level, it owed to the strength of the Gulf Stream and its effect on their speed and course.

Usually, the gathering of naval forces before the Battle of the Chesapeake is described as a simple strategic problem, as if fleets' courses were simply pointers on a map. Historians can judge decisions, whether appropriate or not, as well as results, but in doing so they run the risk of overlooking the most important factors for the movements of fleets: seasons, winds, and the sea. To take them fully into account, the historian ought to be a sailor or to turn to sailors for help. This is precisely what has been done in the PRODROMES project and the author's work with the French Naval Academy. Together, and with the help of the US Naval Academy, the movement and management of Admiral de Grasse's fleet are being studied in detail. For that reason, this essay and that of my colleague Jean-Marie Kowalski are connected and aim at presenting readers with two essential aspects of the common research program: de Grasse's sailing to the Chesapeake and the Battle of the Capes of Virginia.

Three liminal questions direct this inquiry:

Why was the Chesapeake such an unforeseen destination?
How was it possible to turn weather difficulties into an advantage?
To what extent was a sea current able to change the course of history?

Why Was the Chesapeake Such an Unforeseen Destination?

The Chesapeake Bay was not included in the instructions given to de Grasse by the French king and ministers in March 1781 just before the admiral sailed from Brest to the French West Indies.[13] The Capes of Virginia only became a possible destination for de Grasse by June or July, not before. Thus, it is no wonder that British intelligence overlooked such an improbable case. It seems that the Chesapeake was suggested by the French minister plenipotentiary to the United States, M. de La Luzerne, and taken up later by General Jean-Baptiste de Vimeur, comte de Rochambeau, commander of the French troops in Newport (Rhode Island), as a possible and later highly convenient meeting point for the French army and fleet.[14]

To begin, it is worth reading the instructions given to de Grasse dated March 3. These instructions are very different from those issued during the previous naval war against Britain, the Seven Years' War. In 1781 French leaders insisted on the necessity of winning the war and ending it as quickly as possible. De Grasse's instructions are also very original because they leave him with an unusual strategic freedom.[15] It was officially taken for granted that Versailles was too far from the West Indies to monitor continually French naval operations in the Caribbean. After some disappointments the king and his ministers (the marquis de Castries, Naval Secretary, and the comte de Vergennes, Secretary for Foreign Affairs) had chosen to turn back to what can be called an "indirect strategy": trying to defeat Britain in America instead of in Britain. But a better coordination with Spain was imperative. For that reason, the main French fleet was sent not to North America but to the Caribbean to join forces with the Spanish against British colonies, especially Jamaica. De Grasse was explicitly told he was to act as an auxiliary[16]—a phrase later used by Rochambeau in responding to the British general Charles O'Hara when Yorktown surrendered. Nevertheless, it was expected in Versailles that de Grasse's fleet could also sail to North America with Spanish consent in order to build naval superiority there and help the Continental Army. The marquis de Castries dined aboard de Grasse's flagship at Brest before it sailed, and he probably mentioned to de Grasse his recent meeting at Lorient with Colonel John Laurens, the emissary Washington sent to report the desperate condition of his Continental Army.[17] The difficult North American military situation would concern de Grasse himself or the commander of the naval force he would dispatch north from his main fleet. Nothing more precise was stipulated except that de Grasse ought to consult on any movement north with M. de Rochambeau and the American general (i.e., Washington). The same instructions had anticipated that de Grasse would be given the choice as to where to steer to on the American coast. He did not have to ask Versailles beforehand, just obtain the agreement of the Spanish governor at Havana. Thus, Versailles left him with a very wide and flexible scope for action. When de Grasse decided to steer with his whole fleet to the Chesapeake, he remained within the instructions he had received.

Why and when did he choose that destination? The decision that triggered everything was the one taken in Versailles not to send a second convoy of men and weapons to double Rochambeau's troops supporting the American insurgents. This decision was known in Newport on May 10. Its consequences were far-reaching: first, French reinforcements had to be ferried not from France directly but from the French West Indies by de Grasse's fleet; and second, this piece of information remained unknown to British intelligence so that the British admirals in America continued to wait for a French convoy sailing directly from Brest to Newport, as it had the previous year.[18] Only a week after leaving Brest for the West Indies, de Grasse wrote to Rochambeau asking him to send a sizable number of American pilots who would be able to guide his fleet to North America as he hoped to reach it by July. His letter did not reach Boston before June 11.[19] De Grasse's preference for some movement north was clear, but at that time nobody, even among the French, was able to imagine which naval operation his vessels could take part in and where exactly on the American coast.

While witnessing the British campaign in the Carolinas, the French diplomat M. de La Luzerne, anxious about the consequences of these operations, told Admiral Barras and General Rochambeau (in Newport) as early as May 1781 that it was necessary to move as soon as possible to the threatened south. At that time Rochambeau, as well as Barras and Washington, had completely different plans. Rochambeau did not inform Washington of the possible arrival of de Grasse, and Washington did not inform Rochambeau that he had heard about it. However, at the end of May, knowing that de Grasse was in the West Indies, all French officers agreed to stay in Newport. On June 4 La Luzerne wrote to de Grasse urging him to sail to the Chesapeake.[20] A week later de Grasse's letter asking for pilots reached Newport.

As summer approached, the decision to steer to the Capes of Virginia took shape. The Spanish, who had taken Pensacola in May with the help of French vessels, did not foresee any other attack in the West Indies in the following months. Above all, the hurricane season was approaching. The Caribbean climate as well as de Grasse's instructions provided him with the opportunity to sail to North America with some of his ships or the whole fleet. After receiving the agreement and financial assistance of the Spanish—thanks to don Francisco Saavedra de Sangronis more than one million livres were borrowed at Havana to pay Rochambeau's troops—de Grasse was allowed to go with his whole strength for two months, leaving the French Indies under Spanish protection and French merchant ships waiting there for a naval convoy back to the continent.[21]

De Grasse chose his North American destination during the second half of July. Arriving at the Cap Français on July 16, he found the pilots Rochambeau had sent him on board the frigate *La Concorde*. On July 28 he sent a letter to Barras telling him he would steer to the Chesapeake. De Grasse did not have authority over Barras, nor did he have authority over the French squadron at Newport. But with twenty-four vessels he was able to establish French superiority in North American waters and consequently gain victory. Informed of the contents of de Grasse's letter to Barras, Rochambeau succeeded in convincing Barras to support de Grasse and sail to the Capes of

Virginia to meet him, as well as persuading Washington to give up his plan for attacking New York and instead go south.[22] As a result, the Chesapeake Bay surprisingly became the final allied meeting point, catching the British off their guard.

How Was It Possible to Turn Weather Difficulties into an Advantage?

If one asks how it was possible to turn the weather difficulties into an advantage, the answer lies with the Caribbean climate. The rainy season (*hivernage* in French) lasts from July to December. September is a particularly dangerous month, unfit for sailing, because of hurricanes. Not only are military and naval operations suspended during the period, but the very presence of fleets in the region exposes them to serious damage. The previous year, in 1780, the Caribbean experienced a hurricane that proved as violent as the famous Katrina in 2005. The Royal Navy lost five vessels with all hands, something like the toll of a naval defeat (and the exact number of vessels the French were to lose at the Battle of the Saintes in 1782). Therefore, as midsummer 1781 waned, it seemed urgent for both the French and British navies to steer away from the West Indies as soon as possible.[23] How such a constraint was turned into an opportunity remains to be ascertained.

That opportunity was a result of de Grasse's and British admiral Samuel Hood's naval courses from the Caribbean to North America. De Grasse left Fort Royal (Martinique, French Îles du Vent) on July 5 and entered the Cap Français (on Saint-Domingue, today's Haiti) on July 16. He stayed there until August 4 before heading to Cuba through the Old Bahamas Channel (between the northeast coast of Cuba and the Great Bahamas Bank). He reached Matanzas Bay on August 17, meeting the frigate *L'Aigrette* which carried the money for soldiers' pay borrowed at Havana. Then he steered north. Only at that time did crews and troops understand that they were sailing to North America.[24]

The August departure date from Cap Français was particularly well chosen since it was the best possible time in the year for sailing to the Chesapeake based on the prevailing winds. The Cap is the northernmost harbor in the French West Indies and the nearest to Havana, the heart of Spanish power in the Caribbean. The prevailing winds during the period push ships toward the northeast and the Bahamas Channel, and from there they blow

SEASONS, WINDS, AND THE SEA / 107

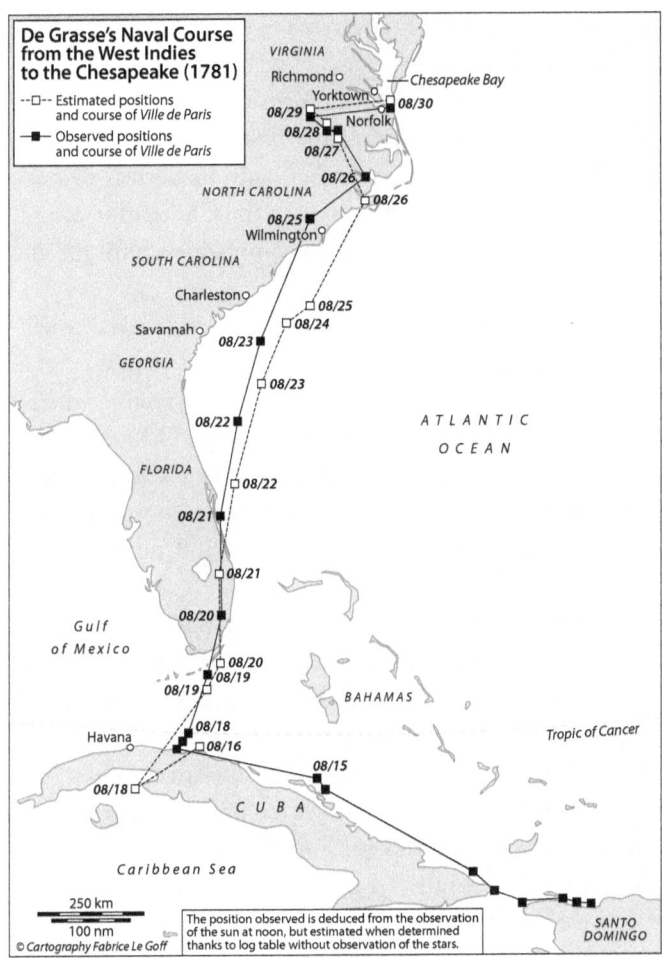

Map 1. De Grasse's naval course from the West Indies to the Chesapeake. Bearings' errors put some of his recorded positions far inland. (Map created by Fabrice Le Goff)

in the same direction, exactly as the Florida and Gulf Stream currents move. August is therefore the best period for sailing to the Chesapeake. September is less favorable because the prevailing wind along eastern Florida blows contrary to the current during that month. Had de Grasse's departure been delayed, his campaign's outcome would probably not have been as successful. The conclusions he and other officers drew from the ill-fated attack on Savannah in 1779,[25] and the advice given by American pilots as well as

Spanish sailors in Havana, all probably suggested to him to take advantage of the natural conditions of August.

These natural elements were known to the British, too, who could reasonably hope that time was running against the French. It was obvious to Sir Henry Clinton in New York that September, with its decreasing heat, would enable the British to operate more easily on the Chesapeake coast.[26] A false sense of security reigned over the British commanders until the end of August.[27]

De Grasse's route remained largely unnoticed by British naval intelligence. Since Pensacola's surrender (May 10), the north and central areas of the Caribbean had been free from British forces, except for Jamaica, where a merchant convoy waiting for the best moment for sailing to Britain needed an escort. De Grasse's course made it possible for him to reach the Chesapeake without crossing Hood's much more easterly route to North America. And his vessels seized the three British ships they saw and thus remained undetected.[28]

Hood's starting point was Antigua, in the British Leeward Islands. Leaving the West Indies from that station made it possible to sail more directly to North America without the western curve the French had to follow. But it is worth emphasizing that neither Admiral George Rodney, who was sick and hesitated over the necessity of steering to America rather than sailing back to Britain, nor Hood, whose first duty in July was to protect the arrival of a convoy from Britain in Jamaica and who was informed of Rodney's decision to return to Portsmouth as late as July 31, had any knowledge of the strength of the French and of their route.[29]

Rodney, commander of the British Leeward Island squadron, had been unable to prevent de Grasse from reaching the French West Indies, and later he proved unable to intercept him.[30] He preferred to remain at St. Eustatius, the Dutch island he had conquered and plundered in February, and he delegated Hood to face de Grasse. British naval intelligence remained at fault during July and August and was unable to deliver precise information that could be used for decision making.[31] The *Nymphe* had noticed that de Grasse left Fort Royal, probably for Le Cap Français, with a convoy of two hundred merchant ships (an overestimate) for France. But a brief reconnaissance of Fort Royal from afar in July only succeeded in misleading British admirals who were convinced that the four ships that remained there—in fact four merchant ships—were to protect a French landing in Saint Lucia.[32]

The lack of accurate intelligence exacerbated Rodney's and Hood's incorrect analyses of de Grasse's decisions.[33] However, it should be noted that their reasoning was sound and logical, although based on wrong premises. Unfortunately for them, de Grasse's reasoning was completely different from their assumptions. First, Rodney was convinced that de Grasse would go back to France escorting the merchant ships that gathered at Fort Royal and sailed to the Cap Français. The example of Guichen's actions in the previous year could justify such a view.[34] Rodney—unlike de Grasse, whose relationship to merchants had never been excellent—did not imagine that his French opponent could delay or cancel a merchant convoy as he in fact did. Rodney underestimated the French threat and understood only on July 31 that de Grasse intended to sail to the Capes of Virginia when he got intelligence that a French frigate was arrived at the Cap Français with thirty pilots from Virginia.[35] But he did not warn the British commanders in New York before August 13, only then sending the frigate *Pegasus* to Graves. That same day he decided to return to Britain.

Second, Joseph Hunt, Hood's secretary, wrote to Charles Middleton that de Grasse would dispatch from his fleet only the twelve best ships, the copper-bottomed ones, and have them sail to North America.[36] Hunt had rightly understood the main weakness of the French fleet, which was its heterogeneity. He believed that de Grasse could not keep ships that were not copper-bottomed for a long time in the West Indies without significant damage. The year 1782 was to prove him right, but not 1781.

In such conditions the British believed that sending Hood with fourteen ships of the line to North America would be enough to maintain British superiority in those waters.[37] Even if de Grasse could sail or dispatch twelve ships, the British would be able to arrive faster from Antigua and reach the Capes of Virginia, the Bay of Delaware, or New York, before their enemies, thus frustrating their plans.

But de Grasse's improbable route and strength caught his enemies by surprise. De Grasse had taken two seemingly unthinkable decisions of importance to take advantage of the rainy season without delay, ignoring trade and merchant convoys, and he kept his whole fleet with him, except for a small number of ships. In doing so, he intended to establish French ascendancy in North America as he was ordered to do. Avoiding being slowed down by an easy-to-spot convoy of troops transports, he chose to embark the three thousand soldiers from Saint-Domingue on board his own warships. All his ships were necessary to ferry them. After those choices were made, which fleet would reach North America first was still uncertain.

To What Extent Was a Sea Current Able to Change the Course of History?

According to the traditional historiography surrounding the forces gathering before the Battle of the Chesapeake, Hood, who left Antigua on the August 10, was the first to reach the Capes of Virginia on the twenty-fifth. He did not then see the French fleet inside the bay and went further north to Delaware Bay in search of it; he finally moored at Sandy Hook, New Jersey (the entrance to New York Harbor) on August 28. He never saw the frigates Admiral Graves had sent from New York to meet him. De Grasse did not reach the Chesapeake before August 30, eluding Hood as well as Graves.

Two distinct sea routes converged on the Capes of Virginia: Hood's from southeast to northwest and de Grasse's from the southwest to northeast. But the two fleets never met in August because the French were five sailing days southwest of Hood. They first saw each other on September 5 when Hood steered back to the capes with Graves, whom he had joined in New York.

Yet that commonly held explanation does not stand up to the scrutiny of the French and British logbooks, a source that historians have not fully exploited. The route the French followed after they took the Bahamas Channel could not be the one historians have imagined for the simple reason that the French got lost. Despite their American pilots, they were unaware of the true strength of the currents: first the Bahamas current and then the Gulf Stream made them drift heavily to the northeast. Except for one of their ships, the *Saint-Esprit,* they did not have a sea clock to assess their longitude correctly.[38]

Reading French logbooks alone is probably not sufficient to perceive their drift. It was only after mapping out positions gathered from the French fleet's logbooks on a GIS that the problem became apparent. Rémy Thibaud (of the French Naval Academy), a specialist in GIS, drew the author's attention to a series of absurd positions that located de Grasse's flagship, the *Ville de Paris,* many miles inland but at the latitude of the Capes of Virginia. The GIS revealed another oddity: the absurd positions were lined up south-north from the eastern coast of Florida and then east of the Carolinas.[39] Obviously that mistake had its own logic.

SEASONS, WINDS, AND THE SEA / III

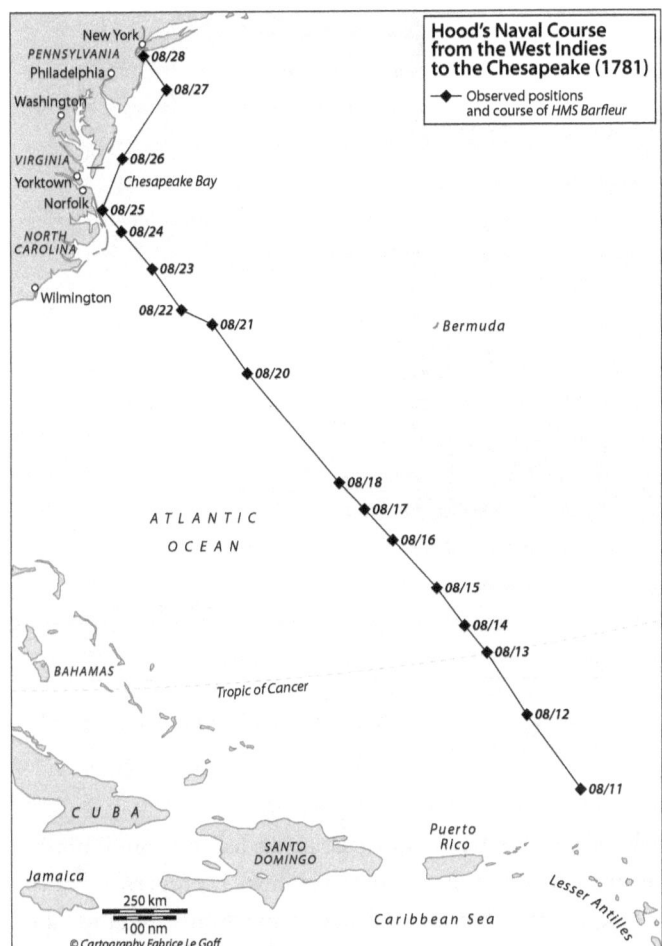

Map 2. Hood's (*HMS Barfleur*) naval course from the West Indies to the Chesapeake. (Map created by Fabrice Le Goff)

Returning to the logbook of the *Ville de Paris* held by Lieutenant de vaisseau Leveneur de Beauvais, it was noticed that when the ship sailed into the Bahamas Channel, the weather became stormy and then very overcast. This prevented French officers from seeing sunrise and sunset clearly for about one week, and consequently they were unable to assess their position correctly.[40] Even Captain de Chabert, commander of the *Saint-Esprit*, had only a very rough idea of their location. Nevertheless, every day from August 20 onward, de Grasse asked him about the longitude he could

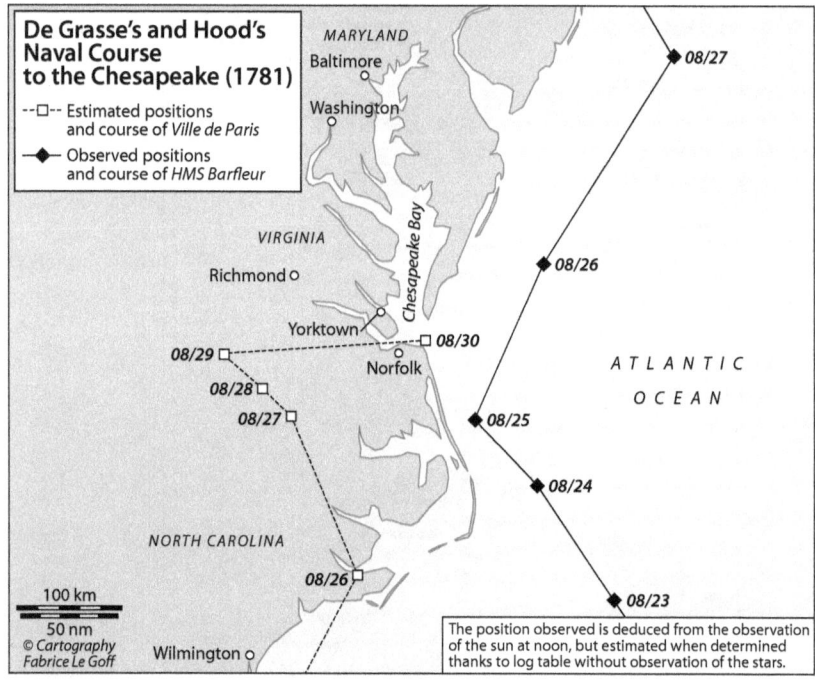

Map 3. Positions of *Ville de Paris*, the French flagship, and *HMS Barfleur*, Admiral Hood's flagship. (Map created by Fabrice Le Goff)

estimate.[41] French officers like Leveneur de Beauvais had obviously noticed the current's strength but were quite unable to evaluate it properly.[42] For five days, August 24–29, the French fleet was lost east-northeast from the capes, convinced they were not very far from the American coast while discovering unintentionally how strong the current was. For that reason, from August 26 onward, de Grasse, now aware of his shift, started tacking westward to find the American coast. He tried to sound and determine the depth of the water and only reached the sea bottom on the morning of the twenty-eighth. Therefore, after moving far more quickly (and eastward) than they anticipated, the French moved very slowly because they had to sound the bottom of the sea frequently.

Today, we know that at the end of August the Bahamas current runs toward the northeast at two knots, thus generating a drift of 1.4 nautical miles to the north and east every hour. But on board de Grasse's vessels, it was impossible to assess the current's strength and the fleet's longitude accurately. De Grasse, carried off toward the northeast, had passed by the Capes of Virginia but was completely unaware of it. (Cape Charles's latitude is N 37°08′, its longitude W 75° 57′; and Cape Henry's latitude N 36°55′ and longitude W 76°1′.)

In that time of uncertainty, in their unforeseen neighborhoods, the logbooks show that the French and British fleets were nearer than they could imagine. At half past three in the afternoon of August 26, Hood's flagship, *HMS Barfleur,* as well as Chabert's *Saint-Esprit* and de Grasse's *Ville de Paris,* saw "strange sails" exactly at the same time. One cannot simply conclude that they saw each other; it may be that they did, but their respective locations seem to make that difficult.[43] Locations remained quite uncertain, all the more so since the French did not know where they were. Each fleet was large enough and spread out enough to be, at least partly, in sight of the other. After this sighting, no more was seen of remote sails on the horizon, thus precluding the possibility of counting them. This would mean that the routes of two fleets perhaps crossed each other northeast of the capes on August 26 and that a completely unforeseen battle could have taken place then. Before night the French sailed in order of battle, and they later lost sight of the strange sails. Neither the French nor the British tried to chase away these mysterious sails. The French watched for the Virginia capes, while the British were convinced that their enemies were further north. It must also be taken into account that these sails were very small on the horizon and that the waters near the American coast were frequented by many ships.

Another crossing is more certain. Rodney had sent a frigate, the *HMS Pegasus,* to escort a convoy from St. Eustatius to New York, which reached Sandy Hook September 3, after Graves and Hood had sailed to the capes.[44] Twice before its arrival at Sandy Hook, on August 28 and, more critically, August 31, the *Pegasus* was chased by French warships. De Grasse was then soon moored near Cape Henry, and the *Pegasus* was soon further north. One may wonder which ships had chased the *Pegasus*. Review of the logbooks shows that it was certainly Barras's squadron, which had left Newport August 26 sailing to the south. The logbooks of the *Pegasus* and the French *Neptune* fit very well together, giving that solution.[45]

The drift to the northeast by de Grasse's French fleet had far-reaching consequences. As de Grasse's fleet was unable to reach the capes before Hood's vessels and remained invisible on the twenty-fifth, the British followed their route toward Delaware and New York, always fearing something like a French attack against New York effected by Barras's fleet. British false intelligence sent by the Admiralty had made Graves steer away from New York from July 21 to August 16 in order to intercept a hypothetical French convoy sailing to Newport.[46] So Graves did not learn before August 28 that de Grasse had sailed and that Hood was arriving as he did a few hours later.[47]

The unforeseen powerful effects of the northeast current on de Grasse's route and the inaccurate British interpretation of the scarce intelligence about French moves and strength made it possible for twenty-four French vessels to moor without any incident inside the Chesapeake Bay on August 30. Clinton, Graves, and Hood in New York were too late in understanding the true destination of the French.

Several concluding points are clear. Gathering such distant ships and troops at a meeting point fixed belatedly inside the Chesapeake was a real challenge that distance, delays, and weather conditions made somewhat improbable in the age of sail. It was the result of a genuine allied cooperation between the French, the Spanish, and the Americans as well as good decisions by de Grasse and the consequence of pure chance. Even the surprise of the Gulf Stream's drift was a lucky strike for de Grasse's fleet, enabling it to avoid its enemies.

On the other hand, it is worth noting that Rodney's and Hood's understanding of the situation was not at all illogical but insufficiently backed by effective, valuable naval intelligence. British strategic planning and operational analysis were too rational and rigid to integrate the vagaries of sailing and the surprises of such a progressive decision-making process as de Grasse's choice of steering to the Chesapeake and, moreover, with almost his whole strength.

De Grasse's naval campaign may rightly be held as an example of bold strategic maneuvering. But it was first a matter of ships at sea, enjoying fine weather or unable to take a bearing because of winds, eluding the enemy, or seeing strange sails.

The very concrete maritime data available from logbooks comprise more than mere details. They cast a new light on de Grasse's North American naval campaign. The example of the Battle of the Capes of Virginia described by Jean-Marie Kowalski in the next essay gives an even more striking illustration of it.

As these sources are consulted more thoroughly, they can enrich historians' understanding of multiple, significant maritime and military engagements, not to mention diplomatic efforts. Undoubtedly future work will continue to enhance and revise the historiography.

Annex

THE MISSION OF THE ADMIRAL DE GRASSE DEFINED BY THE MARQUIS DE CASTRIES, FRENCH SECRETARY OF THE NAVY.

Letter from Castries to Vergennes, Brest, March 16, 1781:

> I thought that I would not depart from the King's intentions by leaving it to Mr. de Grasse to determine the degree of force to be added to the Spanish forces, on the basis of the operations he has agreed with the generals of that nation and the number of ships that the British have retained or that they may assemble. I will recommend, however, that he reserve the right to give the Northern Squadron a superiority in the waters of North America that circumstances may make even more necessary. I thought it was necessary to let Mr. de Grasse free to choose the part where he would prefer to sail. This freedom is all the more necessary because Mr. de La Motte-Piquet has remained ill on the way, that he will not be able to join before the fleet leaves; and that I have given him Mr. de Bougainville as second in command, the only squadron leader who was here and who did not command enough to start with a commander in chief.
> Archives Nationales, Marine B^4 216, f°201 r.–205 v.

Letter from Castries to de Grasse, Brest, March 17, 1781:

> The King's intention is that you would contribute to the projects of the Court of Spain, so as to ensure their execution. However, it will be necessary for you to try to reconcile what concerns Western America [the West Indies and the Caribbean] with the superiority in vessels that the King should acquire on the coasts of North America [. . .].
> In the operations which shall be proposed to you by the Spanish generals, the King's intention is that you should not use your rank or seniority in the same rank to claim command in chief, you

should act as an auxiliary and you should contribute with all your power both through your advice and your actions to the success of their operations.

It may be that the Spanish Court thinks that the most advantageous operation the squadron that will carry out in the North will be to take Hallifax; but in this regard you will follow, you or the general officer who will command it, what is prescribed to you by your instructions to combine an enterprise with Mr. de Rochambeau and the American general. This provision is all the more essential to note that only they can contribute by their land forces to the enterprises to be tempted in the North.

Archives Nationales, Marine B⁴ 216, f°199 r.–200 v.

Notes

1. About the French intervention, see Henri Doniol, *Histoire de la participation de la France à l'établissement des Etats-Unis d'Amérique: Correspondance diplomatique et documents* (Paris: Imprimerie nationale, 1890), 4:627–56; Jonathan R. Dull, *The French Navy and American Independence. A Study of Arms and Diplomacy, 1774–1787* (Princeton, NJ: Princeton University Press, 1975), 238–49, and Dull, *The Diplomatic History of the American Revolution* (New Haven, CT: Yale University Press, 1985). For a recent example of using these earlier works, see Richard Middleton, *The War of American Independence, 1775–1783* (Harlow: Pearson, 2012), 275–92.

2. James Brown Scott, ed., *Correspondence of General Washington and Comte de Grasse* (Senate Document 211, 71st Congress, 2nd Session, 1931), and *De Grasse à Yorktown* (Baltimore: Johns Hopkins University Press, 1931); Charles Lee Lewis, *Admiral de Grasse and American Independence* (Annapolis, MD: Naval Institute Press, 2014; orig. pub. 1945), 117–55.

3. A destroyer followed, built from 1972 to 1977, and it was commissioned from 1977 to 2013. *USS de Grasse* was a destroyer of the Spruance class laid down in 1975, commissioned 1976, and decommissioned 1998.

4. Jean-Jacques Antier, *L'amiral de Grasse, héros de l'Indépendance américaine* (Paris: Plon, 1965).

5. About the Battle of the Capes of Virginia itself and the events that led to it, see (in French) Georges Lacour-Gayet, *La marine militaire de la France sous le règne de Louis XVI: La guerre de l'Indépendance américaine* (Paris: Teissèdre, 2007 [1905]), 389–414; François Caron, *La Victoire volée:La bataille de la Chesapeake—1781* (Paris: Service historique de la Marine, 1981), 376–98; Patrick Villiers, "La stratégie de la marine française de l'arrivée de Sartine à la victoire de la Chesapeake," in *Les Marines de guerre européennes xviie–xviiie siècles,* eds. Martine Acerra, José Merino, and Jean

Meyer (Paris: Presses Universitaires de Paris-Sorbonne, 1998 [1985]), 211–47. In English, French Ensor Chadwick, ed., *The Graves Papers and Other Documents Relating to the Naval Operations of the Yorktown Campaign, July to October 1781* (New York: Naval History Society, 1916); Harold A. Larrabee, *Decision at the Chesapeake* (London: William Kimber, 1965), 123–36; Kenneth Breen, "Graves and Hood at the Chesapeake," *Mariner's Mirror* 66 (1980): 53–65; J. A. Sullivan, "Graves and Hood," *Mariner's Mirror* 69 (1983): 175–94; David Syrett, *The Royal Navy in American Waters, 1775–1783* (Aldershot, England: Scolar Press, 1989), 177–94; Colin Pengelly, *Sir Samuel Hood and the Battle of the Chesapeake* (Gainesville: University Press of Florida, 2009), 96–123.

6. Olivier Chaline, "Une nouvelle approche historique de l'opérationnel naval et de l'histoire du commandement: L'exemple de l'armée navale de l'amiral de Grasse (1781–1783)," in GIS d'histoire maritime, *La maritimisation du monde, de la préhistoire à nos jours* (Paris: Presses universitaires de Paris Sorbonne, 2016), 611–22; Olivier Chaline, "Le comte de Grasse à la tête de son armée navale," in *Les Marines de la guerre d'Indépendance américaine (1763–1783): II—L'opérationnel naval*, eds. Olivier Chaline, Philippe Bonnichon, and Charles-Philippe de Vergennes (Paris: Presses universitaires de Paris Sorbonne, 2018), 295–311; Olivier Chaline and Jean-Marie Kowalski, "French Naval Operations," in *The American Revolution: A World War*, eds. David K. Allison and Larrie D. Ferreiro (Washington, DC: Smithsonian Books, 2018), 52–65.

7. Nineteenth-century French archivists believed these documents far too technical and rather useless and did not keep them. Fortunately, the various logbooks gathered and produced at the trial of the Saintes in 1784 were not destroyed and remained in the French Old Regime Naval Archives.

8. Karl Gustaf Tornquist, *The Naval Campagns of Count de Grasse during the American Revolution, 1781–1783*, trans. A. Johnson (Philadelphia: Swedish Colonial Society, 1942), 53–58. A French officer who signed under the name of M. de Goussencourt also left an account, *The Operations of the French Fleet under the Count de Grasse in 1781–1782, as described in two contemporary journals* (New York: Bradford Club, 1864). Some army officers on board French ships have also left diaries: for example, Lieutenant Calixte Labat de Lapeyrière published in *La glorieuse campagne du comte de Grasse 1781–1782* (Paris: Société en France des Fils de la Révolution américaine, SPM, 2010).

9. Patrick Villiers, *La Marine de Louis XVI, I, de Choiseul à Sartine* (Grenoble: Jean-Pierre Debbane, 1985); Patrick Villiers, *Marine royale, corsaires et trafic dans l'Atlantique, de Louis XIV à Louis XVI*, 2 vols. (Dunkerque: Société dunkerquoise d'Histoire et d'Archéologie, 1999); John B. Hattendorf, *Newport, the French Navy, and American Independence,* (Newport, RI: Redwood Press, 2004); N. A. M. Rodger, *The Command of the Ocean: A Naval History of Britain, 1649–1815* (London: Penguin Allen Lane, 2004); Olivier Chaline, Philippe Bonnichon, Charles-Philippe de Vergennes, eds., *Les Marines de la guerre d'Indépendance américaine (1763–1783): I-L'instrument naval, II-L'opérationnel naval* (Paris: Presses universitaires de Paris Sorbonne, 2013, 2018).

10. For example, Jean Boudriot, *The Seventy-Four Gun Ship: A Practical Treatise on the Art of Naval Architecture*, trans. David H. Roberts, 4 vols. (Annapolis, MD: Naval Institute Press, 1986–1988); Sam Willis, *Fighting at Sea in the Eighteenth Century: The*

Art of Sailing Warfare (Woodbridge, Suffolk: Boydell Press, 2008); Olivier Chaline, *La mer et la France: Quand les Bourbons voulaient dominer les océans* (Paris: Flammarion, 2016).

11. Jean Mascart, *La Vie et les travaux du chevalier Jean-Charles de Borda (1733–1799): Episodes de la vie scientifique au XVIIIe siècle* (Paris: Presses Universitaires de Paris Sorbonne, 2000 [1919]); Jean Bourgoin, "L'hydrographie française au XVIIIe siècle," in *La mer au siècle des Encyclopédistes,* ed. Jean Balcou (Paris-Genève: Champion-Slatkine, 1987), 291–309; *Ferdinand Berthoud (1727–1807): Horloger mécanicien du roi et de la marine* (La Chaux-de-Fond: Musée international d'horlogerie, Paris: Musée de la Marine 1984); Dava Sobel, *Longitude: The True Story of a Lone Genius Who Solved the Greatest Scientific Problem of His Time* (New York: Walker, 1995); Olivier Chapuis, *À la mer comme au ciel: Beautemps-Beaupré & la naissance de l'hydrographie moderne. L'émergence de la précision en navigation et dans la cartographie marine* (Paris: Presses universitaires de Paris Sorbonne, 1999).

12. Kew, National Archives (UK), Public Record Office (now NA PRO), 30/11/68, f°25 r.

13. The text of the instructions is not preserved, but their content is known thanks to two letters of marquis de Castries, the Naval Secretary, the first from March 16 to the French foreign secretary, comte de Vergennes, and the second, from the following day, to de Grasse. Paris Archives nationales (now AN), Marine B4 216, f°201 r.–205 v. and 199 r.–200 v. Other instructions, from March 7, 1781, AN Marine B4 184, f°37 r.–40 r., are not political at all.

14. La Luzerne, who hoped to compensate for American expected discouragement when they heard of the cancellation of the second French convoy to Newport, wrote Barras and Rochambeau to send ships and troops to the Chesapeake to stop British progression in Virginia. Dull, *French Navy,* 240, May 20, 1781. See also AN Marine B4 191, f°159–160. The 4th of June, La Luzerne urged de Grasse to steer to the Chesapeake. AN Marine B4 192 f°284 r. The letters from Rochambeau in June are quoted by Doniol, *Histoire de la participation,* 4:633.

15. AN Marine B4 216, f°201 r.–205 v.

16. AN Marine B4 216, f°199 r.–200 v.

17. Leonard W. Labaree et al., eds., *The Papers of Benjamin Franklin,* 43 vols. to date (New Haven, CT: Yale University Press, 1959–), 34:433–34.

18. The dispatch from May 22 sent by the Admiralty reached New York on July 19; see Chadwick, *The Graves Papers,* 24.

19. AN Marine B4 191 f°90–91.

20. AN Marine B4 192 f°284 r.

21. Saavedra de Sangronis's role in assisting de Grasse is discussed in Nathaniel Philbrick, *In the Hurricane's Eye: The Genius of George Washington and the Victory at Yorktown* (New York: Viking, 2018), 137–44, 150–51.

22. See letters in AN Marine B4 191: de Grasse to de Barras, July 28, 1781, f°91–92; de Rochambeau to de Barras, August 15, 1781, f°120–121; de Barras to de Grasse, August 19, 1781, f°129–130.

23. Names, naval station, and condition of the British ships in North America and in the West Indies from January to October 1781 are given in *The Sandwich Papers, IV, 1781–1782,* G. R. Barnes and J. H. Owen, eds. (London: Publications of the Navy Records Society 1938), vol. 78, 126–27.

24. See, for example, Leveneur de Beauvais's logbook on board de Grasse's flagship, *La Ville de Paris,* AN, Marine B4 258, from f°292 r. (sailing from Fort Royal) to 316 r. (mooring inside the Chesapeake Bay). Note that some of the positions recorded in the logbooks, if precisely mapped as shown, would place the French flagship *Ville de Paris* on land, but while not accurate by modern standards, the logbooks certainly record the general route of the French fleet.

25. Antier, *L'amiral de Grasse,* 136–38; Rémi Monaque, *Suffren, un destin inachevé* (Paris: Tallandier, 2009), 161–64; Alexander A. Lawrence, *Storm over Savannah: The Story of Count d'Estaing and the Siege of the Town in 1779* (Athens: University of Georgia Press, 1951); Dan L. Morrill, *Southern Campaigns of the American Revolution* (Mount Pleasant, SC: Nautical & Aviation Press, 1993), 41–66.

26. NA PRO 30/11/68, f° 43 v. and 44 v., Sir Henry Clinton to Earl Cornwallis, New York, July 11, 1781. About Clinton's relations with Cornwallis, see William B. Willcox, *Portrait of a General: Sir Henry Clinton in the War of Independence* (New York: Alfred A. Knopf, 1964).

27. NA PRO 30/11/68, f°25 r., Sir Henry Clinton to Earl Cornwallis, New York, June 19, 1781: "I am however under no great apprehensions as Sir George Rodney seems to have the same suspicions of Le [sic] Grasse's intention that we have and will of course follow him hither. For I think our situation cannot become very critical unless the enemy by having the command of the sound should possess themselves of Long Island; which can never be the case whilst we are superior at sea."

28. AN Marine B4 258, f°313 r. They were the *Cormoran,* twenty-four guns, the *Queen Charlotte,* eighteen guns, and a yacht. Later, the *Sandwich* was also taken.

29. Graves to Philip Stephens, July 20, 1781, Enclosure C, copy of the intelligence of Sir Geo B. Rodney to RA Graves (to be delivered by the sloop *Swallow*), Sandwich Barbados, August 7, 1781: "As the Enemy has at this time a Fleet of 28 Sail of the Line at Martinique, a part of which is reported to be destined to North America [. . .]. In case of my sending a Squadron to America I shall order it to make the Capes of Virginia, and proceed along the coast to the Capes of Delaware, and from them to Sandy Hook, unless the intelligence it may receive from you should induce it to act otherwise." Chadwick, *The Graves Papers,* 39.

30. Andrew O'Shaughnessy, *The Men Who Lost America: British Command during the Revolutionary War and the Preservation of the Empire* (London: Oneworld Publications, 2013), 308–9.

31. Graves to Sandwich, *London* off Sandy Hook, July 4, 1781: "The intelligence obtained in this country confirming the connexion as well as dependence of Mons. de Barras upon the French admiral at Martinique makes it very much to be apprehended that something material will be attempted as the hurricane season renders it necessary for fleets to quit the West Indies, so that our preservation must turn upon the succours

we may receive." *Sandwich Papers* 4:173. Rodney to Hood, July 9: "Whereas I have received intelligence that a very considerable squadron of the Enemy's Line of Battle Ships are intended to reinforce the French Squadron in America, and it being absolutely necessary that a Squadron of his Majesty's Ships should reinforce his American Squadron," 47; Rodney to Hood, July 24: "Having sent the said convoy [to Jamaica] in safety as above, you are to make the best of your way towards the coast of North America with the Remainder of the Line of Battle Ships," 48. Chadwick, *The Graves Papers*.

32. Hood to Drake, Barfleur off St. Kitts, August 2, 1781, in *Letters of Sir Samuel Hood in 1781-2-3*, ed. David Hannay (London: Publications of the Navy Records Society III, 1895), 27.

33. Kenneth Breen, "Divided Command: The West Indies and North America, 1780–1781," in *The British Navy and the Use of Naval Power in the Eighteenth Century*, eds. Jeremy Black and Philip Woodfine (Leicester: Leicester University Press, 1988), 191–206; "Sir George Rodney and Naval Operations in the Caribbean in the American War of Independence, 1780–1782," *Les Marines française et britannique face aux Etats-Unis (1776–1865)*, VIIes journées franco-britanniques d'histoire de la Marine (Vincennes: Service historique de la Marine, 1999), 45–60.

34. After a campaign in the West Indies against Rodney from March to July 1780, the French admiral Luc-Urbain du Bouëxic, comte de Guichen, returned to Europe. François Jahan and Claude-Youenn Roussel, *Guichen: L'honneur de la marine royale* (Paris: Guénégaud, 2012) 247–63.

35. Chadwick, *The Graves Papers:* Copy of Intelligence referred to in the order to Rear Admiral Samuel Hood, St. Eustatius, August 1, 50. It seems that Rochambeau had sent twenty-five pilots.

36. Joseph Hunt to Charles Middleton, August 29, 1781, in *Letters and Papers of Charles, Lord Barham, Admiral of the Red Squadron, 1758–1813*, ed. John Knox Laughton, 3 vols. (London: Navy Records Society, 1907–1911), 1:122–23: "From the state of the French fleet in the West Indies, I imagine they will not venture to detach more than twelve sail (about the number they had coppered), it is very probable we may find ourselves in superior force."

37. Twenty-two ships of the line were potentially available in the British West Indies: see Kenneth C. Breen, "A Reinforcement Reduced? Rodney's Flawed Appraisal of French Plans, West Indies, 1781," in *New Interpretations in Naval History: Selected Papers from the Ninth Naval History Symposium*, eds. William R. Roberts and Jack Sweetman (Annapolis: Naval Institute Press, 1991), 161–72.

38. See the memorandum written by the captain of the *Saint-Esprit*, the marquis de Chabert: *Mémoire sur l'usage des horloges marines, relativement à la navigation et surtout à la géographie, où l'on détermine la différence en longitude de quelques points des îles Antilles & des côtes de l'Amérique septentrionale, avec le Fort Royal de la Martinique, ou avec le Cap François de Saint-Domingue, par des observations faites pendant la campagne de M. le comte d'Estaing en 1778 & 1779, & celle de M. le comte de Grasse en 1781 & 1782, Extrait des Mémoires de l'Académie royale des Sciences pour l'année 1783* [Memorandum on the use of marine clocks, relative to navigation and especially to

geography, where the difference in longitude of some points of the West Indies and the coasts of North America is determined, with the Royal Fort of Martinica, or with the French Cape of Saint-Domingue, by observations made during the campaign of M. le comte d'Estaing in 1778 & 1779, & that of M. le comte de Grasse in 1781 & 1782. Extract from the Mémoires de l'Académie royale des Sciences for the year 1783] (Paris: Imprimerie royale, 1785), 4–5, 6–8 for the Bahamas Channel, and 17–19 for the route to Virginia.

39. French longitudes are given according to the Paris meridian line, which is 2° 20′ 13.82″ east of the Greenwich one.

40. AN, Marine B4 258, f°311

41. AN Marine B4 184, f°85 r. for example.

42. AN, Marine B4 258, f°311 v.–313 v. One young Swedish naval officer, Carl Gustaf Tornquist, on board the *Vaillant* wrote: "The same night [August 17] we began to tack up into the Bahama channel, between Florida and the Bahamas Islands, whose greatest width is 10 German miles. The constant current which always flows northward with great speed brings it about, that, although the wind may be contrary, one does not consider it remarkable to find oneself in 24 hours from 20 to 30 German miles more northerly than the most careful calculation would indicate [. . .] this current [. . .] then favored us, so that we on August 22nd were already out of the channel, that is to say the current had taken us 90 leagues farther than our calculations indicated, during three and a half days's sailing." *The Naval Campaigns of Count de Grasse*, 54.

43. NA ADM 50/11, f°38 v. and 39 r.; AN Marine B4 184, f°85 v.; Marine B4 258, f°314 r.

44. NA PRO 30/11/68, Cornwallis Papers, 19 June 1781, f°77 r and v.

45. NA Admiralty (ADM now) 52/1905:

HMS Pegasus sailing N:

Friday 31/08:

At daylight [31/08] saw a fleet of 25 sail in the SW standing southwards

At 9 made the signal for the convoy of its being an enemy fleet

At 12 seeing the enemy ships come up the convoy made the signal for gun to the convoy to disperse and act as the thought most probable to avoid their falling into the enemys hands. 7 sails of enemy ships in chace of us.

Lat : 38° 14′, Long unknown.

AN Marine B4 252, f°177 r.–183 v.:

Le Neptune sailing S:

At 6 h 30 morning, seen 7 sails in the East, distance 3 or 4 leagues, At 5 h 30 we have set all sail outside and went to the port tack, the ship was difficult to steer, and it was sometimes impossible to do it.

At 9 the breeze freshened a little from WNW, we sat all sail outside inclusive studding sails high and low and steered to E ¼ NE sailing to the ships we had discovered.

At noon the ships we chased stay at about 3 leagues or 3 and half.

46. NA ADM 1/489, Letters from Commanders-in-Chief North America (Graves Papers), Graves to Philip Stephens, London at Sandy Hook, August 20, 1781, f°409 r. An intercepted letter (kept in the Graves Papers) from an inhabitant from Le Havre to a French officer around Lafayette induced the British to imagine that a second French fleet (six ships of the line and many transports) led by La Motte Piquet would ship reinforcements: Rumour or disinformation? ADM 1/489, f°407 r.

47. Historians have stressed that Graves was not at all informed of what happened in the Caribbean: "Various misfortunes overtook the attempts Rodney actually made to notify his fellow admirals." Larrabee, *Decision at the Chesapeake*, 161; Pengelly, *Sir Samuel Hood*, 103–7. First, the sloop *Swallow* was captured by American privateers and Rodney's dispatches destroyed, NA ADM 1/489 Graves Papers, Graves to Philip Stephens, London at Sandy Hook August 20, 1781, f°409 v. Second, the brick *L'Active*, sent back by Hood to New York, was taken, too. Hood's letter finally reached New York but too late. Third, Rodney, after leaving the Leeward Islands, had sent the frigate *HMS Pegasus* to New York, but she arrived only on August 30. Nevertheless, none of these dispatches would have informed Graves and Clinton that de Grasse had sailed with twenty-four vessels to the Chesapeake.

The Battle of the Chesapeake from the Quarterdeck
From an Admirals' Quarrel to Scholars' Consensus

JEAN-MARIE KOWALSKI

There was such controversy among British admirals and strategists after the Battle of the Chesapeake (September 5, 1781) that this dispute paradoxically resulted in a kind of consensus (a flawed one) among scholars about the key factors of the British defeat. This consensus was reinforced by the fact that the French victory was not actually so decisive: what can be seen as only a minor tactical success eventually turned into a great strategic victory as one month later the British were defeated in Yorktown.

These events can be better understood by starting from a perspective that historians have failed to plumb adequately. I will not discuss strategic decisions here. Instead, I undertake a thorough examination of operational issues based on a comprehensive analysis of a large number of original documents. To understand tactical decisions and command practices on both sides, I approach the Battle of the Chesapeake as observed "from the quarterdeck," presenting points of view from the perspective of both a historian and a sailor. Military operations at sea are, first and foremost, maritime expeditions and exercises in navigation that are highly dependent not just on weather conditions but also on human factors and technical devices.[1] Political approaches to naval history usually do not consider operational aspects. Taking such an approach offers not only a better understanding of the Battle of the Chesapeake but an opportunity for historians to better comprehend a host of other military and naval operations. After a brief examination of the historiographical context and a presentation of the new research pioneered in the chapter, the operational context of the battle is addressed, followed by an analysis of the different weather conditions experienced on both sides. These factors make it possible to suggest that pragmatic versatility was of the essence in the eventual French victory.

The Historiographical Context and the New Methods Used in the Essay

One could conclude that there is almost nothing to add about September 5, 1781, since such authors as Alfred Mahan and Julian Corbett have written famous studies on this battle. Yet despite its qualities, Mahan's *Major Operations of the Navies in the War of Independence* is questionable in at least two ways. First, his analysis is mainly based on British sources. He has obviously not read French archives and relies on second-hand information from Onésime Troude's *Batailles navales de la France*.[2] Second, he focuses his attention on the dispute between British admirals but barely pays any attention to operational issues.

One could expect a different approach to the battle within Corbett's *Fighting Instructions, 1530–1816*, but his tactical views are also fully dependent on the personal dispute between British admirals. Corbett quotes Admiral Samuel Hood's papers, arguing that Hood harshly blamed Admiral Sir Thomas Graves: "When the enemy's van was out, it was greatly extended beyond the centre and rear, and might have been attacked with the whole force of the British fleet. Had the centre gone to the support of the van and the signal for the line been hauled down . . . the van of the enemy must have been cut to pieces and the rear division of the British fleet would have been opposed to . . . the centre division." Then he quotes Admiral George Rodney, who, while not present for the battle, also blamed Graves:

> His mode of fighting I will never follow. He tells me that his line did not extend so far as the enemy's rear. I should have been sorry if it had, and a general battle ensued. It would have given the advantage they wished and brought their whole twenty-four ships of the line against the English nineteen, whereas by watching his opportunity . . . by contracting his own line he might have brought his nineteen against the enemy's fourteen or fifteen, and by a close action have disabled them before they could have received succour from the remainder.

The idea of crushing part of the enemy by concentration had replaced the primitive intention of crowding him into a confusion. Both Mahan's and Corbett's views rely on highly biased and partial sources, thus strengthening the argument for building a bottom-up approach based on unexplored archival evidence that combines French and British sources.[3]

Nevertheless, even if Mahan's views were shaped by the personal dispute between admirals, he had some good tactical intuitions when he read in British logbooks that "at 2:30 PM Graves made the signal for the van ship to lead more to starboard—towards the enemy. As each ship in succession would take her course to follow the leader, the effect of this was to put the British on a line inclined to that of the enemy, the van nearest, and as the signal was renewed . . . this angle became still more marked." He comments on this change by concluding that "this was the original and enduring cause of a lamentable failure by which seven of the rear ships, in an inferior force undertaking to attack, never came into battle at all."[4]

Mahan's basic statement is right, but his conclusions are not for at least three reasons: First, he had not read French sources. Second, he had read only part of the British ones. Last, his remarks about operations do not take into account a systemic view of a naval force at sea.

A naval force at sea is a complex system made up of many subsystems (each individual ship), manned by sailors with differing personal skills and circumstances, particular health conditions, and unique interpersonal issues. This complex system is also highly dependent on weather conditions and on the ability of sailors to understand the influence of these upon operations at sea. This is the very first key to a basic understanding of the importance of sea power in history.

The analysis here is based on data collected during about two years spent in archives in both Britain and France. Its global purpose is to assess the evolution of a naval force's capacities by considering human, material, operational, natural, and technical aspects. This will aid reconsideration of the decision-making processes on both sides during the Battle of the Chesapeake. Clearly, decisions were not made by admirals regardless of the environment, the weather, the condition of the ships, human resources, or interpersonal issues.

Importantly, a vast quantity of operational information is available about this battle. After François Joseph Paul, comte de Grasse, was defeated at the Battle of the Saintes on April 12, 1782, his dispute with his officers over responsibility for that defeat ended in a trial in Lorient.⁵ Most of his officers were prosecuted; the French justice system seized the logbooks and kept them. Usually, these types of documents were not preserved in the archives. On the British side, logbooks have globally been well preserved. These sources raise both historical and methodological questions. First, researchers should recognize that the data are not fully reliable as they were not elaborated with precise technical devices. Some of the information may also have been corrupted on purpose or by mistake. Data were provided on both sides by officers who participated in the same action but had no means to communicate and agree on a common story. Last, but not least, a large amount of the data collected required specific technical means to be evaluated. For example, the database created for this analysis was designed to visualize the various ships within a specific Geographical Information System (GIS), which helped to identify some key features of these events. Further complicating matters, some differences remain between French and British logbooks. The British kept two logbooks regarding each vessel: the captain's logbook and the master's, the latter of which usually gives much more accurate information than the former, especially regarding the timetable. In the French navy it was mandatory for each officer to write his own logbook, which was based both on information shared by all officers as well as personal observations. These were usually written after the action, which sometimes resulted in undigested statements.

Operational Context

My analysis of the operations begins with the arrival of the French ships inside the Chesapeake Bay on August 30, 1781. At 11:30 a.m. Admiral de Grasse made a first important decision as he ordered the ships commanding the van, the center, and the rear to come to anchor at the northernmost point of their respective columns; thus, from August 30 the French fleet was moored on a north-south axis on three lines corresponding to the three squadrons, with the leading ships in the middle of each line. De Grasse's decision placed them in the most favorable position to get under sail with the prevailing winds in this area. After the British were spotted on September 5, this decision made it possible for the leading ship of each squadron to get out of the bay quickly. In the late afternoon on August 30, de Grasse also asked his officers to moor their ships with two anchors ahead so that they could keep steady in their respective positions.[6]

On August 31, operations were seriously delayed: bad weather conditions prevented amphibious operations, and the French infantry troops had to remain aboard the ships.[7]

September 1 was a crucial day as the ships' landing craft got underway to the James River carrying troops to support French and American infantry that would besiege Yorktown. They left at night, at 4 a.m., to take advantage of the favorable tidal currents.[8] This is the main operation the French intended to conduct, along with assisting in the transportation of Washington's and Rochambeau's troops to the vicinity of Yorktown. The operation took several days, and a main consequence for the French naval force was that the sailors who manned those landing craft, a large proportion of their ship's crews (up to 30 percent), were still on shore on September 5, the day the Battle of the Chesapeake was fought. This factor alone demonstrates that the operations conducted that day must be examined within a joint and combined operational context.

At the time the infantry was landed on September 1, the Chesapeake Bay was not considered wholly safe for French operations as the British still had light naval assets further up the bay from the French fleet. The situation was so unclear that French officers became highly suspicious of British naval capabilities. At 7 a.m. the merchant ship *La Reine Charlotte* came within firing range of the *Languedoc*. Mistaking the *La Reine* as British, *Languedoc* fired a gun once, fortunately without any damage. One unidentified ship was seen outside the bay late in the afternoon of September 1, and de Grasse ordered his ships to fly a British flag, but the ship that had been spotted did not enter the bay.[9] Besides amphibious operations, de Grasse had to ensure safe navigation on the bay and secure his fleet from any hostile intent. On this day, the British fleet also got underway from Sandy Hook harbor in New York.

On September 2 the French frigate *L'Aigrette* seized two British ships at the mouth of the bay: a three-masted ship and a brig carrying eighteen guns each, as well as carrying sugar and coffee.[10] In the late afternoon of September 4, the corvette *Loyalist* (seized from the British) sailed up the James River to support landing crafts that were stopped by a British schooner. At that time, French logbooks reported winds on the bay equivalent to 5BF (Beaufort force [17–21 knots]) from the north-northeast.[11]

Different Weather Conditions on Each Side

British and French logbooks provide valuable information about the overall weather situation, as data recorded on the day before the battle, when the two fleets were far apart, can be combined. When viewed together, they offer a large-scale picture of the situation. Eventually, they give information that can be merged when the fleets meet on September 5, as the sources prove to be consistent about conditions on that day.

In the late afternoon of September 4, the British fleet was only about 60 nautical miles north of Cape Charles. But the weather conditions that the two fleets experienced at this time were quite different. The master of the British *Intrepid* wrote that the weather was "squally" with lightning and thunder at 5:30 p.m.; heavy rain at 6; and then a "fresh breeze" (5BF, 17–21 knots) at 8 p.m. The *Intrepid* was then sailing at 6 knots.[12] Between 7 and 8 p.m., according to other British logbooks, the wind was light and variable, blowing mainly from the southwest.[13] The average speed of the ships was about 1 knot. At the same time, inside the bay, the French ships experienced a "pleasant breeze" (4BF, 11–16 knots) from the southwest, turning gradually northwest and north in the evening.[14] On the British side, the

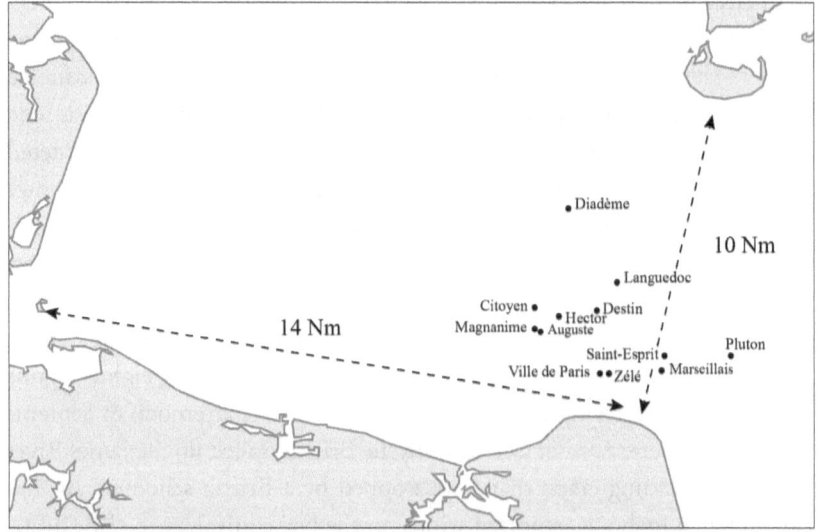

Map 1. Mooring positions of the French fleet (according to French logbooks), September 5, 1781. (Map created by the author)

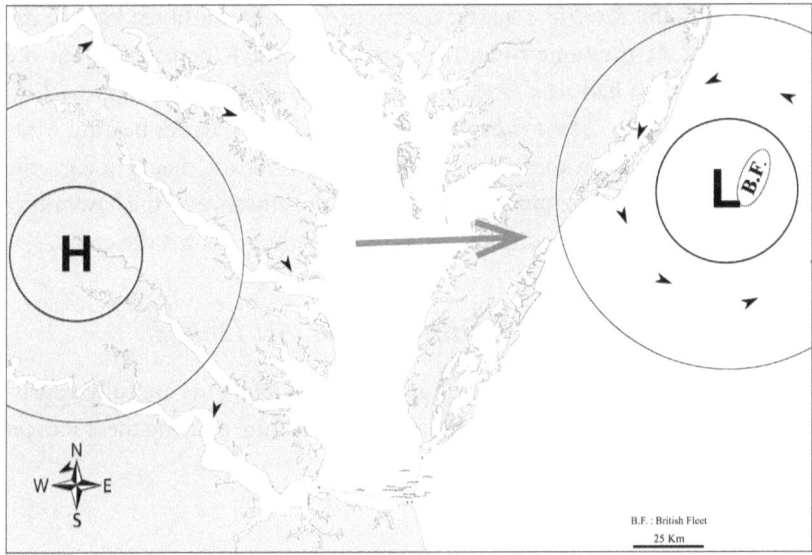

Map 2. Likely weather map of the Chesapeake Bay and eastward, September 4. (Map created by the author)

wind gradually blew from the northwest and north-northwest. At 3 a.m. on September 5, the *London*'s master wrote that the ship was experiencing "fresh gales" (8BF, 34–40 knots) and that the *London* was sailing 6 knots.[15] In such squally conditions, the British ships could not match each others' speed. It is highly probable that such an evolution of the weather conditions was the consequence of a low pressure area located north of the Chesapeake Bay. This phenomenon may sometimes be accompanied by stormy weather conditions, especially along the coast and close to the middle of the depression. That is probably why the British faced different conditions than the French, who experienced rather clear and mild weather.

The French, though, had to face difficulties of their own. During the night the French frigates *La Railleuse* and *l'Aigrette* got under sail for a surveillance mission. The *Railleuse* sailed inside the bay, while the *L'Aigrette* sailed east. Unfortunately, this frigate came aground near Cape Henry and requested other ships' support. She eventually managed to float again without help. During their efforts, the French did not have any naval assets at sea available for patrolling the area and providing the force with intelligence.

On the British side, the fleet was heading southwest, and at 9 a.m. on

September 5 the *Barfleur*'s master mentioned that he could see land to the northwest.[16] At the same time, the *Intrepid*'s master mentioned that the admiral (Graves) had seen land, and they recognized it as the approach to the bay at 10 a.m.[17] The *Princessa*'s master saw Cape Charles bearing west-northwest.[18] Based on these logbook entries, this means that at 9 a.m. the British fleet was approximately in the east of the entrance of the bay, sailing under better weather conditions, after a hard night at sea for the crews.

Victory of Pragmatic Versatility: A Five-Act Drama

At each stage of the battle, French and British documents are fully consistent. This persistent consistency of data is a key feature of using these sources and evidence of their reliability.

1. THE FLEETS COME IN SIGHT

September 5 started with highly unfavorable conditions for the French due to the wind direction and the tidal current, but the situation was balanced by the decisions made by de Grasse on his arrival in the bay. On both sides, lookouts notified their commanders of an enemy fleet. The *Diadème* log notes that the frigate *L'Aigrette* reported a fleet in the east at 9 a.m.[19] Between 9 and 9:30, the lookout of the *Marseillais* notified his commander of a sail in the east.[20]

At the same time (9:30 a.m.), the *London*'s master wrote that the frigate *Solebay* reported a fleet to the southwest.[21] On other ships, the information was reported up until 10 a.m. In other words, it took less than one hour for the fleets on both sides to be fully aware of the presence of the enemy. Unfortunately, sources lack information about the cloudiness when the sightings were reported, which makes it difficult to assess precisely the distance between the enemy ships.

However, both French and British ships gave relevant and consistent information about the weather conditions: the wind was blowing from the north-northeast on the *Alfred* and reported from the northeast on the *Royal Oak*. On the *Auguste*, Truguet le Canet wrote that a strong breeze (6BF, 22–27 knots) blew from the north-northeast. Additionally, the rising tide helped the British sail quickly to the entrance of the bay, while the French ships were moored along a north-south axis and could get out of the bay without tacking.[22]

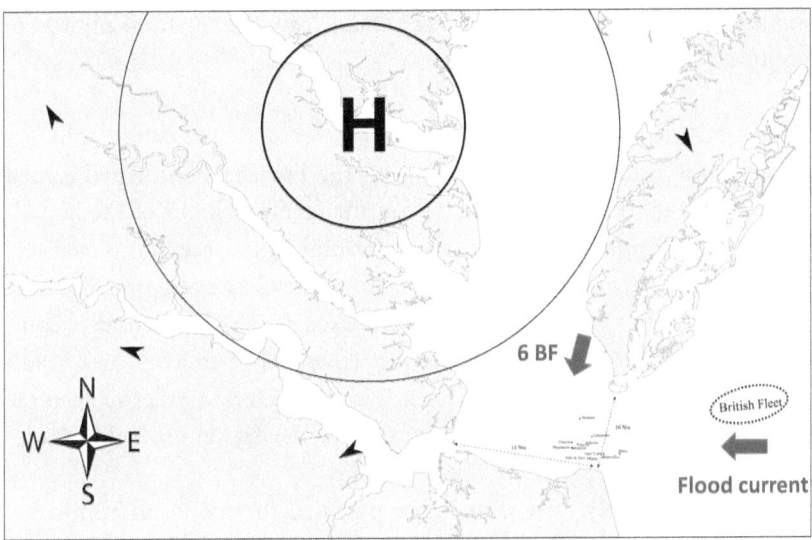

Map 3. Wind speed and direction, c. 9 to 9:30 a.m., September 5, when the fleets come in sight. (Map created by the author)

The arrival of the British forced de Grasse to make emergency decisions. At 10 a.m. he signaled his fleet to prepare for action (*branle-bas*) and called back all craft and boats that were onshore. Most French rowboats were far up the James River, but others were fishing on the bay or were onshore as their crews purchased goods such as meat. At 10:30, without waiting for the arrival of the rowboats, the French admiral gave the order to get under sail and to heave short (*virer à pic*).[23] These operations were carried out between 10:30 and 11:30 a.m. in highly unfavorable conditions. Approximately 1,500 to 2,000 French sailors were away from their ships, and the French ships could not raise their second anchors because this operation could not be completed without a light craft. That is why most logbooks mention that the French left their second anchors with floating buoys in order to collect them after the battle.[24] At 10 a.m. Admiral Graves also gave the order to prepare for action.

The order given by de Grasse on August 30 (that his fleet anchor on a north-south axis) is highly relevant in this situation. On the *Languedoc*, M. de Virgin reported that the northernmost ships got under sail first.[25] Therefore, those commanding the van, the center, and the rear were immediately ready for action: as the wind was blowing from the north-northeast, it was actually much easier to get under sail and leave the bay from a northern position than from the south.

2. THE FLEETS PREPARE FOR ACTION

By noon the situation was improving for the French: the tide had turned about 11:30, and the ebb current helped the French sail out of the bay, although some ships still experienced major difficulties and had to tack several times in order to sail past Cape Henry.[26] De Grasse also organized the communications within the fleet, and he asked the ships that usually commanded the van (*Auguste*) and the rear (*Languedoc*) to keep their traditional positions,[27] with the *Ville de Paris* in the center, in order to keep the basic reliable formation of the fleet in spite of the decision to sail in "order of speed."

At approximately 12:30 p.m., ships prepared for action on both sides. Nevertheless, the situation was highly unbalanced: the British still held a very favorable windward position, with ships sailing in a line at one cable distance. Hood was commanding the van, Graves the center, and Admiral Drake the rear. British logbooks report that the French were getting under sail.[28]

French logbooks confirm this information, but the fleet did not set sail in a conventional way. In this emergency situation, de Grasse revealed a highly creative mind and true improvisation skills based on his former experience. Against all expectations, he ordered his fleet to get underway "*par ordre de vitesse*" (in order of speed).[29] The fastest ships, the ones that were able to set sail as fast as possible, were required to keep the head of the line and form the van. This is actually a highly relevant maneuver, since the best ships joined the van, which was ready to fight first. This decision balanced the lack of speed from the French ships—which de Grasse had noticed during the first encounter with the British on April 29, 1781, on his arrival in the West Indies—and the surprise arrival of Graves's fleet.[30]

The wind direction was steady and the distance between the two fleets short enough to make it possible for each side to identify all the details of the enemy's fleet. From the quarterdeck, the granularity of information was now getting very fine.

On both sides, sailors were doing their best to explain the enemy's maneuvers. The French faced two significant difficulties as they tried to organize the line. First, they were anchored along a north-south axis while they

Table 1. French line of battle v. actual line

Ordinary line	Order of speed
Escadre Bougainville	Avant-garde (Bougainville)
Palmier	*Pluton*
Hector	*Marseillais*
Citoyen	*Bourgogne*
Scipion	*Diadème*
Auguste	*Réfléchi*
Magnanime	*Auguste*
Caton	*Saint-Espirit*
Hercule	*Caton*
Pluton	
Escadre de Grasse	Corps de bataille (de Grasse)
Northumberland	*César*
Zélé	*Destin*
Saint-Espirit	*Ville de Paris*
Triton	*Victoire?*
César	*Sceptre*
Ville de Paris	*Northumberland*
Victoire	*Palmier?*
Solitaire	*Solitaire*
Expériment	*Citoyen*
Souverain	
Escadre Monteil	Arrière-garde (Monteil)
Bourgogne	*Scipion*
Glorieux	*Magnanime*
Vaillant	*Hercule*
Destin	*Languedoc*
Languedoc	*Zélé*
Sceptre	*Hector*
Réfléchi	*Souverain*
Marseillais	
Diadème	
	Did not participate
	Glorieux
	Vaillant
	Triton
	Expériment

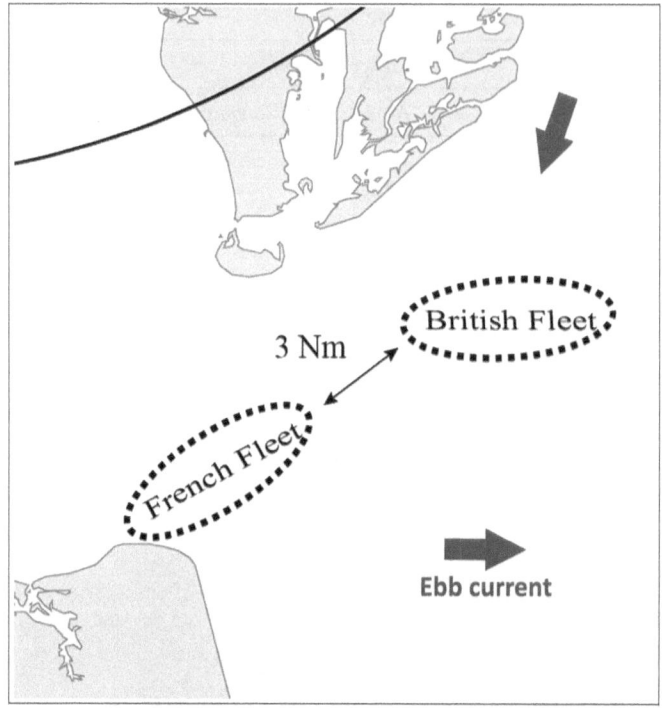

Map 4. The fleets prepare for action, c. 12:30 p.m. (Map created by the author)

had to sail eastward to meet the British. This gave the leading ships the opportunity to sail first, but it made it harder to organize the line. Second, de Grasse first asked his van ships to sail close to the wind, which made the line even more oblique.

As the British were still approaching very fast and heading southwest, some French officers came to think that they intended to cut the line. That is what Préville assumed aboard the *Zélé*, the last ships of the line, which experienced difficulties getting out of the bay, just like the *Hector* and the *Souverain*.[31] These ships were anchored close to Cape Henry, leeward. (There is no evidence of an intention to cut the line in the British logbooks.) At 1:12 p.m. Graves twice ordered the van ships to steer more to the right, but at 2 p.m. he ordered his fleet to veer because they were running up on the middle grounds shoals situated in the northern part of the mouth of the bay.[32] At that time, the estimated distance between the two fleets was similar: 3 miles according to the British, 1 league according to the French.[33]

3. Two P.M.: Sudden Turnaround—The British Veer and Swap Their Van and Rear

At 2 o'clock Graves ordered his fleet to veer and sail on the other tack. The reason, given by the master and the captain of the *Barfleur*, was that they feared running aground on the middle grounds shoals.[34] This is actually why British ships had to veer and swap their van and rear, leaving ageing British ships in front of a French van consisting of some of the best ships of their fleet that were not fully manned but organized in order of speed.

At the same time, the French could barely form a line, with their rear leeward and much space between their ships. But the captains prepared their crews for the fight. De Grasse had first reorganized the line; the captains now reorganized their crews. For example, M. d'Ethy, the captain of the *Citoyen*, wrote at 1:45 p.m.: "I had given the order to place the sailors at their station and to replace those who were missing in the batteries. I also ordered to employ the troops and the officers to replace the sailors, but there were not enough soldiers. I had to disarm the guns on the fore deck [. . .]. There were 200 men and 5 officers absent, dead or ill on that day." With some 25 percent of his crew missing, the captain of the *Citoyen* had to make difficult decisions.[35] The actions of these two captains indicate their priorities: fighting rather than easily maneuvering their ships.

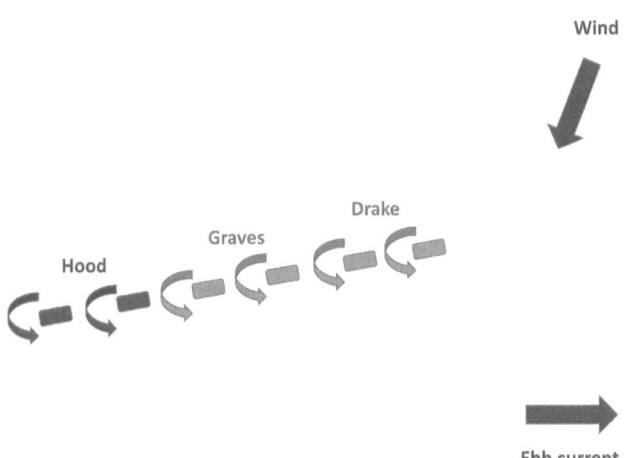

Figure 1. The British veer and swap their rear and van about 2 p.m. (Figure created by the author)

4. Admirals Organize Their Lines and Engage

The wind quickly shifted from northeast to east-northeast. At the beginning, both admirals made good decisions, but de Grasse eventually decided not to engage the fight immediately, as he anticipated a further shift of the wind. This smart tactical decision gave his van a valuable advantage over the British, who had an advantage early in the morning but now had to face unfavorable conditions.

Between 3 and 3:15 p.m., according to both French and British sources, one hour after the British had veered, the weather conditions changed. According to the *Alfred*'s master, the winds turned "right" from northeast (45°) to northeast by east (56°15). In other words, the wind direction shifted to the right and made the ships in both fleets turn slightly to the same direction. On the *Zélé*, M. de Lescure reported that at 3:15 p.m. the winds started shifting to the right and that for this reason de Grasse decided to make the head of the fleet bear away to keep the line ahead. This order is also confirmed by an officer aboard the *Marseillais* (the second ship of the line).[36] If he had not made this decision, the French ships would not have sailed in a line but on parallel lines, which would have made it very difficult to engage the enemy.

Aboard the *Auguste*, M. de Biré reported that the head of the enemy's fleet was also bearing away toward the head of the French van. This statement is confirmed by the *Intrepid*'s master at 3:08 p.m., when he noticed that the *Princessa*, the *Ajax*, and the *Alcide* were given the order to bear away. The *Princessa*'s master noticed at 3:02 p.m. that Graves asked the *Alcide* and the *Princessa* to turn right. The *Barfleur*'s master reported at 3:09 p.m. that Graves asked the *Princessa*, the *Alcide*, and the *Intrepid* to head more on the right. This signal was repeated at 3:17 p.m.[37] This decision kept the British fleet close to the French.

At 3:30 both fleets came once more one point (11°15) to the right. Graves asked the fleet to come on the right. That is confirmed by M. Truguet's logbook on the *Auguste*. There is a slight ambiguity here: all logbooks do not give the same version of the order given by Graves, which was given either to the van or to the entire fleet. On the *Citoyen*, M. d'Ethy wrote that the wind turned east-northeast with a moderate breeze (4 BF, 11–16 knots).[38] In other words, the wind had turned two points (approximately 22°) within about half an hour from northeast to east-northeast, while the fleets had also turned right two points. Both admirals made approximately the same decision at the same time.

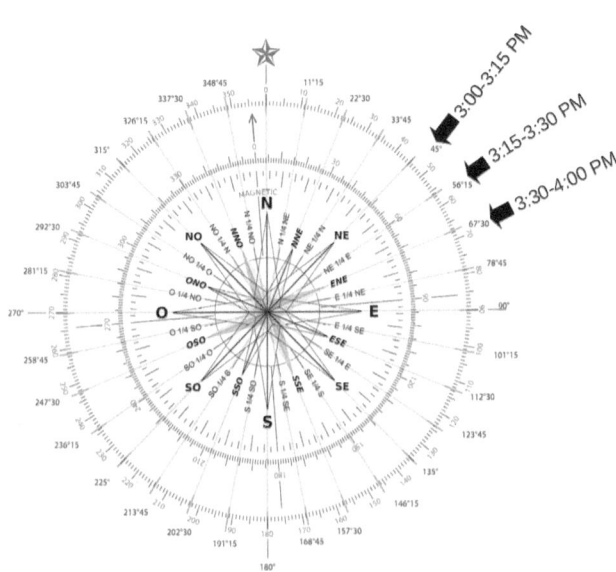

Figure 2. Wind shift during the battle between 3 and 4 p.m. (Figure created by the author)

At 3:45 de Grasse made a crucial decision that gave him the victory. Aboard the *Citoyen*, M. d'Ethy reported that as the wind was still veering forward (turning right), de Grasse decided to make the head of his fleet bear away two points (c. 22°) to restore the line. He also reported that the enemy was arriving obliquely. At the same hour, M. de Villeneuve aboard the *Marseillais*, the second ship of the line, reported the same order. Right after that, the French sailed close to the wind. During this maneuver, some French ships were shot on the left of their stern. These facts were confirmed by M. de Virgin aboard the *Languedoc*. On the British side, the logs report that Graves ordered his entire fleet to bear away and come down to the enemy. The *Alfred*'s master reported that at 4 p.m. the wind had turned east-northeast, just as M. d'Ethy, captain of the *Citoyen*, had reported at 3:30.[39] (Even if the indications they give are not exactly the same, they remain consistent: officers did not always have time to write during the action, and the situation was not exactly the same across the whole area.) At this very critical time of the fight, the two admirals made different decisions: while de Grasse anticipated further changes of the wind, Graves decided to engage the fight. Even if de Grasse took a risk by exposing the sterns of his ships to enemy fire, this turned out to be an excellent decision that enhanced his tactical advantage.

5. "Engage Close" vs. "Bear Away": Tactics Theory vs. Pragmatic Versatility

While de Grasse made wise decisions, there was an apparent misunderstanding among British admirals, but the consequences of this misunderstanding were somehow overestimated afterward, as the situation was already highly critical for the British.

At 4 p.m., some fifteen minutes after the beginning of the battle, Graves raised a signal that was specified neither in the master's nor the captain's logbook aboard the *Barfleur*. The logs just describe it: "The admiral made a signal with a blue and yellow chequered flag with a white pennant over it." Hood obviously did not understand this order. At 4:11 the *London*'s captain reported: "Hauled down the signal for the line ahead that it might not interfere with the signal to engage close."[40] Many historians have focused their attention on this misunderstanding, but it had no real consequence over the outcome of the battle.

Since the wind had veered forward, these two orders—line ahead and engage close—were in fact discordant, but the order to engage close made the British ships even more oblique, angling their bows in front of the French. The damages reported aboard British ships confirm this hypothesis: the ships of the van were badly damaged in their foreparts. On the *Pluton*, M. d'Albert de Rions reported that their opponent, the first ship of the British line (the *Shrewsbury*), had its sails and masts badly damaged, especially its foremast. At 4:55 p.m. the *Intrepid*'s master also reported that the *Shrewsbury*'s main mast and foremast were badly damaged.[41]

The fight engaged first in the van and then spread back to the other ships of the line. At 4:30 M. de Montecler reported that the *Diadème* started fighting at a very close distance with the commanding ship of the enemy's van (*Princessa*). The distance was so short that the *Princessa*'s bowsprit almost tangled with the *Diadème*'s stays. This confirms that the British ships were bearing down on their opponents. At 4:28, aboard the *Princessa*, the captain and the master both reported they started firing at the fourth ship of the French line (the *Diadème*).⁴² All indications can be verified this way by cross-referencing French and British logbooks. (It might be noted that Montecler described the *Princessa* as an eighty-gun ship, although she carried only seventy.)

During the battle de Grasse carried on giving smart tactical orders to follow the evolution of the wind. At 5 p.m. M. de Truguet aboard the *Auguste* and M. de Villeneuve aboard the *Marseillais*, and later, at 5:15 p.m., M. de Montecler aboard the *Diadème*, reported that de Grasse ordered the heading ship to come down two points because she was too far from the rest of the fleet, which was confirmed by the logbooks of *Intrepid*'s master and captain, which recorded the time as 5 p.m.⁴³ This order seems highly relevant: Montecler, aboard the *Diadème*, reported that at 4:30 the wind carried on veering forward. At the same time, Graves maintained the order for close action. While Graves stubbornly persisted in ordering close action, de Grasse smartly took the changing weather conditions into account: his decisions make it clear that his priority was to keep the line before fighting rather than engaging the fight first, as giving the van the order to bear away means increasing the distance between the first ships and the enemy.

Only the French van really participated in the fight, in part because of the changing weather conditions: at 5:15 M. d'Ethy, captain of the *Citoyen*, wrote that the wind has turned east and east-northeast (just as Montecler reported at 4:30 p.m.) and that it had become weak and variable. He reported that the rear of the French fleet was now oblique because of this change of the wind direction and speed.⁴⁴

At 6:10 p.m. the *Princessa*'s logs report that the firing ceased as the French van bore away.

Sporadic rounds were shot from far in the middle. At 6:23 Graves ordered the signal for close action to be hauled down and the signal for a line ahead to be raised. At 6:15 he had sent two frigates—the *Solebay* to the rear and the *Fortune* to the van—to let them know that he wanted his line to stay parallel to the French during the night. This message was received by the *Alfred* at 10 p.m. The battle ended at 7 p.m. (The discrepancy between these recorded times is probably due to inaccuracies of the officers' reports but also can be ascribed to the time needed for the orders to be executed in the entire fleet.) At 7 p.m. a moderate breeze (4BF, 11–16 knots) was said to blow from the east-northeast according to an officer aboard the *Destin*.⁴⁵

Losses

The battle lasted approximately three hours. This was not as long as the Battle of the Saintes, which lasted an entire day, but the fight had to come to an end before nightfall. Drawing a comparison of the losses is difficult because French and British figures are not based on identical data. On the British side, 90 men were killed and 246 injured, while 200 were either killed or injured among the French. Most French losses occurred aboard the *Diadème*, which had experienced friendly fire from the *Auguste* commanded by Bougainville: 22 were killed and 68 injured, while 13 were killed and 65 injured on the *Auguste*.[46]

The *Marseillais* fired 755 rounds, but the *Pluton* only fired 387 as it was too far from the line to be effective.

Five British ships were badly damaged. One of them, the *Terrible*, had to be scuttled. The most significant British losses occurred on the *Shrewsbury* (14 killed and 52 injured) and on the *Intrepid* (21 killed and 35 injured).

Conclusion

This was not actually a crushing victory for the French. The losses were moderate on both sides, but the strategic consequences were overwhelming as Graves, bloodied, did not again seek to enter the bay.

This "forensic analysis" of the different stages of the battle shows that the French turned a highly probable disaster into a victory that owes much to de Grasse's clever decisions. These decisions were based on his learning from his first operations in the West Indies on top of a very good knowledge of his officers' skills and an outstanding analysis of the weather conditions that helped him make the right tactical decisions. The situation was so desperate on September 5 that his very versatile and pragmatic approach to command let his officers give the best of themselves. Nevertheless, the global frame of the decisions he made was based on a clear view of his priorities: set to sail before fighting, man as many batteries as possible with the crew he had, and always anticipate the change of weather.

Consideration might now be given to Mahan's and Corbett's views. Mahan is partially correct when he says Graves did not make the right decisions, but he could have reported de Grasse's clever analysis of the situation. He should also have considered human factors and weather conditions—key factors of the operational potential of a fleet at sea. Corbett is also correct when he reports the dispute between British admirals, but this dispute had no influence over the outcome of the battle, as this battle was mainly fought in the van.

In other words, the primary sources studied in preparation of this essay—very particular sources that have not previously been adequately considered—offer an outstanding opportunity for historians who are eager to understand operational issues. They also provide fascinating means of understanding decision-making processes, styles of command, and leadership. Similar analyses of other conflicts using similar sources will undoubtedly provide a wide field for refining our understanding of maritime history.

Such an approach requires the historian to engage several disciplines to succeed in putting in proper relation the elements of a huge and complex archive. The ship of the line encountered in the operational archives, such as these logbooks, is no longer a sheer technical object; it becomes a singular item with its own characteristics in the hands of a crew whose expertise and skills must be understood and assessed over an extended period. Given the course of battles, the fortunes of the sea, and the hazards of maintenance issues, these naval assets and their potential evolved. In turn, they influenced the potential of the naval forces in which they were integrated. The history of operations, the history of science and techniques, thus meet the arts of navigation, strategy, tactics, command practices, sociology, meteorology, oceanography, geographic information, and even naval architecture to provide the framework for a new approach to the history of naval operations.

Notes

1. See Olivier Chaline, "Season, Winds, and the Sea: The Improbable Route of de Grasse to the Chesapeake," in this work.

2. Alfred Thayer Mahan, *The Major Operations of the Navies in the War of American Independence* (London: Sampson Low, Marston and Co., 1913), 179–83; Onésime Troude, *Batailles navales de la France*, vol. 2 (Paris: Chalamel Aîné, 1867), 107. For example, the information Mahan gives about a French frigate that supposedly saw the British fleet at 8 a.m. on the day of the battle (*Major Operations*, 179) is wrong but was first mentioned by Onésime Troude.

3. Julian S. Corbett, *Fighting Instructions, 1530–1816* (Navy Records Society, 1905), 212.

4. Mahan, *Major Operations*, 180.

5. Michel Hervé, *Une bataille jugée: La Défaite des Saintes (12 avril 1782) et le conseil de guerre de Lorient* (PhD diss., Lucien Bély [dir.], University of Paris-Sorbonne, 2007).

6. Archives Nationales Marine B4 258 f°316 r, 316 v.

7. The signal for landing troops was cancelled at 4 p.m. as the weather conditions became thundery. Ibid.

8. Archives Nationales Marine B4 258 f°371 r.

9. Archives Nationales Marine B4 258 f°317 r.–v.

10. Archives Nationales Marine B4 258 f°317 v.

11. Archives Nationales Marine B4 258 f°318 r. The Beaufort scale was developed in 1805, but it is used here to assist modern researchers (and seamen) in understanding the conditions.

12. Royal Navy Ships' Logbooks, National Archives (Kew, UK), ADM 52/1807.

13. See the *Princessa*'s master's logbook (National Archives, ADM 52/2468) or the *Alfred*'s master's logbook (ADM 52/2125).

14. Archives Nationales Marine B4 241 f°113 r.

15. National Archives, ADM 52/2383.

16. National Archives, ADM 52/2160.

17. National Archives, ADM 52/1807.

18. National Archives, ADM 52/2468.

19. Archives Nationales Marine B4 244 f°12 r.

20. Archives Nationales Marine B4 251 f°21 r.

21. National Archives, ADM 52/2383.

22. National Archives, ADM 52/2125 and 52/2428; Archives Nationales Marine B4 234 f°160 v.

23. Archives Nationales Marine B4 258 f°318 r.

24. M. de Préville, captain of the *Zélé*, says that 90 officers and 1,500 crew were missing in the fleet: Archives Nationales, Marine B4 259, f°30 v.; 100 officers and men on the *Diadème,* according to Courcelles, Marine B4 244, f°195 r.; 2,000 crew in the fleet according to Biré, Marine B4 236, f°156 r.

25. Archives Nationales Marine B4 247, f°121 r. On this ship, 220 crew members were missing (over 25 percent of a normal crew contingent).

26. See M. d'Ethy, captain of the *Citoyen,* Archives Nationales Marine B4 238 f°427 v.

27. See the *Magnanime*'s pilot's logbook, Archives Nationales Marine B4 249, f°313 v.; M. du Canet aboard the *Marseillais,* Marine B4 251 f°135 r.; and M. de Lescure aboard the *Zélé,* Marine B4 259 f°135 r.

28. See the *London*'s logbooks, National Archives, ADM 51/552 and 52/2383; and the *Princessa*'s logbooks, ADM 51/732 and 52/2468.

29. See M. de Castellane, captain of the *Marseillais,* Archives Nationales Marine B4 251 f°21 r.; or M. de Préville, captain of the *Zélé,* Marine B4 259, f°30 v.

30. Archives Nationales Marine B4 258 f°2598 v.

31. Archives Nationales Marine B4 259 f°30 v.

32. National Archives, ADM 51/552 and 52/2383.

33. National Archives, ADM 51/552 and 52/2383; and Archives Nationales Marine B4 259, f°30 v.

34. National Archives, ADM 51/552, 52/2383, 51/88, and 52/2160.

35. Archives Nationales Marine B4 238 f°428 r.

36. National Archives, ADM 52/2125; Archives Nationales Marine B4 259 f°108 r.; Marine B4 251 f°324 v.

37. Archives Nationales Marine B4 236 f°156 r.; National Archives, ADM 52/1807, 52/2468, and 52/2160.

38. National Archives, ADM 51/552 and 52/2383; Archives Nationales Marine B4 235 f°161 r.; Marine B4 238 f°428 r.

39. Archives Nationales Marine B4 238 f°428 r.; B4 251 f°406 r.; B4 247 f°121 v.; National Archives, ADM 51/552, 52/2383, and 52/2125; Archives Nationales Marine B4 238 f°427 v.

40. National Archives, ADM 51/88, 52/2160, and 51/552.

41. Archives Nationales Marine B4 253 f°222 r.; National Archives, ADM 52/1807.

42. Archives Nationales Marine B4 244 f°12 v.; National Archives, ADM 51/732 and 52/2468.

43. Archives Nationales Marine B4 235 f°161 r.; Marine B4 251 f°406 r.; Marine B4 244 f°12 v.; National Archives, ADM 51/475 and 52/1807.

44. Archives Nationales Marine B4 238 f°428 v.

45. National Archives, ADM 51/732, 52/2468, 51/552, 52/2383, 51/34, and 52/2125; Archives Nationales Marine B4 241 f°113 r.

46. *Magazine of American History* 7 (1881): 370; Archives Nationales Marine B4 244 f°195 v.; Marine B4 236 f°156 r.

Conflicted Allies

Spain and Portugal in the American War for Independence

One of the classic problems of the American Revolution is whether it is a democratic revolution (Gordon Wood) or almost a baronial war, more about who rules at home than home rule (to paraphrase the question posed by Carl Becker). However one resolves that debate, it is important to remember that some of America's European "friends" were pointedly not supporting a colonial war of independence from monarchy. In the extreme, as Kathleen DuVal and Gonzalo M. Quintero Saravia explain through the lens of Bernardo de Gálvez, Spain viewed the war as a war for empire. Gálvez became the image of a successful Spanish courtier benefitting from the eighteenth-century Bourbon reforms that sought to improve the efficiency and effectiveness of a Spanish Empire that, by the middle of the century, was suffering a deep malaise that weakened the country in spite of its remarkably profitable American colonies. As a strong and loyal supporter of King Carlos III, Gálvez was no revolutionary and in many respects made a curious European friend of the American Revolution. Yet his considerable success on the southern frontier played an important role in draining British resources and influencing the negotiations that finally ended the war. DuVal and Quintero Saravia also effectively dismiss the allegations brought against Gálvez after his death that he somehow hoped to make himself the monarch of an American empire independent of Spain. "Bernardo de Gálvez: Friend of the American Revolution, Friend of Empire" reminds us of the varied interests held by the European friends of the American Revolution, each of which was pursuing its own advantage through the complex game of Atlantic military conflicts, trade, and politics.

Timothy Walker explores the very understudied issue of how Portugal—a firm British ally since 1386—sought to maintain and develop its own trade with the United States during the American Revolution without seeming to support openly the American War for Independence, reflecting Portuguese policies that continued after the Revolution through the antebellum period. Playing a careful diplomatic game, Portugal experienced considerable success in its effort. While never directly a "friend" of the American Revolution in the military conflict—that would have been unthinkable—Portugal carefully cultivated good relations throughout the period and beyond: for example, it ordered its navy to protect American ships from Barbary pirates for a period of time. Even if indirectly, Portugal's support of American trade benefitted the fledgling nation. Unfortunately, as Walker explains in "Old Partners and Intersecting Interests: Trade and Diplomacy between Portugal and the United States during the Era of George Washington (c. 1781–1805)," diplomatic niceties (perhaps not fully appreciated by the new nation still struggling to understand the intricacies of European court practice) complicated Portuguese and American relations for years as the United States sought to send a lower-ranked representative to Queen Maria I's court, much to the chagrin of the latter.

Bernardo de Gálvez
Friend of the American Revolution, Friend of Empire

KATHLEEN DUVAL AND GONZALO M. QUINTERO SARAVIA

On April 12, 1781, thirty-four-year-old Bernardo de Gálvez rode his horse through his camp on the north shore of Pensacola Bay. In the same month that General Charles Cornwallis was making his fateful decision to turn his army toward Virginia and ultimately Yorktown, General Gálvez was trying to take a colony away from the British. The Spanish general's impressive force of four thousand white and Black soldiers, sailors, and laborers was building fortifications, ferrying supplies from its ships, and setting up tents. Less than two miles away sat Gálvez's next targets: the town of Pensacola and the fortifications that guarded it. Pensacola was the capital of British West Florida. If Gálvez could seize it, West Florida would fall. The victory would not only be sweet for Spain—it would particularly trouble Britain because West Florida was one of its few mainland colonies that was not rebelling. Losing it would raise the stakes for the imperiled British Empire.[1]

Gálvez had traveled by ship, canoe, horse, and on foot over four thousand miles from his home in the mountains of Andalucía in southern Spain. Now just a short distance remained between him and the glory of seizing West Florida from the British. If he succeeded, he would secure his reputation as a brilliant military commander and his future as a favorite of the Spanish crown.

Ambitious Spanish men had served the empire for nearly three centuries since Christopher Columbus returned to Spain with glowing reports of the Caribbean Islands in 1493. Thus, Gálvez followed an old tradition, but he was a new kind of colonial officer. As a man of the Enlightenment, he believed that the future of the Spanish Empire lay in rational, even scientific, governance. When the British won the Seven Years' War and took Spanish

East Florida and French West Florida, they bragged that Spain's day had passed and that the world was England's now. When he was sent to govern Spanish Louisiana, Gálvez hoped that it would serve as the base for Spanish expansion into British colonies in North America and the Caribbean and an opportunity to disprove the British boasts. The American Revolution would give him his chance.

Like the marquis de Lafayette, Bernardo de Gálvez would aid the American Revolutionary War in battle and in European courts. Yet, Gálvez was no friend of revolution or republicanism. He was a man of and for the Spanish Empire. Gálvez and his king joined the war effort in order to support France and to take advantage of Britain's troubles. As the rebellious colonies fought a war against empire, Gálvez led a Spanish war *for* empire, a war to win as much of the British Empire as possible, although never imagining that the war would threaten European colonialism itself; Spanish officials hoped to use it to make the Gulf of Mexico a Spanish lake again. To them, as to most of the world, the American War for Independence was just one of the multiple theaters of operations of a much larger, almost global war between empires, a war that would be fought in Europe (Minorca, Gibraltar, and even a joint Spanish and French attempt to invade the British Isles), the Caribbean, India, and the North American continent. At the time, the rebellion of the thirteen colonies against Britain was, borrowing from David Lean's movie *Lawrence of Arabia,* just "a sideshow of a sideshow."[2]

Training

Bernardo de Gálvez was born on July 23, 1746, to María Josefa de Madrid and Matías de Gálvez y Gallardo in the province of Málaga, in the village of Macharaviaya. After the Catholic Reconquista of the Iberian Peninsula, Catholic farmers eventually took over Muslim farmers' fields and homes and built churches where mosques had stood, just as the Muslims had built their mosques where the Visigothic chapels had been, and as Visigoths had built over Roman temples. One of the king's military commendations for Bernardo de Gálvez traced his ancestry back to men "who notably served the state and my honorable predecessors with arms, and letters, and were present at the conquests of the cities and towns of Teruel, Madrid, Cordoba, Granada, Santaella, and others."[3] The Gálvez family claimed to be a noble line (*hijosdalgo,* literally "sons of someone"). Their claim of nobility may have been much enriched by a subsequent genealogist generously rewarded by his wealthy patrons. In any case, when he was born Bernardo's family was poor. The 1753 census noted that "all residents of this place [Macharaviaya] are day laborers, since none can live on [the produce of] their farms."[4]

But Bernardo de Gálvez's father and uncles took advantage of new opportunities in the eighteenth-century Spanish Empire. The Bourbon King Carlos III concentrated secular power and encouraged talented young men to join his administration. The connections that served Bernardo best were his uncle's. José de Gálvez embarked on what would be a brilliant career as the lawyer of the French Embassy in Madrid, and through this connection he was able to secure for his nephew an appointment as a lieutenant in the French army.[5]

Connections were essential, but in this era of relative meritocracy, Bernardo needed to earn his own reputation through service to the crown. The empire was still based on force, used against both imperial rivals and Indigenous American subjects. In 1762 Bernardo joined the Royal Cantabre Regiment, a French military unit raised in the Basque country of France. The regiment joined the Spanish forces in the invasion of Portugal during the Seven Years' War, but Bernardo saw little or no action.[6]

After the war, Bernardo entered the Spanish army with the rank he had in the French force. He was posted as captain to the Regimiento de la Corona de Nueva España, the crown's regiment in New Spain. He crossed the Atlantic and in April 1769 presented himself in Chihuahua, where the headquarters of the forces led by Lope de Cuellar were concentrating to launch a campaign against the Apaches in the province of Nueva Vizcaya.[7]

Captain Gálvez fought the Apaches, was wounded, and distinguished himself in combat, but he also used his time to study them and Spain's Native allies in the conflict. He wrote *Notes and Considerations on the War with the Apache Indians in the Provinces of New Spain,* in which he not only narrated his experiences in combat but also considered the real causes of the war, its features, and the best means to end it. Instead of succumbing to the warmongering climate prevailing in the region, he insisted that his countrymen "be impartial and acknowledge that if the Indians are not our friends it is because they don't owe us any benefits and if they take revenge on us it is only in just compensation for the affronts we have caused them . . . , the lies we have told them and the tyrannies they had suffered from us."[8] He clearly stated that the two main causes of Native war against the Spaniards were either "hate or necessity": hate born from the vengeance for the affronts the Spanish had caused and a necessity triggered by "the extreme need in which they live, while they don't sow, nor farm the land, nor they breed cattle for their survival, they meet their needs by stealing from the Spaniards."[9] On their reputation for cruelty he wrote that "the Spaniards accuse the Indians of being cruel, but I don't know what their opinion about us is, but most probably it wouldn't be better and much better founded."[10]

Bernardo also studied Native combat tactics, and he suggested that for the Spanish to prevail, they must adopt new ways to confront the Apaches. He insisted that mobility was essential; he wanted his troops, the *Presidiales*, to be rid of most of their heavy equipment. About the soldiers, he did not follow the widespread notion that "the Americans lacked the spirit and generosity required to be good soldiers." For him the "Americans" (i.e., the Spanish-American soldiers) were no less brave than their enemies. The familiarity they showed to their officers was because they were "raised in freedom and accustomed to independence," so they had to be led differently from regular Spanish army troops. "The *Presidiales* soldiers know the reason why they must obey, but they also want to be commanded by reason." He concluded, "What does the King care if the one who serves him well is white or black if the color of the face is refuted by the nobility of his heart? . . . I have seen a flag more victorious and better protected in the black hands of a mulatto than in other which could be whiter but feebler."[11] Bernardo's experience with the Apaches and in the northern frontier of New Spain's viceroyalty would prove extremely useful during his later career, in both Louisiana and Mexico.

The years in Apache country turned Gálvez from an inexperienced officer to a battle commander, from a provincial Iberian to a worldly veteran who had coordinated with Indigenous allies and fought the formidable Apaches. He returned to the Iberian Peninsula in 1772 and was assigned to the Sevilla Infantry Regiment, from which he almost immediately took leave, probably to join his uncles José and Miguel, who at the time were thriving in their respective careers in Madrid. José had served as the visitor general of New Spain, and in 1776 the king appointed him minister of the Indies, the official charged with overseeing the entire empire in the Americas. In 1774 his uncle Miguel became the *ministro togado* (legal counselor) to the Supreme Council of War. One of the council's most important members was the powerful Irish-born general Alejandro O'Reilly. In January 1774 O'Reilly founded the

Royal Military Academy in Ávila, designed not only to provide the best possible military education to young officers but also to give them the necessary knowledge when they became governors of strongholds in Europe or America. The first class of students was selected from among "the officers whose rapid instruction interests the Army most because of their talent, application, behavior and prospects to be promoted as generals."[12] Among them was Bernardo de Gálvez, probably helped by his uncle Miguel's position. The students of Ávila's military academy formed a sort of elite of enlightened officers who relied more on the knowledge of the art of war instead of the blind courage that the old military thinking previously treasured.

In 1775 Gálvez volunteered for General O'Reilly's expedition to Algiers, on the North African coast. In a rare failure for O'Reilly, the Algerians prevailed, and Spain lost over two thousand men. Gálvez, according to O'Reilly, "long remained with his men even after being wounded, and did not retreat from the field until specifically ordered to do so."[13] Despite the loss, Gálvez had impressed his commanding officers, including O'Reilly, whose recommendation earned him promotion to lieutenant colonel.[14]

Louisiana

In July 1776, as Thomas Jefferson sweated over the Declaration of Independence, King Carlos III was deciding on the next man to command his troops in Louisiana and serve as the colony's governor. The debacle at Algiers and Britain's victory in the Seven Years' War, including its temporary seizure of Havana, had only strengthened the king's resolve to enlarge his military forces. He needed officers who would lead the empire to a new era of expansion. The governor of Louisiana was a key position. In 1768 Louisiana's first Spanish governor, Antonio de Ulloa, heard from a passing British ship that "the troubles in New England continue to spread" and threatened Massachusetts's royal governor Thomas Gage. Eight long years before the signing of the Declaration of Independence, Ulloa was already convinced that Bostonians were "determined on total independence from old England."[15] Only three weeks after hearing of New England's unrest, Ulloa himself was overthrown as French residents of Louisiana chased him out of New Orleans. The French rebels resented the coming of Spanish rule after the Seven Years' War and complained about restrictions on trade and the enforcement of tax codes. In response, the king put Alejandro O'Reilly on the job. In 1768 the general sailed from Havana with nearly three thousand troops. When the French Louisianans saw themselves outnumbered, they did not put up a fight. O'Reilly tried and publicly executed some of the rebellion's leaders, opened direct trade with Cuba, standardized land grants, and established a *cabildo*, a town council representing the prominent families of New Orleans. Demonstrating both the power and the opportunities of empire, he ensured that the rebellion of 1768 would be no American Revolution.[16]

By 1776 the king wanted a man for "that important position" of Louisiana governor who would "provide for the defense, and . . . increase the population and commerce of the Province of Louisiana." With José's and Miguel's patronage and Alejandro O'Reilly's encouragement, the king appointed Bernardo de Gálvez commander of the New Orleans battalion and acting governor of Louisiana.[17]

For the previous fourteen years, Bernardo de Gálvez had been making his way rapidly upward through the Spanish imperial ranks by impressing powerful patrons. Some might have thought Louisiana was an unfortunate posting, far from more prominent and lucrative colonial centers. Thirty-year-old Gálvez disagreed. Louisiana was a colony on the fringes of the Spanish Empire, but he saw it as essential for guarding against British advances into New Spain. Doing well here would mean other promotions, to more important colonies such as Mexico, Cuba, or Peru, or to the colonial ministry back in Spain.[18]

Spanish opinions differed as to the importance of Louisiana. In the wake of the French uprising in New Orleans, some administrators argued that Spain should give Louisiana back to France because it was too much trouble to run such a huge province inhabited by powerful Native nations and few Spanish or even French settlers. O'Reilly believed "Louisiana does not merit defense in time of war," and if attacked, the governor should pull back to "protect the presidios of Mexico on that frontier." But an important minister of the king, the conde de Aranda, believed Louisiana was "indispensable" and that the Mississippi River was the ideal border between British and Spanish Americas. During the Seven Years' War the British had captured Havana, the empire's most important port and its third largest American city after Mexico City and Lima. Spain got Havana back in the postwar negotiations, but the crown would not forget the importance of defending against the British. Many believed that Louisiana was key to the defense of Mexico and its lucrative silver mines.[19]

Gálvez would be a different sort of governor from O'Reilly. The general had dictated and ruled with a show of military strength. He had ordered his subordinates to make Indians "understand that they owe submission only to the King." He had returned to Spain without learning that Spanish officials at posts beyond New Orleans—such as Natchez, Arkansas Post, and Natchitoches—could not possibly carry out his dictates. They had a handful of soldiers surrounded by thousands of Indians who allowed their posts to exist only because European trade was useful. In addition to Gálvez's familiarity with American Natives, his language skills and knowledge of France and French surely made him seem like less of an outsider to Louisiana's French residents than most Spanish governors had been, and he married into a prominent New Orleans French family.[20]

The importance of his wife in Bernardo's life and success cannot be overstated. Even though Felicité de St. Maxent was the daughter of one of the most prominent merchants of New Orleans, her family lacked the aristocratic credentials that Bernardo's uncle and father would have considered necessary for a suitable wife. The couple would always remain extremely close. For example, in blueprints for the viceroyal summer palace in Chapultepec, near Mexico City, which was designed under Bernardo de Gálvez's close supervision, the couple shared a bedroom, contrary to the custom among noble families. Felicité, who Hispanicized her name to Feliciana, would accompany her husband even to his hardship postings: she would give birth to their son Miguel in Guarico (Saint-Domingue, now Haiti) while Bernardo was in command of the joint French and Spanish forces that were about to set sail for the invasion of British Jamaica.[21]

Based on his experience in Apache country, the new governor understood his constraints in Louisiana, where most people were Indigenous and most colonists were French. In January 1777, on the day he took office, he confided to his uncle José that "it is not possible to resist the least impulse of the enemies without the neighboring Indians being on our side." Gálvez hoped that with gifts and assurances that the Spanish were the real heirs of France, he could lure Native nations from the English side. In 1778 he advised that by "keeping Indians friendly" with goods and respectful treatment, the king could "keep them very contented for ten years with what he spends in one year in making war on them."[22] In Apache country and in North Africa, Gálvez had seen the cost of war in blood and treasure. During the Apache war and in his first months in Louisiana, he learned he could make valuable allies by understanding Indigenous customs and meeting Indigenous demands. Still, Gálvez's acknowledgement of Native power should not be confused with advocacy of Native sovereignty. He represented the Spanish Empire, and his reasons for cooperating with Indians were to serve Spanish goals, not Indian ones. Despite his opposition to Britain, Gálvez was no supporter of Native or colonial independence.

Rebellion

By the time Gálvez arrived in Louisiana in 1777, relations between Britain and some of its American colonies had dramatically deteriorated, and the conflict promised Spain an opportunity to strike back at Britain after the humiliation of the Seven Years' War. The six Spanish objectives for the war against the British were enumerated in Article 7 of the Treaty for the Defensive and Offensive Alliance between the Crowns of Spain and France against the one of England, signed at Aranjuez on April 12, 1779. The first was reconquering Gibraltar, the second was taking possession of the river and the fort of Mobile, and the third was "the restitution of Pensacola with all Florida's coast to the Bahamas Channel, till all foreign presence there is expelled."[23] From his position in Louisiana, Bernardo de Gálvez would play a key role in the war to come.

During the four years between the start of the American Revolution and Spain's declaration of war on Britain, the Spanish would officially proclaim their neutrality while doing everything they could to help the rebels' cause. Spain's support aimed at weakening the British more than strengthening the Americans since it was clear to everyone that rebellion could set a dangerous precedent for Spanish possessions in the Americas. It was a version of the old axiom that "the enemy of my enemy is my friend," which so many times in history has produced odd couples. On this occasion it led to an alliance of interests between an absolute monarch and the American revolutionaries, who soon would proclaim that all men are created equal.[24]

In March 1778 Governor Gálvez announced that Spanish neutrality "would not compromise her hospitality" to the Americans.[25] This hospitality allowed him to carry out all sorts of covert actions in their support. A few months later, he confirmed that this policy would continue, "until the fate of the war is decided."[26] He slowly began to build up his forces. He increased the size of the free Black militia and lured the upper class of New Orleans into joining the war effort by establishing an elite cavalry order called Carabineros de la Luisiana, complete with their own fancy uniforms. He sent diplomats with presents to Native towns and held a congress with Native nations of the lower Mississippi valley, including Natchitoches, Opelousas, Atakapas, Chitimachas, Pascagoulas, Biloxis, and Alabamas. As he explained to his uncle, the "generosity distributed on behalf of His Majesty has caused a lot of admiration, and in recognition of that they have offered to stay loyal." To prove it, they gave Gálvez the medals they had received from the English, even though he did not have any Spanish ones on hand to give to them. He renewed his plea "that a portion of them be sent to me as soon as possible" for formalizing the alliances.[27]

By the middle of the eighteenth century, the practice of presenting medals to Native leaders was so common that when Louisiana passed into Spanish hands, the new rulers had no choice but to continue it. In the autumn of 1769, the Spanish governor Alejandro O'Reilly had a meeting with representatives of several Indigenous groups, during which they asked that the new authorities continue to extend the same benefits and favors that they had received from the French. The meeting concluded with O'Reilly "bestowing medals hanging from a scarlet ribbon around the necks of several Indian chiefs."[28] The medals given by O'Reilly were ones known as *al mérito* (for merit), first coined in 1764. Some samples of these medals are still found in private collections and museums in the United States, and they represent both the authority of the particular chief who received the medal and his group's loyalty to Spain, although individual recipients defined "loyalty" according to their own political and military objectives.[29]

But the 1764 Spanish Indian peace medal had a flaw. In 1771, when Fernando de Leyba, representative of the Spanish crown in Upper Louisiana, presented one of these medals to Cazenonpoint, chief of the Quapaws, he refused it and asked instead for the French medal, since it was bigger. To avoid a repeat of such a snub, Bernardo de Gálvez asked for larger medals to be coined. Almost immediately, on August 22, 1777, an order was sent from the royal court to the royal mint to produce a new *al mérito* medal having a diameter of about two inches rather than the usual one and a half inches. The design by Tomás Francisco Prieto, official engraver of his Catholic majesty, is very similar to the old design; the main difference is that the bust of

King Carlos III is adorned with the insignia of the Order of the *Toisón de oro* (Golden Fleece), and the coin bears the signature of the artist. This new medal is commonly called the big *al mérito* medal, the first of which were coined in April 1778.[30]

Even as the new governor was seeking to ingratiate himself to surrounding Native nations, Gálvez secretly funded the American rebels with the support of the crown. In the spring of 1777 he sent some $70,000 worth of munitions to the American commander of Fort Pitt in Pennsylvania. In July 1777 American Indian affairs agent George Morgan wrote Gálvez proposing that the United States send a force to seize Pensacola and Mobile, with Spanish support. Gálvez replied that he could not directly assist the effort but that he would give Congress's agent "my permission and all the aid that I can notwithstanding that I shall apparently feign not to understand anything about the matter."[31]

Gálvez also revamped Louisiana's trade policy. Officially, only Spanish ships could do business at the Port of New Orleans, but illegal British trade had been pervasive. Gálvez ordered the seizure of British vessels, and he had gunboats built to defend the lower Mississippi. The long-standing Spanish policy of fighting contraband was selectively used to hurt the British merchants on the Mississippi while turning a blind eye to the not always legal business dealings of New Orleans merchants.[32]

The privileges granted to Louisiana's merchants left their British counterparts with few alternatives. Some decided to continue their business with a little more caution. It was not always easy, as Robert Ross and John Campbell, a pair of Scottish merchant-smugglers, found out when they lost everything and their partner, Alexander Grayden, landed in a Cuban jail. Others opted to join the winning side, including James Jones, who took the pledge of allegiance to Spain while his brother remained a loyal British subject, at least until the die of the American Revolution was finally cast. As historian John Walton Caughey writes, "As a consequence of the new Spanish commercial policy as interpreted by Gálvez, English contraband trade with Louisiana was almost extinguished even before Spain's entrance in the war against Great Britain in 1779 put a final stop to it."[33]

As Gálvez and the Spanish crown looked toward the nineteenth century, they saw the opposite of imperial decline. Whether they entered the war or not, the Revolution could damage Britain and accelerate a renaissance of the Spanish Empire.

War

In 1779 King Carlos III declared war on Britain. He ordered the governor of Cuba to assist Gálvez with "whatever land and sea forces it is possible to assemble in those dominions" for an attack on Mobile and Pensacola, "the keys to the Gulf of Mexico," as well as challenging British posts on the Mississippi.[34]

The rebel Americans were thrilled at the news. Thomas Jefferson, then governor of Virginia, wrote that Spain's declaration "has given us all the certainty of a happy issue to the present contest of which human events will admit."[35] Late in 1779 Congress appointed John Jay minister to the Spanish court, and Jay headed to Spain eager to negotiate a treaty of alliance. An alliance with Bourbon France against Britain, however, was not an alliance with Americans, and the Spanish crown saw little reason to show respect to rebels against monarchy and did not officially recognize Jay or at first even receive him at court.[36]

In terms of the war with Britain, it was not clear that Gálvez had enough forces to take any of West Florida. Despite his efforts, the loyalties of Louisiana's majority-French colonial population were far from clear. Some of them had rebelled against Spanish rule only eleven years before. Gálvez would need to persuade Louisiana's men and women, especially the French majority, that the Spanish Empire could better protect them and advance their ambitions.

On August 20, 1779, Gálvez addressed the inhabitants of New Orleans in the Place d'Armes in front of the Cabildo building. He falsely announced that Spain had recognized the independence of the United States and, further hiding the truth, said that "there was still peace and Spain wanted to keep the peace as long as England did not break it." New Orleans was in danger, he claimed, because the British might "start hostilities with us just as they did with the French." Gálvez also told them that the mail had brought a letter promoting him to brigadier general. To accept the king's appointment, Gálvez explained, he would need to take an oath "to defend the province." But he was not sure that he could, in good conscience, take that oath.[37]

The crowd murmured, wondering how their brave young governor could hesitate when the king called him to service. Gálvez assured the people of New Orleans that even without swearing an oath, he would "shed the last drop of my blood in sacrifice for my Sovereign." Where he balked was in swearing to defend Louisiana, given "the unfortunate state of the colony" with "the few troops" that he had. It would surely be a hollow oath, he told the crowd, unless the people of Louisiana "promised me to fulfill it." They took the bait. Showering him with effusive compliments and assurances of their fidelity, "they almost carried me in their arms to the Cabildo, forcing open the doors without waiting for the keys." Inside, they hailed him with "the greatest acclamations of joy" and "promised me they would sacrifice their lives in service to the King and do the same with their property."[38] A few days later Gálvez rode out of the city alongside his officers, with his regulars and militia behind him, to recruit more followers in the French and American Indian communities north and west of New Orleans.

In the morning of September 7, 1779, Gálvez was addressing another crowd, not far from the British post of Manchac. Over six hundred militiamen were in the crowd, including French-speaking Louisianans, British refugees, immigrants from the Canary Islands, and members of the free Black and mixed-race militias who served in segregated units led by their own officers. The Spanish troops included about five hundred regulars and twenty light cavalry. About 160 Houmas, Six Towns Choctaws, and Alabamas showed up, along with seven self-proclaimed Americans, marching under an American battle flag.[39]

Once Gálvez began to speak to the troops, they learned the startling news that he had kept secret: King Carlos had declared war on Britain, and he expected the people of Louisiana to join the fight. With loud cheers, the men followed Gálvez as he lifted his sabre and turned his horse toward British Manchac.[40]

Over the coming weeks Gálvez's forces took Manchac, Baton Rouge, and Natchez. His naval forces seized control of Lake Pontchartrain and Lake Maurepas, thus cutting off British posts on the Mississippi River from reinforcements from the Gulf. In recognition, the crown promoted him to the rank of *mariscal de campo* (one-star general). In the early months of 1780, Gálvez laid siege to the British fort at Mobile, which surrendered on March 12, 1780.[41]

Gálvez went personally to Havana to request more troops for the siege of Pensacola. By March 1781 he had assembled 1,500 men to attack Pensacola. On March 18 Gálvez himself led the lead ship through enemy fire into Pensacola Bay. Two weeks later 2,300 more troops arrived from New

Orleans and Mobile, and a French-Spanish joint fleet from Havana finally arrived on April 22. The total force under his command came to 5,500 foot troops and 2,200 men from both navies who volunteered to join the attack. After a sixty-one-day siege, Spanish artillery fire finally ignited a gunpowder magazine, and Spanish forces poured in through the gap. After some bloody fighting, British general John Campbell raised the white flag and surrendered all of West Florida to the Spanish.[42]

Next, Gálvez gathered a force of over twenty thousand white and Black troops and a fleet of ships on the north coast of Hispaniola, where he waited for French admiral François Joseph Paul de Grasse to join him after Yorktown for their next conquest. However, British admiral George Rodney won an important victory over the French fleet at the Battle of Dominica (Battle of the Saintes) in the Lesser Antilles in April 1782 and captured Admiral de Grasse. When Gálvez learned the news from Dominica, he delayed other ventures but still sent a force to the Bahamas. On May 8, 1782, Spanish forces captured New Providence, the main island of the Bahamas—a conquest that later would prove useful at the peace negotiation table, where it would be exchanged for East Florida.[43]

New Providence

The expedition against the Bahamas illustrates the Spanish frustration with the American rebels and continuing doubts throughout the Spanish hierarchy about the benefits of a Spanish-American alliance. The idea of conquering New Providence was consistent with the general objectives of the war in the American theater, which included expelling the British from all of the Gulf of Mexico, and while waiting for everything to be ready to get the real prize—Jamaica—it seemed a good idea to "meanwhile" take New Providence. "Meanwhile" was the actual word used by Francisco Saavedra in his diary when referring to the expedition, and it clearly conveys its purpose as a sort of training or rehearsal for Jamaica.[44] Bernardo de Gálvez had received strict orders from his uncle that, while he was the supreme commander of all forces, he must appoint other officers for those operations of "lesser importance."[45] Yet Gálvez was tempted to lead his men this time, too. It took all the diplomacy of his friend Saavedra to persuade him that the size of the force—one thousand men—demanded a colonel and not a general, and that in his absence the preparations for the expedition against Jamaica would inevitably suffer delay. Gálvez reluctantly agreed and appointed Juan Manuel de Cagigal in charge of the attack against New Providence.[46]

By January 1782 the men were ready but not the ships, so everything had to be postponed. As time passed and ships were not to be found anywhere, Cagigal suggested accepting the offer of the American seamen Alexander Gillon and William Cock to provide an escort for the transport vessels that had been already supplied by the Royal Treasury. By mid-April 1782, in the words of Juan Ignacio de Urriza: "After much work, and personally begging the resources from the merchants and inhabitants of the city [Havana], I have it ready for sail just waiting a Northern wind." The expedition against New Providence would have two thousand men, instead of the one thousand initially planned, on board fifty-seven vessels, forty-five of which were Spanish and twelve American.[47]

On May 6 the fleet arrived in front of Nassau, the capital of New Providence Island. At that precise moment, the captain of the *South Carolina*, Alexander Gillon, informed the Spanish commander that "in case of the signature of capitulations by the [British] general one of his [Gillon's] officers should be always present." Moreover, he "demanded his frigate to be insured for 300,000 pesos," and required that the Spanish "paid all costs made for the ship to be ready, about sixty or seventy thousand pesos."[48] He also threatened that if he was not paid in full and on the spot, he would not move his ships blocking the entrance of the port for the rest of the squadron. In the end, the British garrison would surrender without much problem. But the incident with Captain Gillon had consequences: both Havana and Madrid would thereafter seriously question the "Anglo-American" participation in a Spanish military operation.[49]

The problem had deeper implications than just an American captain with an attitude. If the operation was considered to be a joint one, it would contravene specific orders that clearly stated that while Spain was allied with France in their war against Britain, and while Spain shared with the United States a common enemy, that country should not be considered an ally. In a *oficio reservadísimo* (a secret instruction, equivalent today to a top-secret communique) dated April 6, 1782, from José de Gálvez to Bernardo de Gálvez, interpreting and developing the November 16, 1781, Royal Order, he clearly stated that Bernardo de Gálvez and José de Solano should "never agree to help the American colonists with the Arms or the Navy of His Majesty for the war against their metropolis," although, "if in the course of the operation against Jamaica, this was demanded by the French, that problem should not prevent them from being joined to the French generals."[50] In other words, they were never to help the American rebels unless asked to do so by the French, in which case Solano and Gálvez would have to do everything to keep the joint force together. Much easier said than done. Luckily for the two Spanish commanders, such a demand never happened. With this precedent, it was not surprising that Bernardo de Gálvez was asked about his reasons for not having used the Spanish navy in the operation against New Providence. Gálvez received the request and passed it to Juan Manuel de Cajigal for him to answer as commander of the expedition. Confident in his victory, Cajigal declared with panache that the operation "was carried out with fortune and skill (not by American chief as the commander says, but Spaniard, and very much Spaniard)."[51] That settled the matter.

Hero of Empire

For leading the northward expansion of the Spanish Empire, King Carlos awarded Bernardo de Gálvez with the title conde de Gálvez: "To perpetuate in your posterity the memory of the heroic action in which you, alone, forced your entry into [Pensacola] Bay, you may put as a Seal in your coat of Arms . . . the Motto: 'YO SOLO.'" (I alone).[52]

By the end of the American Revolution, Spain held West Florida and had extended its claims so that its territory stretched from the Pacific to the Flint River in Georgia and from the Gulf of Mexico to the Great Lakes. In the eyes of Spanish officials, they had succeeded in their war for empire. While these claims seem outrageously extensive, the ambitions of the United States looked even less reasonable in 1783. The Continental Army's victory at Yorktown had been possible only because of European allies. The new nation owed debts to the Dutch, French, and Spanish and had no means to repay them. Under the Articles of Confederation, Congress could not impose taxes or levy duties on imports and exports. Native Americans from the Ohio valley were raiding the western parts of the colonies from North Carolina to Pennsylvania, and they were coordinating with the British better than at any time earlier in the war. With the exception of the Cherokees, southeastern Indians had fought very little during the war. They had built new alliances with one another and with northern Indians to ward off uninvited settlers, and they were eager to establish an alliance with Spain that would maintain Native control on the ground. The weak United States hardly seemed likely to be the dominant power after war ended. Spain, on the other hand, had joined the war to expand its empire, and it seemed to be working.[53]

Any worries that the Spanish monarchy had at the start of the war about the American Revolution being a threat to empires seemed disproven. Gálvez's victories and success in inspiring loyalty among French and British colonists in the Mississippi valley promised a strong and growing Spanish presence in North America. At the same time, Spanish troops had defeated the Túpac Amaru and put down other rebellions elsewhere in Spain's empire, while in Europe, Geneva, Sweden, Poland, and the Dutch and Venetian republics were proving too unstable to remain independent much less republican, while parliamentary reform had failed in England and Ireland. The 1780s looked like a good time to have an American empire.[54]

Mexico

Gálvez carried his visions of a Spanish colonial renaissance to Mexico. His father, Matías, became viceroy of New Spain after the war but died in office in November 1784, and the king named Bernardo as his successor. Now Bernardo de Gálvez's jurisdiction stretched from the Californias to Cuba and from Panama to the border of British Canada. On May 21, 1785, Gálvez landed at the port of Veracruz with his wife, Feliciana, and three children. From there they traveled to Mexico City, the capital of the Spanish New World for over 250 years and the ancient city of the Aztecs before that. Louisiana had brought glory to Gálvez and his empire, and now he held the highest office in the colonies, an office that stretched back to Hernán Cortés himself. His empire seemed bound for a future as long and splendid as its past.[55]

From the very beginning of his time in Mexico City, Bernardo de Gálvez displayed a new style of government. His reputation as a military leader, his youth, his wife's famed beauty and charm, his presence in the streets, and his willing participation in bullfights, dances, and festivities made him very popular. This popularity was the origin of a later "black legend" accusing him of coveting the royal crown of an independent Mexico. His tenure as viceroy was deeply affected by the so-called famine year in 1785. A series of weather phenomena destroyed most of the crops in Mexico, so Bernardo de

Gálvez had to use all the resources of the Spanish administration to try to feed the starving inhabitants of the most populated viceroyalty in America. He prosecuted hoarders and black marketers who abused "those unhappy people that, although poor, are the ones who fatten the rich giving them with one hand what they received with the other, and the ones who make the wealth of kingdoms working with their arms, fighting the wars, and paying taxes."[56] An empire could not run without the common people, who were "the strength and vigour of the State."[57]

While Gálvez directed most of his attention against the famine, he started several profound and long-lasting reforms. Among them arguably the most important was the Instruction for the Government of the Internal Provinces of August 1786, which laid the foundation of a new policy concerning the expansion and settlement of the northern frontier of Mexico, today's southwest United States. As a commander in New Mexico and governor of Louisiana, Gálvez had learned the importance of Native alliances in running an overstretched empire. He designed a new policy toward Native Americans based on trade and cultural assimilation instead of confrontation. He made peace first with the Comanches in 1786 and then with individual Apache bands. In the east he sought alliance with others who would oppose the Americans, especially the strong Native nations that had recently been British allies.[58]

In November 1786 Bernardo de Gálvez fell ill. Prayers went up from the cathedral and crowds gathered on the streets outside. He died before sunrise on November 30 at the age of forty. After his uncle José de Gálvez died the following year and his numerous enemies felt free to attack him without fear or restraint, rumors appeared that Bernardo de Gálvez had intended to leave the empire he had served.[59] The oldest reference to Bernardo de Gálvez's "black legend" is from Alexander von Humboldt. In his *Political Essay on the Kingdom of New Spain*, first published in French in Paris in 1811, he referred to a rumor heard during his travels through Mexico in 1803 that "Count Bernardo de Galvez has been accused of having conceived the project of rendering New Spain independent from the peninsula."[60] Humboldt rejected the idea, arguing that

> the Count of Galvez belonged to a family that King Charles the Third had suddenly raised to an extraordinary degree of wealth and power. Young, amiable, and addicted to pleasures and magnificence,

he had obtained from the munificence of his sovereign one of the first places to which an individual could be exalted; and consequently, it could not be becoming in him to break the ties, which for three centuries had united the colonies to the mother country.

Humboldt also argued that "in a great revolutionary commotion, it would never have been forgiven him that he was not born an American."[61]

Of course, Humboldt's argument that Gálvez's movement for independence could not be successful does not preclude the possibility that he could have that intention or idea. Yet no contemporary documentation suggests that Bernardo de Gálvez wanted to become king of Mexico. All the references to the conspiracy date from well after his death, the first one being Humboldt, who heard about it in 1803, twenty years after the fact, at a time when Mexico was in a completely different political situation than in the 1780s. There was no feeling favorable toward independence mature enough in 1786 to be able to appear during Bernardo de Gálvez's mandate as viceroy.[62] Thus, the idea that he was working for the independence of Mexico must have been born well after his death, not by coincidence precisely when Mexico was trying to find an historical legitimacy for its own already achieved independence.[63] Humboldt was right that the Gálvez family's success came from and depended on the king, and there is no evidence that Gálvez ever was anything but loyal to the empire.

Conclusion

Today, outside the New Orleans Cabildo, there is a plaque that was erected by the Daughters of the American Revolution in 1930. It reads: "To the French patriots of 1768 who, in revolt against the transfer of the province of Louisiana from France to Spain, first voiced in America the principle of self-determination of nations." Gálvez would be shocked if he knew this memorial stands so close to where he once wielded power, as he probably would be at the rumor that he wanted to lead a Mexican independence movement. Gálvez spent years persuading the French rebels of 1768 and the populace of Mexico that the Spanish Empire was the best protector of their economic opportunities and political rights.

Despite his assistance to the American Revolution, and despite later rumors that he himself was a revolutionary, to Gálvez the Spanish Empire was the way of the future, likely to outmaneuver and outlast the American experiment in self-determination and republicanism. When he died in 1786, that vision was still intact.

Notes

1. Many contemporaneous sources on the siege of Pensacola survive, including Bernardo de Gálvez, *Diario de las operaciones que ejecuta la expedición del mariscal de campo general de ella del 9 de marzo al desembarco en la isla de Santa Rosa*, n.d., n.p., no signature, Archivo General de Simancas (AGS), Simancas, Valladolid, Spain, SGU, 6913, Exp. 12; Bernardo de Gálvez, *Diario de las operaciones de la expedición contra la Plaza de Panzacola concluida por las Armas de S. M. Católica bajo las órdenes del Mariscal de Campo D. Bernardo de Gálvez*, n.d., n.p., BPR, III/6526 (2) and National Library of Spain, Madrid, 2/12654; *Diario del Jefe de la Escuadra D. José Solano, Toma de Panzacola, April y May 1781*, AGS, Marina 422; Francisco de Miranda, *Diario de lo más particular ocurrido desde el día de nuestra salida del puerto de La Habana*, Francisco Miranda Archives (AFM), Caracas, Venezuela, Viajes, t. III, ff. 70–75 and ff. 99–102; *Diario de lo ocurrido en la escuadra, y tropas, que al mando del Jefe de Escuadra Don Josef Solano; y del Mariscal de Campo Don Juan Manuel de Cagigal, salieron de La Habana el 9 de Abril de 1781, para socorrer al ejército español, que atacaba la plaza de Panzacola . . .*, AFM, Viajes, t. III, ff. 80–98. (For an English translation, see Donald E. Worcester, ed., "Miranda's Diary of the Siege of Pensacola, 1781," *Florida Historical Quarterly* 29.3 [January 1951]: 163–96.) Francisco de Saavedra, *Diario de don Francisco de Saavedra*, ed. Francisco Morales Padrón (Sevilla: Universidad de Sevilla / Consejo Superior de Investigaciones Científicas, 2004), 124–200. (English translation, Francisco Morales Padrón, ed., *Journal of Don Francisco Saavedra de Sangronis during the Commission He Held in the Charge from 28 June 1780 Until the 20th of the Same Month of 1783* [Gainesville: University of Florida Press, 2009.])

2. General Murray's opinion about the Arab revolt in the movie *Lawrence de Arabia*. David Lean, dir., Columbia Pictures, 1962.

3. Ramón Zazo y Ortega, *Blasón y genealogía de la casa de los Gálvez de Macharaviaya* (Málaga: Diputación Provincial de Málaga, 1971), 29.

4. Catastro de Ensenada, 1753, Respuestas Generales del lugar de Macharaviaya, AGS, Dirección General de Rentas, Iª Remesa, Libro 296, ff. 524–48.

5. Stanley J. Stein and Barbara H. Stein, *Apogee of Empire: Spain and New Spain in the Age of Charles III, 1759–1789* (Baltimore: Johns Hopkins University Press, 2003); Gabriel B. Paquette, *Enlightenment, Governance, and Reform in Spain and Its Empire, 1759–1808* (New York: Palgrave, Macmillan, 2008); John W. Caughey, *Bernardo de Gálvez in Louisiana, 1776–1783* (Berkeley: University of California Press, 1934), 68.

6. Zazo y Ortega, *Blasón y genealogía*, 20; Caughey, *Bernardo de Gálvez*, 61.

7. Service record of Captain Bernardo de Gálvez, December 1774, Capitán Bernardo [de] Gálvez, AGS, ID Persona 10032, Secretaría de Guerra, 2653, exp. 8, f. 18;

Stein and Stein, *Apogee of Empire*, 108–10; Caughey, *Bernardo de Gálvez*, 62; Jacques A. Barbier, "Charles III's Empire: Conjuncture and Structure," in *Charles III: Florida and the Gulf*, ed. Patricia R. Wickman (Miami: Count of Gálvez Historical Society, 1990), 10–12.

8. Bernardo de Gálvez, *Notes and Considerations on the War with the Apache Indians in the Provinces of New Spain—Noticia y reflexiones sobre la guerra que se tiene con los indios apaches en las provincias de Nueva España*, (Madrid, c. 1771), in OSÉS, Blas, documentación varia, Mss., México, 1817, Hill Museum and Manuscript Library, Steiner Collection, Bush Centre, John's University, Collegeville, MN, Steiner 27, Blas Osés, Manuscritos, n. 2, 35–66, 43. English translation in Elisabeth A. H. John, "A Cautionary Exercise in Apache Historiography—Notes and Reflections on the War with the Apache Indians in the Provinces of New Spain—by Bernardo de Galvez, ca. 1785–86," *Journal of American History* 25 (1984): 301–15. Also see Elizabeth A. H. John, "Bernardo de Gálvez on the Apache Frontier," *Journal of American History* 29 (1988): 427–30.

9. Gálvez, *Notes and Considerations on the War with the Apache Indians*.

10. Ibid., 39.

11. Ibid., 60–61.

12. Herbert Ingram Priestley, *José de Gálvez, Visitor-General of New Spain (1765–1771)* (Berkeley: University of California Press, 1916); David J. Weber, *Bárbaros: Spaniards and Their Savages in the Age of Enlightenment* (New Haven, CT: Yale University Press, 2005), 2; Stein and Stein, *Apogee of Empire*, 53; Thomas E. Chavez, *Spain and the Independence of the United States: An Intrinsic Gift* (Albuquerque: University of New Mexico Press, 2002), 9–10; Serafín María de Sotto, count de Clonard, *Memoria histórica de las academias y escuelas militares de España, con la creación y estado presente del Colegio General establecido en la ciudad de Toledo* (Madrid, 1847), 63; Alejandro O'Reilly, *Relación sucinta que explica el método y reglas bajo las cuales prosiguen sus estudios los oficiales que concurren a la Escuela Militar de Ávila, que ha erigido S.M. en el año de 1774, fiándome la dirección de ella*, Archivo General Militar de Madrid (AGMM), formerly known as Archivo Central del Servicio Histórico Militar, Madrid, Colección Conde de Clonard, leg. 10. The *Presidiales* were the troops garrisoned in the *presidios*, the forts that Spain constructed along the northern frontier of the viceroyalty of New Spain to protect the Spanish settlers from attacks, mainly, but not only, from Native American groups.

13. Alejandro O'Reilly to José de Gálvez, Puerto de Santa María, May 7, 1776, Archivo General de Indias (AGI), Sevilla, Spain, Santo Domingo, 2586, carpeta 11, ff. 927r.–928v.

14. Eric Beerman, "'Yo Solo' Not 'Solo': Juan Antonio de Riaño," *Florida Historical Quarterly* 58 (1980): 175–76.

15. Allan J. Kuethe, "Charles III, the Cuban Military and the Destiny of Florida," in Wickman, *Charles III: Florida and the Gulf*, 65. Antonio Ulloa to Jerónimo Grimaldi, October 6, 1768, *Spain in the Mississippi Valley, 1765–1794*, ed. and trans. Lawrence Kinnaird (Washington, DC: GPO, 1946–49), 1:71–72.

16. Ned Sublette, *The World That Made New Orleans: From Spanish Silver to Congo*

Square (Chicago: Lawrence Hill Books, 2008), 93–94; Paquette, *Enlightenment, Governance, and Reform,* 122–23; Caughey, *Bernardo de Gálvez,* 8–35.

17. Bernardo de Gálvez's appointment as colonel of the Louisiana Fixed Infantry Regiment (Regimiento de Infantería Fijo de la Luisiana), AGI, Santo Domingo, 2586, Carpeta 11, ff. 930r.–v.; O'Reilly to José de Gálvez, Puerto de Santa María, May 7, 1776, AGI, Santo Domingo, 2586, Carpeta 11, ff. 927r.–928v.

18. *Reales Cédulas en que el Rey se sirve haver merced del Título de Castilla, con la Denominacion de Conde de Gálvez* (1783), photostat in *Tribute to Don Bernardo de Gálvez: Royal Patents and an Epic Ballad Honoring the Spanish Governor of Louisiana,* ed. Ralph Lee Woodward Jr., 21; Bernardo de Gálvez to José de Gálvez, January 28, 1777, Audiencia de Santo Domingo, AGI, leg. 2547, doc. 1, reel 13, Historic New Orleans Collection (HNOC); Samuel Wilson Jr., "Architecture in Eighteenth-Century West Florida," in *Eighteenth-Century Florida and Its Borderlands,* ed. Samuel Proctor (Gainesville: University Press of Florida, 1975), 126–27, 135; Robert R. Rea, "British West Florida: Stepchild of Diplomacy," in Proctor, *Eighteenth-Century Florida and Its Borderlands,* 65–67.

19. O'Reilly to Grimaldi, September 30, 1770, in Kinnaird, *Spain in the Mississippi Valley,* 1:185; Paquette, *Enlightenment, Governance, and Reform,* 117–23.

20. O'Reilly to François Desmazellières, November 15, 1769, "The First Spanish Instructions for Arkansas Post, November 15, 1769," ed. Gilbert C. Din, *Arkansas Historical Quarterly* 53 (1994): 317; Kathleen DuVal, "The Education of Fernando de Leyba: Quapaws and Spaniards on the Border of Empires," *Arkansas Historical Quarterly* 60 (2001): 1–29; Kathleen DuVal, *The Native Ground: Indians and Colonists in the Heart of the Continent* (Philadelphia: University of Pennsylvania Press, 2006), chs. 4–5.

21. For the very interesting life of Feliciana Saint Maxent de Gálvez, see Eric Beerman, "La bella criolla Felicitas de Saint Maxent, viuda de Bernardo de Gálvez, en España," in *Norteamérica a finales del siglo XVIII: España y los Estados Unidos,* coord. Eduardo Garrigues, eds. Emma Sánchez Montañés, Sylvia L. Hilton, Almudena Hernández Ruigómez, and Isabel García-Montón (Madrid: Fundación Consejo España–Estados Unidos and Editorial Marcial Pons, 2008), 281–96; Eric Beerman, "Governor Bernardo de Galvez's New Orleans Belle: Felicitas of St. Maxent," *Revista Española de Estudios Norteamericanos* (Madrid) 7 (1994): 39–44; Eric Beerman, "El conde de Aranda en la tertulia madrileña (1788–90) de la viuda de Bernardo de Gálvez," in *El Conde de Aranda y su tiempo, Institución Fernando el Católico Excma. Diputación de Zaragoza,* dir. José A. Ferrer Benimeli, coords. Esteban Sarasa and Eliseo Serrano (Zaragoza: Diputación de Zaragoza, 2000), 349–62; Eric Beerman, "The French Ancestors of Felicite of St. Maxent," *New Orleans Genesis* 17 (September 1968): 403–7, also published in *Revue de Louisiana* 6 (Summer 1977): 69–75. Blueprints for the second floor of Chapultepec's Royal Palace, Plano Superior del Real Palacio de Chapultepec, c. 1787, AGI, Mapas y Planos, México, 407. Miguel de Gálvez baptism certificate—Certificación de partida de bautismo de Miguel de Gálvez Maxent [sic], in Autos de las pruebas para caballero de la orden de Calatrava que pretende Don Miguel de Gálvez y Satmagent [sic], cadete de la compañía Americana de Reales Guardias de Corps, aprobado en mayo de

1797, Archivo Histórico Nacional (AHN), Madrid, Órdenes Militares Caballeros de Calatrava, Exp.1009, ff. 47v.–48v.

22. Bernardo de Gálvez to José de Gálvez, January 28, 1777, Audiencia de Santo Domingo, AGI, leg. 2547, doc. 3, reel 13, HNOC.

23. Treaty of Alliance between France and Spain, concluded at Aranjuez, April 12, 1779, in *European Treaties Bearing on the History of the United States and Its Dependencies*, vol.4: *1716–1815*, ed. Charles Oscar Paullin (Washington, DC: GPO, 1937), 145–47.

24. Miguel Alonso Baquer, "Los ministros de Carlos IV frente a la revolución francesa," *Revista de Historia Militar* 14.29 (1970): 79–99.

25. Bernardo de Gálvez to the inhabitants of the colony of Louisiana, draft copy, New Orleans, March 3, 1778, AGI, Cuba 112.

26. Bernardo de Gálvez to Baltasar de Villiers, official letter n. 43, New Orleans, January 2, 1779, AGI, Cuba 112.

27. Bernardo de Gálvez to José de Gálvez, September 19, 1777, Audiencia de Santo Domingo, AGI, leg. 2547, doc. 90, reel 13, HNOC; Stuart to Howe, October 6, 1777, Guy Carleton, 1st Baron Dorchester, Papers, British National Archives, Kew, England, microfilm copy at University of North Carolina, Chapel Hill; John Blommart to John Stuart, August 18, 1777, fr. 711, v. 78, reel 7, pt. 1, Records of the British Colonial Office, Library of Congress, Washington, DC; Henry Stuart to John Stuart, August 11, 1777, abstract, in *Documents of the American Revolution, 1770–1783 (Colonial Office Series)*, ed. K. G. Davies (Shannon, Ireland: Irish University Press, 1972–81), 13:184; Bernardo de Gálvez to José de Gálvez, May 27, 1779, doc. 288, reel 14, leg. 2547, Audiencia de Santo Domingo, AGI, HNOC.

28. Daniel H. Usner, "American Indians in Colonial New Orleans," in *Powhatan's Mantle: Indians in the Colonial Southeast*, 2nd ed., eds. Gregory A. Waselkov, Peter H. Wood, and Thomas Hatley (Lincoln: University of Nebraska Press, 2006), 163–88.

29. Elvira Villena, "The First Spanish Military Decorations: Tomás Francisco Prieto's al Mérito Medals," *The Medal* 36 (Spring 2000): 25–32; John C. Ewers, "Symbols of Chiefly Authority in Spanish Louisiana," in *The Spanish in the Mississippi Valley 1762–1804*, ed. John Francis McDermott (Urbana: University of Illinois Press, 1974), 272–86; John C. Ewers, *Plains Indian History and Culture: Essays on Continuity and Change* (Norman: University of Oklahoma Press, 1998); Weber, *Bárbaros*, 25, 187.

30. Kathleen DuVal, "The Education of Fernando de Leyba: Quapaws and Spaniards on the Border Empires," *Arkansas Historical Quarterly* 60 (Spring 2001): 1–29; Bernardo de Gálvez to José de Gálvez, several letters dated 1777 and 1778, AHN, Estado 3884 bis, exp. 7, nos. 1–8; dossier of the minting of the "al Mérito" medal, Madrid, 1777, AHN, Fondos Contemporáneos Ministerio de Hacienda, Madrid, 7870, Exp.3, in Steve Cox, "The Rare Spanish Carlos III, Al Mérito Medals: A Chronology 1764 to 1783," *MCA Advisory: The Newsletter of Medal Collectors of America* 13 (July 2010): 4–12: Golden silver medal. Obverse: bust of the King's profile to the right and legend CARLOS III. REY DE ESP.EMP DE LAS INDIAS (Charles the Third. King of Spain and Emperor of the Indies). Back: AL MERITO surrounded by a laurel wreath.

Signed under the bust T. PRIETO. Diameter 56 mm. (2.126 inches). Uncirculated. Although few have survived, one is preserved at the Lázaro Galdiano Museum in Madrid, Medal Collection, inventory n. 5213. Also see Barry D. Tayman, Tony Lopez, and Skyler Liechty, "Tomás Prieto's al Mérito Spanish Indian Peace Medals," in *Peace Medals: Negotiating Power in Early America*, ed. R. B. Pickering (Norman: University of Oklahoma Press, 2012), 19–31. Stack's Bowers Galleries auctioned another in 2009, selling for $17,250. Stack's, 123 W. 57th St., New York, *The Americana Sale*, 1 (Dec. 2009), Lot n. 5012. http://legacy.stacks.com/Lot/ItemDetail/25474.

31. Bernardo de Gálvez to George Morgan, August 9, 1777, reel 1, Mississippi Provincial Archives: Spanish Dominion, 1759–1804, comp. Dunbar Rowland, Jackson, MS; James Alton James, *Oliver Pollock: The Life and Times of an Unknown Patriot* (Freeport, NY: Appleton-Century, 1937, reprint,1970), 105–6.

32. Bernardo de Gálvez to Marquis de la Torre, May 6, 1777, vol. 1, 14–16, Gálvez Cartas al Capitán General de Habana, 1777–81, Transcripts from the Archivo Nacional de Cuba, Ayer Collection, Newberry Library; Bernardo de Gálvez to José de Gálvez (and attachments), September 15, 1777, Audiencia de Santo Domingo, AGI, leg. 2547, doc. 86, reel 13, HNOC; Peter Chester to Bernardo de Gálvez, June 10, 1777, in Davies, *Documents of the American Revolution*, 14:107; Royal Decree to Extend Free Trade, February 2, 1778, in Kinnaird, *Spain in the Mississippi Valley*, 1:250–54; *Tribute to Don Bernardo de Gálvez*, xviii–xix; Caughey, *Bernardo de Gálvez*, 71, 91–92, 136; Robin F. A. Fabel, "Anglo-Spanish Commerce in New Orleans during the American Revolutionary Era," in *Anglo-Spanish Confrontation on the Gulf Coast during the American Revolution*, ed. William S. Coker and Robert R. Rea (Pensacola: Historical Pensacola Preservation Board, 1982), 34–35.

33. William Stiell to William Howe, Pensacola, June 3, 1777, in Historical Manuscripts Commission, *Report on American Manuscripts in the Royal Institution of Great Britain* (London, 1904), 1:115–16; Fabel, "Anglo-Spanish Commerce in New Orleans," 41–43; John Walton Caughey, "Bernardo de Gálvez and the English Smugglers on the Mississippi, 1777," *Hispanic American Historical Review* 12 (February 1932): 58.

34. José de Gálvez to Navarro, August 29, 1779, AGI, Cuba, 1290; Statement of Expenses of the Province of Louisiana, May 31, 1787, in Kinnaird, *Spain in the Mississippi Valley*, 2:209; Joseph Barton Starr, *Tories, Dons, and Rebels: The American Revolution in British West Florida* (Gainesville: University Press of Florida, 1976), 78–121; Kinnaird, introduction to *Spain in the Mississippi Valley*, 1:xxv; Caughey, *Bernardo de Gálvez*, 90–92.

35. Thomas Jefferson to Bernardo de Gálvez, November 8, 1779, in Kinnaird, *Spain in the Mississippi Valley*, 1:362; Founders Online, https://founders.archives.gov/documents/Jefferson/01-03-02-0174.

36. Notes of a Conference between the Count de Florida Blanca and John Jay, Sept. 23, 1780, *The Selected Papers of John Jay*, ed. Elizabeth M. Nuxoll et al. (Charlottesville: University of Virginia Press, 2012), 2:265–72.

37. Spain would not officially recognize the independence of the United States until after the signature of the peace treaty by the United States and Great Britain in

1783. Bernardo de Gálvez to José de Gálvez, October 16, 1779, 3:357–66, Gálvez Cartas al Josef de Galvez, 1777–1781, Transcripts from the Archivo Nacional de Cuba, Ayer Collection, Newberry Library.

38. Bernardo de Gálvez wrote in third person (probably after the fashion started by Julius Cesar in his *The Gallic Wars*) in *Account of the Campaign against the English Settlements along the Mississippi* (Relación de la campaña que hizo D. Bernardo de Gálvez, contra los ingleses, en la Luisiana, Septiembre 1779), which accompanied his letter Bernardo de Gálvez to José de Gálvez, New Orleans, October 16, 1779 (2nd of this date), AGS, SGU, LEG, 6912,1. Gálvez's manuscript is in the National Library of Spain, Madrid, Manuscritos que fueron de la Biblioteca de Ultramar, n. 14. Gálvez's account served as the basis for the report that appeared in the December 12, 1778, edition of the *Gaceta de Madrid*. It has been published in *Documentos históricos de la Florida y la Luisiana: Siglos XVI al XVIII*, ed. Manuel Serrano y Sanz (Madrid: Librería General de Victoriano Suárez, 1913), 343–52. It is also interesting to compare Gálvez's account with the report made by Diego José Navarro in *Extracto de lo acaecido en la expedición hecha por el brigadier d. Bernardo de Gálvez, gobernador de la provincia de Luisiana, contra los establecimientos y fuertes que tenían los ingleses sobre el río Misisipi, que consiguió tomarles desalojándolos enteramente*, in Diego José Navarro to José de Gálvez, official letter n. 633, La Habana, November 11, 1779 (1st of this date), AGI, Santo Domingo 2082.

39. Bernardo de Gálvez to José de Gálvez, dispatch, New Orleans, October 16, 1779 (2nd of this date), AGS, SGU, LEG, 6912,1; Bernardo de Gálvez, *Account of the Campaign against the English Settlements*. The same data about the composition on the forces under Bernardo de Gálvez were included in the report sent by Navarro, *Extracto de lo acaecido en la expedición hecha por el brigadier d. Bernardo de Gálvez*, AGI, Santo Domingo 2082.

40. Bernardo de Gálvez to Navarro, September 18, 1779, pp. 1075–78, vol. 8, leg. 1232, Dispatches of the Spanish Governors, 1766–1792, photostats from the Archivo General de Indias, Ayer Collection, Newberry Library; Bernardo de Gálvez to José de Gálvez, October 16, 1779, pp. 357–66, vol. 3, Gálvez Cartas al Josef de Galvez; Gálvez Commendation, October 4, 1779, reel 7, Carleton Papers.

41. José de Gálvez to Bernardo de Gálvez, dispatch, El Pardo, February 16, 1781, AGS, SGU, LEG, 6912, 4; José de Gálvez to Bernardo de Gálvez, dispatch, Madrid, January 6, 1780, AGS, SGU, LEG, 6912, 2.

42. Estado que manifiesta los Buques de Guerra y Comboy [sic], del mando del Capitán de Navío, Don José Calvo de Irazábal en el que se conduce el Ejército que, a las órdenes del Sr. Don Bernardo de Gálvez, Mariscal de Campo, se dirige al socorro de la Movila y conquista de Panzacola, La Habana, February17, 1781, AGS, Marina 421; Estado que manifiesta los Buques en que se han embarcado las tropas destinadas a las órdenes del mariscal de Campo D. Bernardo de Gálvez, que dieron vela el día de la fecha, La Habana, February 28, 1781, AGI, Santo Domingo 2083A; Tropa que se ha embarcado a la orden del Mariscal de Campo Don Bernardo de Gálvez en La Habana, February 28, 1781, AGI, Cuba, 1377; Estado de los oficiales y tropa que, al mando de d. Cayetano de Salla, teniente coronel del Regimiento de Soria, sale de esta Plaza

para la Expedición a Panzacola con expresión de presentes y enfermos, New Orleans, February 28, 1781, AGI, Cuba 563; Estado que manifiesta los oficiales y tropa que de la Nueva Orleans, salieron el 3 de este mes al mando del teniente coronel d. Cayetano de Salla, con expresión de los que quedan en aquel hospital y buques en que va cada uno, a bordo de la saetía San Francisco de paula de Escardó, March 23, 1781, AGI, Cuba 81. For the total of the joint Spanish-French forces present at Pensacola, see Orden para 23 de abril. Ordenes dadas desde el 22 hasta el 25 de marzo a los Destacamentos de La Habana y Movila. Desde dicho día hasta el 21 de abril a los dos expresados y el de Orleans. Y desde el 22 en que se reunió el refuerzo último hasta la rendición de Panzacola, Archivo Ezpeleta, Papeles de Panzacola., F. de Borja Medina Rojas, *José de Ezpeleta, Gobernador de La Mobila, 1780–1781* (Sevilla: Escuela de Estudios Hispano-Americanos / Consejo Superior de Investigaciones Científicas and Excma. Diputación Foral de Navarra, 1980), 766–67. Alexander Cameron to George Germain, October 31, 1780, fr. 625–32, reel 8, Records of the British Colonial Office, Library of Congress; Robert Farmar, "Bernardo de Galvez's Siege of Pensacola in 1781 (As Related in Robert Farmar's Journal)," ed. James A. Padgett, *Louisiana Historical Quarterly* 26 (1943): 311–29; "Spain's Report of War with the British in Louisiana," ed. and trans. Jac Nachbin, *Louisiana Historical Quarterly* (1932): 468–81; Josef de Ezpeleta to Bernardo de Gálvez, July 8, 1780, fr. 2480, rl. 168, leg. 2, Papeles Procedentes de Cuba, P. K. Yonge Library (PKY), University of Florida, Gainesville; Ezpeleta to Bernardo de Gálvez, November 19, 1780, fr. 2308, reel 168, leg. 2, Papeles de Cuba, PKY; Ezpeleta to Pedro Piernas, November 23, 1780, fr. 2311, reel 168, leg. 2, Papeles de Cuba, PKY; Bernardo de Gálvez to Navarro (dft), December 1, 1780, fr. 244, reel 164, leg. 2, Papeles de Cuba, PKY; Bernardo de Gálvez to Navarro, April 24, 1781, fr. 1435 (should be numbered 1444), reel 166, leg. 2, Papeles de Cuba, PKY; Michael D. Green, "The Creek Confederacy in the American Revolution: Cautious Participants," in Coker and Rea, *Anglo-Spanish Confrontation on the Gulf Coast*, 54–75; Starr, *Tories*, 175–215.

43. Henry Clinton to John Maxwell, March 8, 1782, reel 12, Carleton Papers; Archibald Campbell to Clinton, March 8, 1782, reel 12, Carleton Papers; Caughey, *Bernardo de Gálvez*, 243; Eric Beerman, *España y la independencia de Estados Unidos* (Madrid: MAPFRE, 1992), 174–75; John Maxwell to Alexander Leslie, April 17, 1782, reel 12, Carleton Papers. In parallel, the British in the Caribbean saw the war as between their empire and those of France and Spain. Andrew Jackson O'Shaughnessy, *An Empire Divided: The American Revolution and the British Caribbean* (Philadelphia: University of Pennsylvania Press, 2000), 201–10.

44. José de Gálvez to Diego José Navarro, confidential letter, San Ildefonso, August 29, 1779, AGI, Cuba, 1290; Saavedra, *Diario de don Francisco de Saavedra,* October 11, 1781, entry, 222. Francisco de Saavedra was an old friend of Gálvez from the time both were students at the Royal Military Academy at Ávila. Through Bernardo, he entered the circle of José and became a one of his most trusted officials at the Ministry of the Indies. Saavedra's diary and memoirs are an invaluable source not only on Gálvez's life and character, but also on how the Spanish administration worked at the time. Francisco de Saavedra, *Los Decenios, (Autobiografía de un sevillano de la Ilus-*

tración), transcribed, introduced, and annotated by Francisco Morales Padrón (Sevilla: Servicio de Publicaciones del Excmo. Ayuntamiento de Sevilla, 1995); Saavedra, *Diario*. Saavedra played a crucial part in coordinating Spanish and French forces to provide the much-needed reinforcements to conquer Pensacola and was essential in assisting de Grasse in his victorious Yorktown campaign. Nathan Philbrick, *In the Hurricane's Eye: The Genius of George Washington and the Victory at Yorktown* (New York: Viking, 2018), 139–44, 150–51; Gonzalo M. Quintero Saravia, *Bernardo de Gálvez: Spanish Hero of the American Revolution* (Chapel Hill: University of North Carolina Press, 2018), 213–18.

45. José de Gálvez to Bernardo de Gálvez, El Pardo, February 12, 1781, AGI, Santo Domingo, 2083 A.

46. Saavedra, *Diario,* October 11, 1781, entry, 222–23; Bernardo de Gálvez to Juan Manuel de Cagigal, Havana, January 20, 1782, AGI, Santo Domingo, 2085.

47. Juan Ignacio de Urriza to José de Gálvez, confidential letter n. 86, Havana, January 17, 1782, AGI, Santo Domingo, 2084; Juan Manuel de Cagigal to Bernardo de Gálvez, Havana, March 14, 1782, AGI, Cuba, 1318; Juan Ignacio de Urriza to José de Gálvez, confidential official letter n. 97, Havana, April 12, 1782, AGI, Santo Domingo, 2084.

48. Juan Martin Galiano to Juan Ignacio de Urriza, New Providence, May 19, 1782, AGI, Santo Domingo, 2084. On the attack against New Providence, see the map, "Croquis de las inmediaciones a la villa de Nasso [sic Nassau] en la isla de Providencia, de su puerto y sondeo de los canales que forman su callos." Three identical copies have survived: AGI, Mapas y Planos, Santo Domingo,472; AGI, Mapas y Planos, Santo Domingo, 472bis; and AGI, Mapas y Planos, México, 388; "Mapa de la Ysla de Providencia," AGI, Mapas y Planos, Santo Domingo, 470. For more on Gillon, see Victor Enthoven, "'Sir, I have not yet begun to fight!': John Paul Jones's Friends in the Dutch Republic," in this volume.

49. Galiano to Urriza, New Providence, May 19, 1782, AGI, Santo Domingo, 2084. Captain Thomas Southey, *Chronological History of the West Indies* (London, 1827), 2:538; articles of capitulation of New Providence "Artículos de capitulación estipulados en Nassau de Nueva Providencia el 8 de mayo de 1782 entre el Excmo. sr. D. Juan Manuel de Cagigal, capitán general y comandante en jefe de La Habana y el Excmo. Sr. D. Juan Maxwell esqr. Capitán general y comandante jefe de las islas de Bahama, canciller vicealmirante y primado de dichas islas y teniente coronel del ejército de SMB," in Juan Ignacio de Urriza to José de Gálvez, letter n. 965, Havana, June 10, 1782, AGI, Santo Domingo, 2084. Juan Dabán, acting governor of Havana, to José de Gálvez, letter n. 240, Havana, May 27, 1782, AGI, Santo Domingo, 2085 B; Bernardo de Gálvez to José de Gálvez, letter n. 133, Guarico, June 30, 1782, AGI, Santo Domingo, 2085 B. For a discussion of the building and outfitting of the *South Carolina,* see D. E. Huger Smith, "Commodore Alexander Gillon and the Frigate South Carolina," *South Carolina Historical and Genealogical Magazine* 9.4 (1908): 189–219.

50. José de Gálvez to Bernardo de Gálvez, most confidential order, Aranjuez, April 6, 1782 (3rd of this date), AGI, Santo Domingo, 2084.

51. Bernardo de Gálvez to José de Gálvez, letter n. 264, Havana, June 7, 1783,

AGI, Santo Domingo, 2549; Juan Manuel de Cajigal to Bernardo de Gálvez, Havana, May 30, 1783 (version A), AGI, Santo Domingo, 2549.

52. Real Cédula, Aranjuez, May 20, 1783, BN, Mss. 10.639; Asiento de decreto de gracia a nombre de Bernardo Gálvez, sobre merced de título de Castilla para sí, sus hijos y sus sucesores, con revelación de lanzas y media annata para sola su persona, AHN, Consejos 2753, a.1783, n.4.

53. Robert Middlekauff, *The Glorious Cause: The American Revolution, 1763–1789* (New York: Oxford University Press, 1981), 606; Eliga Gould, *Among the Powers of the Earth: The American Revolution and the Making of a New World Empire* (Cambridge, MA: Harvard University Press, 2012), 133; Gregory Evans Dowd, *A Spirited Resistance: The North American Indian Struggle for Unity, 1745–1815* (Baltimore: Johns Hopkins University Press, 1992), 59–61.

54. J. H. Elliott, *Empires of the Atlantic World: Britain and Spain in America 1492–1830* (New Haven, CT: Yale University Press, 2007), 325–26, 355–63; R. R. Palmer, *The Age of the Democratic Revolution: A Political History of Europe and American, 1760–1800* (Princeton, NJ: Princeton University Press), 127–39, 285–320, 358–64.

55. Caughey, *Bernardo de Gálvez*, 252–54.

56. Gálvez's order October 11, 1785, in Eusebio Ventura Beleña, *Recopilación Sumaria de todos los autos acordados de la Real Audiencia y Sala del Crimen de esta Nueva España y providencias de su Superior Gobierno: De varias Reales Cédulas y Órdenes que, después de publicada la Recopilación de Indias, han podido recogerse, así de las dirigidas a la misma Audiencia ó Gobierno, como de algunas otras que por sus notables decisiones convendrá no ignorar* (Mexico: Felipe de Zúñiga y Ontiveros, 1787), 1–5.

57. Bernardo de Gálvez to José de Gálvez, n. 262, Mexico, October 29, 1785 (2nd of this date), AGI, Mexico, 1418.

58. *Instructions for Governing the Interior Provinces of New Spain* (Instrucción formada en virtud de Real Orden de S.M., que se dirige al señor Comandante General de las Provincias internas Don Jacobo Ugarte y Loyola para el gobierno y puntual observancia de este Superior Gefe y de sus inmediatos Subalternos, dada en México, el 26 de agosto de 1786 por el virrey de la Nueva España, Conde de Gálvez). Originals in AGI, Guadalajara, 268 y Ultramar, 714 and AGS, Guerra Moderna, 7041. Published in *Boletín del Archivo General de la Nación* 8.4 (1937): 491–540; Donald E. Worcester, ed., *Instructions for Governing the Interior Provinces of New Spain, 1786*, bilingual ed. (Berkeley: Quivira Society, 1951); and María del Carmen Velázquez Chávez, ed., *La frontera norte y la experiencia colonial* (Mexico: Secretaría de Relaciones Exteriores, 1982); David J. Weber, *The Spanish Frontier in North America* (New Haven, CT: Yale University Press, 1992), 233.

59. Caughey, *Bernardo de Gálvez*, 256–57.

60. John Black's translation of Humboldt's original French text uses "was accused," but the French orginal, "on accusa," in our opinion translates better as "has been accused" than the one offered by Black. Alexander von Humboldt, *Essai politique sur le royaume de la Nouvelle-Espagne* (Paris, 1811), 2:203. (English translation, *Political Essay on the Kingdom of New Spain,* trans. John Black [New York, 1811], 2:103.)

61. Humboldt, *Political Essay on the Kingdom of New Spain*, 2:103.

62. See Brian R. Hamnett, "Problemas interpretativos de la Independencia Mexicana," in *Visiones y revisiones de la independencia americana: México, Centroamérica y Haití*, eds. Izaskun Álvarez Cuartero and Julio Sánchez Gómez (Salamanca: Aquilafuente/Universidad de Salamanca, 2005), 77–92.

63. Andrés Cavo and Carlos María Bustamante, *Los tres siglos de México durante el gobierno español, hasta la entrada del ejército trigarante* (Mexico: Luis Abadiano y Valdés, 1836); José María Lacunza, *Discursos históricos, leídos en la Academia del Colegio de S. Juan de Letran* (Mexico: Imprenta de Ignacio Cumplido, 1845); Lucas Alamán, *Disertaciones sobre la historia de la República Mejicana desde la época de la conquista* (Mexico: Lara, 1849).

Odd Partners and Intersecting Interests
Trade and Diplomacy between Portugal and the United States during the Era of George Washington (c. 1781–1805)

TIMOTHY D. WALKER

The reaction of the Portuguese monarchy and government to the rebellion of the British colonies in North America in 1775 was mixed, shaped by the simultaneous but conflicting motivations of a profound economic interest in North American trade, an abhorrence on the part of the Portuguese Crown toward democratic rebellion against monarchical authority, and a fundamental Portuguese need to maintain a stable relationship with longtime ally Great Britain.

On the eve of the revolution the British colonies in North America, geographically well-placed to benefit commercially from Atlantic wind and currents and the proximity of cod fisheries off the New England coast, absorbed a significant volume of the Portuguese exchange with the British Empire, rising in some years to represent 15 to 20 percent of the total, with goods mainly originating from or shipped through the Madeira and Azores Islands. A number of industries within the Portuguese trade economy—in particular, Madeira wine, salt, olive oil, and citrus fruits, all produced for export—had come to depend on this trade relationship with North America. Since many Portuguese producers had invested heavily to develop goods specifically for that market, exchanged for foodstuffs on which Lisbon depended, the British colonies represented an important leg in the Portuguese network of transatlantic commerce. The escalating rebellion in Britain's North American colonies in 1775 and 1776, then, threatened to disrupt a substantial portion of this well-established and highly lucrative trade.[1]

Despite these abiding commercial interests, the Lisbon regime, led by King José and his prime minister, the marquês do Pombal, initially reacted quite strongly against the Americans' insurrection, anticolonial rhetoric, and bid for independence. Pombal asserted a position of strict neutrality in the conflict but closed all Portuguese national ports to shipping from the rebellious colonies in July 1776 and even denied assistance to American mariners in distress. When the new queen, Maria I, ascended the throne in February 1777, the Portuguese moderated their position, subtly and indirectly supporting the Continentals' cause and facilitating clandestine trade, so as not to damage the broad, long-term political and economic interests of their nation and empire.[2]

This essay examines the economic and political power relationship that developed between Portugal and the United States in the context of the American Revolution and late eighteenth-century Atlantic world, with a view toward explaining the Portuguese imperial perspective on this evolving political and economic framework and expanding the breadth of our understanding of European friends of the American Revolution. For its part, Portugal acted according to demands created by its precarious overseas empire: the need to maximize trading profits, manipulate the balance of power in Europe among nations with overseas colonies, and discourage the further spread of aspirations toward independence throughout the Americas, most notably to Portuguese-held Brazil.[3]

The Portuguese role as a fundamental player in the early modern Atlantic world is chronically underappreciated and understudied in English-language historiography. Despite the significance of Portugal as a first-tier trading partner to the American colonies, and despite the exceptional importance of the Portuguese Atlantic colonial system to British commercial and military interests in the eighteenth century, little scholarly analysis of this subject has appeared in academic journals that regularly consider imperial power dynamics in the Atlantic world or the place of the nascent United States within them.[4] This contribution, then, helps to fill a gap in the historical literature of the long eighteenth century and the Atlantic era of revolution.

Evolution of the Portuguese Position Following the Peace of 1781–1783

Earl Cornwallis's surrender of British forces at Yorktown, Virginia, on October 19, 1781, made independence for the United States virtually a foregone conclusion. But even after American and French arms had forced

George III's government to begin negotiating for a peace settlement, the Portuguese still did not consider themselves free to resume open trading with the United States. Diplomatic propriety tied their hands. Opening Portuguese ports to American merchant shipping would have been tantamount to a recognition of American sovereignty and independence. So long as the British had not officially recognized the United States, the terms of the venerable Anglo-Portuguese alliance, dating to the Treaty of Windsor (1386), prevented the Portuguese from doing so.[5] At least, that is how the Portuguese were disposed to interpret the matter; in fact, there was no clause expressly prohibiting recognition of powers at war with either of the allied partners, but the realpolitik of the situation dictated that Portugal not unnecessarily rile its principal trading partner.

Still, the prospect of renewed commerce with North America remained a compelling goal. On July 1, 1782, Benjamin Franklin quietly approached the Portuguese government again, as he had done earlier during the war, to forward a revised version of his 1777 plea requesting that their ports be opened to shipping from the United States.[6] But Lisbon continued to hesitate; having only just succumbed to Russian pressure on July 13, 1782, to join the League of Armed Neutrality, an agreement widely viewed as anti-British, the Portuguese wanted to avoid any further undermining of their position in London at the Court of Saint James.[7]

In the late fall of 1782, however, a breakthrough in Anglo-US peace negotiations in London gave the Portuguese their chance. Talks between the United States, France, Spain, and Great Britain had been in session since the previous April; by November 3 a preliminary agreement was reached under which Britain accepted the principle of American independence. Certain that a definitive treaty would shortly follow, and acting under pressure from domestic interests impatient to renew trading ties with the former English colonies, Queen Maria I issued a royal decree on February 15, 1783, reopening Portuguese ports to American shipping. The new decree, which abolished Portuguese prime minister Pombal's edict of July 4, 1776, directed that "in all ports of these realms . . . passage and entry shall be given to all ships arrived there from said Northern America . . . to enjoy there all the hospitality and favor enjoyed by the ships of other friendly nations."[8] Significantly, the queen also used this opportunity to reassert the principle of free commerce among neutral parties during times of war and to reaffirm Portugal's adherence to the policy of "armed neutrality" first promulgated by

Russia in 1780. This decree marks the Portuguese government's official recognition of an independent United States, making it only the third nation to do so, following France and the Netherlands. Portuguese recognition came more than six months prior to the official British grant of independence to their former colonies, done on September 3, 1783, with the signing of the Treaty of Paris.[9]

By remaining neutral during the American Revolution, the Portuguese achieved a great diplomatic accomplishment. Throughout the conflict they managed to stay poised on one fulcrum of a general European war, having been ringed by potentially hostile interests, and to emerge with their trade and empire intact. By acting with obvious self-interest, yet with far-sighted restraint and discipline, the Portuguese made the best out of a difficult situation, laying the groundwork for stronger diplomatic and commercial relations in Europe and the Americas and helping to promote the principle of free trade among nonbelligerent nations. This success did not go unnoticed by other Europeans. As the keenly observant English traveler William Beckford noted while visiting Portugal a few years thereafter, "During the fatal contest betwixt England and its colonies, the wise neutrality she persevered in maintaining was of the most vital benefit to her dominions, and hitherto [to 1787], the native commerce of Portugal has attained under her mild auspices an unprecedented degree of prosperity."[10]

The Portuguese-US Treaty of Commerce and Friendship (1786)

Having put the major impediment to commercial relations behind them, both the Americans and the Portuguese were eager to negotiate an accord for the regulation of trade between the two nations. The main impetus came from the US side. In Paris, Benjamin Franklin began to prepare the groundwork for a trade accord in a letter dated June 7, 1783, to Dom Vicente de Sousa Coutinho, the Portuguese minister to Versailles, in which he discussed possible points of departure for a commercial treaty.[11] Ten days later in Philadelphia, Congress passed a resolution "that the treaty with Portugal be entered on immediately," thus revealing the importance the legislature assigned to Portuguese commercial ties.[12] In early August, John Adams, representing American interests in the Netherlands, contacted the Portuguese envoy to The Hague to discuss a trade treaty; Adams invited the Portuguese to appoint an ambassador to the United States and, in return, received assurances that Lisbon had a keen interest in beginning formal commercial negotiations as well.[13]

Talks for the Luso-American trade agreement took place in a complicated political environment. The Portuguese believed that an expeditious exchange of diplomats was a prerequisite for the trade agreement. The Americans, on the other hand, for reasons stemming mostly from their domestic political situation, reversed these priorities, placing the commercial pact ahead of the exchange of ambassadors. This became a source of frustration for both sides. At the same time, both nations were caught up in a conflict with North African potentates whose corsairs preyed on their merchant shipping, a fact that drew both parties together. The American negotiators' position was hampered by political infighting at home, as their fledgling government tried to cope with the legislative and administrative limitations of the Articles of Confederation. Finally, the Portuguese position always encompassed an added dimension: the need to think in terms of their far-flung and valuable but vulnerable colonial empire, not simply the home nation. This perspective was often conspicuously lost on the Americans, based as it was on imperial exigencies that they clearly did not have.[14]

From the beginning, delays dogged the negotiations. As the United States needed to establish its first commercial agreements as a nation with several European countries simultaneously, a general committee of negotiators empowered to conduct trade talks was required. Not until May 7, 1784, was Thomas Jefferson designated to join John Adams and Benjamin Franklin in Europe, thus completing the American negotiating team. Further, Congress insisted on approving a general blueprint for all treaties with the European powers. This took over a year from the conclusion of the peace; a copy of the model treaty did not reach the Portuguese negotiator in Paris, Dom Vicente de Sousa Coutinho, until December 1784. Of course, the real problem lay in the Congress itself, struggling to govern under the Articles of Confederation. The intrigues of regional and ideological factions, combined with the inadequacies of the Articles, had severely impeded the US politicians' ability to conduct business in the national legislature. One result was that the United States had difficulty in putting forth a cogent foreign policy, including the organization of international accords and the dispatch of representatives abroad. The Portuguese were aware of this disarray, courtesy of what Benjamin Franklin called "false and exaggerated reports of the distracted situation of our government" planted by British propagandists.

Franklin thought this accounted for Portuguese foot-dragging at the trade talks in Paris. Actually, the delay in Lisbon was due more to Queen Maria and her ministers' impatience at the Americans' failure to send a diplomat to Portugal.[15]

The Lisbon government, however, was also displeased with the pace of the negotiations, assigning part of the blame to its own minister, conde de Sousa Coutinho. If Thomas Jefferson's assessment is to be believed—Jefferson called him "a torpid, uninformed machine"—then the Portuguese were not wrong to blame him; in any case, given Jefferson's comments, the talks may have slowed or soured because of personal discord among participants.[16] In October 1785 Coutinho was ordered back to Lisbon and Luís Pinto de Sousa was designated as the new negotiator. This shifted the location of the talks to London, where Pinto de Sousa was posted.

Finally, on November 4, 1785, the two key negotiators, Pinto de Sousa and John Adams, met in London to discuss objectives and concerns. (Jefferson, still in Paris, was kept informed by post until he could arrive in person.) The Portuguese minister indicated that his government most desired to import grain, barrel staves and construction timber, masts and spars, pitch, potash, hides, ginseng, and, above all, salted codfish from the United States. Adams replied that the Americans wanted, primarily, wines from Madeira, Oporto, and Carcavelos (a wine region near Lisbon), as well as fruits, olive oil, and salt. Early complications arose because the Portuguese did not wish to import American spermaceti whale oil, since Portugal possessed abundant sources of this product.[17] Also, the Portuguese had hoped that the Americans would take their Brazilian cotton, woolens, and sugar, as well as teas from Asia, but the Americans, perhaps hoping to gain direct access to trade ports in Brazil and being well supplied with tea and sugar by the Dutch, replied that they would normally buy those products only under special circumstances, usually for reexport elsewhere.[18]

Insistent American demands for Portuguese concessions created a greater obstacle. First, because unground cereals ran a much higher risk of spoiling during transport, Adams and Jefferson hoped to pressure the Portuguese into accepting shipments of prepared flour. Needful of protecting their domestic mills, however, the Portuguese resisted repeated American attempts to foist their flour on the Lisbon market.[19]

Second and more significantly, the Americans hoped to negotiate a treaty with the Portuguese that would, as perhaps its main objective, open direct trade between the United States and colonial Brazil. The Portuguese found such a proposition simply too risky. The specter of American interlopers, advantageously situated geographically and with a greater tonnage of merchant ships at their disposal to drain away trade profits, loomed very large in the Portuguese assessment of the matter.[20] Even worse, officials in Lisbon worried that the presence of American seamen loudly espousing the virtues of independence and democracy would serve as a catalyst for Brazilians to stage their own rebellion. The Portuguese correctly foresaw that they stood to lose Brazil altogether.

Free American commercial navigation to Brazil, then, was never open to negotiation. On August 1, 1783, during the opening stages of diplomatic maneuvering, when John Adams, then American representative in The Hague, broached this subject to the resident Portuguese ambassador, he had received a cool lecture on the complete impossibility of the proposition. Such a concession had never been granted to any foreign potentate, Ambassador João de Almeida explained. He continued by pointing out that not even the British, with whom the Portuguese had signed extraordinary trade accords, were allowed access to Brazil.[21] It would take a long while for the Americans to realize that they would never conduct trade legally in Brazil while the Portuguese still ruled there.

As it turned out, the Portuguese had justifiable grounds for concern. In particular, they soon had reason to suspect the motives of Thomas Jefferson, whom Brazilian revolutionaries twice contacted seeking American assistance in a bid for independence. Both encounters occurred in Paris while Jefferson was serving as US envoy to Versailles. In 1786 José Maia e Barbello, who had been educated in Portugal at the University of Coimbra and went by the enigmatic alias "Vendek," told Jefferson that he and his coconspirators wanted to emulate the United States and sever ties with their mother country. Jefferson conveyed a congenial enthusiasm for the ideals of liberty, but when confronted with a direct request for US aid, Jefferson demurred. The Americans hoped to remain isolated from Europe's quarrels while benefitting from Old World trade; Jefferson therefore responded that a conflict with Portugal was not in the interests of the United States.[22]

Three years later, in 1789, when the incipient French Revolution once more inspired Brazilian patriots to action, Jefferson was contacted again. This time his response was more encouraging. A Brazilian medical student at Montpellier, France, José Joaquim da Maia Montenegro, claimed to have obtained a promise from Jefferson of US support for the independence of Brazil. At least, that is what Montenegro reported to his comrades in Minas Gerais, where the news caused great excitement and helped to incite the rebellious uprising of 1789 known as the Inconfidência Mineira.[23]

Although the "Inconfidence" at Minas Gerais failed, Brazilians continued to admire the Americans' democratic principles and the successful revolution those principles had inspired. A steadily growing independence movement in Brazil remained a serious preoccupation for the Portuguese well into the nineteenth century, when their fears became a reality. Two further revolts, known respectively as the Inconfidência Baiana and the Inconfidência Pernambucana, shook the colony in 1798 and 1801.[24] The Portuguese colonial administration tried to quell these aspirations with every means available. To inhibit the flow of ideas, no free printing press was allowed in Brazil until 1807. A special police unit in Lisbon kept detailed files on potential revolutionaries—even future Portuguese ambassador to the United States Abbade José Corrêa da Serra was put under surveillance, suspected as a *jacobino* for being a friend of Thomas Jefferson.[25] Mostly, however, the Lisbon regime tried to staunch the influx of disruptive democratic influences by simply prohibiting direct trade between the United States and Brazil.

In the end, the Americans were forced to accept the unyielding Portuguese positions concerning flour and Brazil. The final version of the first Luso-American Treaty of Commerce and Friendship was signed in London on April 25, 1786. By its very title (in Portuguese, Tratado de Comércio e Amizade), this agreement clearly ranked commercial interests first and friendship as a subsidiary concern. Of the document's twenty-eight articles, twenty involve commercial provisions directly—codifying regulations for trade, establishing consulates, pledging reciprocal most-favored-nation status—while two stipulate further rules for safeguarding goods and merchants in case of an armed conflict.[26]

One noteworthy aspect of the treaty, however, demonstrates an uncommon concern for the common good: Article 24, mandating the humane treatment of prisoners in time of war. By far the longest provision of the treaty, Article 24 stated that prisoners should be well fed, housed comfortably according to their status, and repatriated expeditiously. Further, the accord expressly forbade sending prisoners to "the East Indies, or any other parts of Asia, or Africa," reflecting an aversion at the long-established Portuguese practice of shipping convicts and captives to labor in the colonies of those regions. For the time, this provision was unique; contemporary statesmen on both sides of the Atlantic recognized in it a new level of enlightened relations between nations. Taken together with Article 23, which provided for the protection of resident foreign merchants, their families, and their goods in case of war, the Americans and Portuguese had pioneered a virtually unprecedented human rights standard in an international agreement. As Portuguese negotiator Luís Pinto de Sousa noted with clear admiration in his report on the treaty to his superiors, "These articles are new in the order of public Stipulations; but their principles are very just, and very advantageous for humanity, and it was in our best interests that I not try to change their form."[27]

With the trade treaty signed, the Portuguese focused their US policy on arranging for an exchange of diplomatic representatives between Lisbon and the United States. Without such an exchange, the Portuguese had little inclination to ratify the treaty. This was something Jefferson and Adams understood very well, but the US Congress remained in disarray, willing neither to send a minister to Lisbon nor ratify the treaty.

Meanwhile, in the midst of negotiations concerning the trade treaty, both nations' merchant ships had become subject to attack by Algerian corsairs, but under different circumstances. Naturally, after establishing their independence, the erstwhile American colonials could no longer expect to enjoy the protection of the British Royal Navy under which they had navigated without fear of North African aggression. But the new United States lacked warships to protect its merchant fleet, and, after the Peace of Paris in 1783, no European power was interested in providing such protection.

The Algerian corsairs had been kept at bay for a while by two joint naval expeditions conducted by Malta, Naples, Spain, and Portugal in 1783 and 1784. In 1785, however, the Spanish negotiated a separate peace with Algeria, necessitating the annual payment of a substantial bribe, euphemistically termed a "subsidy," to the Barbary rulers. Portugal attended these negotiations but refused to make peace by paying a bribe. With the most powerful naval force thus removed from the fleet of the allied powers, the Algerians were once again able to cause substantial damage in the Mediterranean and along the Iberian coast. During 1785 and 1786, Portugal and the United States suffered painful losses to the pirates from Algiers: the Portuguese had to ransom thirteen ships and 125 passengers and crewmen, while the Americans lost several ships, including some off the Portuguese coast. On July 24,

1785, the merchantman *Maria* from Boston was taken near the Cape of Saint Vincent; six days later, the *Dauphin* out of Philadelphia was taken eighty miles northwest of Setúbal.[28]

In response to these losses, the United States sent representative John Lamb to Algiers to see if a negotiated settlement was possible, but the Algerians predictably demanded another bribe. The Portuguese, for their part, reacted with greater martial vigor, preparing a powerful fleet that they planned to send the following year, 1786, to patrol the Strait of Gibraltar and the North African coast.[29] While the trade treaty negotiations and the issue of an exchange of diplomatic representatives were still in limbo, American envoy to Spain John Jay believed that the United States might profitably enter a military alliance with the Portuguese against the Barbary States. Although Adams wanted to pay the bribe, Jefferson concurred with Jay's idea, hoping that an exchange of diplomats and a combined military venture would smooth the way for the Luso-American trade accord. Jay therefore put forward his recommendation that Congress dispatch a representative to the Lisbon court immediately to begin work on this plan. Unfortunately, Congress, preoccupied with domestic squabbles, deferred the matter for later consideration.[30]

Meanwhile, in Lisbon, the Portuguese were growing increasingly impatient with the Americans' seeming disregard for diplomatic etiquette. Hoping to influence the United States government favorably and hasten the exchange of representatives, Queen Maria ordered her Mediterranean war fleet to protect American-flagged merchantmen on an equal basis with her own subjects' vessels. Word of this benevolent act reached the American Congress through John Jay on September 26, 1786, but the government of the United States, preoccupied with Shays' Rebellion, did not respond with an official message of gratitude until February 3, 1787. Because the Portuguese still had not approved the commercial treaty, William Stephens Smith, secretary of the American delegation in London, traveled to Lisbon via Paris and Madrid to deliver the letter personally to Queen Maria.[31]

A greater disappointment to the Portuguese queen than the tardiness of the US reply was Congress's continued refusal to send a permanent diplomatic envoy to Lisbon. Smith was well received in Lisbon, but the prime minister, Martinho de Mello e Castro, stonewalled him when he tried to discover why the trade deal negotiated so painstakingly in London had not been approved in Lisbon. Mello e Castro would only reveal that the queen had carefully gone over the agreement, had some doubts about the text, and felt that carrying on negotiations in London through representatives there was "not the best way" to conclude the accord. Mello e Castro then became frank: the queen desired a direct exchange of ministers between the two nations' capitals. Smith apparently missed the significance of this cue. Without realizing the impact his remarks would have, he divulged that Congress was considering the dispatch of a representative, but only at the level of *chargé d'affaires*. Smith then moved quickly on to inquire about what doubts and observations the Queen had about the text of the trade agreement. The Prime Minister, further exasperated by this unexpected news, avoided the question.[32]

Later, after Smith's brief audience with the Queen, Mello e Castro invited him for an intimate walk and conversation in the royal palace's impressive artillery park. He returned to the matter of the commercial treaty, mentioning the need to review some of the negotiated clauses, but emphasizing the necessity of an exchange of ministers at a higher level than simply *encarregado de negócios* (*chargé d'affaires*). Courtiers in Lisbon remarked on this unusual display of attention shown to Smith. The French ambassador, the marquis de Bombelles, observed that by accepting the Americans and wanting to move closer to them diplomatically, Maria I was setting a new foreign policy path for Portugal, distancing herself from the traditional deference shown to English policy goals. Mello e Castro, too, realized that the United States was a rising power of great potential within the Atlantic world. Closer ties with the Americans, he reasoned, could serve to counterbalance the exceptional—even excessive—economic and political influence Great Britain wielded in Portugal.[33]

Still, progress did not come quickly. In London on September 7, 1787, John Adams received a note from Luís Pinto de Sousa saying that, in view of the fact that no response had come from the United States about concluding the commercial accord, the Portuguese government was not especially interested either, but that it would be "very convenient" if both countries would name reciprocal diplomatic representatives with the grade, at least, of resident minister, so that the trade matter could be sorted out. Congress still intended to send only a *chargé d'affaires,* a policy that the legislature defended on financial grounds. Having shown the United States exceptional favor by rapidly recognizing their independence and providing free protection against the Barbary pirates, the Portuguese considered this behavior a severe affront.[34]

Luso-American relations languished at this impasse for nearly three years; the situation could not be improved until the new American Constitution had been ratified, laying the foundations for a more efficient, effective foreign policy.[35] In Lisbon, the *Gazeta de Lisboa* covered these developments in the United States closely. The front page of the June 5, 1789, edition, for example, reported George Washington's election as first president under the new Constitution, described the ratification process, and explained some of the differences between the new federal system and the old Articles of Confederation. On October 10 that year, the *Gazeta* published translations of the "most interesting articles of the new Constitution" for those Portuguese citizens who had "a commercial interest in the *nova Republica Americana*." Predictably, censors of the democracy-averse Portuguese government did not permit editor Félix António Castrioto to reprint the proposed Bill of Rights; rather, he included only those articles pertaining to the regulation of trade, the collection of duties and taxes, and the minting of coinage.[36]

First Exchange of Diplomatic Representatives

With George Washington inaugurated as president on April 30, 1789, and Thomas Jefferson confirmed as his secretary of state shortly thereafter, the new government of the United States was finally in a position to strengthen diplomatic ties with Portugal. Jefferson wrote on August 7, 1790, to Portuguese ambassador Luís Pinto de Sousa, whom he had come to know well in London during negotiations for the commercial accord five years before. Insisting that this contact was personal rather than official, Jefferson penned an extraordinary letter to his former colleague in which he sought to explain and apologize for the difficulties the United States had had in appointing a diplomat to the court in Lisbon. He then offered a new proposal for an exchange of representatives:

> The history of our first experiment in government . . . [resulted in] a want of such tone in the governing powers, as might effect the good of those committed to their care. The nation, become sensible of this, have changed it's [*sic*] organisation, made a better distribu-

tion of it's powers, and given to them more energy & independence. The new government has now for some time been under way: & so far gives a confidence that it will answer it's purposes. . . . at such a distance from Europe, & with such an ocean between us, we hope to meddle little in it's quarrels or combinations; it's peace and commerce are what we shall court; and to cultivate these, we propose to place at the courts of Europe most interesting to us diplomatic characters of economical grade, and shall be glad to receive like ones in exchange. The important commerce carried on between your country and ours, and the proofs of friendly disposition towards us which her majesty has manifested, induce us to wish for such an exchange with her, to express our sensibility at the intimations heretofore recieved [sic] of her readiness to meet our wish in this point, & our regret at the delay which has proceeded from the circumstances before touched on.[37]

Jefferson went on to request that the United States be allowed to send only a *chargé d'affaires* to Portugal, citing the need for thrift as well as the fact that the Spanish court had accepted an American envoy of that rank without difficulty.

The messenger Jefferson chose to deliver this letter was David Humphreys, who had served in London in the 1780s as secretary of the trade accord negotiating team; consequently, he also knew Pinto de Sousa. Upon his arrival in London, Humphreys was astonished to learn that de Sousa had returned to Lisbon as the newly named prime minister and that the Portuguese government had already designated an envoy to the United States with the rank of resident minister. Moreover, the man chosen for this job was none other than Humphreys's former counterpart in the trade negotiations, Cipriano Ribeiro Freire. In view of the situation, Humphreys informed his superiors about the turn of events, wrote a letter of introduction for his old colleague, Freire, to present to President Washington, and then hurried on to Lisbon to meet with Sousa.[38]

Once in Lisbon, Humphreys spoke with the prime minister on November 25, 1790. After some deliberation and consultation with the cabinet, Pinto de Sousa informed the American envoy that diplomatic protocol dictated that representatives of both nations must be of equal rank; the Portuguese would not accept an American *chargé d'affaires* once they had already dispatched a diplomat of higher rank to the United States. Humphreys duly informed Washington and Jefferson of the dilemma, who decided to solve the problem pragmatically by nominating Humphreys to be the US resident minister to Portugal on February 18, 1791. Jefferson prepared a message that Washington directed to Congress explaining the peculiar circumstances; he expressed his wish that the Portuguese regime not be offended and pressed for Humphreys's confirmation at the same rank as Cipriano Ribeiro Freire. The weight of Washington's authority was enough to quiet any opposition; the Senate confirmed Humphreys's nomination on February 21. On May 1, 1791, the American envoy officially learned about his new post. Twelve days later, Humphreys presented his credentials to the queen and court.[39] He would remain the US envoy in Lisbon for the next six years.

Humphreys was a worthy diplomat with long experience abroad; nevertheless, he was something of a novice in his new role as representative to a European court. On the day before his royal audience to present his credentials to Maria I, Humphreys wrote a personal letter to his former colleague, Luís Pinto de Sousa, asking the prime minister for help with directions inside the queen's residence and assistance in overcoming problems Humphreys worried would arise because of his inability to speak Portuguese or French.[40] Pinto de Sousa handled this minor irregularity of protocol with good humor, dispatching an assistant to make sure that the US minister arrived on time to meet the queen.

Humphreys's diplomatic credential, bearing the signatures of Washington and Jefferson, spoke of the desire to "promote a friendly and useful Intercourse" between the United States and Portugal.[41] Luso-American commercial links continued to expand during the 1790s, though the potential volume of this trade was checked due to the wars of the French Revolution and Napoleon, when neutral shipping in the Atlantic Ocean experienced great security hazards from combatants on all sides.

On February 1, 1793, as a consequence of the radical turn of the French Revolution and the beheading of Louis XVI, France declared war on Great Britain, the United Provinces, and Spain. George Washington declared that the United States would remain neutral but carry on trading with the warring parties. Britain refused to recognize the American position, ordering the Royal Navy to seize US merchantmen coming from France. The British also encouraged the Barbary pirates to attack American shipping, falsely informing the Algerians that the Portuguese, who had entered the European coalition against revolutionary France and had drawn off their fleet to transport a Portuguese expeditionary force to engage in the Pyrennees campaign, had rescinded their policy of protecting US ships.[42] In March 1793 David Humphreys was dispatched to Algiers to negotiate with the North African princes. He got as far as Gibraltar, where he heard to his dismay (falsely as it turned out) that Algiers and Lisbon had concluded a peace accord. Hoping to create a rift between Portugal and the United States, the English had lied to Humphreys, as well. The Portuguese fleet soon returned to patrol the Barbary Coast and offer protection to US ships, but not before eleven American vessels and 105 crewmen had been taken prisoner.[43]

The Lisbon regime deeply regretted these events and was angry at having been compromised in a British intrigue. Humphreys understood what had happened and acted quickly to avoid tension over the incident. Once back in Lisbon, he submitted a gracious letter to Prime Minister Luís Pinto de Sousa, dated March 8, 1794, confirming the "infinite satisfaction" of "the President & people of the United States" over Portuguese efforts to protect American shipping from the Barbary potentates. The letter went on to propose a joint naval venture against this common enemy and ended by reaffirming the long-standing "friendly and commercial ties" between Portugal and the United States.[44] Cool-headed diplomacy, and overriding economic and political interests, had prevented a potential break in Luso-American relations.

Meanwhile, Portuguese minister Cipriano Ribeiro Freire had not yet arrived in the United States, having been delayed in London by the war with France. He wrote to his superiors that, due to Britain's refusal to honor American neutrality, hostilities threatened and commercial traffic had been suspended between the two nations. Therefore, Freire had exceptional difficulty in finding safe passage across the Atlantic for himself and his family.[45]

After a tempestuous voyage, Freire eventually arrived in New York on September 14, 1794. He set out immediately for the federal capital, Philadelphia, but an outbreak of yellow fever had closed the port, so Freire was compelled to return to New York until October 9. When he did finally manage to disembark in Philadelphia on October 13, 1794, he found that President Washington was in western Pennsylvania, leading troops against rural farmers who had taken up arms against a tax on distilled spirits. Freire revealed in his diplomatic correspondence that he was deeply impressed with Washington's personal handling of the Whiskey Rebellion, noting with approval the president's resolution in this early test of federal power.[46]

Washington returned to Philadelphia on October 29, 1794; the following day Freire presented the president with his diplomatic credentials. The Portuguese ambassador, long used to the formality of European royalty, was favorably impressed with the relative congenial simplicity of the reception given him by American officials. Freire was seated to Washington's right, in a chair, he noted, that was the equal of the president's. In a further measure of respect, Freire observed that Secretary of State Edmund Randolph's chair was positioned to the left but at a greater distance from the other two.[47]

Washington began by stating forthrightly that the American republic "reciprocates the sentiments of friendship and cordial disposition which Her Portuguese Majesty has shown to the United States." He continued, saying that the queen's "highest virtues inspired veneration" and that "her recognition in America was great because of her protection of American ships from the Algerians." The president concluded by saying that Freire's arrival was "a happy circumstance for the whole nation."[48] Freire felt that he had made a good first impression and that Washington's intentions were sincere.

The following day, Freire's wife, Eulália Carolina Freire, was presented to Martha Washington at her usual Friday afternoon drawing room gathering. The president attended, too, and spent the greater part of the evening in conversation with Freire. The Portuguese ambassador thought this was a good sign but highly unusual, as he had heard that Washington was known for saying little and keeping to himself on these occasions. Freire reported that the special attention shown him "was much remarked upon" by the rest of the assembled company.[49] Encouraged by such auspicious beginnings, Freire settled in to his diplomatic duties.

One of Cipriano Freire's first concerns as Portuguese envoy to the United States was to report on the United States' position in the ongoing conflict between France and England. Freire observed in the early autumn of 1794, before meeting with President Washington, that most Americans in important government positions favored France. However, he was careful to point out that this sympathy for the French cause reflected a practical fear of Britain's enormous maritime power. "The forces of France occupy the forces of England," Freire wrote, "the advantages of which accrue to the U.S., because the U.S. is thereby freed from the force of her [England's] oppressive attentions." That, he reported, was "the fundamental point of the American policy, which in turn aims to free her commerce and navigation from interruption by England." Freire observed that few Americans seemed to be emotionally aligned with the French cause and that "those few republicans who do risk the speculation of sending munitions & stores to France, do so only because they can obtain hard specie for their pains . . . and this activity is done without the formal disapproval of the American Government."[50]

For all the turmoil in Europe caused by the French Revolution and subsequent Napoleonic Wars, the Portuguese diplomatic mission in the United States remained focused primarily on trade issues. Unfortunately for Portugal, with the rising French threat on the continent and the advent of Napoleon's military aggression in the Iberian Peninsula, the Portuguese found themselves caught between two potent camps in a European power struggle with global implications. The Lisbon regime had grown accustomed to living under reliable British protection through the centuries-old Anglo-Portuguese alliance. Portugal thus had virtually no standing army and only a small fleet of capital warships. Vulnerable to French invasion overland through Spain and without adequate resources to defend either their shipping routes or their valuable far-flung colonies, the only reasonable Portuguese recourse was to turn to Britain to defend national security, eventually through direct military intervention during the costly Peninsular campaigns fought between 1807 and 1814.[51]

Growth of Luso-American Trade during the Age of Washington

Following the signing of the Luso-American peace and trade treaty in 1786 and an exchange of diplomatic representatives, the final fifteen years of the eighteenth century saw an ever-expanding volume of trade between the two nations. Tables of ship arrivals to Lisbon harbor, systematically reported in the *Gazeta de Lisboa*, help tell the story: in 1788 the United States, entering with 65 merchantmen, ranked fifth among Portuguese trading partners, following Denmark with 67, the Dutch with 92, France with 161, and England with 357. Two years later, the Americans ranked a close third with 84 ships, just one fewer than the Dutch; the French meanwhile dropped to fourth place with 62 ships, and the British still dominated with 364. The United States held a steady share of the Lisbon trade through 1798; with 95 ships, the Americans ranked fourth behind the Swedes and the Danes, with 181 and 116 merchant vessels, respectively, while the British figure of nearly 500 still led by a wide margin.[52]

While this commerce clearly benefited Portuguese wine merchants, salt producers, citrus exporters, and shippers of goods from the Asian colonies, a severe trade imbalance favored the United States, which exported mainly grain and flour, salted fish, and shipbuilding supplies to Portugal. As early as the summer of 1789, a Portuguese agent in New York wrote to Martinho de Mello e Castro, Secretary of State for Foreign Relations, warning him about new US navigation laws that would put Portuguese merchants at a disadvantage. One Portuguese historian who rigorously examined his nation's external commerce during this period calculated that between 1796 and 1807 the value of American goods entering Portugal was 10,202,011$352 *escudos,* while the Portuguese exported only 5,888,239$037 *escudos'* worth of goods to the United States, amounting to a deficit of nearly two to one and an approximate shortfall of $6.6 million contemporary dollars. The overall national balance of trade remained in Portugal's favor, however—large export surpluses to England, Germany, Italy, and France made good these losses—so the North American deficit was of no great concern.[53] Moreover, the Lisbon government was soon to be too preoccupied with affairs developing in Europe to reopen trade negotiations with the United States, so commerce continued under the terms of the 1786 agreement (which, as events transpired, the US Senate would never formally ratify).

Nevertheless, the Ministério dos Negócios Estrangeiros kept a steady watch over trade developments with the United States, fostering growth in some markets and trying to minimize circumstances wherein commercial exchange was unfavorable. Every year during his tenure, Cipriano Freire prepared a chart of goods imported into the United States from Portugal. He carefully enumerated each product—wine, salt, spirits, cheese, coffee, cotton, wax, coal, soap, pepper, shoes, bindings, and cordage—recorded its point of origin and value in dollars, and remitted this information with his official annual report to Lisbon.[54] The Portuguese government also gathered such information in more clandestine ways. In 1794, Freire's first year of residence in Philadelphia, a confidential memorandum from an unknown American source revealed that US exports to Portugal had grown to a value of nearly one million dollars in 1793, an extraordinary sum at the time.[55]

Increased trade naturally led to consideration of expanding the official

Portuguese presence in the United States. Toward the end of 1794, Cipriano Freire sent a memorandum about the port wine trade to Luís Pinto de Sousa (then serving as both prime minister and secretary of state for war and foreign relations in Lisbon), outlining his opinions on the advantages of establishing an office of the Companhia Geral do Alto Douro, the state monopoly organization responsible for the regulation and promotion of port wine sales, in the United States. Order and shipping records from wine merchants in Oporto and Madeira bear out the contemporary impression that demand for this commodity had expanded markedly since the American War for Independence. As a result, the Lisbon government did open a second diplomatic consulate in New York City, which began operations in late 1795. Four additional Portuguese consulates opened during the 1820s in Boston, New Orleans, Baltimore, and Norfolk.[56]

As the young republic's economy flourished, the Portuguese began to conduct their diplomatic affairs with a view toward gaining American knowledge, workers, or indigenous plants that could be put to use in the Portuguese Empire. For example, Dom Rodrigo de Sousa Coutinho, Minister and Secretary of State for the navy and overseas colonies, directed that Freire send samples of Virginia and Maryland tobacco seeds to Portuguese Africa and Brazil. Freire also contracted with American merchant Peter Tilly to transport the first seeds for Cayenne pepper from North America to the Brazilian province of Pará.[57]

In an attempt to draw skilled whalemen away from Nantucket, New Bedford, and the New England coast for service in the Portuguese whaling fleet, it became Queen Maria's policy, beginning in 1798, to rapidly naturalize those mariners if they signed aboard a Portuguese-flagged vessel, thus giving them some measure of protection against British impressment but also compelling them to remain in the service of the Portuguese crown.[58] Also in 1798, Freire received word from his superiors that a Portuguese agent, the university-trained Hipólito José da Costa Pereira, was to be sent on a journey through the United States and Mexico specifically to gather information about local manufacturing techniques, cultivation, and agricultural products. He was followed in 1812 by the famous naturalist Abbade José Corrêa da Serra, a valued friend of Thomas Jefferson who became the Portuguese envoy to Washington, DC, in 1816.[59]

Facilitating trade and innovation, however, were not Cipriano Freire's only concerns during his tenure in the United States. He also followed

US foreign policy issues, particularly those that pertained to territorial claims on the frontier. For example, Freire corresponded with British diplomats about the forts England continued to garrison along the United States' northwest border, passing information to Lisbon about the Americans' attitudes and his own opinion about how to proceed in this dispute.[60]

The Portuguese minister also took a keen interest in American policy toward Native American peoples. In 1795 Freire forwarded to Lisbon translations of the peace treaties signed during the previous year between the United States and the Cherokee Nation, the Six Nations, and the Oneida, Tuscarora, and Stockbridge Indians. In his accompanying report, Freire was much impressed by the United States government's "peaceful system" and "sincere effort" to "civilize" the Native Americans, but he noted that constant tension and bloodshed on the frontier threatened to undermine what Freire saw as a manifestly humane official policy.[61]

Monitoring illegal Portuguese immigration to the United States also became part of Freire's duties. Portuguese sailors regularly jumped ship in American harbors, seeking better working conditions on Yankee vessels. As trained *marinheiros* were in chronically short supply in Portugal, the Lisbon regime was worried that a serious drain would develop in this valuable labor pool. Seeking a possible diplomatic solution, Freire provided information about US naturalization regulations to his superiors at the Ministerio dos Negócios Estrangeiros.[62] Given the openness of the American policy—sailors were valuable in the United States, as well—and with no way to effectively police American harbors, Freire could do little to correct the matter.

After 1795, until his departure from Portugal on July 25, 1797, the American minister in Lisbon concerned himself primarily with trade issues as well.[63] Prior to Humphreys's departure, Congress had confirmed the nomination of John Quincy Adams as the new American representative in Lisbon. Mirroring the strengthened ties between Portugal and the United States, Adams was given the highest possible diplomatic rank, that of minister plenipotentiary. Adams never arrived to take up his duties, however. His father, John Adams, newly elected president of the United States, recalled him from London for service with the federal government in Philadelphia and subsequently posted him to Berlin as the US ambassador to Prussia.[64]

Adams's replacement was William Loughton Smith, from Charleston, South Carolina, who had spent most of his early life studying abroad. On

July 10, 1797, Adams appointed him to the post of minister plenipotentiary to Portugal.[65] As with his predecessor, the majority of Smith's work in Lisbon involved mediating trade issues. The Americans still hoped to win free access for their flour to the Portuguese market; this served as the catalyst for Smith to propose negotiations toward a second trade agreement between the two nations. (The 1786 trade accord had never been ratified, due mostly to the intervening wars with France, but both sides honored the terms of the agreement.) Since the Portuguese were becoming increasingly concerned about their growing trade deficit with the United States, they welcomed the initiative. Smith was obliged to return to the United States, however, before negotiations could get underway as concerns over the escalating conflict in Europe occupied both governments.[66]

William Loughton Smith spent exactly four years as the American minister plenipotentiary in Portugal; he left Lisbon on September 8, 1801, the anniversary of his arrival in 1797. His tenure was cut short because of domestic politics in the United States. With Jefferson's election to the presidency in 1800, Federalist supporters were suddenly out of favor, and Smith was consequently called home. For the next nine years, during which time Portugal endured an invasion by the French and the entire royal family and court decamped *en masse* to Brazil, the American ambassador's post in Lisbon remained vacant. Only on June 7, 1810, did Thomas Sumpter Jr. arrive in Rio de Janeiro—maintaining the rank of minister plenipotentiary—to renew the United States' diplomatic presence with the Portuguese government.[67]

On July 27, 1798, Cipriano Ribeiro Freire, citing concerns for his health, requested reassignment and a year's leave of absence. His government approved the petition, and Freire left Philadelphia on April 7, 1799, arriving in Lisbon via London in January 1800. No new Portuguese envoy was named to the United States until 1805.[68] The American government does not seem to have officially marked Freire's departure at the time. Six years later, however, once the new Portuguese *chargé d'affaires*, José Rademaker, had arrived in Washington, President Jefferson took the occasion to send a letter eulogizing Freire to the royal court in Rio de Janeiro. Addressing the prince regent, Dom João, Jefferson spoke of the "distinguished prudence, intelligence, and activity, displayed in your service by the Chevalier Cipriano Ribeiro Freire." Jefferson noted "with great satisfaction that his merits have attracted [the prince regent's] notice and bounty."[69]

The "Permanent" Grant of Land for a Portuguese Embassy Building in Washington, DC

By 1797 warming diplomatic relations between the United States and Portugal during the preceding years had convinced the Adams administration that this nation should be the recipient of a choice location on which to build facilities for its diplomatic mission in the new capitol city being built on the banks of the Potomac River. In late spring of that year, Cipriano Freire sent word to his superiors in Lisbon that the American government had offered to provide a plot of land for the construction of a residence for Portuguese ministers to the United States. He enclosed a map of the District of Columbia street plan, showing his suggested locations for the building, and requested instructions on how to respond to this unexpected proposal.[70]

The Lisbon government responded with enthusiasm for the project. On September 21, 1797, Dom Luís Pinto de Sousa, Prime Minister and Secretary of State for foreign affairs, wrote that the queen desired to accept the offer and instructed Freire to proceed by selecting a site and having plans for the building drawn up. In a gesture of respect for the values embodied in the young republic, the residence was to be built "comfortably" but "without luxury."[71]

At the time, of course, the US capital was little more than a collection of lines on a surveyor's map. The United States government would not take up residence there officially until December 1800, and even then, the most essential buildings were still generally in the planning stages. (As late as 1816, the relative vastness of L' Enfant's plan superimposed on largely undeveloped fields prompted Portugal's ambassador, Abbade José Corrêa da Serra, to endow Washington with the enduring epithet, "the city of magnificent distances."[72])

Land, then, was abundant. Moreover, given continued heavy Luso-American trade and dona Maria I's policy of protecting American merchantmen from Algerian corsairs (both of which continued into the nineteenth century, until effectively ended by the Peninsular War and French invasion of Portugal in 1807), American goodwill toward Portugal was high. Freire made the most of the situation: when American officials charged with arranging embassy locations within the new capital requested that he choose a location for the Portuguese residence, he picked a place of honor on "President's Square," immediately accessible to the planned Executive Mansion. John

Adams's commissioners, Gustavus Scott, William Thornton, and Alexander White, were happy to comply and approved the site with little deliberation. On May 31, 1798, the president signed and sealed the indenture officially granting the land to the Queen of Portugal "for the use and purpose of a residence for the Minister of her said Majesty, her Heirs and Successors forever."[73] Cipriano Freire received the indenture upon the symbolic payment of one United States dollar.

The Portuguese had merited a particularly impressive state gesture. The site eventually chosen for this unprecedented gift was a prime lot on the square today known as the Ellipse, between the White House and the Washington Monument. The rectangular plot boasted 281 feet of frontage along the east side of 17th Street NW and extended 319 feet east into the square adjacent to the Executive Mansion. In 1797 this area was actually waterfront property, being just north of the wharves near the point where the Tiber Creek entered the Potomac River.[74]

During his last months as resident minister to the United States, Freire worked closely on the ambassador's residence project. He engaged English architect George Hatfield to design the building (proudly reporting to his superiors that Hatfield was the director and superintendent of all construction works in the new capital city), settled details of the construction budget, and sent updated maps of Washington to Lisbon with annotations marking the project's progress.[75]

The planned residence was, of course, never built. The Portuguese royal family continued to reside in Rio de Janeiro, causing growing discontent in the home country. In the wake of an antiabsolutist *coup d'état* by constitutionalists in 1820, followed by the Brazilian independence crisis (in which privateers from the United States played an active role), and a civil war in Portugal from 1828 to 1834 (the dynastic War of the Two Brothers), diplomatic relations between the two nations grew more strained. After Ambassador Corrêa da Serra's tenure as minister plenipotentiary from 1816 to 1820, there was no Portuguese representative in Washington above the rank of *chargé d'affairs* until 1840, and no full minister plenipotentiary again until 1854.[76] During this rocky period, voices in Congress began to question whether it was appropriate for the Portuguese to have been given such a prominent position near the White House. More importantly, as Washington slowly developed into a bustling center of government, the sheer value of the Portuguese claim became more apparent. Eventually, Congress challenged the legality of President Adams's grant of the land, charging that the president's commissioners had exceeded their authority. By 1851, after a good deal of diplomatic correspondence contesting the issue, the Portuguese government abandoned their pursuit of the matter.[77]

Thus, after exercising an independent neutrality during the American War for Independence, the Portuguese had renewed their relationship with the United States during the late eighteenth and the beginning of the nineteenth century on the same terms and with the same goals as they had always had: Portugal continued to act according to the demands of its overseas empire, with an eye toward maximizing trading profits, manipulating the balance of power in Europe among nations with overseas colonies, maintaining a judicious neutrality, and discouraging the further spread of ideas or movements which might encourage independence for Brazil. But the two nations, one a republic and the other an absolute monarchy, remained a decidedly odd couple: amicable trading partners drawn together by converging commercial and strategic interests in the Atlantic world. That relationship, though, is undoubtedly a key contextual component of the Atlantic history of the American Revolution.

Portugal's national fortunes were severely battered in the early decades of the nineteenth century due to repeated French invasions, devastating military campaigns, internal political conflict, and crippling financial loss consequent to colonial Brazilian independence.[78] More than a century would pass before the Portuguese recovered any semblance of their prior economic or imperial stature, but that, too, would be short-lived, tangled in the web of regicide (1908), a brief unstable republic, and the rise of António de Oliveira Salazar and his fascist dictatorship government, the Estado Novo (1926–74). US-Portuguese diplomatic relations recovered in the mid-twentieth century because of strategic geopolitical interests that converged during World War Two and the Cold War, but only entered a partnership based on compatible political philosophy in 1976, following the fall of the Estado Novo, the implementation of a new democratic constitution, and successful elections with universal suffrage for all adult women and men.[79]

The aim of this essay has been to provide a brief, well-documented account of the birth of diplomatic and commercial relationships between Portugal and the United States, heretofore a neglected aspect in extant English-language historiography of the international dimension of the American Revolution. Exceptional scholarship on this subject has long been available in Portuguese—the present essay draws heavily on works by Jorge Manuel Martins Ribeiro and José Calvet de Magalhães, to cite two key examples. In 2003, historian of the Portuguese world Kenneth Maxwell published a chapter related to this matter in an edited volume that sought to broadly contextualize US independence, and other authors have touched on contemporary Portuguese foreign policy imperatives, but in general Anglophone scholarship of the early modern Atlantic world has not devoted sufficient attention to Portuguese influences and imperial interests during the Age of Democratic Revolutions.[80] One standout exception is the book by Gabriel Paquette, titled *Imperial Portugal in the Age of Atlantic Revolutions: The Luso-Brazilian World, c. 1770–1850* (2013), that offers a comprehensive consideration of how Portuguese interests were shaped and evolved as antimonarchical, anticolonial, and democratic movements spread around the New and Old World territories. Much room remains for additional perspectives and scholarship; my hope is that this essay will inspire new research to further explore these and related themes.

Notes

1. Jorge Manuel Martins Ribeiro, "Comércio e diplomacia nas relações Luso-Americanas (1776–1822)," 2 vols. (PhD diss., Universidade do Porto, 1997), 1:51–59, 61–121; José Mattoso, dir., *História de Portugal,* vol. 4: *O Antigo Regime* (Lisbon: Editorial Estampa, 1993), 103–11; T. Bentley Duncan, *Atlantic Islands: Madeira, the Azores, and the Cape Verdes in Seventeenth-Century Commerce and Navigation* (Chicago: University of Chicago Press, 1972), 1–6, 239–52.

2. See discussion in Timothy Walker, "Atlantic Dimensions of the American Revolution: Imperial Priorities and the Portuguese Reaction to the North American Bid for Independence (1775–1783)," *Journal of Early American History* 2 (2012): 247–85.

3. Ibid.

4. Ibid., 249–50, esp. nn. 5 and 7.

5. Anthony R. Disney, *A History of Portugal and the Portuguese Empire,* 2 vols. (New York: Cambridge University Press, 2009), 1:120–25.

6. James Piecuch, "A War Averted: Luso-American Relations in the Revolutionary Era, 1775–1786," *Portuguese Studies Review* 5.2 (1997): 31.

7. José Calvet de Magalhães, *História das relações diplomáticas entre Portugal e os Estados Unidos da América (1776–1911)* (Lisbon: Publicações Europa-América, 1991), 23.

8. Salvaterra de Magos, "Decreto da Rainha D. Maria I que Marca o reconhecimento da independência dos Estados Unidos da América," February 15, 1783, Arquivo Nacional do Torre do Tombo (National Archive of Portugal, the Torre do Tombo, hereafter ANTT), Colecção de Leis, SP nr. 2230.

9. Ana Cannas da Cunha and Diogo Gaspar, eds., *Católogo de exposição: Relações entre Portugal e os Estados Unidos da América na época das Luzes* (Lisbon: ANTT and the Fundação Luso-Americano para Desenvolvimento, 1997), 51–52.

10. William Beckford, *Italy: With Sketches of Spain and Portugal* (London: Richard Bentley, 1835), 257, cited in Caetano Beirão, *Dona Maria I*, 3rd ed. (Lisbon: Emprêsa Nacional de Publicidade, 1944), 227.

11. Benjamin Franklin to D. Vicente de Sousa Coutinho, Passy, France, June 7, 1783, Founders Online, accessed November 13, 2022, https://founders.archives.gov/documents/Franklin/01-40-02-0072.

12. Piecuch, "War Averted," 31.

13. Magalhães, *História das relações diplomáticas*, 25–26.

14. Ribeiro, "Comércio e diplomacia," 1:285–317.

15. Piecuch, "War Averted," 32; Magalhães, *História das relações diplomáticas*, 28.

16. Piecuch, "War Averted," 32.

17. For detailed analysis of trade between North America and Portugal in the late eighteenth century, see Ribeiro, "Comércio e diplomacia," 1:61–121.

18. Magalhães, *História das relações diplomáticas*, 27–28.

19. "Observations on the Alterations proposed in the Draught of the Treaty between Her Faithful Majesty and the United States of America," London, Spring 1786, ANTT, Ministério dos Negócios Estrangeiros (Ministry of Foreign Relations, hereafter MNE), *caixa* (box, hereafter cx.), 550, nr. 12.

20. Magalhães, *História das relações diplomáticas*, 27, 30.

21. Ibid., 26.

22. Piecuch, "War Averted," 32–33.

23. Pedro Calmon, *História do Brasil*, 3rd ed., 4:1352–54; cited in Joaquim Verríssimo Serrão, ed., *História de Portugal*, 10 vols. (Lisbon: Editora Verbo, 1996), 6:385.

24. Serrão, *História de Portugal*, 6:390–92.

25. Memorandum to the Intendente-Geral of Police, Lisbon, November 6, 1794, ANTT, Intendência Geral da Polícia, Conta para as Secretárias, Book 4, 214.

26. Treaty of Commerce and Friendship between Portugal and the United States of America, London, April 25, 1786, ANTT, MNE, cx. 550, nr. 13.

27. See Timothy Coates, *Convicts and Orphans: Forced and State-Sponsored Colonizers in the Portuguese Empire, 1550–1755* (Redwood City, CA: Stanford University Press, 2002), 3–20; Magalhães, *História das relações diplomáticas*, 34; Attachment to Ofício Nr. 676 from Luís Pinto de Sousa, "Observações sobre alguns artigos do Tratado ajunto," London, May 15, 1786, ANTT, MNE, cx. 550, nr. 12 (author's translation).

28. Magalhães, *História das relações diplomáticas*, 37–41.

29. Ibid., 40–41.

30. Piecuch, "War Averted," 32.

31. Letter of Arthur St. Clair, President of the Continental Congress, to the Queen of Portugal, February 3, 1787, ANTT, MNE, Livro 4: *Correspondência com soberanos estrangeiros* (Casa Forte), 3–4; Magalhães, *História das relações diplomáticas*, 41–42.

32. Magalhães, *História das relações diplomáticas*, 43–44.

33. Marquis de Bombelles, *Journal d'un ambassadeur de France au Portugal, 1786–1788* (Paris: Presses universitaires de France, 1979), 157.

34. Magalhães, *História das relações diplomáticas*, 48–49.

35. Ribeiro, "Comércio e diplomacia," 1:361–66.

36. *Gazeta de Lisboa*, June 5, October 10, 1789.

37. Thomas Jefferson to Luís Pinto de Sousa Coutinho, New York, August 7, 1790, Founders Online, accessed November 13, 2022, https://founders.archives.gov/documents/Jefferson/01-17-02-0016-0006; ANTT, MNE, cx. 410.

38. Magalhães, *História das relações diplomáticas*, 50–55.

39. Diplomatic Credential of David Humphreys, signed by George Washington, President of the United States, and Thomas Jefferson, Secretary of State, February 18, 1791, ANTT, MNE, Livro 4: *Correspondência com soberanos estrangeiros* (Casa Forte), 5–6; Magalhães, *História das relações diplomáticas*, 50–55.

40. David Humphreys to Luís Pinto de Sousa Coutinho, Lisbon, May 12, 1791, ANTT, MNE, cx. 410.

41. Diplomatic Credential of David Humphreys, Philadelphia, February 21, 1791, ANTT, MNE, Livro 4: *Correspondência com soberanos estrangeiros* (Casa Forte), 5–6.

42. José Rodrigues Pereira, *Campanhas navais: A armada e a Europa, 1793–1807*, vol. 1: *A marinha portuguesa na epoca de Napoleao* (Lisbon: Tribuna da História, 2005), 4–10; and Robert K. Sutcliffe, *British Expeditionary Warfare and the Defeat of Napoleon, 1793–1815* (Rochester, NY: Boydell & Brewer, 2016), xii.

43. Magalhães, *História das relações diplomáticas*, 45–46.

44. David Humphreys to Luís Pinto de Sousa, Lisbon, March 8, 1794, ANTT, MNE, cx. 410.

45. Ofícios of Cipriano Ribeiro Freire to Luís Pinto de Sousa Coutinho, London, June 3 and July 8, 1794, ANTT, MNE, cx. 550, nrs. 20–21.

46. Ofício of Cipriano Ribeiro Freire to Luís Pinto de Sousa Coutinho, Philadelphia, November 1, 1794, ANTT, MNE, cx. 550, nr. 23.

47. Ibid., nr. 31.

48. Ibid. (author's translation).

49. Ibid.

50. Ofício of Cipriano Ribeiro Freire to Luís Pinto de Sousa Coutinho, Philadelphia, September 24, 1794, ANTT, MNE, cx. 550, nr. 25.

51. Fernando Dores Costa, "The Peninsular War as a Diversion and the Role of the Portuguese in the British Strategy," *Portuguese Journal of Social Science* 12.1 (2013): 3–24; and Charles Esdaile, *The Peninsular War: A New History* (London: Allen Lane, 2002), 1–23.

52. Ribeiro, "Comércio e diplomacia," 1:153–265; *Gazeta de Lisboa*, January 6, 1789; January 18, 1791; March 26, 1799; Ribeiro, "Comércio e diplomacia," 1:266–84.

53. José Rodrigues da Silva to Martinho de Mello e Castro, New York, August 18, 1789, ANTT, MNE, cx. 550, nrs. 15–19; Fernando A. Novias, *Portugal e Brasil na crise do antigo sistema colonial (1777–1807)*, 348–49, cited in Serrão, *História de Portugal*, 6:429.

54. Chart of products imported from Portugal by the United States of America between October 1795 and September 1796, compiled and sent by Cipriano Ribeiro Freire to Luís Pinto de Sousa Coutinho, Philadelphia, late 1796, ANTT, MNE, cx. 551, nr. 84.

55. Confidential memorandum concerning American exports to Portugal in 1793, United States. c. 1794, Fundação Luso-Americano para Desenvolvimento (Luso-American Development Foundation, hereafter FLAD), Estate papers of the Abbade José Corrêa da Serra.

56. Ofício of Cipriano Ribeiro Freire to Luís Pinto de Sousa Coutinho relating to the trade in Port wine, Philadelphia, December 30, 1794, ANTT, MNE, cx. 550, nr. 45. See also Ribeiro, "Comércio e diplomacia," 1:357–61; order and shipment book, Newman, Land & Hunt Port Wine Company, Vila Nova de Gaia: 1791–96, Historical Archive of A. A. Ferreira, S.A., of Estate of the Hunt Roope Company; and bottle labeling specimen and order book, Funchal, late eighteenth century, Archive of the Madeira Wine Company, S.A. See also David Hancock, *Oceans of Wine: Madeira and the Emergence of American Trade and Taste* (New Haven, CT: Yale University Press, 2009), 107–12; Luis Teixeira de Sampaio, *O arquivo histórico do Ministério dos Negócios Estrangeiros* (Coimbra: Imprensa da Universidade, 1925), 119.

57. Ofício of D. Rodrigo de Sousa Coutinho to Cipriano Ribeiro Freire relating to Virginia tobacco seeds, Lisbon, Palácio de Queluz, July 23, 1798, Biblioteca Nacional de Lisboa (Natonal Library of Lisbon, hereafter BNL), Mss. 60, nr. 6, doc. 85; agreement between Peter Tilly and Cipriano Ribeiro Freire, March 6, 1798, BNL, Mss. 60, Nr. 6, doc. 59.

58. Ofício of D. Rodrigo de Sousa Coutinho to Cipriano Ribeiro Freire relating to whaling, Lisbon, Palácio de Queluz, June 4, 1798, BNL, Mss. 60, nr. 6, doc. 83; and Royal Warrant of Queen D. Maria I, Lisbon, Palácio de Queluz, May 18, 1798, BNL, Mss. 60, nr. 6, doc. 84.

59. Ofício of D. Rodrigo de Sousa Coutinho to Cipriano Ribeiro Freire relating to the products and cultivation of the United States and Mexico, Lisbon, September 22, 1798, BNL, Mss. 60, nr. 6, doc. 83; Richard Beale Davis, *The Abbé Corrêa in America, 1812–1820* (Providence, RI: Gávea-Brown, 1995), 8–12; and Ribeiro, "Comércio e diplomacia," 1:483–512.

60. Ofício of Cipriano Ribeiro Freire to Luís Pinto de Sousa Coutinho, Philadelphia, 1794, ANTT, MNE, cx. 550, nr. 23.

61. Attachment to Ofício nr. 17 from Cipriano Ribeiro Freire to Luís Pinto de Sousa Coutinho: Portuguese translation of peace treaties between the United States

of America and various Native American nations, Philadelphia, February 24, 1795, ANTT, MNE, cx. 550, nrs. 49–52.

62. Ofício of Cipriano Ribeiro Freire to Luís Pinto de Sousa Coutinho about North American naturalization regulations, Philadelphia, August 6, 1795, ANTT, MNE, cx. 550, nr. 97.

63. Sonnet by David Humphreys to the Infante Dom João, Lisbon, July 19, 1797, ANTT, MNE, cx. 410.

64. Magalhães, *História das relações diplomáticas*, 54, 334.

65. Ribeiro, "Comércio e Diplomacia," 1:760–61.

66. Magalhães, *História das relações diplomáticas*, 65–67.

67. Ibid., 67, 334.

68. Ibid., 57, 348.

69. Letter: "Eulogy for Cipriano Freire," Washington, DC, October 16, 1805, ANTT, MNE, Livro 4: *Correspondência com soberanos estrangeiros* (Casa Forte), doc. 18.

70. Ofício of Cipriano Ribeiro Freire to Luís Pinto de Sousa Coutinho, Philadelphia, May 20, 1797, ANTT, MNE, cx. 551, nr. 17.

71. Ofício of Luís Pinto de Sousa Coutinho to Cipriano Ribeiro Freire relating to the construction of a residence for ministers of Portugal in Washington, DC, Lisbon, Palácio de Queluz, September 21, 1797, BNL, Mss. 60, nr. 6, doc. 60.

72. Davis, *Abbé Corrêa*, 54.

73. Instrument of donation of land in Washington, DC, for a residence for the ministers of Portugal, Philadelphia, May 5, 1798, ANTT, MNE, cx. 551, nrs. 70–74.

74. Ibid.; I. Reid, L. Warland, and C. Smith, "Plan of the City of Washington," New York, 1795, ANTT, MNE, cx. 551, nr. 21; attachment to Ofício 117, from Cipriano Ribeiro Freire to Luís Pinto de Sousa Coutinho, Philadelphia, May 20, 1797, ANTT, MNE, cx. 551, nr. 17; and Robert King Sr., "Plan of part of the City of Washington . . . ," made for Cipriano Ribeiro Freire, American, c. 1798, BNL, D. 290 A.

75. Ofício of Cipriano Ribeiro Freire to Luís Pinto de Sousa Coutinho, Philadelphia, December 23, 1798, ANTT, MNE, cx. 551, nr. 146. See also Andrew Ellicot, "Plan of the City of Washington in the Territory of Columbia," engraved by Samual Hill (Boston, 1792), with manuscript notes and references from Cipriano Ribeiro Freire, included in the Ofício of June 10, 1798, to Luís Pinto de Sousa, BNL, C.C. 1200 A; and King, "Plan of part of the City of Washington," c. 1798, BNL, D. 290 A.

76. Sampaio, *O Arquivo Histórico*, 98.

77. Various Ofícios, Lisbon and Washington, DC, 1850–51, ANTT, MNE, cx. 116.

78. Gabriel Paquette, *Imperial Portugal in the Age of Atlantic Revolutions: The Luso-Brazilian World, c. 1770–1850* (Cambridge: Cambridge University Press, 2013), 84–114, 117–34, 187–96.

79. Daniela F. Melo, "Outmaneuvering Kissinger: Role Theory, US Intra-Elite Conflict, and the Portuguese Revolution (1974–1976)," *Foreign Policy Analysis* 15.2 (2019): 224–43.

80. Kenneth Maxwell, "The Impact of the American Revolution on Spain and

Portugal and Their Empires," in *A Companion to the American Revolution*, eds. Jack P. Greene and J. R. Pole (Malden, MA: Blackwell Publishers, 2000), 531–44. See also Jonathan R. Dull, *A Diplomatic History of the American Revolution* (New Haven, CT: Yale University Press, 1987); and Samuel Flagg Bemis, *The Diplomacy of the American Revolution* (New York: D. Appleton and Co., 1935; reprint, Read Books, 2012).

LAFAYETTE AND FRENCH NOBLES

Constitutional Reform in a Revolutionary Voice

In addition to its broader theme recognizing the European friends of the American Revolution, the Sons of the American Revolution conference that was the basis for this volume was also celebrating the 240th anniversary of the Lafayette's arrival in Charleston, South Carolina, on *L'Hermione*, beginning the American saga of the best-known European friend of the American conflict.

In America Lafayette is well remembered and honored for fighting alongside George Washington and developing a unique, almost filial relationship with the US commander-in-chief and first president under the Constitution. He is also known for his effective efforts to encourage French military support that made success possible. (Those efforts were recently memorialized, and popularized, in the song "Guns and Ships" from Lin-Manuel Miranda's musical *Hamilton*.)

Yet after the fighting was over, Lafayette continued to offer important contributions to the struggling new nation during the "Critical Period," as questions of government power and structure and constitution-writing took center stage. Reminding us that his years supporting the Revolution militarily were but a short period in Lafayette's long life, Robert Rhodes Crout explores the marquis's support of the broader, political and commercial American cause in the difficult years after the Revolution and in the early years of the French Revolution. In addition to supporting improved commercial relations between the United States and France, he exemplified the support for a strong nationalist movement among former Continental Army officers. Of course, many of those who fought in the American Revolution understood the dire necessity of increasing the efficacy of the national government that had been hobbled throughout the war by the minimalist Articles of Confederation. But as a Frenchman, Lafayette was also particularly privy to concerns expressed by French and other European merchants, politicians, and diplomats about America's reliability as a commercial and political partner during this time. With this Atlantic perspective, he set out to answer those concerns both by responding to continuing British attacks in France and Europe on the stability of the new United States and, in perhaps a less well-known effort, by calling upon his extensive list of contacts in America to urge effective political reforms in the new nation, perhaps even influencing the skeptical constitutionalist Thomas Jefferson. In "Lafayette and the 'More Perfect Union': Strengthening America in the Confederation Era, 1783–1789," Crout gives us a sense of how deeply Lafayette was committed to both efforts. Even after the Constitution was drafted, the marquis continued his Janus-like labors: urging more reforms in America (a Bill of Rights and restrictions on the president's powers) while applauding the new system and promoting US interests in Europe. Undoubtedly, his efforts to support the American constitutional reforms and communication with American leaders played a role in his work on the Declaration of the Rights of Man in the initial months of the French Revolution.

Of course, while historic memory has focused on Lafayette, other members of the French nobility also came to America and worked in France to support the new nation, not only during the War for Independence but as the United States struggled to gain its feet afterward. As the French Revolution initially crept, and then burst, upon France, Lafayette and other French nobility who had supported the American Revolution found themselves at the center of the republican struggle in their own nation. Among the leaders of those efforts were the Lameth brothers, Charles, Alexandre, and Théodore. Munro Price reminds us, however, that the work of the French nobility in support of the American Revolution was never divorced from arcane French politics. In "Lafayette, the Lambeths, and 'Republican Monarchy,' 1789–1791," the complex interactions of the Lameth brothers and Lafayette are explored. Interestingly, while the Lameth family was more successful in the court of Louis XVI—Lafayette's family suffering from its long-term antipathy to Austria as Louis's Austrian wife, Marie Antoinette, exercised more influence in the court—the Lameths tended to support a more radical approach to establishing a new French republic. Beyond the possible clash of personalities and, perhaps, some jealousy of Lafayette's perceived role in the American and French Revolutions, the Lameths sought a more democratic system for France than did Lafayette (for example, supporting a single legislative chamber rather than bicameralism), and they hoped to make the French king largely ceremonial while Lafayette seemed to try to convince France to emulate many American reforms and create a strong executive power.

While Julia Osman has given us a new way to consider the influence of the American Revolution on the coming revolution in France, Price and Crout remind us that the issues in France were complex and were enmeshed in long-standing and complicated personal and familial relationships.

Lafayette and the "More Perfect Union"
Strengthening America in the Confederation Era, 1783–1789

ROBERT RHODES CROUT

Prominent Frenchman and American major-general Lafayette was celebrating his last visit to America and his first visit to the grounds of the new University of Virginia on November 5, 1824, as the aged and frail Thomas Jefferson accompanied him to the unfinished Rotunda for a dinner. Once there, Jefferson, who was too weak to deliver his remarks, handed them to his friend Valentine W. Southall, secretary of the Board of Visitors, to read to the participants. Jefferson, having followed the newspaper accounts of Lafayette's previous two weeks visiting the Revolutionary War battlefields around Virginia, knew his audience would be familiar with them. His prepared remarks, delivered as much to Lafayette as to the audience, took a different direction.

> His deeds in the war of independence you have heard and read. They are known to you and embalmed in your memories, and in the pages of faithful history. His deeds in the peace which followed that war, are perhaps not known to you, but I can attest to them. When I was stationed in his country, for the purpose of cementing its friendship with ours, and of advancing our mutual interests, this friend of both, was my most powerful auxiliary and advocate. He made our cause his own, as in truth it was that of his native country also.... In truth, I only held the nail, he drove it. Honor him then, as your benefactor in peace, as well as in war.[1]

Most biographers of Lafayette dedicate a significant portion of their volumes to Lafayette's four years of military combat in America during the War for Independence.² Yet, as Jefferson recognized at that memorable dinner, the story of Lafayette and his commitment to and involvement with the American cause—what he called "the cause of all humanity"—extended through the rest of the seventy-six years of his life. It is Lafayette's involvement in the American cause during the years immediately following the American Revolution to 1789 and the beginning of the French Revolution that is the subject of this essay. It concentrates primarily on two subjects: The first is Lafayette's efforts to promote Franco-American relations by shifting the American economy from one dependent on the British to one more closely associated with France. The second is Lafayette's efforts to support a fundamental restructuring of America's constitutional system. Both objectives would strengthen and consolidate the American system and provide it with an opportunity to secure its place in history. He hoped this would enhance lasting ties between the two countries for future generations and continue to provide the chance for the peoples of those two nations to understand each other better.

Usually, in discussing Lafayette's involvement with America, biographers have limited themselves primarily to recounting his battlefield tactics during the American War for Independence. This may be because in our contemporary world we often presume a "wall of separation" between professional soldiers and politics that was not always there. Most of these studies have defined Lafayette narrowly as a "combat soldier" rather than a man of broader abilities. When they concentrate on his battlefield experiences, they usually ignore his other wartime experiences: his keen observation of the workings (or disfunctions) of the Continental and Confederation Congresses, his awareness of the diverse state and local political systems on both a theoretical and practical basis, and his quickly growing personal attachments to Americans throughout the states. He certainly adjusted to different American social and economic structures, developed close relationships with American families (elites and otherwise), and was well aware of the strengths and weaknesses he witnessed in America's multivaried social, political, and economic systems. All of these served him, and America, well in the postwar decade (1781–1789) to support American economic and constitutional developments.

Lafayette's efforts to promote increased Franco-American trade in the 1780s have been the subject of extensive scholarship for a hundred years.³ Lafayette's wartime experiences had a profound effect on his views of both the viability of the economy of the thirteen states and their ability to continue as an independent and unified political system. By the time Lafayette prepared to return to France after the battle of Yorktown, the French consul at Boston could report to his superior that Lafayette had agreed with him that the war had two objectives: first, to destroy English supremacy of the seas; and second, to provide France a market for its manufactures, art, and industry while interesting French merchants in America.[4]

Lafayette had written little about the American economy and on the prospects for increased trade between France and the Americans during the revolutionary years in America. He had complained about his personal issues with the depreciation of American paper currency versus hard currency to his wife in autumn 1777 and to his father-in-law in 1778.[5] He often found that to supply his own troops required his personal credit, which he occasionally asked the French government to assume.[6] However, for the most part, Lafayette's time was consumed with military matters during the combat years and even into the peace negotiations.

Once the preliminary terms of the peace treaty were settled in November 1782 and the projected Franco-Spanish military expedition from Cadiz in which he was to participate was cancelled in February 1783, Lafayette was free to turn his attention to postwar matters. His first attention was directed toward settling into a new residence in Paris. On November 12, 1782, he purchased a townhouse on rue de Bourbon that would provide a suitable location for his new unofficial role as intermediary between the French and the Americans. He established a weekly dinner routine that quickly became the place for pro-Americans to gather, share contacts and information, and promote mutual causes. There Lafayette could informally gather his French friends with the many Americans who were being sent to him and negotiate on their behalf.[7]

By the summer of 1783, Lafayette had even printed formal invitations to his new salon that would serve as a focus for American activity in Paris for the next decade. One young French officer remarked that the place "seemed to be more in America than in Paris." These sessions were so successful that Lafayette resumed them after the French Revolution on Tuesdays at his later Paris residences.[8]

Lafayette was also willing to take on another project, this one relating to cultural exchange and future generations of Americans and French. Lafayette proposed to his American friends (among them Nathanael Greene, Alexander Hamilton, and Henry Knox) that they should send their children to France for an education. In exchange, he promised he would send his son, George Washington Lafayette, to America. Lafayette had very specific views about how the young boys would be taught. They should not be taught at home, or else they might be "spoiled" by the house servants. School would provide the "advantages of equality and concurrence," but the older boys might have a negative effect on the younger ones. All-in-all, he suggested that they "go to the university school, attend at the public lecture, play with the boys in the proper homes and return home to do the work that has been given at school." He offered his home as a residence during holidays and offered to attend to their medical care. He implied that the education of girls in Paris raised a different set of issues. George Washington Greene reached France in the summer of 1788. George Washington Lafayette resided in America from 1795 to 1798 but under very different circumstances than Lafayette anticipated—as a refugee from the later stages of the French Revolution.[9]

In March 1783, to address the prospects for closer commercial relations between the two nations, Lafayette drew up a long memorandum that he sent to French foreign minister the comte de Vergennes and to finance minister Joly de Fleury. In it, he stressed the importance of the French government decreasing its impediments to trade between the two countries. By doing so, France could obtain much more American trade. If, however, France continued its restrictions, it could be in danger of losing most of that trade. He proposed the opening of several French seaports to the status of free ports.[10]

Not all the American diplomats were happy with Lafayette's efforts. John Adams was especially suspicious of Lafayette and complained about his role as a go-between. Yet, by early 1785, even Adams's skepticism diminished, perhaps due not only to Lafayette's effectiveness but also to his unceasing personal flattery toward Adams.[11]

American consul-general Thomas Barclay had no such initial concerns. In fact, when Lafayette expressed a desire to return to America in the summer of 1783, Barclay urged him to remain in France longer. Lafayette had proven to Barclay his importance as an intermediary for the Americans, for example, in a late August after-dinner conversation at Versailles between Barclay, Lafayette, and French minister of navy and colonies de Castries. Matthew Ridley, who witnessed the discussion, noted that the French official had expressed hesitation in encouraging American trade because the

United States might become a potential rival in its West Indies colonies for the carrying trade and as a producer of flour and salt fish. By the end of that conversation, Lafayette had convinced Castries to view the Americans more sympathetically.[12]

Before leaving France for an extended stay in the United States from August to December 1784, Lafayette sought to expand the system of duty-free ports. This time French finance minister Charles Alexandre de Calonne was more resistant to Lafayette's requests, claiming that reduction of duties and fees was a decision for the Admiralty courts, not for the finance department. He further wanted confirmation of Lafayette's requests from the American Congress or its representatives in France.[13]

Lafayette's five months of traveling through ten American states in 1784 provided him with an opportunity to interact directly with American state officials, merchants, congressional members, and the American consumer public. It also gave Lafayette a better grasp of commercial complexities and provided him with contacts with merchants seeking Lafayette's special efforts on their behalf. The visit also strengthened his hopes for a stronger American political system that could provide more uniform commercial and economic policies. During that time he had the opportunity to discuss prospective commercial ventures concerning fisheries and the timber industry with New England merchants and possible grain and tobacco ventures with middle state and upper south merchants.[14]

Fortunately, Lafayette would find on his return to France in January 1785 a willing collaborator, Thomas Jefferson, as the new American minister to France. Here began that compatible partnership that Jefferson would look back towards in his 1824 remarks in Charlottesville—though it was not always easy to see who "held the nail" and who "drove it."

Among the early projects that Jefferson and Lafayette coordinated was a proposal for New England whale oil to light the city of Paris. Pierre Tourtille-Sangrain had held the contract for lighting the city since 1769. A spring 1785 proposal that a prospective American partner Thomas Boylston had made to Lafayette, including elimination of duties on American whale oil, had failed. Jefferson and Lafayette met in November and discussed a different approach that might be more productive. Lafayette pursued his personal efforts on behalf of Nathaniel Barrett representing Governor James Bowdoin and a group of Boston merchants seeking a general modification of policy. After several months, Lafayette succeeded.[15]

Lafayette was also continuing his efforts through the marshal de Castries (French naval and colonial minister who was also in charge of the French consular system) to encourage the French navy to purchase American timber for masts and spars. This involved competing against Baltic state producers who had traditionally dominated the French market at a time when the British navy dominated New England markets. Lafayette's initial efforts seem to have sprung from his conversations with Nathanael Greene in Newport during the 1784 American tour. Due to Greene's untimely death in June 1786, that project was modified and merged with an earlier proposal from Nathaniel Tracy. When Castries stepped down as minister in 1788, his successor, the comte de Luzerne, faced a reduced naval budget and growing tensions with Britain that eventually led to the outbreak of war in 1791. The project collapsed, and Tracy died in 1796.[16]

Lafayette's most daunting commercial venture was to engage the Americans in the French tobacco business, especially with a difficult and entrenched bureaucracy known as the Farmers General (*fermiers généraux*). Lafayette's efforts in 1783 to create free ports at Lorient and Bayonne had provided an opportunity for the Farmers General to purchase tobacco from American ships arriving in those ports, and French foreign minister the comte de Vergennes insisted that the monopoly discontinue purchases from Britain. But Benjamin Franklin tried to steer such purchases toward his political ally Robert Morris and his grandnephew Jonathan Williams.[17]

In June 1785 Lafayette sent Jefferson a copy of the projected contract with Morris and Williams in hopes that Jefferson could encourage a counterproposal promoting a more open trading system. When Franklin left France in July, Jefferson began an effort in earnest to reform the tobacco purchasing system. Jefferson unfortunately knew little about French politics, and the effort ground to a halt. Lafayette had been traveling through central Europe on America's behalf. He returned in November to find Jefferson at a stalemate. Lafayette met with Vergennes to learn his side of the logjam and requested that any decision be postponed until some alternatives could be developed. Jefferson later reported to Monroe that Lafayette had been especially helpful in his advice.

> He offered his services with that zeal which commands them on every occasion respecting America. He suggested to me the meeting two or three gentlemen well acquainted with this business. We met.

They urged me to propose to the Ct. de Vergennes the appointing a committee to take this matter into consideration. . . . The consequence was the appointment of a committee, and the Marquis as a member of it.[18]

In early February 1786 a twelve-member committee to promote American trade (referred to informally as the "American committee") was created under the chair of a member of the French councils of finance and commerce and former intendant of finance, Jean-Nicolas de Boullongne, an unimpeachable authority on the French economy. Membership included two councillors of state, five masters of requests, two commissaries of trade, a farmer-general (*fermier-général*), and two outside members, one of whom was Lafayette himself. Two other Farmers General attended occasionally. Though its official purpose was to study the full range of Franco-American commerce, its attention quickly settled on the tobacco trade. Before the committee first met, the other outside member, Simon Bérard, sent Vergennes a memorandum critiquing the Morris contract that Vergennes forwarded to finance minister Calonne. Such contracts encouraging monopoly, Bérard claimed, conflicted with American values, encouraged trade with Britain, and appeared to be anticompetitive. All of which created an opportunity for Lafayette.[19]

In March, while Jefferson was visiting London, Lafayette undertook his most audacious effort, an essay that was a full assault on the Farmers General itself, making multiple copies of the pamphlet with a new form of printing, the Hoffman process. His *Résumé de mon avis au comité du commerce avec les Etats-Unis lorsque la question des tabac nous a été présentée* was a critique of the Farmers General and the Morris contract.[20] Lafayette complained that the current arrangement had resulted in exorbitant profits for both the Farmers and Morris. He then proposed (consistent with Jefferson's view) that the monopoly of the Farmers General should be abolished and a free trade policy replace it, subject to a low import duty that would generate the same revenue for the kingdom (with a higher volume of imports) and still prove a lower price for consumers. In the cover letter that he sent to Jefferson including a copy of the *Résumé,* Lafayette noted, "Everybody is so much affraid [*sic*] of the farm that none dare to think of it unless I keep their names a secret, so that I stand alone."[21]

Not only was Lafayette isolated by his criticism of the Farmers General, but he had three angry members of the Farmers responding to his document. One went so far as to recommend cancelling the Morris contract with a return to the old system of buying in French ports (with an additional fee). Lafayette preferred negotiating an exclusive contract with Virginia and Maryland to build Franco-American trade. When the committee reconvened on April 8, it returned to the original question: Should the Morris contract be renewed? Though the committee decided to reject the Morris contract, the Farmers General countered by issuing a memorandum on May 1 that responded to the original complaints.[22]

Yet before this could take place, Lafayette played his trump card with Vergennes. On April 22 he sent Vergennes a report to remind him of the larger issues in stark terms. "You have our opinion on all the matters of trade with the United States. After having advance time during the war and after the peace, it would not be happy if the English who left so late arrived before us." Lafayette sweetened the proposal for free trade by adding at the end an additional possible arrangement with the firm Le Couteulx to purchase furs from the United States payable in French goods. Until then the British had dominated the fur trade with France and demanded cash payment.[23]

Upon his return to France on April 30, Jefferson showed himself unusually defiant toward the committee negotiations—freedom of trade or nothing. Lafayette—at first hesitant to adopt such a hard line—conceded the tactic to Jefferson. As Jefferson wrote to Monroe, "Any palliative would take from us all those arguments and friends who would be satisfied with accommodation. The Marquis, tho differing in opinion from me in this point has however adhered to my principle of absolute liberty or nothing."[24]

To break the resulting impasse, Calonne ordered the committee to meet at his country estate at Berni outside Paris on May 24. Also attending were Vergennes and two members of the Farmers General, Paulze and Saint Amand. They discussed six alternatives and reached a temporary decision (to expire at the end of 1787) that the Morris contract would not be renewed, that the Farmers would buy an additional amount of tobacco carried directly from the United States (not Britain) in French or American ships, and that all terms would be presented to the Americans. Vergennes sent notice of what would be called the "Berni decision" on May 30 to Jefferson, who quickly forwarded multiple copies of the text to John Adams in London, American consular agents in France, the Congress, and the governors of Virginia and Maryland.

Word spread throughout America through the newspapers. The *Maryland Gazette* interpreted the Berni decision as a success due to Lafayette: "An event, which while it reflects great honour on the Marquis, must prove extremely advantageous to our planters and merchants."[25] Yet the Berni decision was not a complete victory for Jefferson or Lafayette; it had neither ended the tobacco monopoly nor eliminated the Morris contract altogether. Nevertheless, it had strengthened the French market for American tobacco. Historian Jacob Price calculated that French import of American tobacco grew from 6.4 million pounds in 1784 to 24.7 million in 1786 and 32 million in 1787.[26]

With an apparent pro-American advantage in the royal council now, Lafayette also decided the time was right to make a more comprehensive Franco-American trade policy proposal to Castries; he probably sent him the relevant memorandum in mid-June 1786. The proposal covered a range of issues: whale oil, the fur trade, naval stores, and continuation of the packet boat system between France and America. The original system of speedy packet boats across the Atlantic established by a royal order of June 28, 1783, had intended to provide faster mail delivery and passenger service across the Atlantic with the hope of improving relations. Yet in their operation, they had not been as efficient as proposed, and there were rumors they might be eliminated. Instead, consistent with Lafayette's proposal, an order by the royal council on December 14, 1786, though reducing the crossings from twelve to eight, not only continued the system but added the French West Indies to the destinations.[27]

The French government's response to the various proposals that autumn covered more than tobacco. As noted, Calonne formally notified Jefferson of the Berni decision in a letter dated October 22, a letter that Jefferson forwarded the next day to Congress (through John Jay as its secretary of foreign affairs) for publication throughout America. Jefferson's cover letter added:

> The assistance of the M. de la Fayette in the whole of this business has been so earnest and so efficacious that I am in duty bound to place it under the eye of Congress, as worthy their notice on this occasion. Their thanks, or such other notice as they should think proper, would be grateful to him without doubt. He has richly deserved and will continue to deserve it whenever occasions shall arise of rendering service to the U.S.

Calonne's official letter, however, was a comprehensive one, enumerating the history of all the French government's efforts to support Franco-American trade. It listed past concessions—the expansion of free ports, stabilization of the tobacco trade regulations, improved treatment of American whale oil and timber, reduced export fees on brandies and wines—and it promised to encourage the import of rice from South Carolina. Calonne's letter appeared in newspapers in New York on December 30, 1786; Philadelphia, January 3, 1787; and Boston, January 8. News of the favorable treatment of rice reached Charleston on March 8.[28]

The Berni decision provided a temporary solution to the problem of the tobacco trade, and Calonne's letter covering other French policies boded well for the future of Franco-American trade, but they were soon jeopardized by unforeseeable events. Lafayette had struggled on America's behalf through a French bureaucracy of personalities he had known for a decade. In February 1787 Vergennes died; in April Calonne was removed as finance minister; and in August Castries stepped down as minister of the colonies and navy. The French political system itself was becoming increasingly destabilized. In February 1787 Louis XVI called for an assembly of notables to propose reforms to the French government. Though Lafayette would participate in that assembly, his criticisms of the bureaucracy would alienate him from his old administrative friends and more importantly from the king and queen. Jefferson himself had already noted the unstable status at court of Lafayette, whose name was first added to participation in the assembly, then removed, then added back. Jefferson's main French ally was becoming a subject of controversy, and Lafayette's allies at court were disappearing.[29]

When Jefferson met with intendant of finances Douet de la Boullaye in August, with Lafayette as "translator," he learned there was no greater possibility of establishing Franco-American trade on the basis of free trade than before. The new controller of finance, Charles Claude Guillaume Lambert, appointed Pierre-Samuel Dupont to report on the status of American trade. Dupont returned with a voluminous report in mid-October 1787, concluding that Jefferson's proposal for abolition of the tobacco monopoly was too far from French traditions.[30] Jefferson, Lafayette, and Lambert then met several times to try to draft additional orders on tobacco, whale oil, and other commodities. However, Lambert did not have the power that Calonne possessed to press the matter to success through the royal council. The result was that progress halted. Lambert was forced by the council to backtrack, and on December 29, two days before the Berni decision expired, Lambert wrote to Jefferson, enclosing a copy of the council's order, which largely confirmed the terms of Calonne's earlier October 1786 letter.[31]

Political turbulence was overtaking France in 1788. The royal administration (including the Farmers General) was in both a financial crisis and institutional chaos. Lafayette was also tied up in dealing with the constitutional pressures for reform in France, which in the summer of 1789 included a divided political constituency, part of which was demanding a written constitution, another part calling for continuation of royal prerogative. Not only was he caught up in drafting and debating an introductory statement of rights for a constitution in a new national assembly, but Lafayette also found himself in command of the Paris National Guard, a semipolitical, semimilitary organization saddled with daily (indeed, hourly) problems of securing peace and order in the city as much as possible amid the chaos. There was also a steady trickle of American merchants coming to France to seek special arrangements and concessions. These Americans continued to appear at his soirées even as he found himself increasingly absent with the business of the security of Paris and dealing with the escalating national politics of a country increasingly at war with itself on a continent not comfortable with constitutionalism. At the same time, Lafayette's ally in promoting Franco-American trade had his own agenda. Jefferson left France in September 1789 and became Washington's secretary of state, never returning to Europe.

The brief period from the end of hostilities in 1781 to the outbreak of the French Revolution had not allowed enough time and stability to create a viable alternative to British domination over the American economy. As difficult as it was to wean American merchants from British credit instruments and trading partners, it was equally difficult to break French traditional preferences in governmental policies, business practices, and consumer preferences. Even more would this be true as both America and France were engaged in fundamental changes of their attitudes about the role of government and its relationship to society and to their economies. Yet that trade would eventually blossom, and with it, Lafayette's hopes would eventually be realized.[32]

As Lafayette was working on behalf of Franco-American trade, he was also regularly reminded of the structural weaknesses of the American political system under the Articles of Confederation. Sovereignty was vested in the states, which had independent trade policies, currencies, even navies, and to some extent foreign policies. Lafayette had of course witnessed the resulting difficulties firsthand in the conduct of the revolutionary military campaigns. Though much has been written on Lafayette and his efforts to strengthen both Franco-American relations and the American economy, little has been written on Lafayette and his efforts to assist the reform of the American constitutional system.

As a general officer who was often serving at Washington's side, Lafayette had learned quickly about the weaknesses of congressional government under the Articles of Confederation.[33] Washington's regular, often unanswered, appeals for support from Congress undoubtedly were a frustrating experience witnessed by his general staff, truer for Lafayette during his summer 1781 campaign in Virginia. This may be a reason why so many senior officers in the Continental Army provided the strongest support for a significant revision of the Articles of Confederation and promoted the cause of more effective power for the American central government. Merchants involved in trade and transport were also aware of the hodgepodge of inconsistent state regulations and multiple currencies that stymied and impeded the growth of American commerce.[34]

Additionally, Lafayette was familiar with the complaints from French diplomats in America about the difficulty of America as a dependable partner in war and in trade. From the French foreign ministry Lafayette heard and shared concerns about the weakness of the American government as a single entity. These assessments by French consuls led some French diplomats to conclude that France might have to negotiate separately with the states or regionally rather than uniformly through Congress. Several American states had already established their own commercial laws that would make trade with the Americans a complex of contradictions for any French merchant considering trade with multiple American states.[35]

Following the Yorktown campaign, Lafayette returned to France early in 1782 to prepare for the next stage of the war, not realizing that major combat in the American states had ended. The signing of peace preliminaries at the end of 1782 soon made the Atlantic secure and unleashed Lafayette's actions to strengthen the American union, especially through his correspondence. To Robert Livingston, he advised in a private letter of February 5, 1783, "Let me tell you that our Articles of Confederation ought to be revised and measures immediately taken to invigorate the Continental union." To Nathanael Greene he made a similar appeal:

> The Articles of Confederation are in my opinion very imperfect. Now is the time when the powers of Congress, the means of internal issues, the rights and limits of the states ought to be established. I wish the states would appoint proper persons with instructions to meet in a few months, then to propose whatever amendments would insure a state of union, vigor, and independence.

In a letter to Washington the same day, he urged him to use his influence to induce the American people to "strengthen their federal union." A month later Lafayette repeated the same appeal to Livingston: "Every American patriot must wish that the foederal union between the states may soon receive an additional strength. Upon that intimate eternal union, their happiness, their consequence depend [sic]."[36]

Lafayette's 1784 tour of American states provided him with an opportunity personally to visit ten states and make his direct appeals in public and in private for a stronger union that could also lead to a more secure commercial relationship with France. Though he was not in charge of any negotiations, traveling in a private capacity only, he offered his good offices to the Americans. His ultimate objective for the Americans was a government that could survive, thrive, and secure its principles for the future. Lafayette made that clear in his address to the Confederation Congress near the end of the tour.

In his private correspondence with American friends, Lafayette did not hesitate to share his opinion. To Washington's former aide David Humphreys, who was in France at the time, Lafayette wrote from the United States in late October 1784: "This winter is an important crisis for the interior arrangements of America, so far at least as respects federal union, commercial system, and militia establishment."[37]

Lafayette also spoke publicly, appealing to a range of American opinion. In September at a public event in Baltimore, he reminded his hosts, "Attending to American concerns, gentlemen, it is to me a piece of duty as well as a gratification to my feelings." Announcing to his audience the opening of four free ports in France, he concluded, "A new convenience is thereby offered to a commercial intercourse which every recollection must render pleasing." To the sympathetic Pennsylvania Assembly, he offered congratulations "upon the just sense which, as it supports the national consequence, and of course the commercial wealth of America, as it cherishes that sacred friendship between states, which is so necessary, will shew to the greatest advantage, the blessings of a free government." Even before the obstinate governor and general assembly of Rhode Island (which sought to limit the power of the national government), he urged, "May these rising states unite in every measure, as they have united in their struggles; and may their wealth and consequence be so much founded on federal union, baffle the calculations of jealousy, and fulfill the enthusiastic hopes of patriotism." Before the moderate New Jersey Council and House, Lafayette reflected, "The blessings of this revolution, so nobly purchased, will be eternally secured in the united strength and wisdom of the federal republic."[38]

Lafayette reserved his most important remarks for his appearance before the Confederation Congress meeting in Trenton. Here he addressed the legacy of America's revolution:

> In unbounded wishes to America, sir, I am happy to observe the prevailing disposition of the people to strengthen the Confederation, preserve public faith, regulate trade, and in a proper guard over Continental magazines and frontier posts, in a general system of militia, in foreseeing attention to the Navy, to insure every kind of safety. May this immense temple of freedom ever stand a lesson to oppressors, an example to the oppressed, a sanctuary to the rights of mankind and may these happy United States attain that complete splendor and prosperity which will illustrate the blessings of their government and for ages to come rejoice the departed souls of its founders![39]

Once back in France, Lafayette took up his pen to continue his appeal for a reform of America's constitutional structure. In a letter of January 7, 1785, Nathanael Greene had asked Lafayette's opinion on the effect in Europe if Congress had powers to regulate trade and restore public credit. Lafayette replied, "The effect, my dear sir, would be greater than can be imagined." Lafayette further remarked to Greene that he wished that those in America who were opposing such matters could be on the European side of the Atlantic. He concluded by urging that "no time may be lost in ensuring the consequence and prosperity of the American confederation." Lafayette also wrote to the president of the Congress, Richard Henry Lee, that same day. "Above all, my dear sir, do attend to the Confederation, to union, and harmony, to every regulations [*sic*] that can give security to the commerce, energy to the government, faith to the public creditors."[40]

In midsummer 1785 Washington gave Lafayette his views on the prospects for reform in two letters. Washington predicted that British actions to restrain American trade would have the reverse effect. They would encourage Congress to seek powers to regulate the "trade of the union" that would not otherwise have happened for half a century. "The mercantile interests of the *whole* union are endeavoring to effect this, & will no doubt succeed; they see the necessity of a controlling power & the futility, indeed the absurdity, of each state's enacting laws for this purpose independent of one another. This will be the case also, after a while, in all matters of common concern."[41]

Before Lafayette had received these letters, he had already undertaken an initiative with US minister Thomas Jefferson to counter European claims about American weakness. Writing from a travel stop in Vienna, he urged Jefferson to launch a newspaper campaign immediately on "the strength of the union, the powers of Congress, the dispositions of the people, and the principles of trade" at the same time as these matters were developing in America. Lafayette's proposal was based in part on discussions that he had with King Frederick the Great of Prussia and his minister Girolamo Lucchesini during visits to observe Prussian military maneuvers in the summer of 1785 and a visit with the Austrian emperor Joseph II and his minister Prince Wenzel Anton Kaunitz. Lafayette's concern arose from questions from the European leaders that he felt would not have been answered "properly" by the Duke of York and Cornwallis, who were there with Lafayette to observe military maneuvers.[42]

In his letters to Washington, Lafayette repeated many of his concerns with America's weak central government under the Confederation. However, to Washington he emphasized the role that British diplomats were playing in spreading such negative reports about America, newspapers in promoting them, and then the British diplomats confirming the very same reports. "The fact is these people, generally speacking [*sic*], know very little of the advantages of democratical [*sic*] governments, of the resources to be found in a free nation." Lafayette warned that Americans could lose the respect gained by their revolution if they did not strengthen the Confederation, empower Congress to regulate trade, and begin to pay off their debt. He told

Washington that he intended to give "very frankly" his opinions to Congress and to his friends "on that side of the Atlantic." Washington soon replied on May 10, 1786, and was forced to admit to the Frenchman that though these accounts were exaggerated, "yet our conduct has laid the foundation for them." Washington mused that one of the evils of democracies was that the people, "not always seeing and frequently misled, must often feel before they can act right." The frustrations implied in that statement were getting the better of Washington. By late summer he had foresworn making any further remark to Lafayette or others on the matter. "Perhaps it is best to be silent since I cannot disguise or palliate where I might think them erroneous." Lafayette also appears to have followed Washington's lead by avoiding public debates over the proposed constitution, preferring to use his influence in private correspondence.[43]

Washington's and Lafayette's concerns appear to have been exacerbated by the appearance between August 1784 and March 1785 of two English editions and a French edition of Richard Price's *Observations on the Importance of the American Revolution and the Means of Making It a Benefit to the World*. Included as an appendix to the book was a March 1778 letter to Price from the former French controller general Turgot (who had since died). Turgot had complained about the tendency of American state constitutions to imitate English patterns of what we would call checks-and-balances. Turgot complained that it tended to hinder a government's ability to respond effectively to crises; he believed that such a check could be necessary for the enormous size and complexity of a monarchy but not for small republics founded on the principle of the equality of citizens. He concluded that Americans had not yet sensed the "truths" of this potential problem.[44] To physiocrats and potential French business partners, the book suggested further hindrances to the opening of their commercial relationships with individual American states.

Lafayette soon launched a series of letters to friends and to the Confederation Congress. He now looked to one of the "friends," Franklin, who was back in America, to assume a major role in the constitutional reform movement. He confirmed Franklin's suspicions about the European opponents of America: "I wish no ground was left for our enemies to broach those lies . . . . [that] it is a matter of doubt . . . if free constitutions can support themselves." As to Franklin's acceptance of the presidency of Pennsylvania, Lafayette was ecstatic. "Nothing but that could speedily restore internal union and remove the jealousies against neighbors. You will encourage federal measures, regulations for trade, a general system of militia. . . . [These matters] want to be set a going."[45]

To an influential figure in Congress, John Jay, Lafayette expressed his pain at the bad effect that the lack of a federal union, effective finances and commercial arrangements, and an established military had on the "minds of European nations . . . for which I could not but acknowledge within myself there was some ground, although it was so unfairly broached upon by the enemies of the United States."[46]

Lafayette soon passed word to John Adams that the constitutional reform effort was underway in America and that Virginia had appointed commissioners for a meeting (what became known as the Annapolis Conference). Yet to Adams, he now raised a new concern, one of balance: "I hope Congress will have those powers that are necessary to give energy to the confederation without encroaching on those rights which it is proper to leave within states so far distant, and so differently circumstanced." This was the first time Lafayette expressed concern for a balance, and there is no documentary source for what precipitated that remark. Perhaps it came from the myriad American newspapers he was receiving at the time. Adams's prompt response was to bemoan the calling of a convention; Congress could have "done as well, at a less expense & in a shorter time."[47]

When Lafayette returned from summer military maneuvers in Alsace in 1786, Jefferson greeted him with an update from America (apparently from Monroe). The proposal for the Confederation to be given the authority to impose a 5 percent impost lacked only New York's assent, and the Articles of Confederation required unanimity for any amendments. In fact, delegates from only five states attended the proposed conference in Annapolis to consider a Virginia plan for a commercial convention. Lafayette promptly responded by sending Jefferson reports that Britain was intent against "the trade, the federal union, the navigation, and the peace of America."[48]

Lafayette had relished his 1784 visit to America, which was not simply a triumphal tour but provided opportunities for him to promote what he considered the political agenda of the American Revolution. Looking back on the success of his tour, Lafayette began planning his next tour to America tentatively scheduled for spring 1787. He had already informed James McHenry, William Stephen Smith, and Anthony Wayne of his planned travel; this time he appeared to set his sights on a tour southward that would include South Carolina. It would be logical to assume that he would have had a similar agenda for his second tour—public and private appeals for a stronger union. The project appears to have been postponed and eventually cancelled when Louis XVI summoned an Assembly of Notables for the spring of 1787. Lafayette's next campaign for American constitutional reform—unlike that of 1784—would have to be conducted entirely through correspondence.[49]

As news arrived in early January 1787 through a letter from John Adams to Jefferson about Shays' Rebellion, Lafayette expressed the hope that governments would take no measures that might lead to popular opposition to the movement for reform; Lafayette saw the rebellion as a "temporary evil" that might lead to a greater good and reverse the hostile reaction from America's enemies—probably implying Britain. In the absence of fresh news from Washington, Lafayette wrote to confirm to the general that he had already heard of the rebellion and that it concerned him, not so much in terms of Americans losing confidence in constitutional reform but from the impact the news could have in Europe by undercutting America's friends (such as Lafayette himself). He hoped that Congress would not get involved. Lafayette repeated the same concerns to William Stephens Smith: "It is important not to arm the people against federal ideas."[50]

Finally, by early February 1787, word reached Paris of a constitutional convention to be held in Philadelphia. Lafayette promptly sent his concerns and his hopes to John Jay:

> May every Americans know the blessings of their own constitutions, and from comparison judge that if they are to correct, it would be madness in them to destroy! I hope the convention in Philadelphia will answer essential and urging purposes of the confederation, the commerce, the establishment of an uniform and republican militia. Each state has within itself the means fully sufficient to set to rights the opinions of mistaken citizens. . . . Every wrong measure of theirs would hurt not only the consequence of the United States, but also the cause of liberty to be.

Lafayette repeated this last point the same day in a letter to Washington. Not only should Americans be "most seriously interested in preserving their happiness at home" but also "their consequence abroad."[51]

John Jay, while not a delegate to Philadelphia himself, announced to Lafayette that a new convention was not only in planning but that some states had appointed "distinguished characters" to represent them at it. Nevertheless, there was significant division over it. More details of the coming convention arrived shortly in a letter from Washington. Washington reported that most of the delegates had been appointed and that they would meet in Philadelphia on the second Monday in May to "revise and correct the defects of the federal system. . . . What may be the result of this meeting is hardly within the scan of human wisdom to predict." Washington considered it the last attempt to modify the existing form.[52]

With no idea of how long the Philadelphia convention would take, Lafayette wrote to Jay about his best hopes for its results on May 30, 1787: "May the Convention be the happy epoch of federal, energic [thus], patriotic measures! May the friends of America rejoice! May her enemies be humbled, and her censors be silenced at the news of her noble exertions in continuance of those principles which have placed her so high in the annals of history and among the nations of the earth!"[53]

As Lafayette waited into the summer to learn the results of the convention, he suddenly received a letter from Washington. Washington had been elected president of the convention on May 25. After less than two weeks he broke the general silence of delegates pursuant to a rule of secrecy to report to Lafayette that he had once again entered public affairs. The usually restrained Washington announced to his young friend that the convention would determine "whether we are to have a government of respectability under which life, liberty, and property will be secured to us, or are to submit to one which may be the result of chance, or the moment, springing perhaps from anarchy and confusion, and dictated by some aspiring demagogue." Having perhaps already written too much, Washington drew back. "What may be the result of the present deliberations is more than I am able at present if I was at liberty to inform you."[54]

Observing the convention not only from the outside but from the distance of New York, Henry Knox speculated to Lafayette that "whether the propositions of the convention will be as perfect as the occasion may require is a discovery to be made by time. But from the characters who compose the convention it may be fairly presumed that the result of their deliberations will be as wise as could be expected from men under the same circumstance."[55]

Upon receiving Washington's report, Lafayette replied to remind Washington again of the rapid decline of opinion about America. He bemoaned the declining reputation of America, the pleasure it gave to America's enemies: "Her dignity is lowering. Her credit vanishing, her good intentions questioned by some, her future prosperity doubted. Good God! Will the people of America . . . stumble in the easy path?" Two days later Lafayette wrote to Madison (also serving in Philadelphia), asking him to forward the news in his letter to Hamilton, Knox, and Richard Henry Lee, "to whom I will write also in a few days." Lafayette repeated the concerns he had written to Washington. He also rephrased his worst fear: "Should [our fellow citizens] be deficient in that glory and happiness which I expect for them, I feel that the tranquility of my life will be poisoned."[56]

What was the official position of the French government throughout this era of controversy over the new constitutional proposal in the United States? French foreign minister Armand Marc, comte de Montmorin, seemed to have a very different view than his predecessor Vergennes's policy of interventionism. In his October 10, 1787, instructions to the French minister to the United States, comte de Moustier, he stated that if the Confederation collapsed, the complete independence of the states from each other would have no ill effects for France. Therefore, he urged a policy of complete neutrality toward the proposed constitution.[57]

By early October, Lafayette had still received no news from America about the status of the proposed government. He again wrote to Washington, reminding him that America was not receiving the "consequence" it deserved in Europe. He hoped that this opportunity for reform would neither lead America away from democracy nor toward monarchy or aristocracy. "We are to expect that so many enlightened, experienced, and virtuous senators will have hit the very point where the people will remain in possession of their natural rights, of that perfect equality among fellow citizens and yet government . . . will be able to provide with efficacy and act with vigor."[58]

Lafayette's and Washington's letters had passed each other in crossing the Atlantic. By the time Lafayette had written, Washington's letter of September 18 (the day after the constitutional convention closed) was already on its way to France. Washington's letter to Lafayette announced that the proposed constitutional text was completed: "It is now a child of fortune, to be fostered by some and buffeted by others." Washington declared he would not speak for or against it. He also enclosed a printed copy for Lafayette, adding with his wry sense of humor that it "will occupy your thoughts for some time." The following month Henry Knox also sent Lafayette a copy of the document. While he admitted that the proposal would be the subject of a year to fifteen months of debate, he found the changes (though not perfect) a significant improvement, "and from my soul I wish them God speed." However, he admitted that if the process were begun again (a proposal floated by some antifederalists), probably the states would not allow such latitude to their representatives: "Such an agreement could not again be produced even by the same men."[59]

Lafayette received his copy of the proposed constitution about Christmas 1787; he sent a copy on to Jefferson for his comment. Lafayette's first reaction was opposition to the powerful presidency it included, which he probably compared to monarchy without using the word. Yet he was willing to support it with the expectation of Washington first assuming the office of president. In a New Year's letter to Washington, Lafayette expressed that reservation and one other—the need for a "declaration of rights" (a proposal also being championed by Jefferson). As to the latter concern, he suggested that the American people could still add such a bill of rights. He urged Washington, "You only can settle that political machine, and I foresee it will furnish an admirable chapter in your history."[60]

Within the first month of the year 1788, Lafayette had joined Jefferson and Thomas Paine in debating among themselves the need for additional amendments, news that he sent in a letter to Knox and that he asked Knox to share with Hamilton. In a letter to Washington the same day, he raised the same concerns with the general and some indications of what those amendments might include—trial by jury, necessary rotation of the office of president, and concern about executive powers. Based on Lafayette's appeals of October 9 and 15, Washington finally expressed his concerns about the proposed constitution in a very frank letter of February 7. His two major concerns were first, that the central government contain no more powers than indispensably necessary; and second, that those powers would be so distributed among executive, legislative, and judicial branches as to forestall government degenerating into a monarchy, an oligarchy, or an aristocracy—so long as the people were virtuous. He expressed concern about the summoning of another convention for further revisions as was being advocated by some. There was, then, no alternative to ratification of the proposal except anarchy.[61]

Now Lafayette's concerns turned to the ratification process. Lafayette learned of the deep conflicts among Americans from John Jay. To James Bowdoin and John Jay, he expressed his satisfaction with the proposed new constitution and suggested that the new document should be accepted (and secured) before seeking amendments. Lafayette now revealed his concern that already the process had dragged on so long that part of America's consequence had been lost since the war, and he stated his resolve not to rest easy until it had recaptured those advantages.[62]

Yet Lafayette had not witnessed the changes already taking place in America. Washington admitted to the Frenchman that he himself was stunned by the pace of change in American attitudes over the previous eighteen months: "It is impracticable for you or anyone who has not been on the spot to realize the changes in men's minds and the progress towards rectitude in thinking and acting which then have been made."[63]

Washington continued his expression of exuberant optimism in his next letter to Lafayette:

> There never was so much labor and economy to be found before in the country as at the present moment. If they persist in the habits they are acquiring, the good effects will soon be distinguishable. When the people shall find themselves secure under an energetic government, . . . when every one (under his own vine and fig-tree) shall begin to taste the fruits of freedom—then all these blessings . . . will be referred to the fostering influence of the new government. . . . You see I am not less enthusiastic than ever I have been.

Yet Lafayette continued to press his friends for a "few amendments" perhaps in the first session of Congress. Those of Lafayette's friends such as Robert R. Livingston who had been occupied with the Constitution and its ratification now began to contact him with the good news of its ratification and expressed their hopes for the future.[64]

Lafayette, finally comfortable with the state of American politics, could now apply his own hand to constitution-making, certainly using the example of his American friends by so acting. He would begin the year of 1789 with optimism by beginning to draft a Declaration of Rights for France. Washington also could share in the optimism on his side of the Atlantic by writing to his young French friend, "I really entertain greater hopes that

America will not finally disappoint the expectations of her friends than I have at almost any former period."[65]

While it is true than Lafayette did not sit in the American constitutional convention or debate on the floor the various proposals, he had a significant though distant influence on the outcome between 1783 and 1789. For six years he had reminded Americans of what was at stake in reforming their government and strengthening their trade relations as well as their overall relationship. Years before the new American Constitution, he had traveled through the roads and pathways of ten American states supporting constitutional reform in all kinds of assemblies, including state legislatures. He probably would have done so again in 1787 if conditions in France had allowed such a trip. Upon returning to Europe in 1785, he undertook an intense correspondence directed toward constitutional and commercial reform—encouraging, cajoling, even warning—while seeking to respond to inflated reports of America's very real weakness.

Lafayette did not distinguish between strengthening Franco-American trade and reforming the American constitutional system—both were important links in securing the legacy of the American Revolution. Indeed, he sought to strengthen the alliance of these two countries and peoples on a firmer and more permanent foundation both commercially and politically. These actions were unfolding on a much larger stage that would soon encompass not only France and America but also the rest of the Atlantic world and beyond on a new path toward free trade, self-governance, and the other liberal principles for which Lafayette had originally come to America. As he had written his wife before his arrival in 1777:

> I trust that, for my sake, you will become a good American. Besides, it is a sentiment made for virtuous hearts. The welfare of America is intimately connected with the happiness of all mankind; she will become the respectable and safe asylum of virtue, integrity, tolerance, equality, and a peaceful liberty.[66]

The purpose of this brief essay has not been to deal with Lafayette in the French Revolution. That would require too much for this piece. Historiographical conflicts over the meaning of the French Revolution and Lafayette's role have raged since the events themselves and continue to reflect the sharp lines of French politics and academics. Since the nineteenth century these interpretative lines have divided royalists, Bonapartists, reactionaries, and latter-day "Jacobins" (radicals who saw themselves as the heirs of the Jacobin tradition and who saw figures such as Marat, Danton, and Robespierre as their heroes). Through much of the twentieth century, this last group came to dominate interpretations of late eighteenth- and early nineteenth-century French historical writing. It was reflected in the dominance by scholars such as Georges Lefebvre, most notably his *Coming of the French Revolution* (1947). Despite a major challenge to this general interpretation by François Furet in *Interpreting the French Revolution* (1981), Furet and his disciples did not include Lafayette as part of their revisions but continued the old formulaic interpretation of him.[67] Some recent French studies on Lafayette have begun to emerge from this sharp ideology in innovative collections of essays such as Philippe Bourdin's *La Fayette, entre deux mondes* (2009), which received a mixed review from Marc Belissa. Belissa diplomatically pronounced the collection of new interpretations a "complex portrait." Still, the fixation on Lafayette in the French Revolution has tended to miss his important role between the American and French Revolutions. As Belissa notes, Bourdin's volume avoided analysis of the Lafayette of the 1780s.[68] Hopefully, this essay can begin to address that lacuna.

Notes

1. Thomas Jefferson, Address at the University of Virginia, November 5, 1824, Founders Online, accessed November 10, 2022, https://founders.archives.gov/documents/Jefferson/98-01-02-4662.

2. For example, popular biographies such as Harlow Giles Unger, *Lafayette* (New York: Wiley, 2002) and Gonzague Saint-Bris, *La Fayette* (Paris: Filipacci, 2006) spend a significant portion on Lafayette in the American war. Even the scholarly work by Laura Auricchio, *The Marquis: Lafayette Reconsidered* (New York: Vintage, 2014), dedicates one-third of its pages to it. Etienne Taillemite, *La Fayette* (Paris: Fayard, 1989), the standard scholarly French source, covers those four years in one-fifth of its length. Jean-Pierre Bois, *La Fayette* (Paris, 2015), an exception, concentrates half its length on the French Revolution and Napoleonic era. The latest significant French biography, Laurent Zecchini, *Lafayette: Héraut de la liberté* (Paris: Feyard, 2019) covers the American war in about one-fourth of its length. The exception to all, with the keenest analysis of Lafayette's life, though admittedly a collection of thoughtful essays rather than a simple narrative, continues to be Lloyd Kramer, *Lafayette in Two Worlds: Public Cultures and Personal Identities in an Age of Revolutions* (Chapel Hill: University of North Carolina Press, 1996), which spends a dozen pages (one essay) on the American war.

3. The standard interpretation of Lafayette for this period continues to be Louis R. Gottschalk, *Lafayette between the American and the French Revolution (1783–1789)* (Chicago: University of Chicago Press, 1950). Other studies concentrate on the commercial relations between France and the United States during the era. Some credit Lafayette; others, while citing his actions, never mention his name. These include: Henri Sée, "Commerce between France and the United States, 1783–1784," *American Historical Review* 31.4 (July 1931): 732–52; Frederick L. Nussbaum, "American Tobacco and French Politics, 1783–1789," *Political Science Quarterly* 40.4 (December 1925): 497–516; Frederick L. Nussbaum, "The Revolutionary Vergennes and Lafayette versus the Farmers General," *Journal of Modern History* 3.4 (December 1931): 592–604; Albert Mathiez, "Lafayette et le commerce franco-américaine à la veille de la Révolution," *Annales historiques de la Révolution française* 3.17 (September/October 1926): 474–84; Louis R. Gottschalk, "Lafayette as Commercial Expert," *American Historical Review* 36.3 (April 1931): 561–70; John F. Stover, "French-American Trade during the Confederation, 1781–1789," *North Carolina Historical Review* 35.4 (October 1950): 399–414; Paul Walden Bamford, "France and the American Market in Naval Timber and Masts, 1776–1786," *Journal of Economic History* 12.1 (Winter 1952): 21–34; Jacques Godechot, "Les relations économiques entre la France et les Etats-Unis de 1778 à 1789," *French Historical Studies* 1.1 (1958): 26–39; Jacob M. Price, *France and the Chesapeake: A History of the French Tobacco Monopoly, 1674–1791*, 2 vols. (Ann Arbor: University of Michigan Press, 1973), esp. 740–833. For American foreign relations during the decade, see Mary Giunta et al., eds., *The Emerging Nation: A Documentary History of the Foreign Relations of the United States Under the Articles of Confederation*, 3 vols. (Washington, DC: National Historical Publications and Records Commission, 1996). From the French perspective, see Peter P. Hill, *French Perceptions of the Early American Republic, 1783–1793* (Philadelphia: American Philosophical Society, 1988). More recent scholars on these relations—Americans such as Alan Potofsky and Paul Cheney—have emphasized the social and intellectual aspects of the subject.

4. Philippe-André-Joseph Letombe to the naval and colonial minister, the marshal de Castries, December 19, 1781, Archives Nationales de France (hereafter AN), Archives des Affaires Etrangères, B3, 441. These are the consular archives; consuls served under the French naval and colonial ministry rather than the foreign minister.

5. Lafayette to Adrienne de Lafayette, October 29 [1777], Stanley J. Idzerda and Robert Rhodes Crout, eds., *Lafayette in the Age of the American Revolution: Selected Letters and Papers, 1776–1790*, 5 vols. to date (Ithaca, NY: Cornell University Press, 1977–) (hereafter *LAAR*), 1:137; Lafayette to the duc d'Ayen, September 11, 1778, box 16, folder 19, Dean Collection, Cornell University, Ithaca, NY.

6. Lafayette to Nathanael Greene, April 17, 1781, *LAAR*, 4:38; Lafayette to La Luzerne, April 22, 1781, *LAAR*, 4:55; Lafayette, Promissory Note to William Smith, Hugh Young, William Neill, and Daniel Bowly, July 1, 1781, Lafayette Manuscripts, Morgan Library, New York.

7. Vente d'un hôtel, November 12, 1782, Etude LVIII, 512, Minutier central des notaires de Paris, AN. The contract that same date for the contents of the house is in

the author's manuscript collection. The house and contents were confiscated in 1792 by the radical revolutionary government (T 333, AN).

8. Xavier de Schomberg to his mother, January 14, 1787, E 3151, Archives départementales des Yvelines, Montigny-le-Bretonneux, France. From 1818 until his death, Lafayette's residences in Paris were on rue d'Anjou. Chantal de Tourtier-Bonazzi, *Lafayette: Documents conservés en France* (Paris: Archives nationales, 1976), 216 n. 1.

9. See Lafayette to Greene, Hamilton, and Knox (*LAAR*, 5:302, 317, 322, 441, and 442). Lafayette's detailed suggestions for the children's education are in Lafayette to Nathanael Greene, June 12, 1785, summarized in Richard K. Showman et al., eds., *The Papers of Nathanael Greene*, 13 vols. (Chapel Hill: University of North Carolina Press, 1976–2005), 13:539–40; and *LAAR*, 5:442. Available scanning technology when the Greene Papers and Lafayette Papers projects were operating did not allow for the full reconstruction of the text of this letter because of its poor condition (due probably to insect damage).

10. Lafayette to Joly de Fleury, March 19, 1783, *LAAR*, 5:110–12.

11. Adams revealed his concerns about Lafayette in a letter to James Warren, April 16, 1783: "I see in that youth the seeds of mischief to our country, if we do not take care" (*LAAR*, 5:123). Despite Lafayette's repeated assurances, Adams continued his suspicions until early 1785. For Adams' transformation, see ibid., 201–3, 211–12, and his private letter to John Jay, January 31, 1785, Founders Online, accessed November 10, 2022, https://founders.archives.gov/documents/Adams/06-16-02-0298. Adams's letterbook copy was confirmed by the recent appearance of Jay's received copy, Sotheby's, New York, *Books and Manuscripts, Sale No. 8211 . . . June 15, 2006*, lot 179.

12. Entry for August 29, 1783, Matthew Ridley, Diary and Journal, box 5, volume 15, Matthew Ridley Papers, Massachusetts Historical Society, Boston. See also Ridley to Robert Morris, September 12, 1783, E. James Ferguson et al., eds., *The Papers of Robert Morris, 1781–1784*, 9 vols. (Pittsburgh: University of Pittsburg Press, 1973–99), 8:509.

13. Lafayette to Joly de Fleury, March 19, 1783, *LAAR*, 5:110–12; Lafayette to Vergennes, March 19, 1783, ibid., 5:112–13; Calonne to Lafayette, June 16, 1784, ibid., 5:225.

14. About his 1784 tour, see my essay, "Bridges to Freedom: Lafayette's Use of Revolutionary Rhetoric in the Political Strategies of His Tours," in *Lafayette in Transnational Context: Identity, Travel, and Nationalism in the Revolutionary Atlantic World*, ed. Jordan Kellman (Lafayette: University of Louisiana Press, 2015), 75–103.

15. Benjamin Bothereau, "Illuminated Publics: Representations of Street Lamps in Revolutionary France," *Technology and Culture* 61.4 (October 2020): 1056; Gottschalk, *Lafayette between the American and the French Revolution*, 208–9. See Jefferson's account of his conversation with Lafayette in reaching a general strategy on negotiation with French officialdom, Jefferson to Adams, December 10, 1785, Founders Online, https://founders.archives.gov/documents/Jefferson/01-09-02-0083. On the negotiations over this contract, see *LAAR*, 5:321n.2, 349–50, 356, where the editors incorrectly identify the addressee of Lafayette's November 4 letter as Boylston rather than Barrett.

16. Paul Bamford, *Forests and French Sea Power, 1660–1789* (Toronto: University of Toronto Press, 1956), esp. 190–95. Though Bamford cites Gottschalk's Lafayette

biography as a source, he avoids entirely mentioning Lafayette's name, preferring to cite Castries's favorable efforts.

17. The officials of Bayonne responded by declaring Lafayette a "citizen," for which he thanked them on his return to France. Lafayette to officials of Bayonne, [undated, but February 8, 1785], Aldé, *Lettres & manuscrits autographes . . . le jeudi 4 et vendredi 5 novembre 2010* [Paris], 23, lot 117. The date is confirmed by an archival transcription (BB 113, no. 25 [2]), Bibliothèque Municipale, Bayonne.

18. Jefferson to Vergennes, August 15, 1785, Founders Online, accessed November 10, 2022, https://founders.archives.gov/documents/Jefferson/01-08-02-0306; Lafayette to Vergennes, November 16, 1785, *LAAR,* 5:350–51; Jefferson to Monroe, May 10, 1786, Founders Online, https://founders.archives.gov/documents/Jefferson/01-09-02-0413.

19. Bérard to Vergennes, January 10, 1786, vol. 31, fols. 31–43, 54, Correspondance Politique, Etats-Unis (hereafter AAE, CP, EU), Centre des Archives diplomatique du ministère des Affaires étrangères, La Courneuve, France; Vergennes to Calonne, February 11, 1786, ibid., fol. 86.

20. The full text is at Founders Online, accessed November 10, 2022, https://founders.archives.gov/documents/Jefferson/01-09-02-0303, with a date of March 6. See Frederick Nussbaum's explanation for dating it February 15 and his edition of the text in the *Journal of Modern History* 3.4 (December 1931): 592–613. Gottschalk, *Lafayette between the American and the French Revolution,* 225, dates it as February 20. Lafayette later claimed that Condorcet had helped him in its drafting. Lafayette to Benjamin Constant, mercredi [c. March 1829], Lafayette Collection, Lafayette College, Easton, Pennsylvania. Louis Gottschalk, *Lafayette: A Guide to the Letters, Documents, and Manuscripts in America* (Ithaca, NY: Cornell University Press, 1976), 104, suggests the approximate date of the letter as August 8, 1792. Due to the later handwriting and Constant's important speech on the tobacco monopoly to the Chamber of Deputies on March 18, 1829, after seeing Lafayette, I have suggested the above date. On the Hoffman process for producing multiple copies of texts, see Founders Online, accessed November 10, 2022, https://founders.archives.gov/documents/Jefferson/01-10-02-0234 -0001.

21. Lafayette to Jefferson, March 19, 1786, Founders Online, accessed November 10, 2022, https://founders.archives.gov/documents/Jefferson/01-09-02-0302. In his letter, Lafayette also refers to the immediate reaction to his remarks during the committee session as "a hot skirmish."

22. Balthazar-Jacques Paulze, "Mémoire," AAE, CP, EU, vol. 31, fols. 225–47; Farmers General, "Mémoire," May 1, 1786, ibid., fols. 268–79.

23. Lafayette to unidentified count, but probably Vergennes, April 22, 1786, Christie's, New York, *Fine Printed Books and Manuscripts including Americana . . . 5 December 2017,* 60, lot 62. On the fur proposal, see Jefferson to John Jay, May 27, 1786, Founders Online, accessed November 10, 2022, https://founders.archives.gov/documents /Jefferson/01-09-02-0476. Le Couteulx soon decided to send a family member (Louis-Etienne Le Couteulx de Caumont) to America, and Lafayette wrote a letter of introduction on his behalf. Lafayette to [unknown], October 8, 1786, R. R. Auctions,

Boston, *Catalog 1008, Auction of May 21, 2020*, lot 7456. The name is variously spelled by Americans and French as "Le Coulteux" or "Le Couteulx." I have adopted modern usage.

24. Jefferson to Monroe, May 10, 1786, Founders Online, accessed November 10, 2022, https://founders.archives.gov/documents/Jefferson/01-09-02-0413 .

25. The text of the decision is in ibid., https://founders.archives.gov/documents/Jefferson/01-09-02-0490; for Jefferson's May 31 letters to the governors, see ibid., https://founders.archives.gov/documents/Jefferson/01-09-02-0494. The *Maryland Gazette* (Frederick), August 9, 1786; the *Pennsylvania Packet* (Philadelphia), August 14, 1786; the *Daily Advertiser* (New York), August 31, 1786. The *Columbian Herald* (Charleston) published the news on October 12, 1786.

26. Price, *France and the Chesapeake*, 2:737, 773.

27. Lafayette to Castries, [probably after June 15, 1786], GLC 04799, Gilder Lehrman Institute of American History. Lafayette appears to have written it after Jefferson's June 15, 1786, letter to Lafayette, proposing Honfleur as a free port, Founders Online, accessed November 10, 2022, https://founders.archives.gov/documents/Jefferson/01-09-02-0538. On the packet boat system, see Henri Tristant, *Les premiers paquebots français de la ligne de New-York, 1783–1793* (the first French packet boats of the New York Line, 1783–93) (n.p., 1985).

28. Calonne to Jefferson, October 22, 1786, Founders Online, accessed November 10, 2022, https://founders.archives.gov/documents/Jefferson/01-10-02-0332; Jefferson to Jay, October 23, 1786, ibid., https://founders.archives.gov/documents/Jefferson/01-10-02-0337; *Independent Journal* (New York), December 30, 1786; the *Pennsylvania Packet* (Philadelphia), January 3, 1787; and the *American Herald* (Boston), January 8, 1787; *Charleston Morning Post*, March 8, 1787, had published the document through Gov. William Moultrie's forwarding of Jefferson's letter the previous May to Congress.

29. "His education in our school [that is, American beliefs] has drawn on him a very jealous eye from a court whose principles are the most absolute despotism." Jefferson to Edward Carrington, January 16, 1787, Founders Online, accessed November 10, 2022, https://founders.archives.gov/documents/Jefferson/01-11-02-0047.

30. One version from the French foreign ministry archives was published in the Jefferson Papers. It does not appear in Founders Online, but see Julian Boyd et al., eds., *The Papers of Thomas Jefferson*, 45 vols. to date (Princeton, NJ: Princeton University Press, 1950–), 13:57–75. Another version titled "Mémoire de Monsieur Dupont sur le Commerce des Etats-unis" is in the consular archives; see AN: AAE, B3:442, fols. 219–375.

31. Lambert to Jefferson, December 29, 1787, with the enclosed text of the council's order, Founders Online, accessed November 10, 2022, https://founders.archives.gov/documents/Jefferson/01-12-02-0481.

32. As an example, see the emergence of a strong trade between Americans and the city of Bordeaux in Silvia Marzagalli, "Establishing Transatlantic Trade Networks in Time of War: Bordeaux and the United States, 1793–1815," *Business History Review* 79.4 (Winter 2005): 811–44. Her larger study is *Bordeaux et les Etats-Unis, 1776–1815:*

Politique et stratégies négociantes dans la genèse d'un réseau (Bordeaux and the United States, 1776–1825: Policy and merchant strategies in the beginning of a network) (Geneva: Librairie Droz, 2015).

33. See, for example, Herbert A. Johnson, "American Constitutionalism and the War for Independence," *Early American Studies* 14.1 (Winter 2016): 140–73; Michael J. Klarman, *The Framers' Coup: The Making of the United States Constitution* (New York: Oxford University Press, 2016), though exhaustive of American perspectives, cites Lafayette only twice, both times as recipient of George Washington letters.

34. On Lafayette's appeals to Virginia officials for support in the summer 1781 campaign, see, for example, Lafayette to Thomas Nelson, August 12, 1781, *LAAR,* 4:314–15; to William Davie, August 13, 1781, Executive Department, Governor's Office, Letters Received, Library of Virginia, Richmond; to Davie, August 14, 1781, Lafayette Mss., Lilly Library, University of Indiana, Bloomington; to von Steuben, August 13, 1781, *LAAR,* 4:320–21; to Daniel Morgan, August 15, 1781, ibid., 4:323–24. Finally, Lafayette asked La Luzerne for Lauzun's Legion, letter to La Luzerne, August 14, 1781, ibid., 4:321–22.

35. The French consul at Boston, Philippe-André-Joseph de Létombe, wrote to Castries on April 16, 1784, that the New England states—Massachusetts, Rhode Island, and New Hampshire—would become a commercial republic like Genoa, Venice, or Holland, AN: AAE, B1 209, fols. r.–v. 302. François Barbé de Marbois compiled a 174-page general "Mémoire concernant le commerce entre France et les Etats-Unis," in early 1784 that divided the confederation into three distinct entities, AN: AAE, B3 441. French reactions to the individual, often contradictory, state legislation constitute much of an entire carton of documents, AN: AAE, B3 440.

36. Lafayette to Livingston, February 5, 1783, *LAAR,* 5:88; Lafayette to Nathanael Greene, February 5, 1783, Richard Showman et al., eds., *The Papers of General Nathanael Greene,* 13 vols. (Chapel Hill: University of North Carolina Press, 1976–2015), 12:415; Lafayette to Washington, February 5, 1783, Founders Online, accessed November 10, 2022, https://founders.archives.gov/documents/Washington/99-01-02-10575; Lafayette to Livingston, March 2, 1783, *LAAR,* 5:106.

37. Lafayette to David Humphreys, October 31, 1784, *LAAR,* 5: 277.

38. Reply to the Citizens of Baltimore, September 1, 1784, *LAAR,* 5:240–41; remarks of August 12/13, 1784, *Political Intelligencer* (New Brunswick, NJ), August 24, 1784; also *Pennsylvania Gazette* (Philadelphia), August 18, 1784; *Maryland Gazette* (Annapolis), August 26, 1784; remarks of October 26, 1784, *Providence Gazette* (Rhode Island), October 30, 1784; response of December 11, *New-Jersey Gazette* (Trenton), December 27, 1784, reprinted in the *New-York Journal,* December 30, 1784; *Political Intelligencer* (New Brunswick), January 4, 1785; *Maryland Gazette* (Annapolis), January 6, 1785; and the *Essex Journal* (Newburyport, MA), January 12, 1785. For more on the importance of the newspaper as a medium by which Lafayette "democratized" and expanded his political messages to wider, larger, and more diverse audiences during the 1784 tour, see my "Bridges to Freedom," in Kellman, *Lafayette in Transnational Context,* esp. 75–84.

39. *LAAR*, 5:281.

40. Lafayette to Nathanael Greene, March 16, 1785, *LAAR*, 5:304. Greene's January 7, 1785, letter to Lafayette has not been found; see ibid., 5:318n.3. Lafayette to Richard Henry Lee, March 16, 1785, ibid., 5:308.

41. Washington to Lafayette, July 25, 1785, Founders Online, accessed November 10. 2022, https://founders.archives.gov/documents/Washington/04-03-02-0143; Washington to Lafayette, September 1, 1785, ibid., https://founders.archives.gov/documents/Washington/04-03-02-0201.

42. On Lafayette's summer 1785 visits with the Austrians and Prussians, see *LAAR*, 5:333–49; and Gottschalk, *Lafayette between the American and the French Revolution*, 182–201; Lafayette to Jefferson, September 4, 1785, Founders Online, accessed November 10. 2022, https://founders.archives.gov/documents/Jefferson/01-08-02-0370.

43. Lafayette to Washington, February 6, 1786, Founders Online, accessed November 10. 2022, https://founders.archives.gov/documents/Washington/04-03-02-0461; Washington to Lafayette, May 10, 1786, ibid., https://founders.archives.gov/documents/Washington/04-04-02-0051; Washington to Lafayette, August 15, 1786, ibid., https://founders.archives.gov/documents/Washington/04-04-02-0200.

44. On Richard Price, see Allan Potofsky, "Le Corps consulaire français et le débat autour de la 'perte' des Amériques: Les intérêts mercantiles franco-américains et le commerce atlantique, 1763–1795," *Annales historiques de la Révolution française* 363 (2011): 33–57, esp. 41–43; and Will Slauter, "Constructive Misreadings: Adams, Turgot, and the American State Constitutions," *Papers of the Bibliographical Society of America* 105.1 (2011): 33–67. Washington did not receive his copy of Price's book until after Lafayette had already left America; see Washington to Benjamin Vaughan, February 5, 1785, Founders Online, accessed November 10. 2022, https://founders.archives.gov/documents/Washington/04-02-02-0235 .

45. Lafayette to Franklin, February 10, 1786, Benjamin Franklin Papers, American Philosophical Society Library, Philadelphia. This document is not in Founders Online, but see Jared Sparks, ed., *The Writings of Benjamin Franklin*, 10 vols. (Boston, 1836–40), 10:247–49.

46. Lafayette to John Jay, February 11, 1786, *Selected Papers of John Jay Digital Edition*, ed. Elizabeth N. Nuxall (Charlottesville: University of Virginia Press), https://rotunda.upress.virginia.edu/founders/JNJY-01-04-02-0132.

47. Lafayette to John Adams, June 16, 1786, Founders Online, accessed November 10. 2022, https://founders.archives.gov/documents/Adams/06-18-02-0183; Adams to Lafayette, June 26, 1786, ibid., https://founders.archives.gov/documents/Adams/06-18-02-0190.

48. Jefferson to Lafayette, August 24, 1786, Founders Online, accessed November 10. 2022, https://founders.archives.gov/documents/Jefferson/01-10-02-0211; Lafayette to Jefferson, August 30, 1786, ibid., https://founders.archives.gov/documents/Jefferson/01-10-02-0230.

49. Lafayette to James McHenry, October 26, 1786, photostat, Papers of James McHenry, Manuscript Division, Library of Congress, Washington, DC; Lafayette to

William Stephen Smith, December 20, 1786, Rosenbach of the Free Library, Philadelphia; Lafayette to Anthony Wayne, December 20, 1787, Wayne Papers, Historical Society of Pennsylvania, Philadelphia. See also Gottschalk, *Lafayette between the American and the French Revolution*, 273.

50. Lafayette to Adams, January 5, 1787, Founders Online, accessed November 10, 2022, https://founders.archives.gov/documents/Adams/06-18-02-0282; Lafayette to Washington, January 13, 1787, ibid., https://founders.archives.gov/documents/Washington/04-04-02-0442; Lafayette to Smith, January 16, 1787, DeWindt Collection, Massachusetts Historical Society, Boston.

51. Lafayette to John Jay, February 7, 1787, *Selected Papers of John Jay Digital Edition*, https://rotunda.upress.virginia.edu/founders/jnjy-01-04-02-0215; Lafayette to Washington, February 7, 1787, Founders Online, accessed November 10, 2022, https://founders.archives.gov/documents/Washington/04-05-02-0010.

52. John Jay to Lafayette, draft, February 16, 1787, Founders Online, accessed November 10, 2022, https://founders.archives.gov/documents/Jay/01-04-02-0218; Washington to Lafayette, March 25, 1787, ibid., https://founders.archives.gov/documents/Washington/04-05-02-0103.

53. Lafayette to John Jay, May 30, 1787, Founders Online, accessed November 10, 2022, https://founders.archives.gov/documents/Jay/01-04-02-0238.

54. Washington to Lafayette, June 6, 1787, Founders Online, accessed November 10, 2022, https://founders.archives.gov/documents/Washington/04-05-02-0200.

55. Henry Knox to Lafayette, draft, July 25, 1787, Gilder Lehrman Institute of History, New York City, NY, GLC02437.03616.

56. Lafayette to Washington, August 3, 1787, Founders Online, accessed November 10, 2022, https://founders.archives.gov/documents/Washington/04-05-02-0259; Lafayette to Madison, August 5, 1787, ibid., https://founders.archives.gov/documents/Madison/01-10-02-0082.

57. Montmorin to Moustier, October 10, 1787, "Correspondence of the Comte de Moustier with the Comte de Montmorin, 1787–1789," *American Historical Review* 8.4 (July 1903): 710–14. Montmorin wrote in part: "Le comte de Moustier aura vu dans la correspondance du S. Otto que les Américains sont occupés d'une nouvelle constitution. Cet objet n'intéresse que faiblement la politique du Roi. Sa Majesté pense, d'un coté, que les délibérations n'auront aucune succès par la diversité des affections, des intérets et des principes des différentes provinces. . . ." (The comte de Moustier will have seen in the correspondence of Monsieur Otto that the Americans are busy with a new constitution. This object interests the policies of the king only slightly. His Majesty thinks, on the one hand, that the proceedings will be unsuccessful due to the diversity of affections, interests, and the principles of the different states.) (Translation by author). See also Clyde Augustus Duniway, "French Influence on the Adoption of the Federal Constitution," *American Historical Review* 9.2 (January 1904): 304–9. On Montmorin, see Orville T. Murphy, *The Diplomatic Retreat of France and Public Opinion on the Eve of the French Revolution, 1783–1789* (Washington, DC: Catholic University of America Press, 1998).

58. Lafayette to Washington, October 9, 1787, Founders Online, accessed November 10, 2022, https://founders.archives.gov/documents/Washington/04-05-02-0332. Lafayette wrote a similar inquiry seeking to learn the results of the convention to Adams on October 12, 1787, ibid., https://founders.archives.gov/documents/Adams/99-02-02-0238; and to John Jay on October 15, 1787, ibid., https://founders.archives.gov/documents/Jay/01-04-02-0277; and to Adams, October 30, 1787, ibid., https://founders.archives.gov/documents/Adams/99-02-02-0262.

59. Washington to Lafayette, September 18, 1787, Founders Online, accessed November 10, 2022, https://founders.archives.gov/documents/Washington/04-05-02-0309. There were two possible printings of the Constitution that Washington may have sent to Lafayette, one approved on September 12, the other including the changes of September 13–17. Knox to Lafayette, draft, October 24, 1787, Gilder Lehrman Institute of America History, New York City, GLC02437.03680.

60. Lafayette to Jefferson, Tuesday [December 25 [?], 1787], Founders Online, accessed November 10, 2022, https://founders.archives.gov/documents/Jefferson/01-12-02-0470; Lafayette to Washington, January 1, 1788, ibid., https://founders.archives.gov/documents/Washington/04-06-02-0003. Boyd states that Washington had also written to Jefferson on September 18, and that letter, enclosing a copy of the proposed constitution, arrived on December 19, 1787; see the note in ibid., https://founders.archives.gov/documents/Washington/04-05-02-0308.

61. Lafayette to Knox, February 4, 1788, Gilder Lehrman Institute of American History, New York City, GLC 02437.04105. Lafayette to Washington, February 4, 1788, Founders Online, accessed November 10, 2022, https://founders.archives.gov/documents/Washington/04-06-02-0071.Washington to Lafayette, February 7, 1788, ibid., https://founders.archives.gov/documents/Washington/04-06-02-0079.

62. Jay to Lafayette, April 26, 1788, Jay Papers, Butler Library, Columbia University, New York City. This letter does not appear in Founders Online, but it does appear in Henry P. Johnston, ed., *The Correspondence and Public Papers of John Jay*, 4 vols. (New York, [1890–93]), 3:327–29. Lafayette to James Bowdoin, May 25, 1788, Bowdoin-Temple Collection, Massachusetts Historical Society, Boston; Lafayette to John Jay, May 30, 1788, Founders Online, accessed November 10, 2022, https://founders.archives.gov/documents/Jay/01-04-02-0337.

63. Washington to Lafayette, May 28, 1788, Founders Online, accessed November 10, 2022, https://founders.archives.gov/documents/Washington/04-06-02-0264 .

64. Washington to Lafayette, June 18, 1788, Founders Online, accessed November 10, 2022, https://founders.archives.gov/documents/Washington/04-06-02-0301; Lafayette to Jeremiah Wadsworth, after August 25, 1788, Trumbull Collection, Connecticut Historical Society, Hartford. Lafayette had written to Elias Dayton, "God grant it may be unanimous; it is the way for America to preserve her glory and insure her happiness for which no heart is more fervently praying than that of your humble servant and sincere friend, Lafayette." Lafayette to Dayton, September 5, 1788, Christie's, New York *Printed Books and Manuscripts . . . Sale 7700 . . . June 9, 1993*, 119, lot

220. Robert R. Livingston to Lafayette, draft, September 7, 1788, Robert R. Livingston Collection, New-York Historical Society.

65. Jefferson to Madison, January 12, 1789, Founders Online, accessed November 10, 2022, https://founders.archives.gov/documents/Madison/01-11-02-0302; Washington to Lafayette, January 29, 1789, ibid., https://founders.archives.gov/documents/Washington/05-01-02-0198.

66. Lafayette to Adrienne de Lafayette, June 7, 1777, *LAAR*, 1:58–59.

67. Georges Lefebvre, *Coming of the French Revolution*, trans. Robert R. Palmer (Princeton, NJ: Princeton University Press, 1947); François Furet, *Interpreting the French Revolution*, trans. Elborg Forster (Cambridge, MA: Harvard University Press, 1981). See also, for example, Patrice Guennifey's entry on "La Fayette" in François Furet and Mona Ozouf, eds., *A Critical Dictionary of the French Revolution*, trans. Arthur Goldhammer, 2 vols. (Cambridge, MA: Harvard University Press, 1989), 224; and—among other critics—Guennify's vitriolic review of Lloyd Kramer's *Lafayette in Two Worlds* in the *Journal of Modern History* 70.3 (September 1998): 707–9.

68. Philippe Bourdin, ed., *La Fayette, entre deux mondes* (Clermont-Ferrand: Presses universitaires Blaise-Pascal, 2009). According to Belissa, "It is nevertheless a pity that recent historiography has more or less abandoned the specific study of his politics. For example, his activity as 'lobbyist' in the commercial field in favor of the United States in the years 1783–1789 has stirred no new research" (254), *Annales historiques de la révolution française* 364 (April/June 2011): 252–54.

Lafayette, the Lameths, and "Republican Monarchy," 1789–1791

Munro Price

Both during and after the American Revolution, many observers were convinced that France's decision to support the thirteen colonies in their struggle against Britain had created a general climate of opinion in favour of "American" ideas of liberty that helped prepare the revolution of 1789. They noted the significant number of French revolutionary leaders who had previously fought in America, most obviously Lafayette, but also the three Lameth brothers, the duc de Lauzun, the vicomte de Noailles, and the comte de Ségur. As Thomas Paine put it in *The Rights of Man,* "The French officers and soldiers who went to America . . . were . . . placed in the school of freedom, and learned the practice as well as the principles by heart."[1]

From the mid-nineteenth century, a distinguished historical tradition has analysed the connections between the American and French Revolutions, beginning with Tocqueville, and continuing through Palmer and Godechot to François Furet and Patrice Higonnet in the 1980s and 1990s.[2] Yet the main concern of these works is the grand sweep of the history of ideas and social movements, and they generally have a wide geographical range. In contrast, much less work has been written that applies these insights at the level of individuals and small groups and analyses, on a case-by-case basis, just how far those Frenchmen who fought in America and went on to lead their own revolution were shaped by "American" ideas. An exception is Louis Gottschalk's six-volume biography of Lafayette, but this is unfinished, going only up to 1790, and some of its arguments can be disputed.[3] For those other French revolutionaries who served in America, neglect is the rule. There is, for example, no scholarly biography of any of the Lameth brothers: Charles and Alexandre, leading radical deputies in the constituent assembly and luminaries of the Jacobin club, and Théodore, who collaborated with them politically and left important memoirs.[4] This is remarkable, since along with Lafayette they were the most prominent French revolutionaries to have fought in the American War of Independence. This paper compares the "American" influence on the conduct both of Lafayette and the Lameths in the French Revolution and assesses just how crucial this was.

Lafayette's role in the War for Independence is too well known to recount in detail here. Having early embraced the American cause and been offered the rank of major-general in the Continental Army, he landed in South Carolina on June 13, 1777, and almost immediately upon his arrival at the army camp in Massachusetts struck up a remarkable rapport with George Washington, who came to treat him virtually as his adopted son. He was wounded at the Battle of Brandywine, endured the hardships of Valley Forge, and captured one of the two key British redoubts defending Yorktown, helping to ensure Cornwallis's surrender. The part played by Alexandre, Charles, and Théodore de Lameth in the war is less familiar but was also distinguished. All three brothers served in comte de Rochambeau's expeditionary force, Charles from 1780 and Alexandre and Théodore from 1782. Charles's record was the most brilliant; he was one of the general's aides-de-camp and received two bullets in the knee during the storming of the second redoubt at Yorktown.

From that point on, however, a rivalry grew up between Lafayette and the Lameths that became increasingly bitter during and after the French Revolution. Lafayette devotes only a few, not very revealing, pages to the Lameths in his memoirs. However, the one Lameth who did write memoirs, Théodore, implies that the conflict sprang directly from the War for Independence and from his and his brothers' jealousy at Lafayette eclipsing his compatriots as its greatest French hero. While conceding that Lafayette had captured a redoubt at Yorktown, Théodore could not resist adding a footnote minimizing this achievement: "The more important one was taken by the baron de Vioménil. Charles de Lameth . . . first opened the communication trench and the head of a hundred grenadiers who were almost all hit; he himself was struck twice by gunfire."[5]

Circumstances, and personalities, clearly played some part in determining the conduct of, and explaining the conflict between, Lafayette and the Lameths during the French Revolution. However, they were also motivated by strongly held political ideals. The most concrete way of examining and comparing these is to analyse Lafayette's and the Lameths' differing positions on the constitution worked out by the French national assembly between July 1789 and September 1791. To gauge any American influence on these, the US Constitution, ratified only four years earlier, forms an obvious point of reference.

Lafayette's views on the developing French constitution between 1789 and 1790 can be fairly clearly established through his memoirs and through his correspondence. It is also easy to demonstrate the connections between these ideas, a substantial part of which he managed to put into practice, and those of the Declaration of Independence and the US Constitution. This link was embodied by the author of the Declaration of Independence himself, Thomas Jefferson, who was in Paris as American minister to France during the first two years of the revolution and in regular communication with Lafayette.[6]

Lafayette's most important contribution to the French constitution eventually promulgated in 1791—and through this to many subsequent ones throughout the world—came with the Declaration of the Rights of Man. As early as January 1789 he began working on this project, explicitly modelled on the Declaration of Independence, to encapsulate the political changes gathering pace in France. He was later to call this, rather grandiloquently, a "profession of faith, fruit of my past, pledge of my future." Jefferson certainly commented on the first draft, which he passed on to Madison back in the United States. Six months later Lafayette produced a second draft, which he presumably also discussed with Jefferson, since the latter annotated it and kept a copy in his papers.[7] Significantly, Lafayette chose to unveil it to the national assembly on July 11, 1789, when it seemed for a moment that Louis XVI might be about to reassert his authority by force. Presumably, if the king did resort to violent measures and reimpose the old order, Lafayette wanted to leave some form of political testament for the record.

The basis of Lafayette's declaration was that nature had made all men "free and equal," and that distinctions between them could only be made if "based upon general utility." The source of sovereignty lay "imprescriptibly" in the nation; the separation of powers between executive, legislature, and judiciary was laid down, and legislative power should be exercised by a large representative assembly, regularly and frequently elected. Freedom of speech and religion were guaranteed. In words unmistakeably modelled on Jefferson's in the Declaration of Independence, Lafayette listed among the "inalienable rights of man" "life," "liberty," and "the pursuit of happiness."[8]

Lafayette's declaration of rights was not the only one presented to the assembly in these crucial days—indeed, he specifically asked his colleagues to present others of their own—but it was the first. When debates on the constitution resumed after the fall of the Bastille, therefore, his text retained particular importance despite competing versions from such luminaries as Mirabeau, Sieyès, and Mounier. Ultimately, of the seventeen articles of the Declaration of the Rights of Man endorsed by the national assembly on August 26, 1789, the first nine were based principally on his draft. As Louis Gottschalk concludes, "In sum, as Lafayette claimed about forty years later, the Declaration of the Rights of Man and the Citizen of 1789 was based more upon his project than upon any one other, and the greater part of his was incorporated in it."[9]

In contrast to the volumes written on Lafayette, there are almost no studies, and certainly none of book length, devoted to the Lameth brothers. In their absence, the most helpful modern source is Sylvia Delannoy's article of 2010, "Les frères Lameth, de l'engagement aux désillusions." Delannoy's research in the departmental archives of the Val d'Oise, which contain some Lameth papers, makes it clear that little in the brothers' background predisposed them to become revolutionaries. They were well-connected court nobles, related through their mother to the prestigious Broglie family; indeed, their uncle, the maréchal de Broglie, was to be one of the most prominent counter-revolutionaries after 1789. They also benefited financially from their status at Versailles; as the publication of the *Livre Rouge* of the court revealed to their embarrassment in January 1791, they and their mother were recipients of 60,000 livres worth of pensions.[10]

The process by which the Lameth brothers became radicalized remains obscure. Their participation in the American War of Independence may have played a part, but there is no firm surviving evidence for this. The first concrete evidence of one of the brothers embracing what would become the revolutionary cause is a pamphlet written by Alexandre de Lameth just before the elections to the Estates-General. The date usually ascribed to it is early 1789, but since it refers to the second assembly of notables as still being in session, it was more likely published in December 1788. It took the form of a reply to a previous pamphlet, entitled *Le Bon Sens*, written by the naval officer and future Girondin deputy to the convention, the comte de Kersaint.[11] The pamphlet, *Lettre à M le Comte de * * *, auteur d'un ouvrage intitulé Le Bon Sens,* was certainly not a denunciation of Kersaint's; both men supported broadly liberal measure such as guarantees of individual, religious, and press freedom, and consent to taxation. However, it respectfully but firmly took issue with Kersaint on two crucial issues—the extent of the royal authority and the composition of the legislature under a future constitution. Here, Alexandre de Lameth's stance prefigured both his own and that of his brothers during the revolution and served notice that until 1791 at least, their position on the political spectrum would be markedly on the left.

It is significant that the first major reproach Lameth levels at Kersaint is that of Anglomania or, as the pamphlet delicately puts it, being "a little too enthusiastic about the English constitution." For Lameth, importing the British constitution wholesale into France would have two disadvantages. The first is that it gave the king too much power through allowing him undue influence over the legislature: "In proposing that the king of France should be able to collaborate in legislation, you invite the corruption with which the English constitution has so justly been reproached." The second was that the British constitution ignored the separation of powers, especially between the executive and the legislature, which Lameth strongly upheld: "By mixing up the different powers, one encourages permanent warfare between them, which ends by destroying the government. On the contrary, one cannot be too careful to define their respective limits."[12] This is the only hint in the pamphlet, an oblique one it is true, that Lameth found the US Constitution, with its stricter distinctions between executive, legislative, and judicial power, superior to its British counterpart.

The necessity for dramatic limitations to the royal authority, which was to become such a theme of Alexandre de Lameth's speeches and actions during the revolution, is clearly set out in the *Lettre*. It concedes that the king should remain titular commander-in-chief of the army and navy and that war should be declared, peace made, and justice handed down in his name.[13] However, Lameth strongly implies that he sees these attributions as merely courtesies and that the real decisions in these areas should be made respectively by the military chiefs, deputies, and independent judges appointed for life. For Lameth, rigorously restricting the king henceforth to the executive sphere was simply a means of subordinating him firmly to the legislature.

The extent of this hostility to the old regime monarchy from someone whose family had been so closely associated with it is striking. It was certainly to lay Alexandre and his brothers open to much attack during the revolution. One possible explanation is that advanced by Daniel Wick, first in his article of 1980, "The Court Nobility and the French Revolution: The Example of the Society of Thirty," and then in his book published seven years later, *A Conspiracy of Well-Intentioned Men: The Society of Thirty and the French Revolution*.[14] The focus of Wick's work, the Society of Thirty, was an informal political committee founded in Paris in November 1788 to influence the forthcoming elections to the Estates-General in a liberal, even radical direction. The remarkable fact about this oppositional grouping is that it was dominated by court nobles—including Lafayette and Alexandre, Charles, and Théodore de Lameth. What could have alienated them so decisively from the milieu in which they had been brought up?

Wick finds his answer in the increasingly dysfunctional politics of Versailles in the reign of Louis XVI. Louis XIV and Louis XV, he argues, had generally tried to distribute posts and pensions evenly between the competing families and factions at court. In contrast, Louis XVI, and particularly his queen Marie Antoinette, who swiftly acquired unprecedented influence over patronage, concentrated it on a small, unpopular clique headed by the Polignac clan. A major victim of this development was the powerful Noailles clan, of which Lafayette's wife was a member and to which he himself therefore belonged. In Wick's view, the factional battle in court politics between "ins" and "outs" was at least as important as liberal ideology in recruiting not only Lafayette but also his brother-in-law the vicomte de Noailles to the opposition to the old regime.[15]

The case of the Lameths is slightly different from Lafayette's but reflects several of the same themes. The Broglie family, to which their mother belonged, had held high military and political office under Louis XV. Its anti-Austrian views in foreign policy were hardly likely to endear it to the Habsburg Marie Antoinette in the next reign. The Broglies' move into open opposition, however, came late and stemmed from one specific issue, the military reform of 1787. This was the old regime's last effort to remodel the army, and the reforms attacked in particular the court nobility's grip on the officer corps. Its most prominent opponent was the Lameths' uncle, the maréchal de Broglie, one of France's most distinguished soldiers, who refused to implement the reforms in his command at Metz. A few months later, in May 1788, Broglie extended his opposition from the military to the civilian sphere, refusing to join the plenary court set up by the crown as part of its reform of the judiciary. In both of these actions, he was supported by all three of his nephews.[16] It is certainly plausible that this bitter breach explains the references to the crown's "corruption," "despotism," and "perverse ministers" in Alexandre de Lameth's pamphlet published only a few months later.

The second major reproach that Lameth levelled against Kersaint in his *Lettre* concerned not the executive, but the legislature. In *Le Bon Sens* Kersaint had proposed that in the new constitutional dispensation he hoped the meeting of the Estates-General would shortly bring about, the legislature should be divided into two chambers. On the English model, the upper chamber would be drawn from the nobility and the clergy and the lower elected by the people. Lameth unequivocally condemned this plan. Partly this reflected his suspicion of his own order, the nobility, and his conviction that, grouped together in an upper chamber, its members would refuse to give up their privileges for the common good. However, his greatest objection to an upper house, revealingly, centered once again on his abiding distrust of the crown. Giving the privileged orders, already closely linked to the court through patronage, a chamber of their own would, Lameth argued, simply give the monarchy an extra weapon with which to block liberal reform. As he put it rhetorically to Kersaint in his *Lettre:*

> Why, having emphasized the obstacles which the nobility, in some circumstances, poses to the balance of a good constitution, do you confine to a part of that very nobility, the one most devoted to the throne, since it has the greatest access to it, the right to form the first chamber of representatives? Why fill it with archbishops, bishops, magistrates, councillors of state, vice-admirals and marshals of France, who all owe their existence to the king? Giving the hope of being able to corrupt often inspires the wish to do so.[17]

The deep suspicion of royal power expressed in the *Lettre à M de Comte de* *** prefigured the political stance taken by all three Lameth brothers in the first two years of the revolution. This was to change in 1791, as the danger to their political programme posed by the radical Jacobins came to dwarf that presented by Louis XVI. Yet the bitter tone of Alexandre de Lameth's pamphlet is testimony to the depth of the split in 1789 between the monarchy and many of those who should have been its natural supporters, a split that helped make the events of that summer possible.

Although he was a fellow member of the Society of Thirty, Lafayette's views on executive and legislative power differed in certain crucial ways from the Lameths'. Lafayette envisaged King Louis XVI as a relatively strong executive, along the lines of the US president, rather than the mere tool of the legislature proposed by the Lameths. The first sign of this divergence came in the crucial battle in August and September 1789 over whether the king should have an absolute or merely a suspensive veto over legislation. Lafayette was so concerned about the issue's divisive potential that he persuaded Jefferson to invite the leaders of both sides to his house to resolve their differences on August 26, 1789. However, the meeting, at which Lafayette and Alexandre de Lameth were both present, broke up without agreement, and on September 11 the constituent assembly voted overwhelmingly in favour of the suspensive veto. Both Lafayette and the Lameths supported this option, but there were significant nuances between their positions. Lafayette had written to Jefferson that he favoured "a suspensive veto so strong and so complicated as to give the king a due influence."[18] In contrast, Alexandre de Lameth advocated a far swifter procedure: a dissolution of the assembly and fresh elections, after which the king would have to accept the opinion of the new legislature.[19]

The clearest constitutional split between Lafayette and the Lameths came over the composition of the legislature and the foreign policy powers of the executive. The question of whether the national assembly should have one or two chambers was debated at the same time as that of the royal veto, in September 1789. Lafayette advocated a second chamber on the American model. "I am definitely for two chambers," he wrote at the time, "not for a hereditary chamber, but for a senate nominated for six years, or even longer if necessary."[20] Given how strongly he had condemned the idea of a two-chamber legislature a few months previously in the *Lettre à M le Comte de ****, Alexandre de Lameth is curiously absent from the national assembly's tumultuous debate on the subject. He is simply quoted in the record as remarking that "the way the two chambers are organized should be clarified before it can be decided whether two chambers should be preferred to one."[21] Louis Gottschalk, however, argues that at the meeting at Jefferson's house on August 26, Lameth's strong opposition to a second chamber swayed many of his colleagues and contributed significantly to its crushing rejection, by a majority of 490 to 89 (with 112 abstentions) in the Constituent Assembly's vote of September 10.[22]

The last significant passage of arms between Lafayette and the Lameths came in May 1790, over the critical question of whether the right to declare war and make peace should be vested in the king or the national assembly. The trigger was the Nootka Sound crisis, in which Britain and Spain appeared to be about to go to war over possessions on the American Pacific Coast, a conflict into which France would then be drawn as an ally of Spain. When the foreign minister Montmorin requested funds to mobilize the French navy in support of Spain, he was immediately challenged by the radical deputies, and a passionate debate ensued.

Alexandre de Lameth's stance on the issue placed him firmly in the radical camp. The right of making war and peace, he argued, should be removed entirely from the king and vested in the national assembly alone. The reason, once again, lay in his profound distrust of royal power. This had, if anything, increased over the past year, fuelled by recurrent rumours that Louis XVI was prepared to use any means, including military force, to regain his lost authority. Previously, he maintained, absolute monarchs had "sacrificed entire peoples to their personal resentments and despicable whims." Now, he was convinced, the main reason the king hoped to retain the exclusive right to declare war was to use it as a weapon against his own compatriots, in "the cause of kings against peoples."[23]

Lafayette firmly opposed Lameth's position but did not take the lead in denouncing it. That task he left to one of the great orators of the assembly, Mirabeau, whom he was content to support. Mirabeau countered the arguments of Lameth and his allies with an ingenious compromise: the king should have the right to begin war but to be legal, his action would have to be ratified by the assembly. While apparently giving the assembly the deciding power, in fact this proposal gave crucial advantages to the king; it would take a brave assembly to stop a war once the monarch had set it in motion in an atmosphere of national emergency. Mirabeau also could not resist a highly personal sideswipe at the Lameth brothers. Defending himself from charges that he was betraying the popular cause, he reminded his audience that for twenty years he had been "speaking to the French people of liberty, a constitution [and] resistance, while his vile detractors had been sucking up the milk of the court and exploiting all the privileges available."[24]

Lafayette, never a great speaker, could not match this invective. He was, however, warmly applauded when he told the assembly that Mirabeau's plan "suits the majority of a great people, the spirit of a free people, the interests of a numerous people, whose industry, possessions and foreign relations demand effective protection."[25] It is worth noting that the proposition he was supporting gave the French king war and peace-making powers broadly analogous to those of the US president. It was passed, with only slight amendments, on May 22, 1790, and was incorporated into the constitution of 1791.

Clearly Lafayette's American experience strongly influenced his constitutional ideas. It is more difficult to establish that the Lameths' service in the War of Independence did the same for them. Indeed, on some important issues, such as the composition of the legislature and its powers relative to the executive, the Lameth brothers rejected the American example. However, Lafayette's and the Lameths' constitutional ideas did broadly converge on basic principles: the people as the ultimate source of authority, the separation of powers, equal rights under the law, and representative government. These essential points strongly resemble those of the US Constitution. Given this underlying similarity, a wider question arises: Was the French constitution of 1791, as envisaged by Lafayette and the Lameths, essentially republican?

One difficulty immediately presents itself here. Between 1789 and 1792, the period in which Lafayette and the Lameths were so prominent, France was obviously not a republic but a constitutional monarchy. The triumph of republicanism only occurred four years into the revolution with the overthrow of the king on August 10, 1792. Yet several eminent French historians have recently concluded that, despite the retention of Louis XVI as head of state, many of the features of the new France were republican from the start. For François Furet and Ran Halévi, the constitution of 1791 created a "republican monarchy." In a penetrating passage in an essay from 1993, Patrice Gueniffey takes the argument further:

> The advent of the republic does not date from 10th August 1792, and the preceding period does not constitute its prehistory. The French Revolution was republican from the beginning. The proclamation of equality of rights, the collective appropriation of sovereignty, the introduction of representative powers and the limiting of royal authority to a subordinate executive domain, inaugurated in 1789 a republican regime in all but name. 1792 simply saw a change in the form of the executive power, a revolution *within* the republic, part of the history of the Revolution itself.[26]

This striking statement helps to explain one of the key conflicts of the French Revolution. For many French people, at their head Louis XVI himself, the revolution's collective appropriation of sovereignty, and above all the limiting of royal authority to a subordinate executive domain, took constitutional innovation a long step too far and propelled them into counter-revolution. In December 1791, Louis XVI could write of "the absurd and detestable constitution which gives me less power than the King of Poland used to have."[27] He could have added "less power than the President of the United States," since the 1791 constitution had stripped him of the right to initiate legislation. The introduction of "republican monarchy" not only alienated the king decisively from the revolution but split the revolutionaries themselves. It was a major reason why the revolution could never create the political consensus France so desperately needed after 1789.

Interestingly, Louis Gottschalk does not count Lafayette among the supporters of "republican monarchy." He argues that for all his veneration of the American republic, what Lafayette wanted for France during the revolution was "a strong constitutional monarchy, brought about by tempered reform through the willing cooperation of a benevolent king with a moderate constitutional assembly."[28] This is not, however, the whole story. In his memoirs, above all in a neglected section entitled *De la démocratie royale de 1789 et le républicanisme des vrais constitutionnels,* Lafayette does present himself as a defender of the constitutional monarchy, but he significantly qualifies this stance. First, he openly admits that the basic inspiration of the 1791 constitution was indeed republican. In words that anticipate Gueniffey's, he states simply:

> The assertion that France's first constitution [that of 1791] was republican is correct; because when ninety-nine parts of a whole are of one nature, and the last of mixed composition, it fits that description. Therefore I cannot blame MM Burke, Mounier, John Adams, in a word the best-informed publicists who have written against the constitutional party [in France], for having called it republican, and for having defined France since 1789 as a republic.

This still leaves the problem of how any state whose executive is hereditary, as France's remained between 1789 and 1792, can be termed a republic, however republican its basic principles may be. It also raises the question of how Lafayette, who claimed that his heart was "naturally republican" could defend any form of monarchy without risking the charge of hypocrisy. In

De la démocratie royale Lafayette attempted to reconcile these two positions and to defend his own integrity and did so with some skill. France in 1789 was not America in 1776, with a faraway king who could the more easily be repudiated. Despite his essential republicanism, Lafayette claimed, he was forced to recognize that in France centuries of tradition required Louis XVI to remain head of state.[29]

Yet this does not mean that Lafayette wished this settlement, a constitutional monarchy, to continue indefinitely. He hoped that, sooner rather than later, the French people would be sufficiently enlightened to switch to full republicanism in a moderate and peaceful manner. As he puts it, rather obliquely, in *De la démocratie royale:* "I agree that there may have been deputies in the constituent assembly who, having no sentimental preference for a hereditary monarchy, foresaw, perhaps even with pleasure, a near future in which this heredity would cease to be necessary." Lafayette leaves no doubt that he was one of those deputies. In the next sentence, he reveals exactly how long he estimated it would take for France to become a republic: "M Jefferson . . . said many times that [I] was mistaken in [my] calculation that the monarchy would still last for twenty-five or thirty more years."[30] For Lafayette and Jefferson, it was not a question of if, but when, France would become a republic.

Further confirmation of Lafayette's essentially republican view of the French constitution comes, appropriately, from the most distinguished American after Jefferson to witness the French Revolution, Gouverneur Morris. A former delegate to the Continental Congress and later a key framer of the US Constitution, Morris arrived in France in February 1789 as the representative of American tobacco interests. In January 1792 he was to succeed Jefferson as American minister to France. Morris, however, was markedly more conservative politically than his predecessor; he believed in strong executive power and had doubts about democracy, making him throughout his time in France a strong defender of Louis XVI.[31]

Morris's main contribution to the history of the French Revolution is his voluminous diary, eventually published in 1939, and this refers often to Lafayette. Morris first met Lafayette during the American War for Independence and renewed the acquaintance in Paris in 1789. In the early stages of the French Revolution both men moved in the same social and political circles—in May 1789, for example, Morris was elected a member of the constitutionalist Club de Valois, to which Lafayette and the Lameths also belonged. However, Morris felt that Lafayette's abilities were mediocre and his politics too radical for France's present situation, and as a result, the diary's treatment of him is caustic. As early as April 1789, Morris perceived Lafayette's basic republicanism and how sharply this differed from his own prescription for France: "His principles accord best with those of a Republic, mine are drawn only from human Nature and ought not therefore to have much Respect in this Age of Refinement." A few months later, in a letter to William Carmichael, the American *chargé d'affaires* in Madrid, Morris extended this critique of Lafayette to all those of his compatriots who thought the US Constitution was suitable for France. Appropriately, he was writing on July 14:

> I have steadily combated the Violence and Excess of those Persons who, either inspired with an enthusiastic Love of Freedom or prompted by sinister Designs, are disposed to drive everything to Extremity. Our American Example has done them good; but like all novelties, Liberty runs away with their Discretion, if they have any. They want an American Constitution with the Exception of a King instead of a President, without reflecting that they have not American Citizens to support that Constitution.[32]

Despite its slightly patronising tone, this is an extremely acute analysis that chimes perfectly with Lafayette's own admission in his memoirs that the monarchy he sought for France was an American-style republic in all but name. The fact that Morris disapproved so strongly of Lafayette's views, while his predecessor Jefferson had helped shape them, is also very revealing. Two years after its drafting in Philadelphia and a year after its ratification, the battle over the US Constitution was being refought in France, with the Republican Jefferson endorsing a weak executive, while the Federalist Morris actively supported a strong monarchy.

Moving from the arena of principles to that of practical politics, Morris's diary adds important—and neglected—evidence to the controversial question of Lafayette's personal ambitions. Throughout the first years of the revolution, Lafayette's conservative opponents accused him of wishing actually to displace Louis XVI and take supreme power himself. Historians since have tended to discount this charge and to conclude that the form of constitution Lafayette wished for France, while severely limiting the crown's future authority, held no place for a Cromwell.³³ Morris's diary entry for November 18, 1789, written just after a dinner with Lafayette, leaves room to doubt this conclusion. During this conversation, Morris recounts, Lafayette expressed contempt for his fellow-deputies and went on to make a startling prediction: "He says that Mirabeau has well described the Assemblée which he calls *the Wild Ass*. That in a Fortnight they will be obliged to give him Authority which he has hitherto declined. I ask him what Authority. He says a Kind of Dictatorship such as Generalissimo. He does not know exactly what will be the Title.... Here is vaulting Ambition, which o'erleaps itself."³⁴

Of course, this is only one source, but it is a direct quote from Lafayette recorded by a witness who knew him well. It is also highly unlikely that Morris fabricated Lafayette's words in a private diary he did not intend to publish. If one accepts this, it is quite possible that at least once in the revolution's first phase Lafayette did consider assuming some sort of dictatorial power. Whether this would have left Louis XVI as a purely symbolic head of state, or would have displaced him altogether, can only be conjectured.

Whether or not it masked his own designs on power, Lafayette's crypto-republicanism marked one more point of difference with the Lameths. At first glance, this seems paradoxical: the Lameths were far more suspicious of the executive than Lafayette and sought at every turn to subordinate it to the legislature. Yet however much they wished to limit executive power, they were convinced that it should remain vested in the crown. After the flight to Varennes, Lafayette briefly considered whether this was the time to declare a republic, before deciding that at this perilous juncture changing the executive would imperil the entire constitution. The Lameths' response was more forthright. On June 25, 1791, Alexandre de Lameth rose in the assembly to make a ringing declaration of faith in constitutional monarchy: "Sent here to give our country a constitution, we felt that the size of the kingdom and a population of 25 million ... required the unity of power and action which could only be found in a monarchical constitution."³⁵

This speech probably reveals the secret of the Lameths' monarchism: the idea, borrowed from Montesquieu, that monarchy was the system of government best adapted to a large country where coordination over large areas was necessary. None of this, of course, diminished their belief that the form of that monarchy should be constitutional and dominated by the legislature. Significantly, Théodore chose to underscore all the Lameths' loyalty to the crown in his memoirs and to contrast this with what he had always assumed was Lafayette's basic republicanism. At the end of his chapter detailing their long rivalry with Lafayette, he added that they had finally been reconciled during the Hundred Days (in 1815). Since then, he wrote, "my brothers and I have kept up polite relations [with Lafayette], while always firmly opposing him over political ideas and our own unshakeably monarchist beliefs."[36] It was a clash on two levels. During the revolution Lafayette had wanted a strong executive, but in his heart had hoped it would become republican; the Lameths had preferred a weak executive but had always wished it to remain monarchical.

The rifts and rivalries between Lafayette and the Lameths should not obscure what united them. Borrowing from the American example, though Lafayette did so more than the Lameths, they pioneered the introduction into France of principles that now form the basis of its political system. Yet in the short term they failed, in dramatic and tragic circumstances. They did so for many reasons, but one was central—the conundrum, which they never managed to resolve, of the nature and powers of the executive. Grafting the existing king in a largely symbolic capacity onto an essentially republican polity was an experiment doomed to failure, especially when the monarch in question had enjoyed absolute power only two years previously. Louis XVI was prepared to give up many powers, but not simply to become the figurehead envisaged by Lafayette and the Lameths. The contrast with the successful installation of George Washington as US president, in a country that had clearly decided to become a republic and thus felt confident enough to accord its leader powers approaching that of a king, is striking. As the examples of the United States of America, and of France after 1958, show, the monarchical republic has had some substantial success in the modern world. The same cannot be said of republican monarchy.

Notes

1. Cited in A. Potofsky, "The One and the Many: The Two Revolutions Question and the 'Consumer-Commercial' Atlantic, 1789 to the Present," in *Rethinking the Atlantic World: Europe and America in the Age of Democratic Revolutions,* eds. M. Albertone and A. de Francesco (London: Palgrave Macmillan, 2009), 18.

2. R. R. Palmer, *The Age of the Democratic Revolution: A Political History of Europe and America, 1760–1800,* 2 vols. (Princeton, NJ: Princeton University Press, 1959, 1964); J. Godechot, *La grande nation: l'Expansion révolutionnaire dans le monde de 1789 à 1799* (Paris: CNRS, 1956), and *Les révolutions (1770–1799)* (Paris: Presses Universitaires de

France, 1963); J Appleby, "America as a Model for the Radical French Reformers of 1789," *William and Mary Quarterly* 28.2 (April 1971): 267–86; François Furet, *Penser la Révolution française* (Paris: Gallimard, 1979), and "Tocqueville," in *A Critical Dictionary of the French Revolution*, ed. F. Furet and M. Ozouf (Cambridge, MA: Harvard University Press, 1989), 1021–32; P. Higonnet, *Sister Republics: The Origins of French and American Republicanism* (Cambridge, MA: Harvard University Press, 1988). The theme runs through both Tocqueville's major works: *De la démocratie en Amérique* (*Oeuvres, Papiers et Correspondence*), ed. J. P. Mayer (Paris: Gallimard, 1951) vol. 1, and *L'Ancien Régime et la révolution* (*Oeuvres, Papiers et Correspondence*) ed. J. P. Mayer (Paris: Gallimard 1951), vol. 2.

3. L. Gottschalk, *Lafayette Comes to America* (Chicago: University of Chicago Press, 1935); *Lafayette Joins the American Army* (Chicago: University of Chicago Press, 1937); *Lafayette and the Close of the American Revolution* (Chicago: University of Chicago Press, 1942); *Lafayette between the American and the French Revolutions, 1783–1789* (Chicago: University of Chicago Press, 1950); with M. Maddox, *Lafayette in the French Revolution: Through the October Days* (Chicago: University of Chicago Press, 1969); with M. Maddox, *Lafayette in the French Revolution: From the October Days through the Federation* (Chicago: University of Chicago Press, 1973).

4. T. de Lameth, *Mémoires*, ed. E. Welvert (Paris, 1913).

5. Lameth, *Mémoires*, 108 n.2

6. See C. Cruise O'Brien, *The Long Affair: Thomas Jefferson and the American Revolution, 1785–1800* (London: Sinclair Stevenson, 1996), 1–68.

7. Letter to M. d'Hennings, January 15, 1799, in *Mémoires du Général Lafayette*, 6 vols. (Paris, 1837–38), 3:227; Gottschalk, *Lafayette . . . through the October Days*, 14, 89.

8. Ibid., 85–90.

9. Ibid., 225.

10. S. Delannoy, "Les frères Lameth: De l'engagement aux désillusions," in *Les noblesses françaises dans l'Europe de la révolution*, ed. P. Bourdin (Rennes: Presses Universitaire de Renned, 2010), 162.

11. Alexandre de Lameth, *Lettre à M le Comte de ***, auteur d'un ouvrage intitulé Le Bon Sens* (Paris, 1788).

12. Ibid., 8–10.

13. Ibid., 10–11.

14. D. L. Wick, "The Court Nobility and the French Revolution: The Example of the Society of Thirty," *Eighteenth-Century Studies* 13.3 (Spring 1980): 263–84; and *A Conspiracy of Well-Intentioned Men: The Society of Thirty and the French Revolution* (New York: Garland, 1987).

15. Wick, "Court Nobility," 268–71, 279–81.

16. Ibid., 281–87.

17. A. Lameth, *Lettre*, 7–8.

18. Gottschalk, *Lafayette . . . through the October Days*, 228.

19. *Archives parlementaires de 1787 à 1860*, série 1 (1787–1799), ed. M. J. Mavidal, E. Laurent, and E. Clavel (Paris, 1867–1896), 8:572–73.

20. Undated letter, published in *Mémoires du Général Lafayette*, 2:62.

21. *Archives parlementaires*, 8:605.

22. Gottschalk, *Lafayette . . . through the October Days*, 229.

23. Quoted in D. A. Bell, *The First Total War: Napoleon's Europe and the Birth of Modern Warfare* (London: Bloomsbury, 2008), 94.

24. Quoted in G. Chaussinand-Nogaret, *Mirabeau* (Paris: Seuil, 1982), 217–18.

25. *Archives parlementaires*, 15:660.

26. P. Gueniffey, "Cordeliers et Girondins: La préhistoire de la république?," in *Le siècle de l'avènement républicain*, ed. F. Furet and M. Ozouf (Paris: Gallimard, 1993), 205–6.

27. F. Furet and R. Halévi, *La monarchie républicaine: La constitution de 1791* (Paris: Fayard, 1996); Gueniffey, "Cordeliers et Girondins," 205–6; Louis XVI to the baron de Breteuil, December 14, 1791, in *Louis XVI, Marie Antoinette et Mme Elisabeth: Lettres et documents inédits*, ed. F. Feuillet de Conches, 6 vols. (Paris: Plon, 1864–1873).

28. Gottschalk, *Lafayette through the Federation*, ix.

29. *Mémoires du Général Lafayette*, 2:324–25, 326, 329.

30. Ibid., 325.

31. There are three recent studies of Morris, one specifically dealing with his period in France: W. H. Adams, *Gouverneur Morris: An Independent Life* (New Haven, CT: Yale University Press, 2003); J. J. Kirschke, *Gouverneur Morris: Author, Statesman and Man of the World* (New York: St. Martin's Press, 2005); and M. R. Miller, *Envoy to the Terror: Gouverneur Morris and the French Revolution* (Dulles, VA: Potomac Books, 2005).

32. *A Diary of the French Revolution 1789–93, by Gouverneur Morris*, ed. B. C. Davenport, 2 vols. (London: Harrap, 1939), 1:43, 136.

33. See, for example, Gottschalk, *Lafayette . . . through the October Days*, vii–viii: "We consider Lafayette neither a scheming ambitious *arriviste* nor a simple, undeserving *niais* but a competent, well-meaning, patriotic soldier and statesman who, at this stage at least, generally managed to control events, even if they sometimes got out of hand, and in so doing was thrust into a position of leadership, a position he neither diligently conspired to achieve nor earnestly shunned." See also N. Hampson, *Prelude to Terror: The Constituent Assembly and the Failure of Consensus, 1789–1791* (Oxford: Blackwell, 1988), 120–21: Lafayette "was too honourable, where Mirabeau was not honourable enough, for either to be the effective leader of a party. No one trusted Mirabeau, and Lafayette was too trustworthy to consider using his control over Paris to dictate terms to both the Assembly and the king. It was Washington rather than Cromwell every time."

34. Morris, *Diary*, 1:306.

35. J. Hardman, *The Life of Louis XVI* (New Haven, CT: Yale University Press, 2016), 395; *Archives parlementaires*, 27:519.

36. Théodore Lameth, *Mémoires*, 144.

Studying Atlantic History with Jacques Godechot and Robert R. Palmer

European friends of the American Revolution is, after all, a topic within the broader field of Atlantic history. With that in mind, the Sons of the American Revolution conference was particularly honoring the important contributions of Robert R. Palmer and Jacques Godechot, intellectual godfathers of Atlantic history, as Marie-Jeanne Rossignol persuasively shows. While the field has moved well beyond its early beginnings, Rossignol calls on scholars to reflect on the continuing importance of the foundational contributions of Palmer and Godechot. The principles that they embraced in their work are now being applied to a much broader field, including especially the Haitian Revolution and the slave trade. The expansion of Atlantic history has produced a rich result, a microcosm and reflection, perhaps, of the enormous enrichment to our civic culture that occurred as the principles of the American Founders have been applied to a broader group of people, from African Americans, to women, to Native Americans, and beyond.

Beginning in 1955, Godechot and Palmer started articulating the foundations for what became the new field in an effort to understand the Age of Revolutions. Of course, through the years their early insights faced considerable criticism, explicit and implicit. For example, during the academic reaction to the Cold War, stressing the links between the American and French Revolutions was often seen as an American trope, especially in Europe (and in extreme instances, seen as a CIA plot). Other developments questioned or minimized any apparent relationship between the two revolutions. Social and cultural interpretations of both revolutions that became more dominant also saw the literature on both sides of the Atlantic focusing inward as bottom-up histories and microhistories proliferated. The growth of neoprogressive history, questioning the radical nature of the American Revolution, also tended to move the focus away from seeing deep linkages between the American and French Revolutions, much less with developments in the rest of Europe.

Still, the foundation that Palmer and Godechot built never fully disappeared. Initially, what came to be known as Atlantic history was dominated by British-American relations, but more recently it has expanded, especially in the study of the slave trade and African influences. With increased focus on the Haitian Revolution, the interest in democratic revolutions of the eighteenth century has come full circle, putting these developments and questions of the progressive and modernizing impact of the Age of Revolutions again at the center of Atlantic history as Palmer and Godechot initially suggested all those years ago. By reminding us of the roots of Atlantic history, Rossignol suggests that study of the American Revolution still offers important insights for the broader field. The essays in this volume by a broad group of Atlantic scholars demonstrate the value of that approach.

More generally, Rossignol reminds students and historians alike that it is worth revisiting some "classics" of history. While such foundational works are often so easily forgotten in the rush to stay apace with a flood of current and trendy literature, those earlier works still provide enormously important insights and frame our historic understanding. Certainly, this is true in the works of Godechot and Palmer, as Rossignol shows in "In Search of Global Democracy: Revisiting the Historical work of Jacques Godechot and Robert. R. Palmer, Founders of Atlantic History."

In Search of Global Democracy
Revisiting the Work of Jacques Godechot and
Robert R. Palmer, Founders of Atlantic History

MARIE-JEANNE ROSSIGNOL

Most of my research since 2006 has been concerned with the history of antislavery in North America and France in the late eighteenth century, culminating with the translation and new edition of *Some Historical Account of Guinea,* the 1771 antislavery bestseller written by the French-born Philadelphia Quaker and antislavery activist Anthony Benezet.[1] This prolonged interest in transatlantic abolitionism has enabled me to see some of the major protagonists of the War for Independence from the angle of their opposition to slavery. Both George Washington and the marquis de Lafayette eventually came to believe that slavery was wrong, and both made a point of turning their convictions into commitments. Lafayette tried to emancipate slaves in the late 1780s in the French Caribbean, before the events of the French Revolution engulfed him in other activities. He remained convinced that slavery was wrong throughout his life, though. As for Washington, he freed his slaves upon his death (although not the dower slaves that returned to Martha Washington), as is well known, though recent publications have also documented his prior support for slavery as a social system.[2]

Apart from this research interest in antislavery, alongside a number of other French scholars I have developed a project focusing on historians of the past.[3] Too often, contemporary historians spend their time reading only the latest books and lose sight of what previous important historians had to say on similar topics in the past. Questioning that approach, my contention is that the works of past historians, such as Robert R. Palmer and Jacques Godechot, the objects of this essay, can still offer highly valuable, even provocative, insights and analyses. Although methods and questions may change and sometimes improve the reliability and complexity of what we know about the past, the contribution of great historians of the past is too precious to be dismissed, especially as they can still offer new insights when read after a few decades have elapsed.

In this essay on two historians, one French, one American, I will first focus on Godechot, Palmer, and the concept of Atlantic history, which they were instrumental in developing but which has considerably evolved since they elaborated the concept in 1955. I will then present their lives and work more specifically to highlight the specificity of their approach. In a third and final part, I will insist on why we should read them today: Palmer and Godechot did not simply launch the study of Atlantic history, a thriving field today; by emphasizing the Age of Revolutions, they also critically articulated Atlantic history with a defense of global democracy and infused it with deeply felt progressive political meaning.

Godechot, Palmer, the Concept of Atlantic History, and the Atlantic "Paradigm"

I had read Jacques Godechot and Robert R. Palmer at the time I was writing my dissertation in the late 1980s.[4] Then, Godechot and Palmer were mainly well known for their work on the "Western" revolutions of the late eighteenth century, books that had been written from the late 1940s to the late 1960s and that presented the Western revolutions as connected, with the United States leading the way and many European countries following, most prominently France.[5] But such transatlantic views were not fashionable in the 1980s at a time when narratives of the French and American Revolutions highlighted the national aspects of the events rather than their global repercussions; some historians did study the French and American Revolutions, but mainly to compare and oppose the two events.[6] In the 1980s in France, the history of the French Revolution had come to be dominated by François Furet, who highlighted the Terror as a major problem in the French Revolution and did not put connections between the American and French Revolutions at the heart of his analysis. Placing the French Revolution in a long French chronology that embraced the Ancien Régime and nineteenth-century political progress, his goal was to turn the French Revolution into a cold, dispassionate topic of analysis and to prevent any further appropriation of the event by historians for their own political ends.[7]

Bernard Bailyn, who revolutionized the study of the American Revolution in the United States in the late 1960s by focusing on its intellectual and ideological origins, stressed the deep-seated connections of the American revolutionary moment with the "radical social and political thought of the English Civil War and the Commonwealth period"; although not discounting the influence of French Enlightenment philosophers, he did not consider them as essential.[8] In the United States the 1980s saw the culmination of a radical and social interpretation of the American Revolution, which focused on national, even local, social, ethnic, and racial conflicts, generally speaking disconnecting the study of the Revolution from that of the War for Independence (and thus global war and cooperation), a trend that is only being reversed now.[9] As a result, this new generation of specialists of the American Revolution in the United States was also not interested in connections with the French Revolution. Their vision of their own revolution as essentially conservative can even be said to have confirmed some French historians' belittling view of American events, sometimes dismissed as the mere rebellion of white settlers against metropolitan authorities with little social impact, while their own French Revolution took on a much larger stature and was portrayed as a central political, social, and geopolitical turning point.[10]

Consequently, the perspective of Palmer and Godechot, that of an Age of Revolutions that joined the United States, France, and Western Europe as a whole in a common democratic movement, was no longer popular either in France or the United States by the mid-1980s.[11]

But right at a time when Palmer and Godechot as "Atlantic" historians had gone out of fashion together with a transatlantic vision of the Age of Revolutions, both were somehow about to enjoy a second life, primarily because of a new focus in the historical profession on Atlantic history. The rise of Atlantic history was made very visible in 1995 with the establishment of a specific seminar at Harvard by Bernard Bailyn, who had made his mark as a historian through influential studies of the origins of the American Revolution and of British migrations to North America. Through the establishment of the "International Seminar on the History of the Atlantic World, 1500–1825," which lasted from 1995 to 2010, Bailyn created an international (but mainly Western) network of young scholars who exchanged research bearing on various parts of the Atlantic world, and he started discussions on a number of issues common to nations and colonies around the Atlantic world.

There is no denying that the seminar fostered real transatlantic intellectual and professional dynamics.[12]

In a book he wrote in 2005 assessing the experience of the international seminar, *Atlantic History: Concepts and Contours,* Bailyn pinned the intellectual origins of Atlantic history on a paper given jointly by Godechot and Palmer at an international history conference in 1955: "Le problème de l'Atlantique du XVIIIè siècle au XXè siècle."[13] He explained that the Palmer-Godechot connection was originally due to their being both specialists of the history of the French Revolution, but the relationship had crystallized in 1954 and 1955 when Palmer, a Princeton professor, invited Godechot to stay at Princeton as a visiting fellow.

As Godechot himself recalled the event in the preface of his 1983 book *La Grande Nation,* both men had been asked to present a special report on Atlantic history at the World Historical Congress in Rome in 1955 as the North Atlantic Treaty had been signed in 1949, and NATO headquarters were established in Paris in 1951. Godechot assumed he had been chosen on the strength of his 1947 book on the Atlantic, and Palmer probably as a result of a paper the American historian had published in 1954 on "The World Revolution of the West." Their report provided a broad vision of Atlantic history and insisted on the fact that the climax of Atlantic confluence was reached at the time of the "democratic revolutions." When it was presented, it ran into strong opposition, and the two historians were accused of being CIA agents, promoting the revolutions of the West in order to strengthen the new diplomatic and military alliance.[14]

The very idea of Atlantic history thus seemed to rhyme with North Atlantic Treaty to the ears of a number of Marxist historians who listened to the two men's presentation. Yet in spite of a lasting opposition to their "Atlantic Revolution thesis"—opposition that was of course always more vocal in France than in the United States given the different Cold War political context in the two countries—Godechot and Palmer stuck to their vision of an age of Atlantic democratic revolutions in their later careers, publishing major works that developed this notion, mainly in the late 1950s and 1960s.[15] And we will get back to their publications later in this essay.

However unpopular their views on democratic revolutions may have been in certain circles between the 1950s and 1980s, the notion of Atlantic history experienced a phenomenal development starting in the mid-1990s.

Although French historians initially resisted it, as the concept reminded them of the initial political criticisms voiced in 1955 or because its early historiography was dominated by the British Atlantic, even they progressively embraced the notion as they could see how beneficial Atlantic history could be in the redefinition of imperial and colonial French history in the New World.[16]

Atlantic history was eventually adopted in France as one stage in the more general development of "world" and "connected" histories, a trend that was welcomed by historians as one way to move beyond national narratives of the first globalization and to include the perspectives of Native peoples and enslaved men and women. Like the kind of Atlantic history advocated by Godechot and Palmer in the 1950s and 1960s, the new Atlantic history highlighted connections between both sides of the Atlantic, but while Godechot and Palmer had focused on political history and the history of democratic revolutions, the new specialists of Atlantic history stressed trade (Silvia Marzagalli); immigration (Alison Games); connections between the coast and the hinterland, Natives, and settlers (Daniel K. Richter); and slavery, making Africa a central part of the new narrative, something Godechot and Palmer had definitely not done.[17]

The new Atlantic history as practiced and written from the 1990s onward spanned many centuries, from the arrival of Europeans in the Americas to the end of the Atlantic slave trade progressively after the American Civil War, as the titles of many major monographs and reference works testify.[18] For the new school of Atlanticists, studying the first globalization meant breaking established chronologies and covering a very long period. But although Godechot and Palmer embraced a long period in their initial reflections on the Atlantic paradigm, their later research mainly bore on the age of democratic revolutions.

Interestingly, that particular topic was mainly lost sight of in the new Atlantic history, or it was engulfed in vaster preoccupations. Indeed, the new Atlantic history did not pay much attention to the Age of Revolutions proper if we are to judge from the list of Atlantic history seminars organized by Bernard Bailyn at Harvard. Quite symbolically, one recent reference work on Atlantic history pays no heed at all to the French Revolution as one major event in the history of the Atlantic world. Another recent survey (*The Age of Revolutions in Global Context, c. 1760–1860*) blurs the lines between democratic revolutions, imperial revolutions, and crises so much that a real sense of the distinct specificity of democratic revolutions is lost, as one critic contended.[19]

However, due to the focus on slavery and migrations from Africa in the new Atlantic school, one Atlantic revolution that did receive increasing attention on the part of historians starting in the 1990s was the Haitian Revolution. The flurry of publications covering the Haitian Revolution, starting with Laurent Dubois's history in 2004 (*Avengers of the New World*), fits in with Godechot's and Palmer's Age of Revolutions in its chronological reach and corresponds to the brand of Atlantic history that they had tried to promote as defined by Jürgen Osterhammel, even if they did not give pride of place to the Haitian Revolution as part of their panorama of Western revolutions: it fit with "the concept of a common origin of modernity, spanning both sides of the Atlantic, in an age of revolution between the 1760s and the 1820s." Numerous books have since been published dealing with various aspects of this very Atlantic revolution, such as the flood of refugees it poured out on the shores of the United States (Ashli White), reactions all around the Atlantic (Alejandro Gomes), or the memory of it in Haiti itself (Le Glaunec), and more recently the impact it had on Cuba (Ada Ferrer).[20]

Godechot, Palmer, and Democratic Revolutions

Given the recent prominence of at least one Atlantic revolution, it is worth revisiting the works of Godechot and Palmer, as their specific vision of an Atlantic revolution has not been explicitly challenged or rediscussed in the past twenty years of Atlantic history activities, after being originally criticized for having downgraded "the uniqueness of the French Revolution by diluting it into a vague general international disturbance," as a rather bitter Palmer put it in 1990.[21] A short biography of both historians and a presentation of their major works is thus a requisite preliminary.

Robert Roswell Palmer was born in 1909 in Chicago. As reported by Isser Wolloch, his graduate work bore on the history of the French Revolution and the role of American independence, a harbinger of his later interest in Atlantic history, though he never published his dissertation. His first book was on the religious history of France in the eighteenth century.[22] As the United States entered the Second World War in 1941, he published a monograph on the Committee of Public Safety, the twelve men who ruled France during the Terror. This book, entitled *Twelve Who Ruled*, is still in print today and was translated into French on the occasion of the 1989 bicentennial of the French Revolution, under the very aegis of François Furet, who wrote a preface. According to Isser Wolloch, it is still the best book on the French Revolution published by an American historian. Wolloch describes the "moral scope" of the book as an attempt at putting forward his idea of "liberal democracy." Within the scope of this essay, it is worth analyzing the book in some detail as it somehow reveals what democratic revolutions meant to Palmer. Indeed, Palmer tries to explain the Terror, underlining its positive dimensions without exonerating the twelve committee members who ruled over France between September 1793 and July 1794 of the crimes that were committed under their rule.[23]

The main strength of the Terror, according to Palmer, was its commitment to efficiency and modernity in management. Because France was surrounded by foreign armies, the committee members focused their energy on reviving morale in the army and reorganizing it. They visited regiments stationed on French borders, getting rid of inefficient and undisciplined aristocratic officers, promoting young men of promise, and having them share the tents of the soldiers in a display of equality and fraternity. Under the control of Jean Bon Saint André, a former protestant minister, the navy in Brittany was energized, with the seaport city of Brest concentrating on the building of ships and the upholding of revolutionary principles.

By contrast, the enemy armies were divided over strategy, slow in reaching decisions, and could not rely on an army of citizens, as the French did. As a result, the European monarchical foes of France were defeated. The committee of twelve ruled as a group; there was no cult of personality. Instead of a rabid and bloodthirsty terrorist, Robespierre is described as a moderate, trying to quell the excesses of dechristianization and to maintain religious toleration and diversity in the face of an anticlerical opposition. However, because it used terror to rule, the committee of twelve did not manage fully to regenerate society. To Palmer, terror discredited the valuable republican principles that the committee of twelve tried to inject in the country.

Although the book dealt with France, not with democratic revolutions as a whole, Palmer's overall position was that the French Revolution was a progressive event with global repercussions, as he made clear in the foreword to a later edition, which concluded on the theme of racial equality and the French abolition of slavery in 1794:

[T]he year of the Terror was the year of the guillotine, but it was also the year when many democratic ideas were made clear and were proclaimed throughout the world, even if they were not implemented immediately. Those who prefer to refer to the American Revolution should not forget that the French revolutionaries introduced universal suffrage, shaped a system of public education and decreed the abolition of slavery. If this book were written today, more would be said on the movement for racial equality which culminated in February 1794.[24]

Palmer's full commitment to Atlantic history and an Atlantic history of democratic revolutions was his *Age of Democratic Revolution, 1760–1800,* the first volume of which, entitled *The Challenge,* was published in 1959 and received the Bancroft Prize.[25] Covering all the revolutionary events from the British North American colonies in the 1770s to the French Revolution, Palmer's position was that the Age of Revolutions, starting in North America and spreading to Europe, was a progressive movement, uniting enlightened leaders and people across the Atlantic against Ancien Régime institutions and thought.

The second volume, *The Struggle,* published in 1964, was devoted to the European revolutionary struggles caused by the advent of the French Revolution. Once again, Palmer stressed the opposition between patriotic and democratic forces against counter-revolutionary and conservative forces. Such a broad vision of the revolutionary era, Isser Wolloch suggests, is what explains his being awarded a prestigious Italian prize in 1990.[26] But unlike Godechot, who considered that the Napoleonic era had preserved many of the achievements of the French Revolution, Palmer thought that the age of democratic revolutions came to an end in 1800 when Napoleon's and Jefferson's rise to power sent signals of political stabilization in France and the United States.

In his later works Palmer reverted to studies of the French Revolution proper, even translating works by French scholars into English. His last project was to have been a study on the Abbé Grégoire, the French revolutionary who fought on behalf of equal rights for Jews and, most famously, against slavery. Once again, from the standpoint of Atlantic revolutions, Palmer could envision the more global consequences of the Age of Revolutions. He died in 2002 without having completed his project.[27]

Jacques Godechot was born two years before Palmer, in 1907, in a family of Jewish merchants of Lorraine, a region then occupied by Germany and where the local inhabitants nurtured strong French patriotic feelings. Like Palmer, he focused as a graduate student on the French Revolution, defending a dissertation in 1938 that studied relationships between the government and the French revolutionary army.[28] As a Jew, the fact that the French Revolution had put an end to the discriminations under which the Jewish population labored in France during the Ancien Régime played a role in his choice of specialization; as he confided later, he had been impressed as a child by the statue of the Abbé Grégoire, the revolutionary-era defender of both Jews and slaves, an inspirational figure that Palmer also revered at the end of his life, as I noted above.

After finding a teaching position in Brest, Godechot made his first foray into Atlantic history by starting work on his *History of the Atlantic,* which was still maritime history in many ways, published in 1947. As a Jew in Vichy France, he was banned from his position as a civil servant during World War II, but he survived by moving to Grenoble in the Alps, then under the control of Italian occupation. As soon as the war ended, he received an appointment as a professor of history at the University of Toulouse in 1945. Then his publications were many, and historian Claude Petitfrère, one of his former students, likes to remember that he was the editor of a "monumental" general history of the French press.[29] But Petitfrère is adamant that Godechot was first and foremost a historian of the French Revolution, and of the age of democratic revolutions.

Even as a graduate student, Godechot had the intuition that the French Revolution could not be studied as an isolated event. His conviction was that, however important the French Revolution might have been and however important it was in the eyes of some other French historians, it was only a central moment in a train of events starting in North America and spreading to the whole of the West. As he wrote in the foreword to the first edition of *La Grande Nation:* "The French revolution is but one aspect of the Western, or more precisely the Atlantic, revolution, which began in the British North American colonies shortly after 1763, was continued in the revolutions of Switzerland, the Netherlands, Ireland, before reaching France between 1787 and 1789. From France, it bounced back to the Netherlands, reached the Rhineland in Germany, Switzerland, Italy, Malta, Eastern Mediterranean, and Egypt."[30]

This conviction was turned into a number of books. In 1956 he published *La Grande Nation* (The Great Nation: The revolutionary expansion of France in the world, 1789–1799) in which he showed how France spread democratic principles into Europe as it was led to invade neighboring countries during its wars against monarchies in the 1790s. In 1963 he published *Les Révolutions (1770–1799)*, an erudite synthesis aimed at graduate students that insisted that the Age of Revolutions did start with the American Revolution and did not stop in fact until the revolutions of 1848 in Europe. The whole book focused on the similarities he could trace between Western societies and ideas, but the 1986 edition included a long chapter discussing the controversy between Godechot and others and those historians opposing the idea of a "Western revolution."[31]

In 1967 Godechot published the sequel to *Les Révolutions*, that is *L'Europe et l'Amérique à l'Époque Napoléonienne* (Europe and America in the Napoleonic era). Determined to stress continuities more than discontinuities in the Age of Revolutions, Godechot presented the years from 1799 to 1815 as the consolidation of all the revolutionary gains of the previous period. Although Napoleon's despotic regime curtailed economic and social rights in France, yet the spread of the French Empire over Europe made it possible for revolutionary democratic ideas and institutions to penetrate Austria and even Russia. Between 1800 and 1815, the decline of feudalism and serfdom made it possible for more people in Europe and the United States to become landowners, even if in North America it was at the expense of Native populations, he noted. Under the administrations of Jefferson and Madison, the United States could consolidate its republican regime and democratic system while Latin America gradually moved toward revolution, independence, and republicanism.[32]

In 1971 Godechot published a collection of documents from the revolutions of 1848 in Europe, thus still adhering to his general view of the Age of Revolutions as having embraced the years 1770 to 1848 in the West. He published many other books on the French Revolution, the counter-revolution, Italian history, and rapidly reconciled with Marxist historians who had so bitterly criticized his "Atlantic thesis" in 1955. In 1959 he became the vice president of a major French revolutionary-era scholarly society, the *Société des études robespierristes,* and he died in 1989, the year of the bicentennial of the French Revolution, having become by then a specialist of the various interpretations of the French Revolution.[33]

Why Should We Read Palmer and Godechot Today?

At a very simple, professional level, the type of history both Godechot and Palmer wrote still reads well today because, like today's historians, they tried to encompass all the dimensions of the revolutionary era, including social, economic, political, and cultural aspects. They rejected an interpretation of the revolutions of the West as based merely on influence and the transfer of ideas. They were social historians, convinced that history was shaped by social and economic realities as well as by the experiences of ordinary people. Palmer, for instance, had little patience with explanations of the revolutionary movement only through the influence of the Enlightenment philosophers or through very general class analyses.

Pleading for ambitious "unifying conceptions for the whole revolutionary movement" in his 1954 article on "The World Revolution of the West," he wrote disparagingly about those two other approaches, thus dismissing the work of some other historians interested in Atlantic revolutions: "It is not enough to have a rough semi-Marxist idea of the 'bourgeois revolution' . . . or to speak vaguely of the 'influence' of France over America." Ideas of liberty and emancipation, he wrote in this same article, derived from "centuries of European thought." Simply now they "applied to the actual conditions of the day," he added.[34]

However, by contrast with many current specialists of Atlantic history, Palmer and Godechot did not consider that the Age of Revolutions was just one dimension of Atlantic history, and that is the main reason why we should read them today. While the Age of Revolutions is often downplayed in general studies of the Atlantic world today, Godechot and Palmer insisted that it was a unique moment and formed the climax of Western development. They were not interested in idealizing the revolutions of the West, though: as historians, they were fully aware of the failings of the era. In his 1954 essay on "The World Revolution of the West," Palmer insisted from the start on the "paradoxes of the French Revolution"; he saw in the French Revolution "the association of liberty with force, of enlightenment and education with propaganda and histrionics, of a sense of progress with a sense of conquest, of soldiers with professors, of a feeling of attachment to the Western tradition with one of angry repudiation of the historical past."[35] However flawed Western revolutions were, certainly they remained a source of inspiration for both men.

As Lynn Hunt put it in a tribute to Palmer in 2011: "He believed that democracy was an absolute good, that it had its origins in European history, and that its rise provided one of, or even perhaps the principal theme of all of modern history. As a consequence, he never lost his sympathy for the French revolutionaries of 1789–1794, however terrible their actions, however much they fell short of living up to their ideals."[36] By placing the rise of democracy at the heart of their narrative and analyses and insisting on the centrality of a movement that encompassed religious toleration, the granting of political rights, the birth of representative government, and a wide franchise in many countries, they sent the message that certain historical themes mattered more than others and that historical research could not be dissociated from ongoing contemporary political discussions.

This is what Lloyd Kramer meant when he praised them in a tribute, saying that their "transnational, synthetic work also gives us a provocative invitation to debate the big historical questions that constantly reanimate our political and cultural lives." As I do now, Kramer thought that the intellectual framework they offered remained inspirational, and his words are worth quoting:

> I strongly believe (fifty years later) that Palmer's general themes still offer provocative starting points for continuing research: the emphasis on an Atlantic world in which ideas moved across national borders and inspired popular political movements in diverse social contexts; the emphasis on a profound, irreversible challenge to aristocratic privileges and legal hierarchies; the emphasis on a new belief in the fundamental equality of all persons . . . and the emphasis on dangers that emerge whenever particular groups claim to embody the ultimate truths of history, religion, or social order.[37]

One question deeply entrenched in the Age of Revolutions, and inevitably linked today to any discussion of democracy, was the question of slavery, and, as Palmer put it, of "racial equality." However, neither of them addressed this issue in depth in their work. Yet probably the most innovative work that has come from Atlantic history in the past two decades has been related to slavery, and quite specifically I think, with the Haitian Revolution. Whether consciously or not, many of those books can be said to follow in the steps of Godechot's and Palmer's tradition of Atlantic history, going further than both men had by taking the Caribbean into account and making race a key ingredient of the democratic challenge of the Age of Revolutions (and of today, as well).

By the end of the 1990s two major books conceptualized race and revolution in the Atlantic world: the first one was *A Turbulent Time: The French Revolution and the Caribbean,* edited by David Barry Gaspar and David Geggus (1997) which insisted on the connection between the impact of the French Revolution and resistance and insurrections in the Caribbean region. These were not totally new ideas, but the concrete links established in the book chapters between the revolution of the West, and the slaves' plight and agency exposed another "age of revolutions," one that could no longer treat slaves as a separate problem, or a subsidiary problem. The year before, Lester Langley's book *The Americas in the Age of Revolution: 1750–1850* (1998) had placed Haiti, as a revolutionary nation, at the heart of a narrative that did not focus on Europe but highlighted "American" revolutions and the specific connections between independence and race.[38]

It would take too much time to analyze all the important books that came out in the 2000s and the 2010s on the Haitian Revolution, and my point here is rather to show the deep-seated connection between this recent emphasis on the Haitian Revolution and the "Atlantic revolutions" thesis expounded by Godechot and Palmer. The work of historian Laurent Dubois is probably one of the best examples of this new revolutionary Atlantic history, as in numerous publications he explicitly raised the questions of the limits, and legacies, of the Age of Revolutions in terms of race, equality, and citizenship, stressing the fact that the slaves themselves used the period to stretch the meaning of universal rights beyond the original intent of many "white" revolutionaries.[39]

Godechot and Palmer would have welcomed such work placing the question of universal rights at the forefront of historical inquiry. Their optimistic, yet critical, approach to the Age of Revolutions is to be found today in the writings of those historians dealing with race and the Age of Revolutions around the Atlantic world. Though Godechot and Palmer were criticized, and maybe not fully understood, when they voiced their thesis on Atlantic revolutions in 1955, their work was recognized, and they were regarded as major figures in their profession. Palmer's book on the Committee of Public Safety has enjoyed remarkable longevity on both sides of the Atlantic, while Godechot established himself as one of the pillars of French revolutionary history; his 1963 book *Les Revolutions (1770–1799)* went through many editions until 1986 and serves as essential reading for all aspiring students working on the Atlantic revolutions. Actually, it was one of the first books my own advisor recommended when I started work on my dissertation in 1985, though she herself was highly critical of Atlantic history and has remained so to this day.

Notes

1. "The Quaker Antislavery Commitment and How It Revolutionized French Antislavery through the Crèvecoeur-Brissot Friendship, 1782–1789," in *Quakers and Abolition*, eds. Brycchan Carey and Geoff Plank (Urbana: University of Illinois Press, 2014); "Jacques-Pierre Brissot, and the Fate of Atlantic Anti-Slavery during the Age of Revolutionary Wars," in *War, Empire and Slavery, 1770-1830*, eds. Richard Bessel, Nicholas Guyatt, and Jane Rendall (Basingstoke, Kent: Palgrave, 2010); Marie-Jeanne Rossignol and Bertrand Van Ruymbeke, eds., *Une histoire de la Guinée* (Paris: SFEDS, 2017); Marie-Jeanne Rossignol and Bertrand Van Ruymbeke, eds., *The Atlantic World of Anthony Benezet: From French Reformation to North American Quaker Activism* (Leiden: Brill, 2016).

2. Lloyd Kramer, in *Lafayette in Two Worlds: Public Cultures and Personal Identities in an Age of Revolutions* (Chapel Hill: University of North Carolina Press, 1996), scrutinizes Lafayette's friendship with abolitionist Fanny Wright, and his support of her endeavours, during his American tour from 1824 to 1826 and lists the various gestures he made toward recognizing the contribution of Blacks toward independence (162–63, 217–18); also see Melvin D. Kennedy, *Lafayette and Slavery: From His Letters to Thomas Clarkson and Granville Sharp* (Easton, PA: American Friends of Lafayette, 1950). For an account of Washington's evolving position on slavery, see Henry Wiencek, *An Imperfect God: George Washington, His Slaves, and the Creation of America* (New York: Farrar, Straus & Giroux, 2003); François Fürstenberg, "Atlantic Slavery, Atlantic Freedom: George Washington, Slavery, and Transatlantic Abolitionist Networks," *William and Mary Quarterly* 68.2 (April 2011); Erica Armstrong Dunbar, *Never Caught: The Washingtons' Relentless Pursuit of Their Runaway Slave Ona Judge* (New York: Atria Books, 2017).

3. *Histoire en marges: Les périphéries de l'histoire globale*, accessed September 2015, http://hdlm.hypotheses.org/.

4. This dissertation was turned into a book that came out in English in 2003: *The Nationalist Ferment: The Origins of U.S. Foreign Policy, 1789–1812* (Columbus: Ohio State University Press).

5. Major publications by Jacques Godechot on the Age of Revolutions include *La Grande Nation: L'expansion révolutionnaire de la France dans le monde, 1789–1799* (Paris: Editions Montaigne, 1956); *Les révolutions, 1770–1799* (Paris: Presses universitaires de

France, 1963); *L'Europe et l'Amérique à l'époque napoléonienne* (Paris: Presses universitaires de France, 1967). Robert R. Palmer's publications on this subject mainly include *The Age of the Democratic Revolution: A Political History of Europe and America, 1760–1800*, 2 vols. (Princeton, NJ: Princeton University Press, 1959–64). Both men published numerous other books, principally on the French Revolution.

6. Susan Dunn, *Sister Revolutions: French Lightning, American Light* (New York: Faber and Faber, 2000); Patrice Higonnet, *Sister Republics: The Origins of French and American Republicanism* (Cambridge, MA: Harvard University Press, 1988).

7. For a general presentation of Furet's influence and the absence of the American Revolution in his analysis of French Revolution, see Marie-Jeanne Rossignol, "The American Revolution in France: Under the Shadow of the French Revolution," in *Europe's American Revolution*, ed. Simon P. Newman (Houndsmills: Palgrave Macmillan, 2006). See also François Furet, *Interpreting the French Revolution* (Cambridge: Cambridge University Press, 1981).

8. Bernard Bailyn, "General Introduction," in Bailyn, ed., *Pamphlets of the American Revolution 1750–1776*, vol. 1 (Cambridge, MA: Belknap Press of Harvard University Press, 1965), 28; and Bailyn, *The Ideological Origins of the American Revolution* (Cambridge, MA: Belknap Press of Harvard University Press, 1967). Recent work by Manuela Albertone has challenged this Anglocentric view of the revolutionary era. See Manuela Albertone and Antonino De Francesco, eds, *Rethinking the Atlantic World: Europe and America in the Age of Democratic Revolutions* (Basingstoke: Palgrave Macillan, 2009), 1; and Manuela Albertone, *National Identity and the Agrarian Republic: The Transtlantic Commerce of Ideas between America and France (1750–1830)* (Farnham, Surrey, UK: Ashgate, 2014).

9. There is no room here for even a brief presentation of the "radical" historiography of the American Revolution, which highlighted the social, ethnic, and racial conflicts at work in colonial America and the role they played in the revolutionary events, but a few iconic works may be mentioned: Alfred F. Young, ed., *The American Revolution: Explorations in the History of American Radicalism* (De Kalb: Northern Illinois University Press, 1976); Gary B. Nash, *The Urban Crucible: Social Change, Political Consciousness, and the Origins of the American Revolution* (Cambridge, MA: Harvard University Press, 1979); and Edward Countryman, *A People in Revolution: The American Revolution and Political Society in New York 1760–1790* (Baltimore: Johns Hopkins University Press, 1981). For recent books mixing an awareness of the global dimensions of the War of Independence with the social and cultural preoccupations of historians of the American Revolution, see Claudio Saunt, *West of the Revolution: An Uncommon History of 1776* (New York: Norton, 2014); and Kathleen DuVal, *Independence Lost: Lives on the Edge of the American Revolution* (New York: Random House, 2015). Gary B. Nash has returned to the study of the radicalism of the American Revolution in *The Unknown American Revolution: The Unruly Birth of Democracy and the Struggle to Create America* (New York: Viking, 2005), and *Revolutionary Founders: Rebels, Radicals, and Reformers in the Making of the Nation*, ed. Alfred F. Young, Gary B. Nash, and Ray Raphael (New York: Knopf, 2011).

10. Marcel Dorigny shares this dismissive view in *Révoltes et révolutions en Europe et aux Amériques (1773–1802)* (Paris: Belin, 2004), 5, 12, 33; while Serge Bianchi concludes on the undeniable democratic and republican foundations of the new nation in the wake of the Revolution in *Des révoltes aux revolutions: Europe, Russie, Amérique (1770–1802)* (Rennes: Presses universitaires de Rennes, 2004), 56.

11. One should still qualify this analysis by remembering that Milan historian Loretta Valtz-Manucci regularly brought together historians of the French and American Revolutions between 1980 and 2000. But the conferences juxtaposed two communities of "radical" historians, each entrenched in its own national specificities, and they were not conducive to a revival of the Atlantic paradigm. For details, see Rossignol, "American Revolution in France," 67n.11.

12. Bailyn, *Ideological Origins*; Bernard Bailyn, *The Peopling of British North America* (New York: Knopf, 1987). The website of the seminar indicates that a total of "336 young historians" were invited, 164 coming from abroad and 202 from the United States, accessed June 14, 2019, http://www.fas.harvard.edu/~atlantic/seminarsabout.html. There were (and still are) other Atlantic seminars, but Bailyn's proved to be the most visible at an international level.

13. Bernard Bailyn, *Atlantic History: Concepts and Contours* (Cambridge, MA: Harvard University Press, 2005), 27. For the reference to the paper: "Le problème de l'Atlantique du XVIIIè siècle au XXè siècle," *Relazioni del X Congresso Internazionale di Scienze Storiche* [Florence, 1955], V (Storia Contemporanea).

14. Jacques Godechot, "Préface de la deuxième édition (1983)," in *La Grande Nation: L'expansion révolutionnaire de la France dans le monde de 1789 à 1799* (Paris: Flammarion, 1983), 7–11; Robert R. Palmer, "The World Revolution of the West, 1763–1801," *Political Science Quarterly* 69.1 (March 1954): 1–14. In addition to his book on the Atlantic, Godechot had also published a paper on the subject in 1954, like Palmer: "La France et le problème de l'Atlantique à la veille de la révolution," *Revue du Nord*, 1954.

15. Bailyn, *Atlantic History*, 24–29. Palmer gives details of this opposition in "American Historians Remember Jacques Godechot" (also contributions by Robert Forster, James Friguglietti, and Emmet Kennedy), *French Historical Studies* 16.3 (Spring 1990): 883–84. The phrase "Atlantic Revolution thesis" is from him.

16. Silvia Marzagalli, "Sur les origines de l'Atlantic History: Paradigme interprétatif de l'histoire des espaces atlantiques à l'époque moderne," *Dix-huitième siècle* 33 (2001). A major critic, but also key practitioner, of Atlantic history in France was Cécile Vidal: see "Pour une histoire globale du monde atlantique ou des histoires connectées dans et au-delà du monde atlantique?," *Annales: Histoire, Sciences Sociales* 67.2 (2012): 391–413.

17. Sylvia Marzagalli, *Les boulevards de la fraude: Le négoce maritime et le Blocus continental, 1806–1813* (Villeneuve d'Ascq: Presses universitaires du Septentrion, 1993); Allison Games, *Migration and the Origins of the English Atlantic World* (Cambridge, MA: Harvard University Press, 1999); Daniel K. Richter, *Facing East from Indian Country* (Cambridge, MA: Harvard University Press, 2003); John Thornton, *Warfare in Atlantic Africa: 1500–1800* (London: University College of London Press, 1999).

18. Nicholas Canny and Philip Morgan, eds., *The Oxford Handbook of the Atlantic*

World, c.1450–c.1850 (Oxford: Oxford University Press, 2011); Thomas Benjamin, ed., *The Atlantic World: Europeans, Africans, Indians, and Their Shared History, 1400–1900* (Cambridge, MA: Cambridge University Press, 2009); Douglas Egerton et al., *The Atlantic World: A History, 1400–1888* (Wheeling, IL: Harlan Davison, 2007).

19. In 2001, the one year the Harvard seminar was devoted to "The Atlantic Revolutions," all revolutions were dealt with on a fairly equal basis (French, North American, Latin American, Haitian), and thus a rich panorama of the Atlantic revolutions was presented. In *The Oxford Handbook of the Atlantic World* (2011), the French Revolution is nowhere mentioned in the table of contents. David Armitage and Sanjay Subramanyam, *The Age of Revolutions in Global Context, c. 1760–1860* (London: Red Globe Press, 2009); for a review, see Annie Jourdan, "David Armitage et Sanjay Subrahmanyam, dir., *The Age of Revolutions in Global Context, c. 1760–1840*," *Annales historiques de la Révolution française* [online], 373 | juillet-septembre 2013, mis en ligne le 03 octobre 2013, accessed June 12, 2019, http://journals.openedition.org/ahrf/12888.

20. Laurent Dubois, *Avengers of the New World: The Story of the Haitian Revolution* (Cambridge, MA: Harvard University Press, 2004); Jürgen Osterhammel, "World History," in Daniel Woolf, ed., *The Oxford History of Historical Writing*, vol. 5 (Oxford: Oxford University Press, 2011), 107; Ashli White, *Encountering Revolution: Haiti and the Making of the Early American Republic* (Baltimore, MD: Johns Hopkins University Press, 2010); Alejandro Gomes, *Le spectre de la révolution noire: L'impact de la révolution haïtienne dans le monde atlantique, 1790–1886* (Rennes: Presses universitaires de Rennes, 2013); Jean-Pierre Le Glaunec, *L'armée indigène: La défaite de Napoléon en Haïti* (Montréal: Lux éditeur, 2014); Ada Ferrer, *Freedom's Mirror: Cuba and Haiti in the Age of Revolutions* (New York: Cambridge University Press, 2015).

21. Palmer, "American Historians Remember Jacques Godechot," 883.

22. Isser Wolloch, "Robert R. Palmer (1909–2002)," *Annales Historiques de la Révolution Française* 330 (2002): 159; Robert R. Palmer, *Catholics and Unbelievers in Eighteenth-Century France* (Princeton, NJ: Princeton University Press, 1939).

23. Robert R. Palmer, *Twelve Who Ruled: The Committee of Public Safety during the Terror* (Princeton, NJ: Princeton University Press, 1941); in French, *Le gouvernement de la Terreur: L'année du comité de salut public* (Paris: A. Colin, 1989). The book was reprinted in English in 1989 and 2005 (with a new preface by Isser Wolloch in the 2005 edition); Wolloch, "Robert R. Palmer," 160.

24. Robert R. Palmer, "Avertissement," in *Le gouvernement de la Terreur*, 14. This "avertissement" was said to date from a 1970 English edition of the book.

25. Robert R. Palmer, *The Age of the Democratic Revolution, 1760–1800*, vol. 1, *The Challenge*, vol. 2, *The Struggle* (Princeton, NJ: Princeton University Press, 1959, 1964).

26. Wolloch, "Robert R. Palmer," 161.

27. Ibid., 163.

28. Information on Jacques Godechot's biography is taken from Claude Petitfrère, "Jacques Godechot," in *Annales historiques de la Révolution française* 281 (1990): 308–17. Reminiscences of Jacques Godechot by American historians are to be found in "American Historians Remember Jacques Godechot," by Robert Forster, R. R. Palmer, James

Frigulietti, and Emmet Kennedy, *French Historical Studies* 61.4 (Fall 1990): 879–92. Another obituary in French is to be found in *Historiens and Géographes* 327 (Mars/Avril 1990), by Robert Marconis and Rémy Pech, 15–17; Jacques Godechot, *Les commissaires aux armées* (Paris: Fustier, 1937).

29. Jacques Godechot, *Histoire de l'Atlantique* (Paris: Bordas, 1954); Jacques Godechot et al., *Histoire générale de la presse française*, 5 vols. (Paris: PUF, 1969–76).

30. Godechot, "Avertissement de la première édition," in *La Grande Nation*, 17.

31. Godechot, *La Grande Nation*. Like *Twelve Who Ruled*, it went through many editions (1956, 1983, and 2004); see "Avant-propos de la première édition (1963)," 5, for Godechot's views on a revolution beginning in 1770 and ending in 1850; for the controversy over Atlantic history, see chapter 2, "Révolution française ou révolution occidentale," in *Les révolutions (1770–1799)* (1963; Paris: PUF, 1986), 287–303.

32. Jacques Godechot, *L'Europe et l'Amérique à l'époque napoléonienne (1800–1815)* (Paris: PUF, 1967).

33. Jacques Godechot, *Les révolutions de 1848* (Paris: Albin Michel, 1971); Christian Amalvi, *Dictionnaire biographique des historiens français et francophones: De Grégoire de Tours à Georges Duby* (Paris: la boutique de l'histoire, 2004), 133; Jacques Godechot, *Un jury pour la révolution* (Paris: Robert Laffont, 1974).

34. Palmer, "World Revolution of the West," 3–4.

35. Ibid., 2.

36. Lynn Hunt, preface to *Historical Reflections/Réflexions historiques* 37 (Winter 2011): v.

37. Lloyd Kramer, "Robert R. Palmer and the History of Big Questions," in ibid., 101–22.

38. See David Barry Gaspar and David Geggus, eds., *A Turbulent Time: The French Revolution and the Caribbean* (Bloomington: Indiana University Press, 1997); and Lester Langley, *The Americas in the Age of Revolution: 1750–1850* (New Haven, CT: Yale University Press, 1998).

39. I cannot mention all of Laurent Dubois's publications on this question. I will just refer to three articles in French that raised the question of the limits of French republicanism and of the Enlightenment and that underlined the ability of slaves and former slaves to claim their rights: Laurent Dubois, "'Citoyens et Amis!': Esclavage, citoyenneté et République dans les Antilles françaises à l'ère révolutionnaire," *Annales. Histoire, sciences sociales* 58.2 (2003): 281–303; "Histoire d'esclavage en France et aux Etats-Unis," *Esprit* 2 (February 2007): 71–80; Bernard Camier and Laurent Dubois, "Voltaire et Zaïre, ou le théâtre des Lumières dans l'aire atlantique française," *Revue d'histoire moderne et contemporaine* 54.4 (2007): 39–69. Of course, his books on the Haitian Revolution and the French abolition of slavery in Guadeloupe also develop these themes.

Contributors

OLIVIER CHALINE (b. 1964) was a student at the Ecole Normale Supérieure, Paris, where he was later associate professor. He was a Professor of Early Modern History at the Université de Haute-Bretagne Rennes, and he now teaches at Université Paris IV, now Sorbonne Université. His fields of research are Early Modern France, the Austrian Habsburg Monarchy, and war history, especially navies. He is the Vice-Director of the Sorbonne University Ocean Institute.

ROBERT RHODES CROUT served as coeditor of the *Lafayette Papers Project* (Cornell University), associate editor of the *Jefferson Papers Project* (Princeton University), and associate editor of the *Madison Papers Project* (University of Virginia). He currently teaches in the History Department of the College of Charleston in South Carolina and is completing a book on Lafayette's 1824–25 tour of the United States.

KATHLEEN DUVAL is a Professor of History at the University of North Carolina, Chapel Hill. She is the author of *Independence Lost: Lives on the Edge of the American Revolution* (Random House, 2015) and *The Native Ground: Indians and Colonists in the Heart of the Continent* (University of Pennsylvania Press, 2006) and coeditor of *Interpreting a Continent: Voices from Colonial America* (Rowman and Littlefield, 2009). She is currently writing a book on the Native dominance of North America from the eleventh to nineteenth centuries.

VICTOR ENTHOVEN was educated and trained as a maritime historian at Leiden University. Until 2017 he taught global history at the Vrije Universiteit Amsterdam. His research focuses on the early modern period, with a particular interest in the Atlantic world. He has published *Riches from Atlantic Commerce: Dutch Transatlantic Trade and Shipping, 1585–1817* (Brill, 2003), *The Navigator: The Log of John Anderson, VOC Pilot-Major, 1640–1643* (Brill, 2010), and *Geweld in de West: Een militaire geschiedenis van de Nederlandse Atlantische wereld, 1600–1800* (Brill, 2013).

PAUL A. GILJE is George Lynn Cross Research Professor Emeritus in the Department of History at the University of Oklahoma. Author or editor of over a dozen books, his most recent publications include *Free Trade and Sailors' Rights in the War of 1812* (Cambridge University Press, 2013) and *To Swear Like a Sailor: Maritime Culture in America, 1750–1850* (Cambridge University Press, 2016). Since his retirement, he has written *Cycles of Life: Bicycling from Brooklyn to Montreal in 1968 and 2018* (Sticky Earth Books, 2019), which compares the world of his youth to more recent times as he describes two four-hundred-mile bicycle trips fifty years apart. Currently he is writing a book on the year 1800 that examines the relationship between politics and the daily lives of ordinary people.

JEAN-MARIE KOWALSKI is an Associate Professor of Ancient History at Sorbonne Université and director of humanities and the military wing at the French Naval Academy. He has conducted research in navigation techniques and naval operations in antiquity, early modern, and modern history. He has been involved for several years in a major research program about the American War of Independence led by Pr. Olivier Chaline. This program is based on a thorough examination of both British and French sources. He has authored several papers and given several lectures about these naval operations.

ANDREW J. O'SHAUGHNESSY is a Professor of History at the University of Virginia and was the Vice President of the Thomas Jefferson Foundation (Monticello), Saunders Director of the Robert H. Smith International Center for Jefferson Studies at Monticello from 2003 to 2022. His book *The Men Who Lost America: British Leadership, the American Revolution, and the Fate of the Empire* (Yale University Press, 2013) received eight national awards including the New York Historical Society American History Book Prize, the George Washington Book Prize, the National Society Daughters of the American Revolution Excellence in American History Book Award, and the Society of Military History Book Prize. He is also the author of *An Empire Divided: The American Revolution and the British Caribbean* (University of Pennsylvania Press, 2000). A Fellow of the Royal Historical Society, in 2009 Dr. O'Shaughnessy was named Teacher of the Year by the Virginia Society of the Sons of the American Revolution (SAR), and he served as the national SAR Distinguished Scholar, with the responsibility of arranging the conference on European allies, in 2015. His most recent book is *The Illimitable Freedom of the Human Mind: Thomas Jefferson's Idea of a University* (University of Virginia Press, 2021).

JULIA OSMAN is an Associate Professor of History at Mississippi State University. She specializes on the French army during the Ancien Régime and is author of *Citizen Soldiers and the Key to the Bastille* (Palgrave Macmillan, 2015), as well as several articles and book chapters. Her current project considers the seventeenth- to eighteenth-century centralization of the French army and its consequences for soldiers and civilians alike. She is also currently the Director for the Institute for the Humanities at Mississippi State University.

MUNRO PRICE is Professor of Modern European History at the University of Bradford, UK, and specializes in late eighteenth- and early nineteenth-century French political and diplomatic history. Among his books are *Louis XVI and the Comte de Vergennes: Correspondence, 1774–1787*, with John Hardman (Voltaire Foundation, 1998), *The Road from Versailles: Louis XVI, Marie Antoinette and the Fall of the French Monarchy* (St Martin's Press, 2003), and *Napoleon: The End of Glory* (Oxford University Press, 2014).

GONZALO M. QUINTERO SARAVIA (PhD in American History, Universidad Complutense, Madrid; PhD in International Law, Universidad Nacional de Educación a Distancia, Madrid) is a member (*académico correspondiente*) of the Spanish Royal Historical Society and the Colombian Historical Society and fellow at the Weatherhead Center for International Affairs, Harvard University, 2015–16. His book *Bernardo de Gálvez: Spanish Hero of the American Revolution* (University of North Carolina Press, 2018) won the 2019 Distinguished Book Award by the Society for Military History as the best biography published in 2018. The biography was published in Spanish by Alianza Editorial in 2020. Other books include *Spain and the American Revolution: New Approaches and Perspectives,* coedited with Gabriel Paquette (Routledge, 2019), *Soldado de tierra y mar: Pablo Morillo: El pacificador* (EDAF, 2017 and Planeta Colombia, 2005), and *Don Blas de Lezo: Biografía de un marino español del siglo XVIII* (EDAF, 2016 and Planeta Colombia, 2002).

JOHN A. RAGOSTA is a historian at the Robert H. Smith International Center for Jefferson Studies at Monticello and a fellow with Virginia Humanities. He is the author of *Religious Freedom: Jefferson's Legacy, America's Creed* (University of Virginia Press, 2013) and *Wellspring of Liberty: How Virginia's Religious Dissenters Helped to Win the American Revolution and Secured Religious Liberty* (Oxford University Press 2010). He published *Patrick Henry: Proclaiming a Revolution* (Routledge, 2017) as a precursor to this current project, *For the People, For the Country: Patrick Henry's Final Political Battle* (University of Virginia Press, 2023). He has taught history and law at the University of Virginia, George Washington University, and Hamilton, Oberlin, and Randolph Colleges.

MARIE-JEANNE ROSSIGNOL is Professor of North American Studies at Université Paris Cité and past president of the European Early American Studies Association (EEASA). Her first book received the OAH Foreign Book Prize (David Thelen Prize) and was eventually translated as *The Nationalist Ferment: The Origins of United States Foreign Policy, 1789–1812* (Ohio State University Press, 2003). Her research has long concentrated on slavery and antislavery in the early American republic. She has edited a collection of essays on Anthony Benezet (*The Atlantic World of Anthony Benezet,* with Bertrand Van Ruymbeke, Brill, 2016) and translated Benezet's *Some Historical Account of Guinea* (also with Van Ruymbeke and other scholars). Her book on antislavery in the United States from 1754 to 1830 (*Noirs et Blancs contre l'esclavage: Une histoire de l'antiesclavagisme aux Etats-Unis*) is forthcoming (CIRESC, Karthala, 2022). She is currently moving to a new project which focuses on the context of Tocqueville's visit to America in light of the new historiography of the age of Jackson and Clay.

TIMOTHY D. WALKER (BA, Hiram College, 1986; MA, PhD, Boston University, 2001) is Professor of History at the University of Massachusetts Dartmouth where he serves on the executive board of the Center for Portuguese Studies and Culture and as graduate faculty for the doctoral program in Luso-Afro-Brazilian Studies and Theory. He is an affiliated researcher of the Centro de História d'Aquém e d'Além-Mar (CHAM), Universidade Nova de Lisboa, Portugal. Walker was a visiting professor at the Universidade Aberta in Lisbon (1994–2003) and at Brown University (2010). He is the recipient of a Fulbright dissertation fellowship to Portugal (1996–97), a doctoral research fellowship from the Portuguese Camões Institute (1995–96), and a fellowship from the Calouste Gulbenkian Foundation in Lisbon (2010–11). Walker is the editor and coordinator of a new volume entitled *Sailing to Freedom: Maritime Dimensions of the Underground Railroad* (University of Massachusetts Press, 2021).

Index

Aan het volk van Nederland (Capellen), 73
Abbé Grégoire, 268–69
Adams, John, 20, 43, 60–62, 85, 252; and Barbary pirates, 184; and Jefferson, 216, 226; and Lafayette, 212, 225, 226, 234n11; and Netherlands, 67; Plan of Treaties, 61; and Portugal, 178–81, 183, 185; as president, 194–95, 196–98
Adams, John Quincy, 194
admirals: British, 102, 104, 108, 123–25, 138, 141; French, 100, 103, 131, 248
Affaires de l'Angleterre et de l'Amérique, 18–19, 20–24, 26, 27
Afghanistan, 3–4
Africa, 10, 182, 193, 265, 266
African Americans, 25, 259; in American Revolution, 2; enslaved, 14, 21
Age of Revolutions, 2, 6, 7, 259, 260, 262, 263, 265–73
Age of Revolutions in Global Context, c. 1760–1840, The (Armitage and Subrahmanyam), 265
Age of the Democratic Revolution, 1760–1800 (Palmer), 268
Aix-la-Chapelle (Aachen, Germany), 78
Ajax (British ship), 136

Alabamas (Native American nation), 155, 158
Alcide (British ship), 136
Alexander I (of Russia), 62
Alfred (British ship), 130, 136, 137, 139
Alliance (American ship), 71–72, 82–84
Almanach Litteraire, 30–31
Almeida, João de, 181
American Revolution: centennial of, 35; complexity of, 11; Dutch friends of, 67–88; European friends of, 1–11, 13–15, 43, 97, 145–46, 176, 205, 259; European influence on, 7; European supplies for, 57, 97; French intervention in, 99; and French Revolution, 259–60, 262–63, 270; French support for, 206, 242; French views on, 24–32; history of, 2, 7, 13, 44, 198; impact on Lafayette, 243–44, 251; international dimension of, 199; interpretations of, 263; League of Armed Neutrality and, 45–46; legacy of, 222, 225, 231; and monarchy, 30, 162; nature of, 145, 260; naval warfare and, 101; origins of, 263; Portugal and, 175–76; slavery and, 39n21; Spanish involvement in, 154–65

Americas in the Age of Revolutions: 1750–1850, The (Langley), 273
Amsterdam: and American Revolution, 67–88; Exchange, 80; merchants of, 73
Ancien Régime, 59, 262, 268, 269
André, Jean Bon Saint, 267
Annapolis, 9
Annapolis Conference, 225
Antigua, 108, 109, 110
Antoine Léonard Thomas: *Jumonville Poème*, 19–20
Apaches (Native American nation), 149–50, 153, 163
Apotheosis of Franklin and Washington, 32
Aranjuez (Spain), 154
army: British, 5, 18, 22–23, 24, 25, 28, 31; citizen, 36, 267; Dutch, 89n3; French, 6, 17, 20, 26, 34, 35, 36, 103, 127, 149, 246, 247, 267, 269; Portuguese, 191; Spanish, 147, 149, 150, 151
Articles of Confederation, 161, 179, 186, 206; Lafayette on, 219–21, 225
Asia, 69, 180, 182
Atakapas (Native American nation), 155
Atlantic History (Bailyn), 264
Atlantic Ocean, 26, 32, 35, 36, 46, 70, 149, 183, 187, 188, 189, 220, 222, 224, 228, 230, 259, 266, 273; packet boats, 217
Atlantic world, 1, 46, 145, 176, 185, 198, 199, 231, 263, 272, 273; British, 265; history of, 265
Auguste (French ship), 130, 132, 136, 139, 140
Austria, 28, 45, 53, 206, 270; diplomacy of, 55–59; and War of the Bavarian Succession, 54
Avengers of the New World (Dubois), 266
Ávila (Spain), 151, 171n44
Azores Islands (Portugal), 175

Bahamas Channel, Old, 106, 110, 111, 154
Bahamas Current, 110, 112
Bailyn, Bernard, 13; and Atlantic history, 262–65; *Atlantic History*, 264
Baltic, 84, 214; Russian, 58
Baltimore (Maryland): Lafayette in, 221; Portuguese consulate in, 193
Barbary pirates, 146, 179, 183–84, 186, 188–90, 196
Barfleur (British ship), 111–13, 130, 135, 136, 138
Barras, Jacques-Melchior Saint-Lauren, comte de, 99, 105, 113, 114, 118n14
Bastille (Paris): fall of, 245
Batailles navales de la France (Troude), 124
Battle of the Chesapeake (1781), 5–6, 9, 97–98, 99, 100, 102–3, 110, 114, 123–41; French fleet, 133; French victory of, 123–24, 140–41; losses, 140
Battle of Saratoga (1777), 5, 23, 77
Battle of the Saintes (1782), 100, 101, 106, 140, 159
Bayonne (France): as free port, 214
Beaufort scale, 142n11
Benezet, Anthony: *Some Historical Account of Guinea*, 261
Berckel, Engelbert François van, 77–78, 81, 84–86
Bergen (Norway), 72
Berkenbosch (Dutch ship), 84
Berni (France), 216; "decision" of, 217, 219
Bill of Rights, 186, 206, 229–30
Biloxis (Native American nation), 155
Bleiswijk, Pieter van, 76–77, 83
blockade: naval, 5, 45, 79, 81, 83, 84
Bonhomme Richard (American ship), 44, 71, 74
bonnet rouge. *See* Phrygian cap
Borel, Antoine: *L'Amérique Indépendante*, 32

Boston (Massachusetts), 24, 25, 77, 84, 85, 105, 184, 218; French consul at, 211; merchants, 213; Portuguese consulate in, 193
Boston Evening-Post, 61
Boston Gazette, 21–22
Bouchet, Denis Jean Florimond de Langlois, marquis du, 35
Bougainville, Louis Antoine de, 115, 140
Bourbons (dynasty), 54; in Spain, 145
Bourdin, Philippe: *La Fayette, entre deux mondes,* 232
Bowdoin, James, 213, 230
Brazil: independence movement in, 181–82, 197–98; Portuguese court at, 195; as Portuguese colony, 176, 193; trade goods from, 180; US trade with, 180–82
Brest (France), 84, 99, 103, 104, 267, 269
British Leeward Islands, 108, 122n47
Broglie, Victor-François, duc de, 245, 247
Broglie family, 245, 247
Burgoyne, John, 23, 24, 28
Burke, Edmund, 252

cabildo, 152, 157, 158, 164
Cádiz (Spain), 211
Cagigal, Juan Manuel de, 160, 161
Calonne, Charles Alexandre de, 213, 215–19
Campbell, John, 156, 159
Canada: British, 162; French, 14, 20
Canary Islands (Spain), 158
Cape Charles (Virginia), 113, 130
Cape Henry (Virginia), 113, 129, 132, 134
Capellen tot den Pol, Joan Derck van der, 73, 74, 76, 78, 87; *Aan het volk van Nederland,* 73
Cape of Saint Vincent, 55, 184
Capes of Virginia, 101, 102–16
Cap Français (Haiti), 105, 106, 108, 109, 121n38

Carabineros de la Luisiana, 155
Caribbean, 5, 10, 115, 122n47, 147, 148, 273; British in, 108, 171n43; climate of, 105–06; French, 261; French naval operations in, 103–4; Spanish power in, 106, 115
Carlos III (of Spain), 145, 148, 149, 150, 151, 152, 153; and Bernardo de Gálvez, 161–64; on coin, 156; declares war on Britain, 157, 158
Carolinas, 110; British campaign in, 105
Castries, Charles Eugène Gabriel de La Croix de Castries, marquis de, 103–4, 115, 118n13, 212–13, 214, 217–18
Catherine the Great (of Russia), 8, 43–44, 45; as Anglophile, 54; diplomacy of, 52–59; and League of Armed Neutrality, 44–63; *Regarding the Principles of Armed Neutrality,* 52, 56, 64n11; and Russian foreign policy, 65n12
Cerf (French ship), 71
Cerutti, Joseph: *The Eagle and the Owl,* 24
Chabert, de (captain), 111
Chaline, Olivier, 7, 9, 97–98
Charleston (South Carolina), 6, 87, 94, 205, 218
Chartier, Roger, 26
Chaumont, Jacques-Donatien Le Ray de, 68, 70–72, 74, 76, 80, 82, 84
Cherokees (Native American nation), 161; treaty with United States, 194
Chesapeake Bay, 98, 99, 102–16, 118n14, 122n47, 126–41
China: and Vietnam War, 4
Chitimachas (Native American nation), 155
Choctaws (Native American nation), 158
CIA (Central Intelligence Agency), 259; agents, 264
Citoyen (French ship), 135, 136–37, 139
Civil War (American), 265

Civil War (English), 263
Clinton, Henry, 99, 102, 108, 114, 122n47
clocks: maritime, 102, 110, 120n38
Cold War, 198, 259, 264
Columbus, Christopher, 147
Comanches (Native American nation), 163
Coming of the French Revolution (Lefebvre), 232
Committee of Public Safety, 266–67, 273
Committee of Secret Correspondence, 75
Common Sense (Paine), 31, 62
Companhia Geral do Alto Douro (firm), 193
Congress, US, 188, 230; and Portuguese embassy, 197–98
consolato del mare, 47–51, 63
Conspiracy of Well-Intentioned Men, A (Wick), 247
Constitutional Convention (US), 226–28, 231
Constitution of 1791 (France), 244–45, 255; republican character of, 251–56
constitutions: of American states, 35, 224
Continental and Confederation Congress, 8, 14, 24, 68, 73, 82, 156, 210, 216, 217, 253; and Articles of Confederation, 161; bonds of, 74; diplomacy of, 157, 213, 220; finances, 84–85, 88; and John Paul Jones, 70; Lafayette and, 222, 224, 226; and Netherlands, 67; and Portugal, 178–86; powers of, 221–24; trade policy of, 60
Continental Army, 6, 21, 23, 27, 73, 104, 127, 161; Lafayette in, 243; officers, 205–6, 220
contraband, 45, 48–49, 51, 56, 58, 156
Conyngham, Gustavus, 80
Corbett, Julian, 124–25, 140–41; *Fighting Instructions*, 124
Cornwallis, Charles, 5, 9, 99, 102, 147, 176, 223, 243

Cortés, Hernán, 162
Costa Pereira, Hipólito José da, 193
Countess of Scarborough (British ship), 71–72, 82–84
Couteulx, Le (firm), 216
Crimea (Russia), 53–54, 55
Crout, Robert Rhodes, 205–07
Cuba, 106, 156, 162, 266; as Spanish colony, 152, 157; trade with, 152
currents, sea: and naval warfare, 103, 114, 127, 130

Daniël Crommelin & Zoonen (firm), 67
Danton, Georges, 232
Daughters of the American Revolution, 164
Dauphin (American ship), 184
Dean, Silas, 68, 69
Declaration of Independence, 1, 24, 30, 38n12, 68, 151, 244
Declaration of the Rights of Man and of the Citizen, 31, 206, 230, 244–45
De Grasse (French ship), 100
De Ijhoek (shipyard), 74
De la Démocratie Royale de 1789 (Lafayette), 252–53
De la Lande & Fijnje (firm), 74, 75, 78
Delaware Bay, 109, 110
democracy, 181, 228, 253; advantages of, 223; evils of, 224; global, 262; liberal, 267; rise of, 272
Democratic-Republicans, 62
Den Helder (Netherlands), 75, 76, 82
Denmark, 45, 53, 191, 192; commercial treaties, 48; diplomacy of, 56–59; and League of Armed Neutrality, 64n11
Destin (French ship), 139
d'Ethy, M., 135, 136–37, 139
Deventer (Netherlands), 73
Diadème (French ship), 130, 138–39, 140
Diderot, Denis, 52
diplomacy, 6, 8–9, 20; alliances, 99; American, 23, 38n17; and American

Revolution, 43–44; European, 52–59; and free trade, 46–52, 60–63; and League of Armed Neutrality, 46; Old World, 63; between Portugal and United States, 178–99; Portuguese, 146, 177–78, 189; revolution in, 60–63; state and private, 67, 72, 88

District of Columbia (DC), 196

Docteur Franklin Couronné par la Liberté, Le (Fragonard), 32

Dordrecht (Netherlands), 73

Drake, Francis Samuel, 132

Dubois, Laurent, 273, 278n39; *Avengers of the New World,* 266

Dull, Jonathan R., 100

Dumas, Anna, 81, 88

Dumas, Guillaume-Frederic, 72, 75–82, 84, 87–88

Dunkirk (France), 72, 84

Dupont, Pierre-Samuel, 218

Dutch Republic. *See* Netherlands

DuVal, Kathleen, 9, 145

Duviquet, Pierre: *Verses on the Peace,* 25

Eagle and the Owl, The (Cerutti), 24

East Indies, 182

Edler, Friedrich, 68

Egypt, 269

Eiffel Tower (Paris), 100

Embargo of 1807, 62

Enlightenment, 14, 47, 49, 61, 147; European, 36; and free trade, 46; French, 36; ideas, 26, 59; limits of, 278n39; philosophes, 51–52, 263, 271

Enthoven, Victor, 7, 44

equality, 1, 212, 231, 273; of citizens, 224, 228; and fraternity, 267; fundamental, 272; racial, 267–68, 272–73; of rights, 251, 268

Estado Novo (Portugal), 198

Estates General (France), 245, 247, 248

Europe, 75, 86, 120n34; American agents in, 75, 179; and American Revolution, 1–3, 17, 52–53; Americans in, 44, 67; balance of power of, 5, 176, 198; colonialism of, 148; commercial treaties, 47–52; courts of, 146, 148, 188; democracy in, 270; diplomacy of, 45–46, 52–59, 60–63; empires of, 171n43; and League of Armed Neutrality, 46, 60–62; major powers of, 17; newspaper correspondents in, 61; and revolutions of 1848, 270; royalty, 190; status of Catherine the Great in, 55–56; US interests in, 206

Explanatory Declaration: between England and Netherlands, 47–48

Farewell Address (Washington), 46

Federal Constitution (US), 186, 205–6, 246, 251, 254; and Constitution of 1791, 244; Lafayette and creation of, 219–31; Morris and, 253; ratification of, 6, 230

Ferreiro, Larrie D., 7

Fighting Instructions (Corbett), 124

Fizeaux, Grand & Co. (firm), 67, 69, 75, 78–79

Florida, 110; eastern, 107, 159; West, 147, 148

Fort Royal (Martinique), 106, 108, 109, 121n38

Fortune (British ship), 139

Fragonard, Jean Honoré: *Le Docteur Franklin Couronné par la Liberté,* 32

France, 43, 109; abolitionism in, 38n10, 278n39; Admiralty courts of, 213; aid for United States, 5, 7–8, 13, 17, 22, 205; alliance with Spain, 154; "American Committee," 215; American minister to, 244; and American Revolution, 1, 3, 9, 17, 19–37; antislavery in, 261; attitude towards Americans, 17–32, 38n17; Caribbean colonies of, 13, 14; commercial treaties, 47–52; constituent assembly, 242, 249, 252,

France (*continued*)
253; constitution of, 35; and democracy, 207; diplomacy of, 52–59, 220; economy of, 215; empire of, 270; Farmers General, 214–16, 219; free ports, 214, 221; government of, 35–36, 70, 71, 76, 83, 211, 212, 218, 228; National Guard of, 35, 219; political stabilization, 268; political system of, 218, 256; public opinion, 18, 23; relations with Netherlands, 69, 75; relations with Spain, 100; relations with United States, 13–15, 76, 100, 205–6, 210, 210–19, 221, 231, 233n3; rivalry with Great Britain, 17; during Terror, 266–67; trade with Portugal, 191, 192; war with Great Britain (1778), 4, 5; war with Great Britain (1793), 62

Franklin, Benjamin, 20, 21, 26, 77, 88; Dumas and, 75; in France, 43, 68, 69, 70, 78, 82, 86; French image of, 25, 29, 32–33; and Jones, 84; and Lafayette, 224–25; *nom de plume*, 71; and Portugal, 177, 178–80; on trade policy, 60, 62, 214

Frederick II (of Prussia), 55, 58, 223

Free Sea, The (Grotius), 50

Freire, Cipriano Ribeiro, 187–90, 192–95

French and Indian War (1754–1763), 8

French Revolution, 6, 10, 27, 53, 181, 205–07, 243; and American Revolution, 8, 13–15, 18, 29, 34–37, 242–43, 259–60, 262–63, 270; bicentennial, 267, 270; causes of, 18, 34–37, 40n50; centennial, 35; and classical imagery, 31; history of, 253, 264, 266, 268; interpretations of, 231–32, 267, 270; language of, 17, 26, 37; radicalization of, 188; refugees of, 212; as republican, 251; turmoil in Europe, 191, 219; and wars of, 188–91

Furet, François, 242, 251, 262, 267; *Interpreting the French Revolution*, 232

Gallic Wars, The (Caesar), 170n38

Gálvez, Bernardo de, 5, 9, 145, 147–148, 171n44; and American Revolution, 154–56; "black legend" of, 162–64; expedition to Algiers, 151; as governor of Louisiana, 148, 152–54; "Instructions for the Government of the Internal Provinces," 163; and Native Americans, 149–50, 153–55, 163; *Notes and Considerations on the War with the Apache Indians in the Provinces of New Spain*, 149–50; and Spanish Empire, 148, 161–65; and war with Great Britain, 157–61; wife of, 153

Gálvez, José, 149, 152, 153, 160, 163, 171n44; as minister of the Indies, 150

Gálvez, Miguel, 151, 152; as *ministro togado*, 150

Gálvez, Miguel (son of Bernardo), 153

Gálvez y Gallardo, Matías de, 148, 149, 162

Gaspar, David Barry: *A Turbulent Time*, 273

Gazeta de Lisboa, 186, 191

Gazette de France, 27–28

Gazette de Leyde, 27, 73

Geggus, David: *A Turbulent Time*, 273

Genêt, Edmé-Jacques, 20

George III (of Great Britain), 54, 70, 177

Germany, 75, 77, 269; states of, 53, 54; trade with Portugal, 192

Gibraltar, 148, 154, 189; Strait of, 184

Gijzelaar, Cornelis de, 73, 76

Gilje, Paul A., 8, 44

Gillon, Alexander, 86–87, 160

Glaunec, Le, 266

Godechot, Jacques, 8, 10, 242, 259–60; and Atlantic history, 36, 261–73; biography of, 269–70; *La Grande Nation*, 264, 269, 270; *History of*

the Atlantic, 269; "Le Problème de l'Atlantique du XVIIIè Siècle au XXè Siècle," 264; *Les Révolutions*, 270, 274; *L'Europe et l'Amérique à l'Époque Napoléonienne*, 270
Goff, Fabrice Le, 111–12
Gottschalk, Louis, 242, 245, 249, 252
Grand, Ferdinand, 68, 75, 77, 78
Grand, George, 68–69, 75, 79
Grande Nation, La (Godechot), 264, 269, 270
Granville (French ship), 71
Grasse, François Joseph Paul de, 115, 118n13, 122n47, 126–27, 159, 172n44; and Battle of the Chesapeake, 99–116, 130–41; and Battle of the Saintes, 125; memorial of, 100
Graves, Thomas, 109–10, 113, 114, 122n46, 122n47, 124–25; and Battle of the Chesapeake, 130–41
Great Britain, 38n12; abolitionism in, 38n10; Admiralty, 114; Baltic fleet of, 71; barbarism of, 19, 21, 22, 24, 25; cabinet of, 86; commercial treaties, 47–52, 180; Commonwealth period, 263; constitution of, 246; and counterinsurgencies, 4; diplomacy of, 52–59, 194, 223; diplomatic isolation of, 56, 60; forts in North America, 194; interregnum, 47; intrigues of, 189; mercantilist system of, 61; naval intelligence of, 103, 108, 109, 114, 119n29, 119n31, 120n35; naval supremacy of, 211; and Nootka Sound Crisis, 250; North American colonies of, 14, 17, 20, 75, 147, 148, 154, 175–76, 268, 269; parliamentary reform, 162; propaganda of, 179; relations with Netherlands, 68, 69, 70–71, 75, 76; relations with Portugal, 175–76, 177, 185, 191; relations with Spain, 147–48, 154–56; relations with United States, 4, 177–78, 225; resources of, 4, 145; Rule of 1756, 49; trade, 156, 191–92, 216; war against France (1778), 4, 45; war against France (1793), 62; war against Spain (1779), 4, 45; and War of Independence, 1, 3–5, 43–44, 45; war with Netherlands (1780), 4, 45, 86; war with Spain, 157–61, 160
Greene, Nathanael, 212, 214, 219–220, 222
Grotius, Hugo, 44, 49–51, 63; *The Free Sea*, 50; *The Rights of War and Peace*, 49–50
Gueniffey, Patrice, 251, 252
Guichen, Luc Urbain du Bouëxic, comte de, 109, 120n34
Gulf of Mexico, 148, 157, 158, 159, 161
Gulf Stream, 102, 107, 110, 114

Haiti, 266, 273
Haitian Revolution, 2, 10, 259–60, 266, 272–73, 278n39
Halifax (Nova Scotia) 116
Hamilton, Alexander, 212, 228, 229
Hapsburg Empire. *See* Austria
Harden, David J., 31–34
Havana, Cuba, 104, 105, 106, 108, 158–59, 160; British occupation of, 151, 152
Hector (French ship), 134
Heemskerck, Willem van, 78
Higginbotham, Don, 28
Higonnet, Patrice, 34, 242
history: American, 63; of American Revolution, 99; of antislavery, 261; Atlantic, 2–11, 36, 97, 176, 198, 259–60, 261–274; bottom-up, 101, 260; of democratic revolutions, 265; diplomatic, 43–44, 100, 115; European, 63, 272; of free trade, 46; French colonial, 265; of ideas, 242; of immigration, 265; of League of Armed Neutrality, 58; maritime, 8, 9, 97–98, 99–100, 114, 123, 141, 269;

history (continued)
    micro, 260; military, 97–98, 99–100, 114, 125, 141; modern, 272; narrative, 100; neoprogressive, 260; of science, 141; of slavery, 265; of social movements, 242, 259; state, 101; of trade, 265; world, 265
History of the Atlantic (Godechot), 269
hivernage, 106
Hommage de l'Amérique à la France (Jouy), 32
Hood, Samuel, 106, 108–14, 120n35, 122n47, 124, 132, 138
Hooft, Hendrik Daniëlsz, 78
Horneca, Fizeaux & Co. (firm), 69
Hortalez and Company (firm), 5
Houmas (Native American nation), 158
Humboldt, Alexander von, 163–64, 173n60; *Political Essay on the Kingdom of New Spain*, 163–64
Humphreys, David, 194, 221; as US minister to Portugal, 187–89
hurricanes, 106; Katrina, 106; season, 105

ideals, 60; of American Revolution, 1; Enlightenment, 59; of liberty, 181, 271; political, 243; revolutionary, 36, 272
identity: American, 17–19, 21–32; French, 18, 19, 26; national, 18
Île de Groix (France), 71
Imperial Portugal in the Age of Atlantic Revolutions (Paquette), 199
Inconfidência Baiana, 182
Inconfidência Mineira, 182
Inconfidência Pernambucana, 182
India, 10, 148; and War of Independence, 5
Interpreting the French Revolution (Furet), 232
Intrepid (British ship), 128, 130, 136, 138, 139, 140
Ireland, 269; parliamentary reform, 162

Italy, 269; mercantile states of, 47; states of, 53; trade with Portugal, 192

Jacobin club, 243, 248
Jamaica, 104, 108, 159–60, 161; invasion of, 153
James River, 127, 131
Jay, John, 157, 184, 217, 225, 226–27, 230
Jefferson, Thomas, 179–81, 193, 206; and Adams, 216, 226; and Barbary pirates, 183–84; and Declaration of Independence, 38n12, 151, 244; and French Revolution, 249, 254; as governor of Virginia, 157; and Lafayette, 209–10, 213–15, 217–19, 223, 225–26, 229; in London, 215; as minister to France, 213; and monarchy, 253; as president, 195, 268, 270; as secretary of state, 186–88, 219; support for Brazilian independence, 181–82
Jeune, J. L. Le Barbier le, 23
Jews, 268–69
John Hodshon & Zoon (firm), 67
John VI (of Portugal), 195
Jones, John Paul, 8–9, 44; in Netherlands, 67–88
Joseph I (of Portugal), 175
Joseph II (of Austria), 55, 57–58, 223
Jouy, 40n44; *Hommage de l'Amérique à la France*, 32
Jumonville, Joseph Coulon de Villiers de, 19; literature on, 27, 29
Jumonville Poème, 19–20

Kalb, Baron de, 10
Kerloguen, Dennis-Nicolas de Brulôt Cottineau de, 71
Kersaint, Armand de, 245–46; *Le Bon Sens*, 245, 248
Key to American Independence, The (Wenger), 7
King Philip's War (1675–76), 26
Knox, Henry, 212, 227–29

Kosciuszko, Thaddeus, 10
Kowalski, Jean-Marie, 7, 9, 97–98, 100, 103, 114

La Concorde (French ship), 105
L'Active (British ship), 122n47
La Fayette, entre deux mondes (Bourdin), 232
Lafayette, George Washington: in United States, 212
Lafayette, Marie-Joseph Paul Yves Roch Gilbert du Motier, marquis de, 1, 10, 148; and Adams, 212, 225, 234n11; and American constitutional reforms, 219–31; and American Revolution, 205–07, 209–10, 242–43, 243–44, 251; American tour (1784), 213, 221, 225–26; American tour (1824–25), 209–10, 274n2; biographers of, 209–10; and Confederation Congress, 222, 224, 226; and Constitutional Convention, 226–28; constitutional ideas of, 248–52; and Constitution of 1791, 229–30, 244–45; as courtier, 247; *De la Démocratie Royale de 1789*, 252–53; European travels of, 214; and Franco-American trade, 210–19, 231; and Franklin, 224–25; and French Revolution, 210, 211, 231–32; and Greene, 212, 214, 220–21, 222; and Hamilton, 212, 228, 229; and Jay, 225, 226–27, 230; and Jefferson, 209–10, 213–15, 217–19, 223, 225–26, 229; and Knox, 212, 227–29; and Lee, 222–23, 228; and Livingston, 220–21, 230; and Madison, 228; and Morris, 253–55; and National Guard, 219; republicanism of, 252–56; *Résumé de Mon Avis au Comité du Commerce avec les Etats-Unis*, 215; rivalry with Lameth brothers, 243–56; on royal power, 248–53; on Shay's Rebellion, 226; and slavery, 261, 274n2; and tobacco trade, 214–18; and Washington, 28, 35, 220–21, 223–24, 226–30, 243
L'Aigrette (French ship), 106, 127, 129, 130
Lake Maurepas and Lake Pontchartrain, 158
Lamb, John, 184
Lambert, Charles Claude Guillaume, 218–19
L'Amérique Indépendante (Borel), 32
Lameth, Alexandre, 10, 206–7; and American Revolution, 242–43; as courtier, 247; *Lettre à M le Comte de ****, 245–46, 248, 249; as monarchist, 255–56; on royal powers, 249–50
Lameth, Charles Malo François, 10, 206–7; and American Revolution, 242–43; as courtier, 247; as monarchist, 255–56
Lameth, Théodore, 206–07, 247; and American Revolution, 242–43; as monarchist, 255–56
Landais, Pierre, 71, 74
Langley, Lester: *The Americas in the Age of Revolutions*, 273
Languedoc (French ship), 127, 131, 132, 137
La Railleuse (French ship), 129
La Reine Charlotte (French ship), 127
Laurens, Henry, 78, 85–86
Laurens, John, 104
Lauzun, Armand Louis de Gontaut, duc de, 242
law: equal rights under, 251; international, 6, 44, 79; as king, 31; of nations, 19, 50, 52, 60, 63; natural, 38n10, 46–47, 50–51
Law of Nations, The (Vattel), 51
League of Armed Neutrality, 4, 8, 43–44, 45–46, 53–59, 86; Americans and, 60–63; history of, 58; legacy of, 62; Portugal joins, 177
Lean, David, 148

Le Bons Sens (Kersaint), 245
Le Docteur Franklin (LeManissier), 25
Le duc de Duras (French ship), 71
Lee, Arthur, 68, 69, 73, 76, 77
Lee, Henry, 28
Lee, Richard Henry, 222–23, 228
Lee, William, 77, 78
Lefebvre, Georges: *Coming of the French Revolution*, 232
Le Havre (France), 122n46
LeManissier (French poet): *Le Docteur Franklin*, 25
L'Enfant, Pierre Charles, 196
"Le Problème de l'Atlantique du XVIIIè Siècle au XXè Siècle" (Godechot and Palmer), 264
Lescure, M. de, 136
Leslie (captain), 22
Lesser Antilles, 159
Lettre à M le Comte de *** (Lameth, A.), 245–46
Lettre Hollandaise [. . .] de la République des Sept Provinces-Unies, 73
L'Europe et l'Amérique à l'Époque Napoléonienne (Godechot), 270
levée en masse, 27–29; National Convention and, 28–29
Lewis, Charles Lee, 100
Leyba, Fernando de, 155
L'Hermione (French ship), 205
liberty, 1, 14, 28, 227, 231, 254; American, 21–22; ancient, 31, 34; Brazil and, 181; cause of, 226; idea of, 242, 271; individual, 246; poles, 31–34; of the press, 246; of religion, 244, 246; of speech, 244. *See also* trade, free
Lima (Peru), 152
L'Indien (French ship), 69–71, 74, 86–87
Lisbon (Portugal), 175, 177, 179; market, 180
Liverpool (England), 84
Livingston, Robert, 220, 230
Livingston, William, 73
Livoncourt, M. de, 75
Livorno (Italy), 84
Livre Rouge, 245
logbooks: ship, 9, 97, 101, 110, 111, 113, 114, 117n7, 125–41
London, 8, 177, 182, 184–87, 189, 194–95, 215–16; Jefferson in, 215; Portuguese minister to, 180; Tower of, 85
London (British ship), 129, 130, 138
Lorient (France), 71, 84, 100, 104, 126; as free port, 214
Lorraine (France), 269
Louisiana, 20, 150; French population of, 153, 157; as Spanish colony, 151–52, 154, 158; trade policy, 156; Upper, 155
Louis XVI (of France), 18, 25, 26, 34, 71, 84, 100, 103–4, 115, 218, 226, 248–49; beheading of, 188; court of, 206; flight to Varenne, 255; and French Revolution, 244, 250–53
Loyalist (British ship), 127
Luchesini, Girolamo, 223
Lumina, Etienne-Joseph Poullin de, 19
Luso-American Treaty of Commerce and Friendship, 182–83, 184, 186, 191
Luzerne, Anne-César de La, 103, 105, 118n14
Luzerne, César-Henri de La, 214

Macharaviaya, 148, 149
Mackesy, Piers, 3–4, 6; *The War for America*, 3
Madeira (Portugal), 175, 193. *See also* wine, Madeira
Madison, James, 62–63, 228, 244, 270
Madrid, 148, 150, 160, 254; French embassy at, 149
Madrid, María Josefa de, 148
Magalhães, José Calvet de, 199
Mahan, Alfred, 124–25, 140, 140n2; *Major Operations of the Navies in the War of Independence*, 124
Maia e Barbello, José, 181

Major Operations of the Navies in the War of Independence (Mahan), 124
Malaysia, 4
Malta, 183, 269
Marat, Jean-Paul, 232
Maria (American ship), 184
Maria I (of Portugal), 146, 176, 177–78, 180, 184–85, 187, 188, 190, 193, 196–97
Marie Antoinette (of France), 206, 218, 247
mariscal de campo, 158
Marseillais (French ship), 130, 136, 137, 139, 140
Marseillaise, 23
Maryland, 215; tobacco, 193
Maryland Gazette, 217
Massachusetts, 151; Continental Army in, 243
Massachusetts Spy, 61
Matanzas Bay, 106
McDonald, Forrest, 34
Mediterranean, 10, 53, 55, 57, 183, 184, 269
Mello e Castro, Martinho de, 184–85, 192
Mercury (American ship), 85
Metz (France), 247
Mexico, 150, 193; famine in, 162–63; as Spanish colony, 152, 162–64
Mexico City (New Spain), 152, 153, 162
Middelburg, Netherlands, 84
Middle Ages: and neutral trade, 46–47
Middleton, Charles, 109
militia, 6; American, 27–28, 222, 225, 226; Black, 155, 158; Connecticut, 27; Louisiana, 158; state, 4
Minas Gerais, 182
Ministério dos Negócios Estrangeiros, 192, 194
Minorca (Spain), 57, 148
Mirabeau, Honoré Gabriel Riqueti, comte de, 245, 250, 255

Mississippi River, 152, 155, 156, 158, 162; British posts on, 157
Mobile (Alabama), 154; British fort at, 158; Spanish attack on, 156, 157
monarchy, 228, 229; absolute, 154, 198, 250; in America, 145; Bourbon, 59; British, 25, 27; constitutional, 251–53; and corruption, 248; and democratic revolutions, 13, 15; French, 25, 27, 31, 70, 86–87, 157, 207, 254; hereditary, 253; Jefferson on, 253; in old regime, 246; and patronage, 248; Portuguese, 175–76, 193; rebellion against, 157; republican, 251–52, 256; Spanish, 115–16, 147, 149, 155, 156, 157, 162; Stuart, 47; Turgot on, 224; war against, 270; Washington and, 30–31
monopoly: on tobacco, 217–18; trade, 215
Monroe, James, 214, 216, 225
Monsieur (French ship), 71
Montagu, John, 4th Earl of Sandwich, 5
Montecler, M. de, 138–39
Montenegro, José Joaquim da Maia, 181–82
Montesquieu, Charles Louis de Secondat, Baron de La Brède et de, 52; on monarchy, 255
Montmorency, Anne Paul Emmanuel Sigismond de, 87
Montmorin, Armand Marc, comte de, 228, 250
Montpellier (France), 181
Morgan, George, 156
Morris, Gouverneur: as Federalist, 254; on Lafayette, 253–55
Morris, Robert, 214; tobacco contract of, 215–17
Motte-Picquet, Toussaint-Guillaume de La, 115, 122n46
Mounier, Jean Joseph, 245, 252
Mount Vernon (Virginia), 50
Moustier, Elénor-François-Elie, comte de, 228

Nantes (France), 70, 80
Nantucket (Massachusetts), 193
Naples (Italy), 45, 58, 183
Napoleon, 188, 268, 270; as emperor of France, 35
Napoleonic Wars, 53, 191, 195; Peninsula campaign, 191, 196
Nassau (Bahamas), 160
Nassau-Siegen, Karl Heinrich, 70
Natchez, 153, 158
Natchitoches (Native American nation), 155
National Assembly (France), 219, 249–50, 255; and Constitution of 1791, 244–45
National Convention (France), 28–29
National Society of the Sons of the American Revolution, 2, 7, 97, 205, 259
Native Americans, 14, 21, 25, 152, 259, 265, 270; in American Revolution, 2; Bernardo de Gálvez and, 149–50, 153–54; as British allies, 19, 153, 163; combat tactics of, 150; imagery of, 32, 38n10; sovereignty of, 154; as Spanish allies, 149, 161–62; and US treaties, 194. *See also specific Native American nations*
NATO (North Atlantic Treaty Organization), 264
Naval Academy: French, 9, 100–101, 103, 110; United States, 9, 101, 103
navy, 101; American merchant, 62, 183; of American states, 220; British, 1, 5, 6, 43, 54, 68, 79, 87, 102, 106, 115, 126–41, 183, 188, 214; Dutch, 89n3; French, 5, 97–98, 100, 103, 106, 110, 126–41, 159, 214, 246, 250, 267; French minister of, 71, 86; Portuguese, 146, 191; Prussian, 58; Russian merchant, 58; Spanish, 5, 159, 161; Swedish, 57; US, 71, 222
Neif, Arie de, 84

Neptune (French ship), 113
Netherlands, 8, 44, 61, 89n3, 269; Adams in, 178; aid for United States, 8; and American independence, 178; and American Revolution, 3, 9, 67–88; commercial treaties, 47–52; diplomacy of, 53–59, 83; Orange party in, 67, 70, 87; relations with France, 75, 79–80, 82–83; relations with Great Britain, 68–69, 70–71, 75, 76, 79–80, 82–83; States General, 68, 69, 70, 74–76, 78, 80–81, 83, 86; States of Holland, 85; support for privateers, 1; trade with United States, 77, 180; war with Great Britain (1780), 4; war with Spain and Portugal, 50
Neufville, John de, 72, 74, 76–77, 80–81, 85–88; supports United States, 67
Neufville-Evans, Anna G., 85, 88
Neufville & Fils, de (firm), 67
neutrality, 43, 228; Portuguese, 176, 198; rights of, 1, 46–52, 53; of shipping, 188; Spanish, 154–55; trade and, 45–46, 46–52; United States and, 188–89
New Bedford (Massachusetts), 193
Newbury (Massachusetts), 77
New England, 14, 151; coast, 175, 193; markets, 214; merchants, 213; states, as republics, 237n35
New France, 20
New Jersey, 73; legislature, 222
New Orleans (Louisiana), 9, 151, 152, 153, 157; militia of, 155; port of, 156
Newport (Rhode Island), 103, 104, 113, 114, 214; French convoy to, 118n14
New Providence (Bahamas), 159–61
New Spain, 149, 150, 152, 166n12; viceroy of, 162
newspapers, 20, 23, 26, 27–28, 73, 87, 217, 218; American, 61, 225; Dutch, 18, 27; Lafayette and, 209, 223, 237n38

New York City, 6, 77, 99, 106, 108, 113, 114, 122n47, 127, 189, 218, 227; and Articles of Confederation, 225; British commanders in, 109; Portuguese agent in, 192; Portuguese consulate in, 183
Noailles, Louis Marie Antoine, vicomte de, 242, 247
Noailles family, 247
Nootka Sound Crisis, 250
Norfolk (Virginia): Portuguese consulate in, 193
North, Frederick (Lord North), 58–59
North Africa, 153
North America, 17, 20, 35, 54, 59, 102; antislavery in, 261; British migration to, 263; coast of, 112, 113, 115, 121n38, 129; Dutch supplies for, 69; East Coast, 77; French fleet at, 104–5; French threat to, 99; and League of Armed Neutrality, 46; and Native Americans, 38n10, 270; Pacific coast of, 250; sailing to, 108, 109–10; Seven Years' War in, 29; Spanish presence in, 162; trade, 175–76, 177–78; waters of, 115
North Atlantic Treaty, 264
North Carolina, 161
Norway, 3, 56
Notes and Considerations on the War with the Apache Indians in the Provinces of New Spain (Gálvez), 149–50
Nueva Vizcaya, 149
Nymphe (British ship), 108

Oberkampf, Christophe Philippe, 40n44
Observations on the Importance of the American Revolution (Price), 224
O'Hara, Charles, 104
Ohio valley, 161
Oneida (Native American nation): treaty with United States, 194
Opelousas (Native American nation), 155

Oporto (Portugal), 193
Oranje family, 89n3
Oranje-Nassau, William, 70, 83
O'Reilly, Alejandro: Algiers expedition, 151; as governor of Louisiana, 151–52, 153, 155; and Royal Military Academy, 150–51
Osman, Julia, 8, 13–15, 207
Osterhammel, Jürgen, 266
Ottoman Empire, 53–54, 55; commercial treaties, 47, 52

Pacific Ocean, 161
Pact of Amity and Commerce, 85
Paine, Thomas, 229; *Common Sense*, 31, 62; *The Rights of Man*, 242
Pakistan: Taliban bases in, 4
Palais de Chaillot (Paris), 100
Pallas (French ship), 71, 74, 81–84
Palmer, Robert R., 8, 10, 242, 259–60; *Age of the Democratic Revolution, 1760–1800*, 268; and Atlantic history, 36, 261–73; biography of, 266–68; on democratic revolutions, 34; and French Revolution, 268; "Le Problème de l'Atlantique du XVIIIè Siècle au XXè Siècle," 264; "The World Revolution of the West," 264, 271; *Twelve Who Ruled*, 267–68
Paquette, Gabriel: *Imperial Portugal in the Age of Atlantic Revolutions*, 199
Pará (Brazil), 193
Paris (France), 8, 13, 20, 69, 213, 253; American commissioners in, 68, 70, 75–76, 88; Lafayette in, 211; NATO headquarters in, 264; security of, 219
Parker, Daniel & Joseph (firm), 77
par ordre de vitesse, 132
Pascagoulas (Native American nation), 155
Passy, 44, 87; Franklin and, 43, 70, 79
patronage: at French court, 247; monarchy and, 248

Paulze, Balthazar-Jacques, 216
Pavlovitch, Konstantin (Grand Duke of Russia), 53
Pearson, Richard, 71–72, 80
Pegasus (British ship), 109, 113, 122n47
Pennsylvania, 156, 161, 189, 224; assembly, 221; Quakers of, 21, 25
Pensacola, 105, 108, 154; Spanish attack on, 147, 156, 157, 158–59, 172n44
Pensacola Bay, 147, 158
pensionaris, 86
Peru: as Spanish colony, 152
Petitfrère, Claude, 269
Peuchot, Éric, 35
Philadelphia, 28, 30, 31, 73, 77, 85, 184, 218; constitutional convention at, 226–28; as seat of federal government, 189–90, 192, 194, 195
Phrygian cap: ancient roots of, 33; as symbol of American and French Revolution, 31–34
physiocrats, 51, 224
Piercy, Thomas, 72
pilots: American, 107, 109, 110, 120n35
Place d'Armes (New Orleans), 157
Plains of Abraham, 13
Plan of Treaties (Adams), 61
Plan of Treaty of Commerce, 78, 84
Pluton (French ship), 138, 140
Poland, 10; first partition of (1772), 54; king of, 252
Polignac family, 247
Political Essay on the Kingdom of New Spain (Humboldt), 163–64
Pombal, Sebastião José de Carvalho e Melo, marquês do, 175–76, 177
Portsmouth (Great Britain), 108
Portsmouth (New Hampshire), 70
Portugal, 8, 45, 58; and American independence, 176–78, 186; and American Revolution, 10, 175–76; Asian colonies of, 192; and Barbary pirates, 183–84; commercial treaties, 48, 178–86; economy, 175–76; empire of, 176, 178, 179, 191, 193, 198; foreign policy of, 185; French invasion of, 195, 196, 198; relations with Great Britain, 146, 175–76, 177, 185, 191; relations with United States, 1, 146, 176, 178–99; royal family, 197; Spanish invasion of, 149; trade, 178, 181, 191–95; US consulates of, 193; war with Netherlands, 50
Potomac River, 196, 197
Pouchot, M., 29
Presidiales, 150, 166n12
presidios, 166n12
Préville, M., 134, 142n24
Price, Jacob, 217
Price, Munro, 7, 206–07
Price, Richard, 21; *Observations on the Importance of the American Revolution*, 224
Prieto, Tomás Francisco, 155
Princessa (British ship), 130, 136, 138–39
Pringle, John, 75
privateers, 48, 74, 84, 87; American, 5, 80, 197; French, 71; in War of Independence, 1
PRODROMES, 100–101, 103
Protestants, 14; German, 40n44
Prussia, 10, 45, 53, 61; diplomacy of, 55–59; military maneuvers in, 223; US ambassador to, 194; and War of the Bavarian Succession, 54
Pulaski, Casimir, 10

Quakers, 21, 25, 28; as abolitionists, 38n10; in Philadelphia, 261
Quapaws (Native American nation), 155
Quebec (Canada), 13, 20

Raadpensionaris, 76
Rademaker, José, 195
Randolph, Edmund: as secretary of state, 190

Ranger (American ship), 70
Realeneiland (Netherlands), 69
Reconquista: Catholic, 148
Regarding the Principles of Armed Neutrality (Catherine the Great), 52, 56, 64n11
regenten, 72
Regimiento de la Corona de Nueva España, 149
religious toleration. *See* toleration, religious
republic, 255; American, 25, 190, 196, 198, 252, 254, 256; ancient, 30; federal, 222; French, 29, 206, 251, 253; instability of, 162; monarchical, 256; size of, 224; United States and Netherlands as, 76, 77, 85
republicanism, 148, 165, 251, 270; French, 278n39; Lafayette and, 252–56
Résumé de Mon Avis au Comité du Commerce avec les Etats-Unis (Lafayette), 215
revolutionaries, 13, 145; American, 18, 59, 61, 104, 154, 156, 157, 159, 161; Brazilian, 181, 182; French, 34, 242–243, 252, 268, 272; Lameth brothers as, 245; white, 273
Révolutions, Les (1770–1799) (Godechot), 270, 274
revolutions: of 1848, 270; Atlantic, 266–74; democratic, 260, 263–69; and race, 272–73; Western, 262, 270
Reynst, Hendrick Pieter, 83–84
Rhineland (Germany), 269
Rhode Island: assembly, 222
Ribeiro, Jorge Manuel Martins, 199
Richter, Daniel K., 265
Ricot, Philippe, 71
Ridley, Matthew, 212
Riemersma, Nicolaas, 83
Riga (Latvia), 86
Rights of Man, The (Paine), 242

Rights of War and Peace, The (Grotius), 49–50
Rio de Janeiro (Brazil), 195, 197
Rions, d'Albert de, 138
Robespierre, Maximilien, 232, 267
Rochambeau, Jean-Baptiste Donatien de Vimeur, comte de, 97, 103, 104, 105, 116, 118n14, 120n35, 127, 243
Rodney, George Brydges, 55, 70, 102, 108, 113, 114, 120n34, 122n47, 124, 159
Ross, John, 80
Rossignol, Marie-Jeanne, 7, 35–36, 259–60
Rousseau, Jean-Jacques, 50
Royal Cantabre Regiment, 149
Royal Military Academy (Spain), 151, 171n44
Royal Oak (British ship), 130
Rule of 1756 (Great Britain), 49
Russia, 45, 74, 270; commercial treaties, 52; diplomacy of, 52–59, 65n12; history of, 52; interests of, 53–59; and neutral rights, 1; and Portugal, 177

Saavedra, Francisco, 159, 171–72n44
Saint-Domingue (now Haiti), 109
Saint-Esprit (French ship), 110, 111, 113
Saint Lucia, 108
Saint Non, Abbé de, 32
Salazar, António de Oliveira, 198
saltpeter, 5, 28
Sandwich, Earl of. *See* Montagu, John, 4th Earl of Sandwich
Sandy Hook (NJ), 110, 113, 127
Sangronis, Francisco Saavedra de, 105
sans culottes, 31
Saravia, Gonzalo M. Quintero, 145; *Bernardo de Gálvez*, 9–10
Sartine, Antoine, 86
Savannah (South Carolina), 107
Savoy: commercial treaties, 48
Saxony: and War of the Bavarian Succession, 54

Sayre, Stephen, 73–74, 88
Schulte Nordholt, Jan Willem, 68
Schuyler, Philip, 24
Scott, Gustavus, 197
Scott, James Brown, 100
Scott, Sam, 34
Ségur, Louis Philippe, comte de, 242
Senate, US, 188, 192
separation of powers, 246, 251
Serapis (British ship), 8, 44, 71–72, 77, 80–84
Serra, Abbade José Corrêa da, 182, 193, 196–97
Setúbal (Portugal), 184
Seven Years War (1756–63), 5, 13–14, 17, 18, 20, 25, 49, 53, 103; British victory in, 147–48, 151, 152, 154; France and, 19; French army and, 36; invasion of Portugal, 149; veterans of, 29
Sevilla Infantry Regiment, 150
Shay's Rebellion (1786), 184, 226
Shovlin, John, 18
Shrewsbury (British ship), 138, 140
Shy, John, 3–4, 6
Sieyès, Emmanuel Joseph, 245
slavery, 265, 266, 272–73; abolitionism, 261; American, 38n10, 39n21; Atlantic trade, 265; French abolition of, 267–68, 278n39; history of, 265; Washington and Lafayette on, 261
Smith, Adam, 51
Smith, Jay, 18
Smith, William Loughton, 194–95
Smith, William Stephens, 184–85, 225, 226
Société des Études Robespierristes, 270
Society of Thirty, 247, 248
Solebay (British ship), 130, 139
Some Historical Account of Guinea (Benezet), 261
Sorbonne University (Paris), 7, 100–101
Sousa, Luís Pinto de, 180, 183, 185, 186–89, 193, 196

Sousa Coutinho, Rodrigo de, 193
Sousa Coutinho, Vicente de, 178–79
Southall, Valentine W., 209
South Carolina, 78, 86–87, 107, 218, 226, 243
South Carolina (American ship), 69, 87, 160
Souverain (French ship), 134
Spain, 8, 43, 191; aid for United States, 7–8; and Algiers expedition, 151; alliance with France, 9, 148, 154, 160; and American independence, 169n37; and American Revolution, 3, 9; colonial ministry of, 152; commercial treaties, 47–48; conquers Pensacola, 105; court of, 155, 157, 187; empire of, 145, 147–48, 149, 150, 151, 154, 156, 157, 161–64; forts in America, 166n12; mint of, 155; and Native Americans, 149, 153, 155, 161–62, 166n12; and Netherlands, 75; and Nootka Sound Crisis, 250; relations with France, 100, 104; relations with Great Britain, 147–48, 154–56; relations with United States, 5; Supreme Council of War, 150; war with Great Britain, 1, 4, 154, 160; war with Netherlands, 50
Spanish East Florida, 147–48
Sparks, Jared, 68
Staats, Arie, 69, 74
stadhouder, 67, 70, 85, 89n3
Staphorst, Jacob van, 67
Staphorst, Nicolaas van, 67
Steuben, Baron von, 10
St. Eustatius, 57, 69, 70, 85, 87, 108, 113, 120n35
St. Maxent, Feliciana de, 153, 162
Stockbridge Indians: treaty with United States, 194
Stockton, Samuel Witham, 77
St. Petersburg, 57, 63
Sumpter, Thomas, 195

Sweden, 45, 53, 61, 192; and American Revolution, 4; commercial treaties, 48; diplomacy of, 56–59
Switzerland, 75, 269; merchants, 79

Tarelinck, Jan van, 78
Tegelaar, Jan Gabriel, 67, 73
Ten Cate (firm), 74
Terrible (British ship), 140
Terror, the, 262, 266–68
Texel (Netherlands), 44; John Paul Jones at, 67–88
The Hague (Netherlands), 72, 75, 76, 77, 80–82, 85; Portuguese minister to, 178–79
"The World Revolution of the West" (Palmer), 264, 271
Thibaud, Rémy, 110
Thornton, William, 197
tobacco, 77, 213; American, 253; trade, 214–18
Tocqueville, Alexis de, 18, 242
Toisón de oro (Golden Fleece), 156
toleration: religious, 267, 272
Tornquist, Karl Gustav, 101, 121n42
Tourtille-Sangrain, Pierre, 213
Tracy, Nathaniel, 214
trade, 25; of America, 61; Baltic, 58; British, 156; European, 153, 181; European treaties, 47–52; between France and United States, 211–19, 231, 233n3; free, 6, 8, 11, 44, 45–46, 46–52, 59, 60–63, 85, 178, 215–16, 218, 231; French, 102; fur, 216, 217; history of, 265; maritime, 43; monopoly, 215; with Native Americans, 163; neutral, 45–46, 56, 59; between Portugal and United States, 191–95; Portuguese, 175–76, 177–78; principles of, 223; regulations, 222; restrictions on, 151; rights of, 60; Russian interest in, 54; slave, 259–60, 265; tobacco, 214–18; and War of Independence, 43

Tratado de Comércio e Amizade. See Luso-American Treaty of Commerce and Friendship
Treaty of Kuchuk-Kainarju (1774), 53
Treaty of Paris (1763), 14, 57
Treaty of Paris (1783), 169n37, 178, 183, 211
Treaty of Utrecht (1713), 46, 48, 61
Treaty of Westminster (1654), 47
Trenton (NJ), 222
Troude, Onésime, 141n2; *Batailles navales de la France*, 124
Truguet, M., 136, 139
Trumbull, Jonathan, 73
Túpac Amaru, 162
Turbulent Time, A (Gaspar and Geggus), 273
Turgot, Anne Robert Jacques, 224
Tuscarora (Native American nation): treaty with United States, 194
Twelve Who Ruled (Palmer), 267–68

Ulloa, Antonio de, 151
United States: and Afghanistan, 3–4; citizens, 254; commercial treaties, 178–86; constitutional reforms, 219–31; debts to European countries, 161; democratic principles of, 182, 270; economy, 62, 193, 210–11, 219, 220; European opponents of, 224–25; flag, 71, 76, 79, 84, 158; foreign policy of, 46, 60–63, 179, 186, 194; and free trade, 44, 45–46, 60–63; French banker of, 75; French merchants in, 211; government of, 6, 186–87, 196; historians, 7; history of, 6, 46; independence of, 1, 2, 53, 62, 97, 99, 100, 157, 169n37, 176–78, 186, 266; museums in, 155; and Native Americans, 194; neutrality of, 188; political system of, 210, 213, 219–20, 268; Portuguese immigration to, 194; presidential powers, 229, 249, 251,

United States (*continued*)
252; relations with France, 70, 100, 205–6, 210, 211–19, 221, 231, 233n3; relations with Great Britain, 4, 177–78, 225; relations with Netherlands, 67–88; relations with Portugal, 146, 176, 178–99; reputation of, 228; and Rule of 1756, 49; territorial ambitions of, 161; trade, 146, 180–82, 191–95, 210–19, 220, 223, 233n3; treaty with France (1778), 1, 18, 30, 31, 61, 76; and Vietnam War, 3, 4

Université Paris Cité, 7
University of Bradford (Great Britain), 7
University of Coimbra (Portugal), 181
University of Toulouse (France), 269
University of Virginia, 209
Urriza, Juan Ignacio de, 160

Vaillant (French ship), 121n42
Val d'Oise (France), 245
Valtz-Manucci, Loretta, 276n11
Van de Perre & Meyners (firm), 84
Varange, Joseph, 71
Vasseur, Jean Charles le, 32
Vattel, Emer de, 44, 49, 51–52, 63; *The Law of Nations*, 51
Vaudreuil, Louis-Philippe de Rigaud, marquis de, 101
Vauguyon, Paul François de Quélen de Stuer de Caussade, duc de la, 72, 74–77, 81, 83, 88
Vengeance (French ship), 71–72, 74, 82–84
Veracruz (Mexico), 162
Vergennes, comte de (Charles Gravier), 14, 17, 20, 21, 23, 103–4, 115, 118n13, 212, 214–15, 216, 228; *Affaires de l'Angleterre et de l'Amérique*, 18–19, 20–24; death of, 218
Vergulde Schol, 69
Versailles (France): court of, 69, 71, 103–4, 212, 245, 247; Portuguese minister to, 178; US minister to, 181

Verses on the Peace (Duviquet), 25
Vestal (British ship), 85
veto: absolute, 249; temporal, 249
Vichy France, 269
Vienna (Austria), 223
Vietnam War, 3, 4
Ville de Paris (French ship), 110–12, 113, 119n24, 132
Villeneuve, M. de, 137, 139
Vioménil, baron de, 243
virer à pic, 131
Virgin, M. de, 131, 137
Virginia, 77, 109, 147, 209, 215; and Annapolis Conference, 225; British forces in, 118n14; tobacco, 193; in War of Independence, 220
Visscher, C. W., 73
Voltaire (François-Marie Arouet), 52
Vrij Temminck, Egbert de, 73, 76–78

Walker, Timothy, 146
War of 1812, 6, 62
War of Independence, 1, 13, 22, 148, 193; and American Revolution, 263; American victory in, 6, 32, 97; antislavery sentiment in, 261; battlefields of, 209; Blacks and, 274n2; extent of, 10, 45, 54; France and, 17, 23, 243; Great Britain and, 3–5; history of, 2–11; Lafayette and, 209–10, 243; Lameth brothers and, 245, 251; nature of, 145; Portugal and, 146, 176, 198; and trade, 43; Virginia campaign, 220
War of the Bavarian Succession (1778–79), 54, 55
War of the Two Brothers, 197
Washington, DC: Ellipse, 197; Executive Mansion, 196, 197; Portuguese embassy at, 196–98; White House, 197
Washington, George, 6, 50, 97; as commander-in-chief, 28, 35, 104, 105, 106, 116, 127, 205; in Constitutional

Convention, 227; correspondence of, 100; as Fabius, 30; *Farewell Address*, 46; imagery of, 32; and Jumonville murder, 19, 29–30; and Lafayette, 220–21, 223–24, 226–30, 243; as literary character, 29–31; as president, 186–90, 205, 229, 256; and slavery, 261

Washington, Martha, 190; and slavery, 261

Wenger, William V.: *The Key to American Independence*, 7

West Indies, 69, 101, 103–9, 115, 120n34, 121n38, 132, 140; British, 120n37; French, 102, 103–4, 106, 108, 213, 217

Whiskey Rebellion, 190

White, Alexander, 197

White, Ashli, 266

Wick, Daniel, 246–47; *A Conspiracy of Well-Intentioned Men*, 247; "Court Nobility and the French Revolution," 247

Wijk, F. W. van, 68

Williams, Jonathan, 214

wine: Madeira, 175, 180

Winter, P. J. van, 68

Wolloch, Isser, 266–68

Wood, Gordon S., 145

World Historical Congress (Rome, 1955), 264

World War II, 3, 198, 269; United States entry, 266

Wright, Fanny, 274n2

yellow fever: in Philadelphia, 189

York, duke of, 223

Yorke, Joseph, 69, 74–76, 80–81, 85–86

Yorktown: naval blockade of, 5, 97–98, 99; siege of (1781), 6, 9, 59, 102, 104, 123, 147, 159, 161, 172n44, 176, 211, 220, 243

zeehelden: Jones as, 80

Zélé (French ship), 134, 136, 142n24

The Revolutionary Age

The Tory's Wife: A Woman and Her Family in Revolutionary America, Cynthia A. Kierner

Writing Early America: From Empire to Revolution, Trevor Burnard

Spain and the American Revolution: New Approaches and Perspectives, Gabriel Paquette and Gonzalo M. Quintero Saravia, editors

The Habsburg Monarchy and the American Revolution, Jonathan Singerton

Navigating Neutrality: Early American Governance in the Turbulent Atlantic, Sandra Moats

Ireland and America: Empire, Revolution, and Sovereignty, Patrick Griffin and Francis D. Cogliano, editors

www.ingramcontent.com/pod-product-compliance
Lightning Source LLC
Chambersburg PA
CBHW022026240426
43667CB00042B/1197